expressions of home
home
plans

W9-DEE-978

Contents

COVER HOME - The house shown on the front cover is Plan #583-023D-0001 and is featured on page 70. Photo courtesy of Chatham Home Planning, photographer; Chris Little, Atlanta, GA

EXPRESSIONS OF HOME - HOME PLANS is published by HDA, Inc. (Home Design Alternatives) 944 Anglum Road, St. Louis, MO, 63042. All rights reserved. Reproduction in whole or in part without written permission of the publisher is prohibited. Printed in U.S.A. © 2005. Artist drawings and photos shown in this publication may vary slightly from the actual working drawings. Some photos are shown in mirror reverse. Please refer to the floor plan for accurate layout.

Current Printing   5   4   3   2   1

Expressions of Home

Expressions of Home is a collection of our best-selling home plans featured in a variety of styles and sizes. A broad assortment is presented to match a wide variety of lifestyles and budgets. Each design page features floor plans, a front view of the house, interior square footage of the home, number of bedrooms, baths, garage size and foundation types. All floor plans show room and exterior dimensions.

Technical Specifications

At the time the construction drawings were prepared, every effort was made to ensure that these plans and specifications meet nationally recognized building codes (BOCA, Southern Building Code Congress and others). Because national building codes change or vary from area to area some drawing modifications and/or the assistance of a professional designer or architect may be necessary to comply with your local codes or to accommodate specific building site conditions. We advise you to consult with your local building official for information regarding codes governing your area.

Blueprint Ordering - Fast and Easy

Your ordering is made simple by following the instructions on page 640. See page 639 for more information on which types of blueprint packages are available and how many plan sets to order.

Your Home, Your Way

The blueprints you receive are a master plan for building your new home. They start you on your way to what may well be the most rewarding experience of your life.

page 527

page 523

page 330

1

Total Living Area: 2,727 sq. ft.

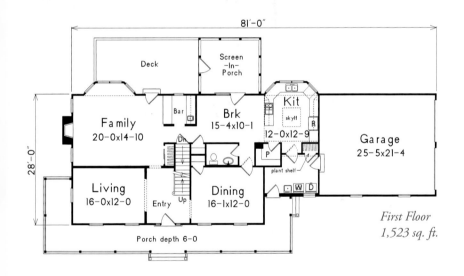

81'-0"

Deck

Screen -In- Porch

28'-0"

Family
20-0x14-10

Bar

Brk
15-4x10-1

Kit
12-0x12-9
skylt
R

Garage
25-5x21-4

Dn

plant shelf
P

Living
16-0x12-0

Entry

Up

Dining
16-1x12-0

W D

*First Floor
1,523 sq. ft.*

Porch depth 6-0

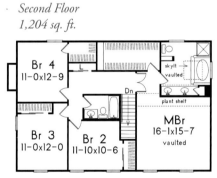

*Second Floor
1,204 sq. ft.*

Br 4
11-0x12-9

skylt
vaulted

plant shelf

Dn

MBr
16-1x15-7
vaulted

Br 3
11-0x12-0

Br 2
11-10x10-6

Plan Features

- Wrap-around porch and large foyer create an impressive entrance
- A state-of-the-art vaulted kitchen has a walk-in pantry and is open to the breakfast room and adjoining screen-in-porch
- Vaulted master bedroom enjoys a luxurious bath with skylight and an enormous 13' deep walk-in closet
- 4 bedrooms, 2 1/2 baths, 2-car side entry garage
- Walk-out basement foundation

Quick & Easy Customizing

Here's an affordable and efficient way to make changes to your plan.

BEFORE

AFTER

Make changes to your Home Plan in 4 Easy Steps

1. Select the house plan that most closely meets your needs. Purchase of a reproducible master is necessary in order to make changes to a plan.

2. Call 1-800-373-2646 or e-mail customize@hdainc.com to place your order. Tell the sales representative you're interested in customizing a plan. A $50 nonrefundable consultation fee will be charged. You will then be instructed to complete a customization checklist indicating all the changes you wish to make to your plan. You may attach sketches if necessary. <u>If you proceed with the custom changes the $50 will be credited to the total amount charged.</u>

3. FAX the completed customization checklist to our design consultant. Within 24-48* business hours you will be provided with a written cost estimate to modify your plan. Our design consultant will contact you by phone if you wish to discuss any of your changes in greater detail.

4. Once you approve the estimate, a 75% retainer fee is collected and customization work gets underway. Preliminary drawings can usually be completed within 5-10* business days. Following approval of the preliminary drawings your design changes are completed within 5-10* business days. Your remaining 25% balance due is collected prior to shipment of your completed drawings. You will be shipped five sets of revised blueprints or a reproducible master, plus a customized materials list if required.

Sample Modification Pricing Guide

The average prices specified below are provided as examples only. They refer to the most commonly requested changes, and are subject to change without notice. Prices for changes will vary or differ, from the prices below, depending on the number of modifications requested, the plan size, style, quality of original plan, format provided to us (originally drawn by hand or computer), and method of design used by the original designer. To obtain a detailed cost estimate or to get more information, please contact us.

Categories	Average Cost*
Adding or removing living space	Quote required
Adding or removing a garage	Starting at $400
Garage: Front entry to side load or vice versa	Starting at $300
Adding a screened porch	Starting at $280
Adding a bonus room in the attic	Starting at $450
Changing full basement to crawl space or vice versa	Starting at $495
Changing full basement to slab or vice versa	Starting at $495
Changing exterior building material	Starting at $200
Changing roof lines	Starting at $360
Adjusting ceiling height	Starting at $280
Adding, moving or removing an exterior opening	$65 per opening
Adding or removing a fireplace	Starting at $90
Modifying a non-bearing wall or room	$65 per room
Changing exterior walls from 2"x4" to 2"x6"	Starting at $200
Redesigning a bathroom or a kitchen	Starting at $120
Reverse plan right reading	Quote required
Adapting plans for local building code requirements	Quote required
Engineering and Architectural stamping and services	Quote required
Adjust plan for handicapped accessibility	Quote required
Interactive Illustrations (choices of exterior materials)	Quote required
Metric conversion of home plan	Starting at $400

*Prices and Terms are subject to change without notice.

Plan #583-007D-0068

Total Living Area: 1,384 sq. ft.

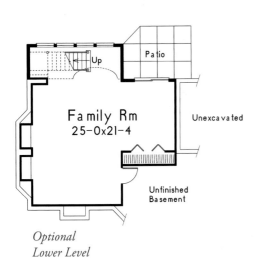

Family Rm
25-0x21-4

Up

Patio

Unexcavated

Unfinished Basement

Optional Lower Level

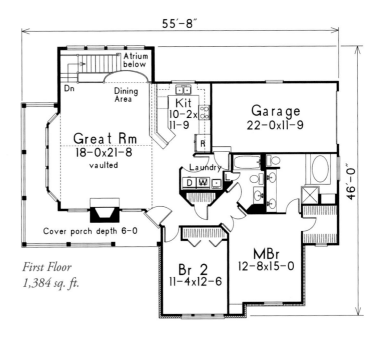

55'-8"

Atrium below

Dn

Dining Area

Kit
10-2x
11-9

Garage
22-0x11-9

Great Rm
18-0x21-8
vaulted

Laundry
D W

R

46'-0"

Cover porch depth 6-0

First Floor
1,384 sq. ft.

Br 2
11-4x12-6

MBr
12-8x15-0

Rear View

Plan Features

- Vaulted great room enjoys a large bay window, stone fireplace, pass-through kitchen and awesome rear views through atrium window wall
- Master bedroom features a double-door entry, walk-in closet and a fabulous bath
- Atrium opens to 611 square feet of optional living area below
- 2 bedrooms, 2 baths, 1-car side entry garage
- Walk-out basement foundation

Paint-By-Number Wall Murals

Solar System
#75902

Photo colors may vary from kit colors

Create a unique room with 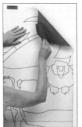 WALL ART™

You will be the envy of friends when you decorate with a Paint-By-Number Wall Mural.

Choose from over 100 custom designs for all ages and transform your room into a paradise.

You don't have to be an artist to paint a Wall Art mural. The whole family can participate in this fun and easy weekend project.

Your Wall Art kit includes everything but the wall!

Wall Art murals are available in a variety of sizes starting at the *low price of $49.97.*

ORDER TODAY!

It's As Easy As 1 - 2 - 3!

1. Tape   2. Trace   3. Paint

To order or request a catalog, call toll-free

1-877-WALLMURAL (925-5687)

24 hours a day, 7 days a week,
or buy online at

www.wallartdesigns.com

Deep Blue Sea
#75002

Route 66
#76305

ROUTE 66

45 ZONE AHEAD

Bug Collection
#75001

Plan #583-001D-0024

Price Code:

A

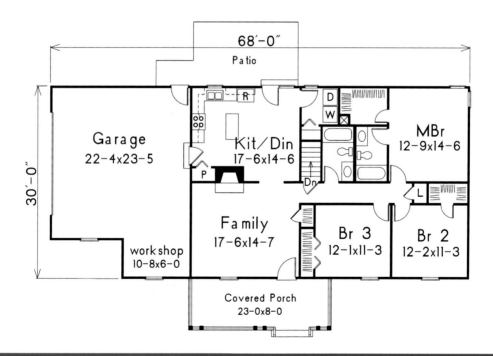

Total Living Area: 1,360 sq. ft.

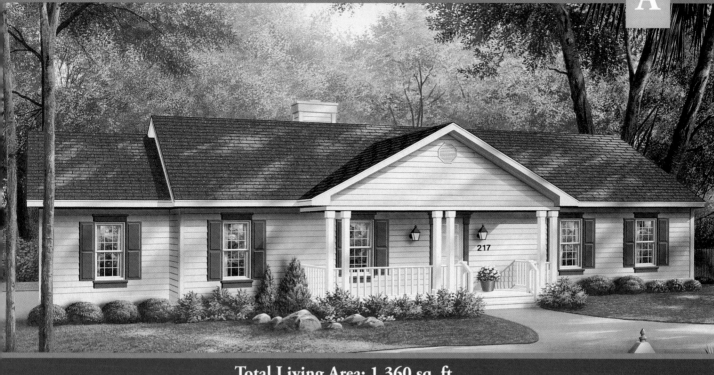

Plan Features

- Kitchen/dining room features island workspace and plenty of dining area
- Master bedroom has large walk-in closet and private bath
- Laundry room is adjacent to the kitchen for easy access
- Convenient workshop in garage
- 3 bedrooms, 2 baths, 2-car side entry garage
- Basement foundation, drawings also include crawl space and slab foundations

To order call toll-free 1-800-DREAM HOME or visit www.houseplansandmore.com

Total Living Area: 1,568 sq. ft.

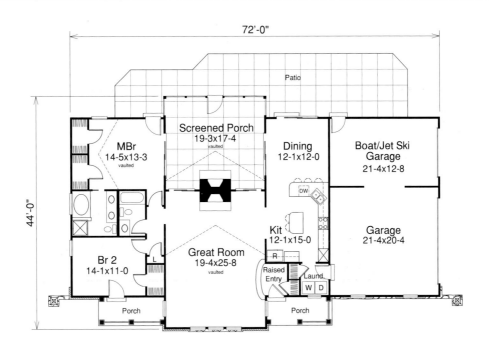

Plan Features

- Multiple entrances from three porches help to bring the outdoors in
- The lodge-like great room features a vaulted ceiling, stone fireplace, step-up entrance foyer and opens to a huge screened porch
- The kitchen has an island and peninsula, a convenient laundry room and adjoins a spacious dining area which leads to a screened porch and rear patio
- 2 bedrooms, 2 baths, 3-car side entry garage
- Crawl space foundation

Total Living Area: 3,368 sq. ft.

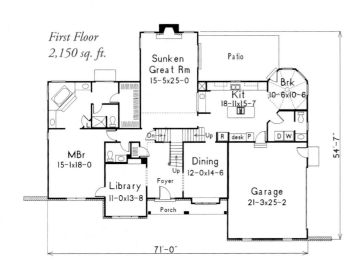

First Floor
2,150 sq. ft.

Sunken Great Rm
15-5x25-0

Patio

Brk
10-6x10-6

Kit
18-11x15-7

Dn   Up   R   desk   P   D W

MBr
15-1x18-0

Library
11-0x13-8

Foyer

Up

Dining
12-0x14-6

Garage
21-3x25-2

Porch

54'-7"

71'-0"

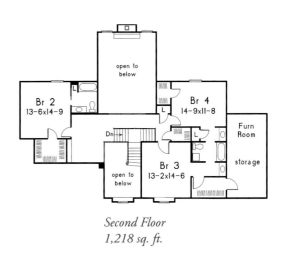

open to below

Br 2
13-6x14-9

Br 4
14-9x11-8

Furn Room

Dn

storage

open to below

Br 3
13-2x14-6

Second Floor
1,218 sq. ft.

Plan Features

- Great room features a cathedral ceiling, wooden beams, skylights and a masonry fireplace
- Octagon-shaped breakfast room has domed ceiling with beams, and a door to the patio
- Private master bedroom has a deluxe bath and dressing area
- Oversized walk-in closets and storage areas in each bedroom
- 4 bedrooms, 3 full baths, 2 half baths, 2-car side entry garage
- Basement foundation

Total Living Area: 3,176 sq. ft.

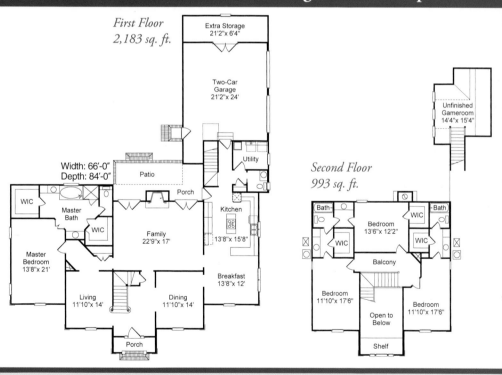

First Floor
2,183 sq. ft.

Extra Storage
21'2"x 6'4"

Two-Car
Garage
21'2"x 24'

Utility

Width: 66'-0"
Depth: 84'-0"

Patio

Porch

WIC

Master
Bath

WIC

Kitchen
13'8"x 15'8"

Master
Bedroom
13'8"x 21'

Family
22'9"x 17'

Breakfast
13'8"x 12'

Living
11'10"x 14'

Dining
11'10"x 14'

Porch

Second Floor
993 sq. ft.

Unfinished
Gameroom
14'4"x 15'4"

Bath

WIC

Bath

WIC

Bedroom
13'6"x 12'2"

WIC

Balcony

Bedroom
11'10"x 17'6"

Bedroom
11'10"x 17'6"

Open to
Below

Shelf

Plan Features

- Formal dining and living rooms flank the foyer for an impressive feel
- Spacious secondary bedrooms include walk-in closets and private bath access
- Fireplace is flanked by French doors leading from the family room to the rear porch
- The unfinished gameroom has an additional 255 square feet of living area
- 4 bedrooms, 3 1/2 baths, 2-car side entry garage
- Slab foundation

What's The Right PLAN For You?

Many of the homes you see may appear to be just what you're looking for. But are they? One way to find out is to carefully analyze what you want in a home. This is an important first step we'll show you how to take.

For most people, budget is the most critical element in narrowing the choices. Generally, the size of the home, or, specifically, the square footage of living area is the single most important criteria in establishing the cost of a new home. Also, in most instances, it's cheaper to build up than to build out (assuming the same amount of square footage). Sprawling ranch houses have twice the foundation and roof area of the multi-level homes covering half the ground area.

Your next task is to consider the style of home you want. Should it be traditional, contemporary, one-story or two-story? If yours is an infill lot in an existing neighborhood, is the design you like compatible with the existing residential architecture? If not, will the subdivision permit you to build the design of your choice?

And what about the site itself? What will it allow you to do and what won't it allow you to do?

Site topography is the first consideration in floor plan development. Slopes, both gentle and steep, will affect the home design you select. If you want a multi-level home with a walk-out basement that appears to be a single-story residence from the street, you need a

lot that slopes from front to back. And what about the garage? Do you prefer access at street level or a lower level?

Next, there is the issue of orientation, that is, the direction in which you want the house to face. Considering the north-south or east-west orientation of the site itself, will the plan you choose allow you to enjoy sweeping views from the living room? Does the design have a lot of glass on the south side that will permit you to take advantage of the sun's warmth in winter?

Now for the tough part; figuring out what you want inside the house to satisfy your needs and lifestyle. To a large extent, that may depend on where you are in life – just starting out, whether you have toddlers or teenagers, whether you're an "empty-nester," or retired.

Next, think about the components of the home. Do you want, or need, both a living room and family room or would just one large great room suffice? Do you want, or need, both a breakfast room and a formal dining room? How many bedrooms, full baths and half baths do you need? How much storage? And what about space for working from home, hobbies or a workshop?

Experts in the field suggest that the best way to determine your needs is to begin by listing everything you like or dislike about your current home.

When you've completed your wish list, think about how you want your home to function. In architectural terms, think about spatial relationships and circulation, or in other words, the relationship of each of the components to one another.

For example, to deliver groceries conveniently, the kitchen should be directly accessible from the garage. To serve meals efficiently, the dining area should be adjacent to the kitchen. The same principle applies to other areas and components of the home. Consider the flow from entry foyer to living, sleeping, and food preparation areas.

As you study your favorite home plan, ask yourself if it's possible to close off certain spaces to eliminate noise from encroaching upon others. For instance, if you enjoy listening to music, you don't want it drowned out by a droning dishwasher or blaring TV being watched by another member of the family nearby. One popular trend, the media room, solves this problem efficiently and beautifully offering a relaxing retreat for enjoying music, films or TV while effectively keeping noise away from the bedrooms with sound-proof walls. Similarly, sleeping areas and bathrooms should be remote from living areas. After you've come to terms with the types and relationship of rooms you want in your dream home, you can then concentrate on the size and features you want for each of those spaces.

If cooking is a hobby and you entertain frequently, you might want a large gourmet kitchen or even the ever-so-popular outdoor kitchen. If you like openness and a laid-back environment, you might want a large family room with picture windows, a fireplace, vaulted ceiling, and exposed wood beams. A central living area directly accessible to an outdoor deck or patio is the ultimate in casual, relaxed style.

Deciding what you want in your dream home, where you want it, and how you want it to look is thought provoking and time consuming, but careful planning and thought will have a great return on investment when it comes to you and your family's happiness.

Total Living Area: 1,525 sq. ft.

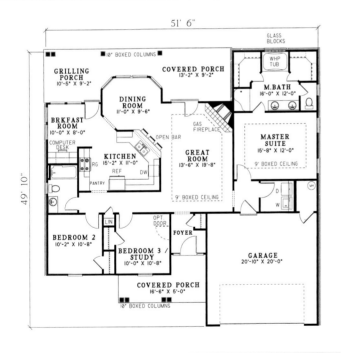

DID YOU KNOW?

A telescopic extension pole when painting high ceilings is an invaluable tool. Trying to balance yourself and a paint tray is a problem that gets eliminated when using this highly functional tool.

Plan Features

- Corner fireplace is highlighted in the great room
- Open bar overlooks both the kitchen and great room
- Breakfast room leads to an outdoor grilling and covered porch
- 3 bedrooms, 2 baths, 2-car garage
- Basement, walk-out basement, crawl space or slab foundation, please specify when ordering

Total Living Area: 1,550 sq. ft.

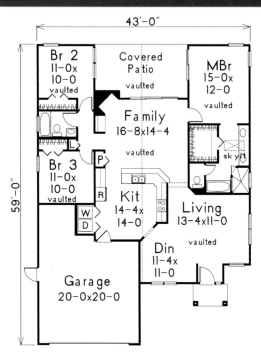

DID YOU KNOW?

Fireplaces are consistently rated as one of the top amenities desired by home-owners. In fact, fireplaces have one of the highest investment returns of any addition to your home. Here are a few tips to keep safe when using your beautiful fireplace: When you light the fire keep the flue fully open, for maximum airflow to feed the flames. Once it's roaring, close the flue to the point where the chimney starts smoking, then open it just a tad for optimal heat. To keep airflow constant and avoid carbon monoxide buildup, open the window closest to the fire by a half-inch. And make sure to keep a fire extinguisher handy, because even a "dead" fire can suddenly emit random, carpet-igniting sparks.

Plan Features

- Alcove in the family room can be used as a cozy corner fireplace or as a media center
- Master bedroom features a large walk-in closet, skylight and separate tub and shower
- Convenient laundry closet
- Family room and master bedroom access the patio
- 3 bedrooms, 2 baths, 2-car garage
- Slab foundation

Total Living Area: 1,400 sq. ft.

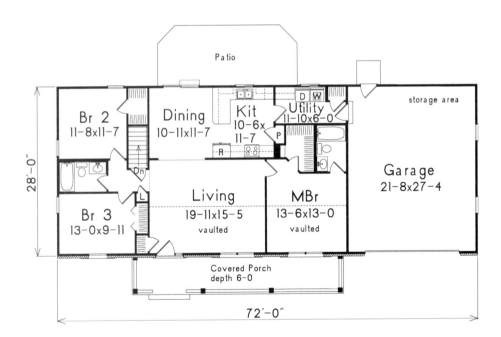

Patio

Br 2
11-8x11-7

Dining
10-11x11-7

Kit
10-6x
11-7

Utility
11-10x6-0

storage area

28'-0"

Dn

Br 3
13-0x9-11

Living
19-11x15-5
vaulted

MBr
13-6x13-0
vaulted

Garage
21-8x27-4

Covered Porch
depth 6-0

72'-0"

Plan Features

- Large utility room has additional cabinet space
- Covered porch provides an outdoor seating area
- Living room and master bedroom feature vaulted ceilings
- Oversized two-car garage has storage space
- 3 bedrooms, 2 baths, 2-car garage
- Basement foundation, drawings also include crawl space foundation

Total Living Area: 2,659 sq. ft.

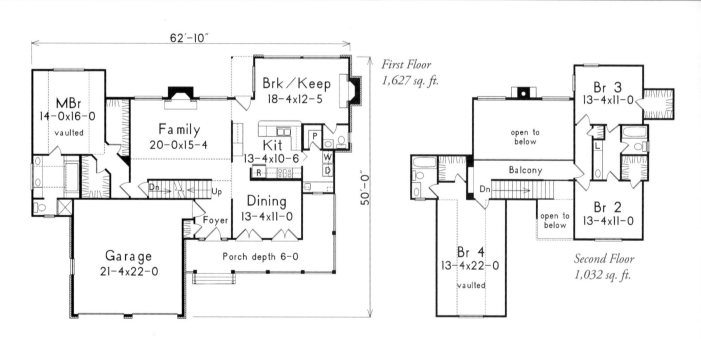

62'-10"

*First Floor
1,627 sq. ft.*

MBr
14-0x16-0
vaulted

Family
20-0x15-4

Brk/Keep
18-4x12-5

Kit
13-4x10-6

P
W
D
R

Dining
13-4x11-0

Dn
Up

Foyer

Garage
21-4x22-0

Porch depth 6-0

50'-0"

open to
below

Balcony

Dn

Br 3
13-4x11-0

L

Br 2
13-4x11-0

open to
below

Br 4
13-4x22-0
vaulted

*Second Floor
1,032 sq. ft.*

Plan Features

- 9' ceilings throughout the first floor
- Private first floor master bedroom features double walk-in closets, a sloped ceiling and a luxury bath
- Double French doors in the dining room open onto the porch
- 4 bedrooms, 3 1/2 baths, 2-car garage
- Basement foundation

Total Living Area: 1,268 sq. ft.

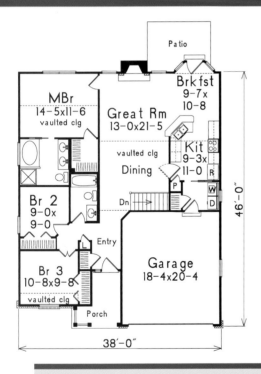

DID YOU KNOW?

Ideally, your central air-conditioning compressor should be located on a shady side of your house because it has to work a little harder in full sun. Studies show that shading a compressor can shave 1% to 2% off cooling costs. However, air flow is much more important because it's the air moving over the compressor's coils that causes them to give up their heat, and that's what makes the system work. It's important to keep fences, shrubs, and anything else that might block airflow at least 24 inches away.

Plan Features

- Multiple gables, large porch and arched windows create a classy exterior
- Innovative design provides openness in great room, kitchen and breakfast room
- Secondary bedrooms have private hall with bath
- 3 bedrooms, 2 baths, 2-car garage
- Basement foundation, drawings also include crawl space and slab foundations

Total Living Area: 2,613 sq. ft.

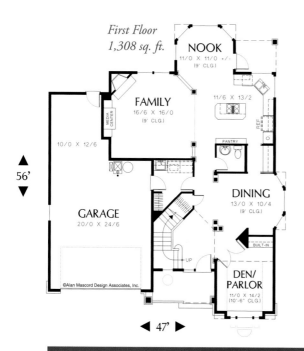

First Floor
1,308 sq. ft.

NOOK
11/0 X 11/0 +/-
(9' CLG.)

FAMILY
16/6 X 16/0
(9' CLG.)

11/6 X 13/2

MEDIA CENTER

10/0 X 12/6

PANTRY

DINING
13/0 X 10/4
(9' CLG.)

56'

GARAGE
20/0 X 24/6

UP

BUILT-IN

©Alan Mascord Design Associates, Inc.

DEN/
PARLOR
11/0 X 14/2
(10'-6" CLG.)

◀ 47' ▶

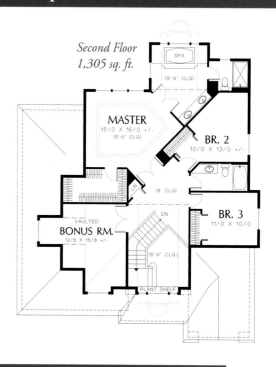

Second Floor
1,305 sq. ft.

SPA
(9'-6" CLG.)

MASTER
15/0 X 16/0 +/-
(9'-6" CLG.)

BR. 2
10/0 X 13/0 +/-

(8' CLG.)

BR. 3
11/0 X 10/0

VAULTED

BONUS RM.
12/6 X 15/8 +/-
(9'-6" CLG.)

DN

PLANT SHELF

Plan Features

- Cheerful breakfast nook features access outdoors
- Sunny master suite is sure to be enjoyed with a deluxe bath
- A quiet den/parlor in the front of the home is a great place to retreat
- Bonus room above the garage is included in the square footage
- 3 bedrooms, 2 1/2 baths, 2-car garage
- Crawl space foundation

Color and psychology meet in the interior decorating world.
Without ever being aware, colors can affect our moods and how we function
while viewing them in a phenomenon known as the

personality of
COLOR

Cool colors include blue, green and violet. These tranquil hues relax, refresh and lift spirits.
They are best used in rooms for rest and relaxation such as the bedroom, living room, spa or sun porch.

calming

Classic and cool, blue has the ability to lower blood pressure and make you feel at ease. Nothing is more peaceful for a bedroom. However, beware of grayish blues which are usually too cold for comfort. Deeper hues leaning toward red or green are warmer and more welcoming.

soothing

Green is the color of hope and rejuvenation and will revive and soothe your spirit. Green rarely feels cold, making it a sound choice for bedrooms or anywhere you seek comfort. Yellow tones are more stimulating and would be good for a kitchen or dining room, while blue tones are more calming.

graceful

Violet in its pure form is indisputably regal. It speaks to the creative and delicate alike. Ranging from meditative lavender to the sophisticated eggplant, this color works well anywhere.

Warm colors include red, yellow and orange. These energetic hues inspire and command attention. They are best used in active rooms such as entryways, dining rooms, and rooms for entertaining.

energizing

You can't miss red; it cannot be ignored. This color stimulates and excites which makes it ideal for rooms you want to encourage lively conversation or hearty appetites. Pared down shades of pink work well for bedrooms, promoting a sense of well-being and happiness. Whatever the shade, red is sure to add a little sizzle.

cheerful

The color of a sunny day, yellow evokes warmth and cheer, giving an instant lift. This color is an excellent choice for an entertaining room, making guests feel welcomed. To stay "happy" versus "warning" lean toward creamy yellows; which are perfect softened with white accents.

lively

The only color that has its own flavor. Everyone warms up to orange. It is dynamic and energetic while being cheerful and welcoming. Orange has a versatility that is stunning, and depending on the shade, can be used anywhere.

stylish

Neutrals (beige, brown, taupe, white, gray and black) are a quiet alternative to color that is rather refreshing. They are perfect for rooms that connect to other rooms for a nice transition. They also are a good option for rooms that spotlight collections, letting your prized possessions speak for themselves.

Total Living Area: 1,393 sq. ft.

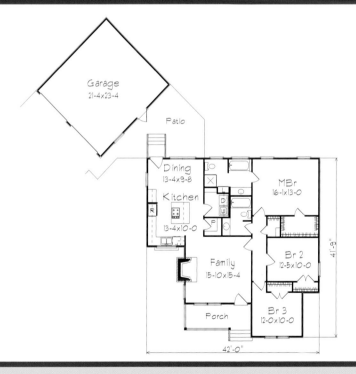

Garage
21-4x23-4

Patio

Dining
13-4x9-8

Kitchen
13-4x10-0

MBr
16-1x13-0

Br 2
12-5x10-0

Family
15-10x15-4

Br 3
12-0x10-0

Porch

42'-0"

41'-9"

Plan Features

- L-shaped kitchen features a walk-in pantry, island cooktop and is convenient to the dining area
- Master bedroom features a large walk-in closet and private bath with separate tub and shower
- Convenient storage/coat closet in hall
- 3 bedrooms, 2 baths, 2-car detached garage
- Crawl space foundation, drawings also include slab foundation

Total Living Area: 1,791 sq. ft.

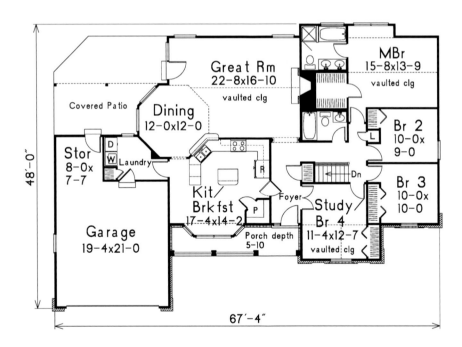

Plan Features

- Vaulted great room and octagon-shaped dining area enjoy a spectacular view of the covered patio
- Kitchen features a pass-through to dining area, center island, large walk-in pantry and breakfast room with large bay window
- The garage includes extra storage space
- 4 bedrooms, 2 baths, 2-car garage with storage
- Basement foundation, drawings also include crawl space and slab foundations

Total Living Area: 4,100 sq. ft.

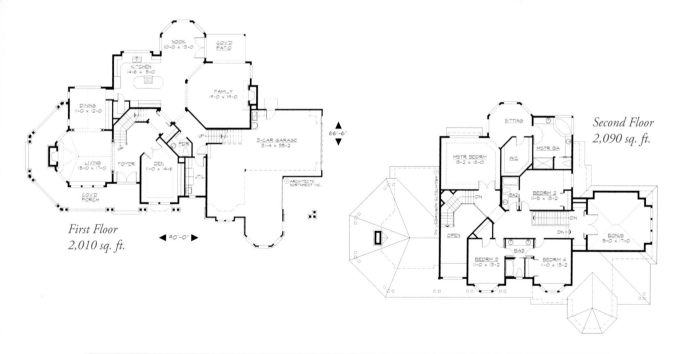

First Floor
2,010 sq. ft.

Second Floor
2,090 sq. ft.

Plan Features

- Family room connects to other casual living areas for convenience
- French doors keep the cozy private den from the rest of the first floor
- A beautiful sitting area extends the master bedroom
- The bonus room on the second floor is included in the square footage
- 4 bedrooms, 3 1/2 baths, 3-car side entry garage
- Crawl space foundation

Total Living Area: 6,088 sq. ft.

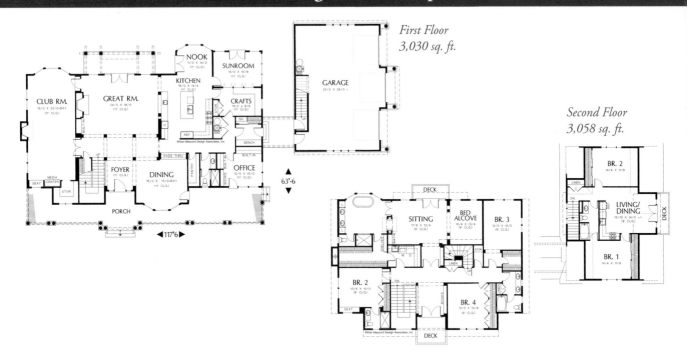

First Floor
3,030 sq. ft.

Second Floor
3,058 sq. ft.

Plan Features

- Master suite has a separate bed alcove and a large central sitting area with a view onto the deck
- The first floor features many amenities including a club room for entertaining, an office with direct deck access and a craft room for hobbies
- The guest quarters feature two bedrooms, a full kitchen and bath
- 6 bedrooms, 5 baths, 3-car side entry detached garage
- Crawl space foundation

Total Living Area: 1,859 sq. ft.

First Floor
1,070 sq. ft.

Second Floor
789 sq. ft.

Plan Features

- Fireplace highlights the vaulted great room
- Master bedroom includes a large closet and private bath
- Kitchen adjoins breakfast room providing easy access to the outdoors
- 3 bedrooms, 2 1/2 baths, 2-car garage
- Basement foundation

One of the first questions to ask yourself when thinking about building your dream home is...

Where's the Money Coming From?

You're going to need a substantial amount of money and chances are you're going to have to borrow most of it. Where and how you borrow it will determine whether you pay a reasonable or an excessive amount for the money you need for your new home.

HOW TO BEGIN

The first consideration of course, is "How much money will I need?"

As long as you have at least one set of blueprints, most building contractors can give you an approximate cost of construction rather quickly. This is especially important when deciding if any design modifications are necessary to stay within your budget.

Let's assume that your property and house will be valued at $180,000 by the lender providing your long-term mortgage. If the land is valued at $30,000, you should need $150,000 to pay your building costs. Therefore, you will probably need to obtain a construction loan.

A construction loan is a short term loan used to pay for building your house. When the house is completed, this loan is paid in full, usually out of the proceeds of your long-term mortgage loan.

Lending institutions usually offer construction loans to builders and developers. The best way for you to get a construction loan is to arrange for a long-term mortgage loan at the same time you ask for the construction loan. This makes you a more desirable customer since you will be paying interest over many years. Also, you may be charged lower interest for your construction loan than if you were to borrow it alone.

If you intend to obtain financing for your home, you need to assemble the following items:

$ Building plans and specifications for your house. High quality drawings, like those available through this publication, are important. Good drawings reduce errors, risks and loss of time.

$ A building permit from your local housing authority. To obtain a permit, submit your plans, specifications and a site layout so the building permit department can verify that you meet local zoning and building code regulations.

$ A list of the licensed building contractors or subcontractors who will help build your house. If you are using a general contractor, his name will usually suffice.

$ A written and signed agreement with your contractor(s) specifying the work to be done and costs.

$ Waivers of Lien signed by your contractor(s) to protect you in the event that they do not pay their workmen and suppliers.

$ Evidence that you have liability insurance against theft, fire or damage to the building and site during construction.

$ Your personal financial statements and records.

FINANCING

As a general rule, you will arrange for permanent financing before you seek construction financing. This is especially true if you are borrowing from two different sources. The commitment to lend money on your completed home is taken as security on your construction loan by the second lender.

If you want your mortgage loan guaranteed by the Federal Housing Administration (FHA) or the Veterans Administration (VA), you need to approach those agencies before going to a lender. Be sure to take your building plans and specifications and your personal financial statements. If the agency approves your application, it will issue a commitment to insure your mortgage loan. This commitment naturally makes you a more attractive risk to any lender.

LOAN SOURCES

There are three principal sources of mortgage loans and allied construction loans: banks, savings and loan associations, and mortgage bankers.

The most important objective in approaching any of these institutions is to shop carefully for your loan. You are going to pay a lot of interest for a long time, so you need to make sure that you pay the lowest possible total interest. Compare total interest costs before choosing your lender.

As you search for financing, just remember that since you are about to make the biggest financial commitment most of us ever make, it pays to be very thorough.

Total Living Area: 3,814 sq. ft.

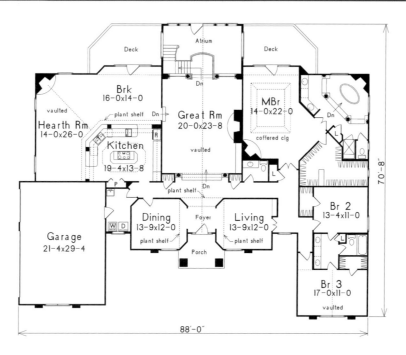

Rear View

Plan Features

- Great room with vaulted ceiling includes balcony overlook of atrium window wall
- Seven vaulted rooms for drama and four fireplaces for warmth
- Master bath is complemented by the colonnade surrounding the sunken tub
- 3,566 square feet on the first floor and 248 square feet on the lower level atrium
- 3 bedrooms, 2 1/2 baths, 3-car side entry garage
- Walk-out basement foundation

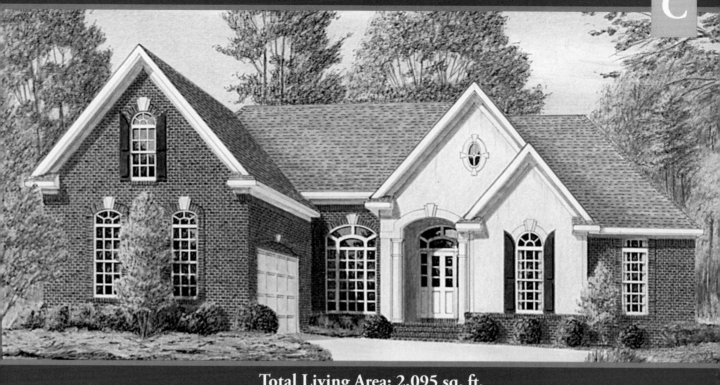

Total Living Area: 2,095 sq. ft.

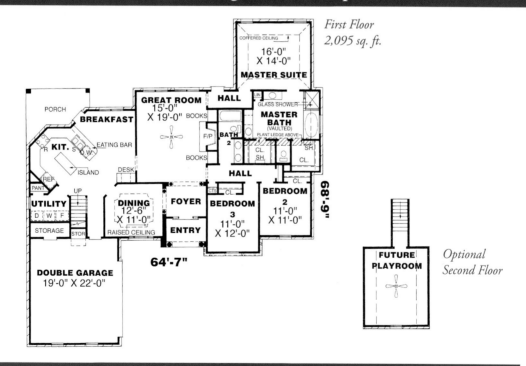

First Floor
2,095 sq. ft.

COFFERED CEILING

16'-0"
X 14'-0"

MASTER SUITE

GREAT ROOM
15'-0"
X 19'-0"   BOOKS

HALL

LIN.

GLASS SHOWER

MASTER BATH
(VAULTED)

PLANT LEDGE ABOVE

PORCH

BREAKFAST

F/P

BATH 2

CL.

SH.

CL.

SH.

CL.

KIT.

EATING BAR

D W

S O W

BOOKS

HALL

CL.

REF

ISLAND

DESK

CL.

BEDROOM 2
11'-0"
X 11'-0"

69'-8"

PANT

UP

DINING
12'-6"
X 11'-0"

FOYER

CTS

CL.

BEDROOM 3
11'-0"
X 12'-0"

UTILITY

D W F

STORAGE

STOR

RAISED CEILING

ENTRY

64'-7"

DOUBLE GARAGE
19'-0" X 22'-0"

FUTURE PLAYROOM

Optional
Second Floor

Plan Features

- Decorative columns add interest to foyer, separating it from the dining and great rooms
- Built-in bookshelves flank a large fireplace
- Stunning U-shaped kitchen design has a substantial amount of space
- Future playroom on the second floor has an additional 231 square feet of living area
- 3 bedrooms, 2 baths, 2-car side entry garage
- Basement or slab foundation, please specify when ordering

Plan #583-007D-0162

Total Living Area: 1,519 sq. ft.

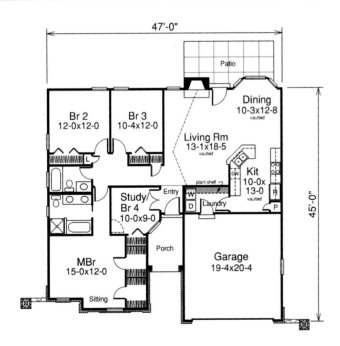

DID YOU KNOW?

Cooking with your kids can be a very scary thought for many parents. But, with a couple of tips it can be a memorable experience for all those involved.

Tips for keeping it safe and fun include:

- Keep a sturdy stool nearby so kids can be a part of the action and aren't reaching for a pan or utensils over their heads.

- Organize a "kid's tools" drawer within their reach so the utensils aren't too sharp. This allows them to take ownership and want to become a part of the cooking.

Plan Features

- The living room has a vaulted ceiling, plant shelf, fireplace and opens to the dining area
- The kitchen has an adjoining laundry/mud room and features a vaulted ceiling, snack counter open to the living and dining areas and a built-in pantry
- Two walk-in closets, a stylish bath and small sitting area accompany the master bedroom
- 4 bedrooms, 2 baths, 2-car garage
- Crawl space foundation, drawings also include slab and basement foundations

Total Living Area: 2,039 sq. ft.

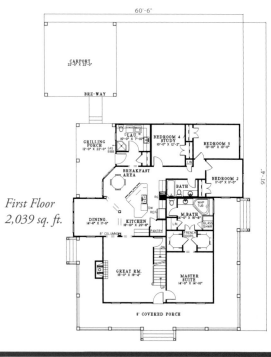

*First Floor
2,039 sq. ft.*

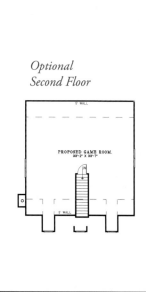

*Optional
Second Floor*

Plan Features

- A walk-in pantry and extra-large island add convenience to the open kitchen
- The luxurious master suite features two walk-in closets and French doors leading to the relaxing master bath
- The optional second floor has an additional 1,155 square feet of living space
- 4 bedrooms, 3 baths, 2-car carport
- Slab or crawl space foundation, please specify when ordering

Total Living Area: 3,426 sq. ft.

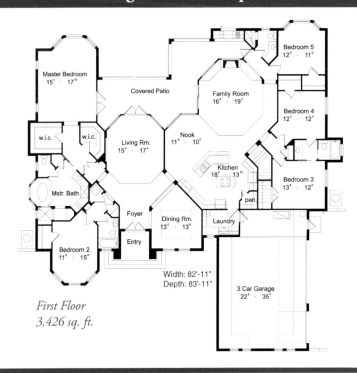

Master Bedroom
15³ · 17¹⁰

Covered Patio

Bedroom 5
12³ · 11³

Family Room
16⁹ · 19³

Bedroom 4
12³ · 12³

w.i.c.

w.i.c.

Living Rm.
15⁹ · 17²

Nook
11⁴ · 10⁰

Kitchen
18³ · 13¹⁰

Bedroom 3
13⁴ · 12³

Mstr. Bath

pan.

Foyer

Dining Rm.
13³ · 13³

Laundry

Entry

Bedroom 2
11³ · 15⁶

Width: 82'-11"
Depth: 83'-11"

3 Car Garage
22³ · 35³

First Floor
3,426 sq. ft.

Optional
Second Floor

w.i.c.

Game Room
15⁴ · 26⁰

Plan Features

- Master bath features two walk-in closets and a whirlpool tub under a bay window
- Angled walls throughout add interest to every room
- The airy kitchen looks into a cozy breakfast nook as well as the casual family room
- Future space on the second floor has an additional 515 square feet of living area
- 5 bedrooms, 4 baths, 3-car side entry garage
- Slab foundation

Total Living Area: 2,880 sq. ft.

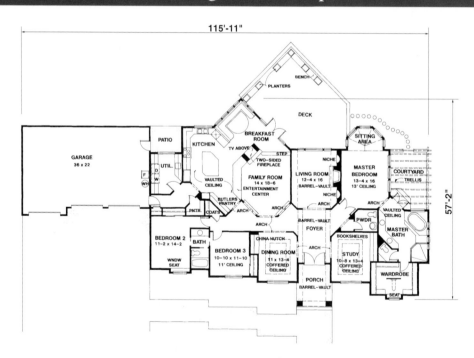

Plan Features

- Varied ceiling heights throughout
- Charming master bedroom features a bayed sitting area, view to the courtyard and an exquisite master bath
- Interesting barrel vaulted living room ceiling
- 3 bedrooms, 2 1/2 baths, 3-car garage
- Crawl space foundation

Rear View

Total Living Area: 1,593 sq. ft.

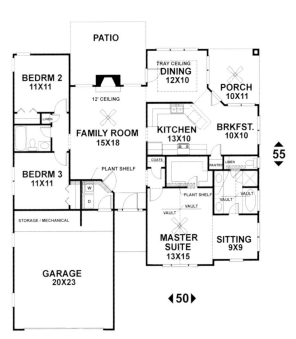

DID YOU KNOW?

The tray ceiling gets its name from its resemblance to an inverted tray. Tray ceilings can be a terrific option when trying to hide recessed lighting in bedrooms.

Plan Features

- Large sitting area is enjoyed by the master bedroom which also features a walk-in closet and bath
- Centrally located kitchen accesses the family, dining and breakfast rooms with ease
- Storage/mechanical area is ideal for seasonal storage or hobby supplies
- 3 bedrooms, 2 baths, 2-car garage
- Basement, crawl space or slab foundation, please specify when ordering

Total Living Area: 1,919 sq. ft.

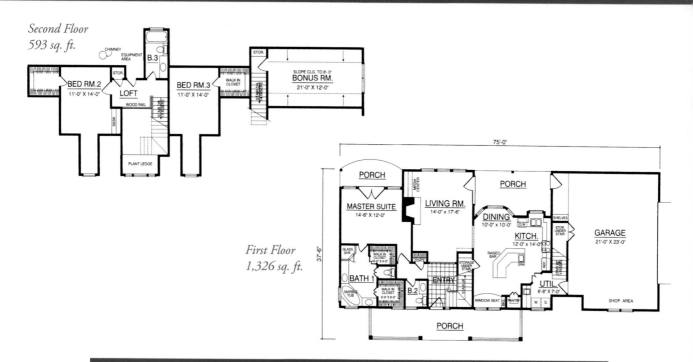

Second Floor
593 sq. ft.

First Floor
1,326 sq. ft.

Plan Features

- The kitchen and dining area feature a bar island with sink, window seat and pantry
- The master suite boasts double-door access to a private porch and a lavish bath
- Both secondary bedrooms include a walk-in closet and charming dormer
- Second floor bonus room has an additional 306 square feet of living area
- 3 bedrooms, 2 1/2 baths, 2-car side entry garage
- Slab or crawl space foundation, please specify when ordering

Total Living Area: 2,684 sq. ft.

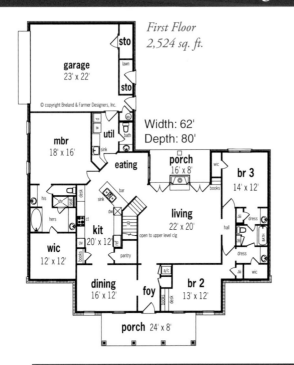

First Floor
2,524 sq. ft.

sto

garage
23' x 22'

lawn

sto

© copyright Breland & Farmer Designers, Inc.

Width: 62'
Depth: 80'

bath

mbr
18' x 16'

util

sink

eating

porch
16' x 8'

wic

br 3
14' x 12'

his

desk

bar

sink

books

hers

ct

dw

kit
20' x 12'

living
22' x 20'

open to upper level clg

hall

dress

BATH

wic
12' x 12'

books

pantry

dress

dining
16' x 12'

a/c

foy

desk

br 2
13' x 12'

wic

porch   24' x 8'

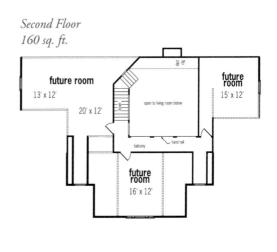

Second Floor
160 sq. ft.

future room
13' x 12'

20' x 12'

open to living room below

future
room
15' x 12'

balcony

hand rail

future
room
16' x 12'

Plan Features

- Formal dining room off kitchen is ideal when entertaining
- Enormous master bedroom has a private bath and walk-in closet
- The second floor has an additional 926 square feet of living area in three future rooms
- 3 bedrooms, 2 1/2 baths, 2-car side entry garage
- Slab foundation, drawings also include crawl space foundation

Total Living Area: 2,590 sq. ft.

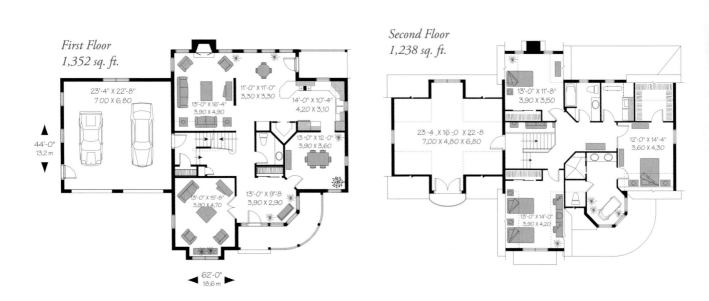

First Floor
1,352 sq. ft.

Second Floor
1,238 sq. ft.

Plan Features

- Energy efficient home with 2" x 6" exterior walls
- Master bedroom has a private bath with double vanity, an oversized shower and a freestanding tub in a bay window
- Bonus room above the garage has an additional 459 square feet of living area
- 3 bedrooms, 2 1/2 baths, 2-car garage
- Basement foundation

Total Living Area: 3,489 sq. ft.

First Floor
2,514 sq. ft.

Second Floor
975 sq. ft.

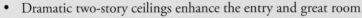

Plan Features

- Dramatic two-story ceilings enhance the entry and great room
- The nook is flooded with sunlight from the large windows and skylights above
- A stovetop island and walk-in pantry add convenience to the large kitchen
- 4 bedrooms, 3 1/2 baths, 3-car side entry garage
- Basement foundation

Total Living Area: 2,331 sq. ft.

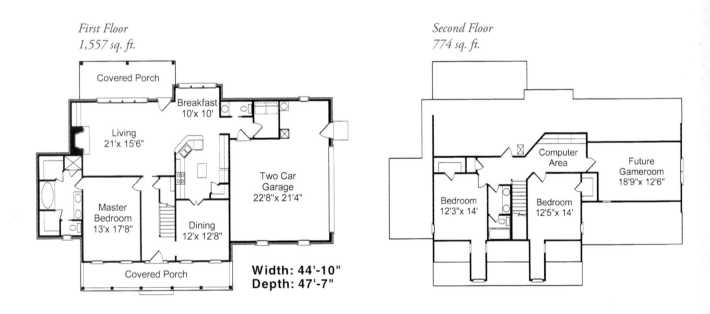

First Floor
1,557 sq. ft.

Covered Porch

Breakfast
10'x 10'

Living
21'x 15'6"

Two Car
Garage
22'8"x 21'4"

Master
Bedroom
13'x 17'8"

Dining
12'x 12'8"

Covered Porch

Width: 44'-10"
Depth: 47'-7"

Second Floor
774 sq. ft.

Computer
Area

Future
Gameroom
18'9"x 12'6"

Bedroom
12'3"x 14'

Bedroom
12'5"x 14'

Plan Features

- Kitchen overlooks living area with fireplace and lots of windows
- Conveniently located first floor master bedroom
- Second floor features computer area with future game room space
- Future gameroom on the second floor has an additional 264 square feet of living area
- 3 bedrooms, 2 1/2 baths, 2-car side entry garage
- Slab foundation

Total Living Area: 1,373 sq. ft.

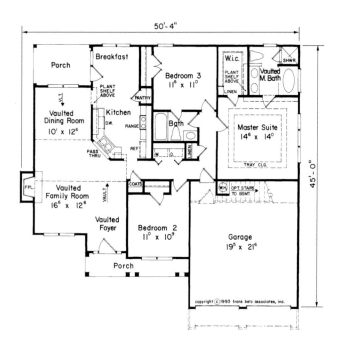

DID YOU KNOW?

The origin of dormer windows goes back centuries to French architect Francois Mansart (1598-1666). Mansart inserted a sequence of windows into the sloping roofs to make the attics inhabitable. This is reflected in the name dormer which comes from the French word dormir which means "to sleep."

Plan Features

- 9' ceilings throughout this home
- Sunny breakfast room is very accessible to the kitchen
- Kitchen has a pass-through to the vaulted family room
- 3 bedrooms, 2 baths, 2-car garage
- Crawl space or walk-out basement foundation, please specify when ordering

Total Living Area: 3,411 sq. ft.

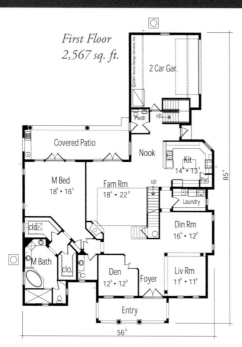

First Floor
2,567 sq. ft.

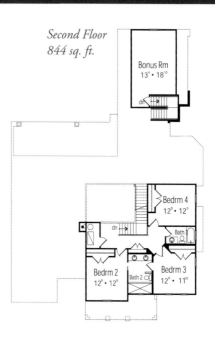

Second Floor
844 sq. ft.

Plan Features

- Secluded living room is a nice conversation area located off the formal dining room
- Breakfast nook looks out onto covered patio
- Framing - only concrete block available
- Bonus room on the second floor has an additional 297 square feet of living area
- 4 bedrooms, 3 full baths, 2 half baths, 2-car side entry garage
- Slab foundation

Plan #583-007D-0058

Total Living Area: 4,826 sq. ft.

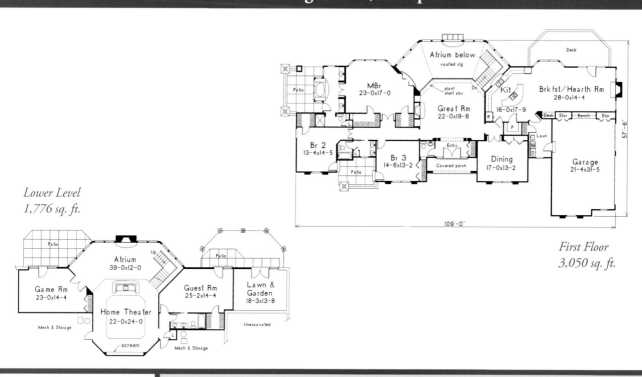

First Floor
3,050 sq. ft.

Lower Level
1,776 sq. ft.

Great Room/Atrium View

Plan Features

- Brightly lit entry connects to great room with balcony and massive bay-shaped atrium
- Kitchen has island/snack bar, walk-in pantry, computer area and an atrium overlook
- Master bedroom has sitting area, walk-in closets, atrium overlook and luxury bath with private courtyard
- 4 bedrooms, 3 1/2 baths, 3-car side entry garage
- Walk-out basement foundation with lawn and garden workroom

Total Living Area: 4,053 sq. ft.

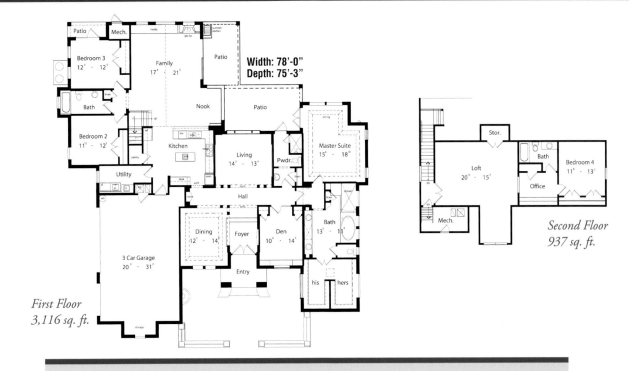

Width: 78'-0"
Depth: 75'-3"

First Floor
3,116 sq. ft.

Second Floor
937 sq. ft.

Plan Features

- The main living areas feature 12' ceilings adding to the spaciousness of this home
- The formal living and dining rooms with arched entrances and decorative columns are located at the entrance for a dramatic first impression
- The informal family room, kitchen and nook combine for an expansive living area
- 4 bedrooms, 4 baths, 3-car side entry garage
- Slab foundation

Total Living Area: 1,992 sq. ft.

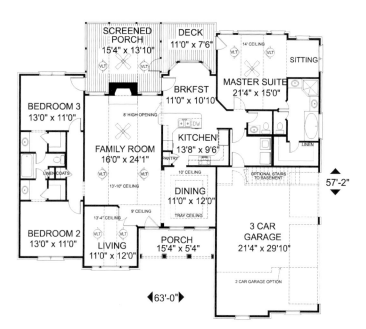

DID YOU KNOW?

The key to a tidy kitchen is efficient storage. Make the most of cupboard space by fixing racks and shelves inside your units — most kitchen suppliers offer a range of clever interior fittings to help you get organized.

Plan Features

- Bayed breakfast room overlooks the outdoor deck and connects to the screened porch
- The formal living room could easily be converted to a home office or study
- A compact, yet efficient kitchen is conveniently situated between the breakfast and dining rooms
- 3 bedrooms, 2 1/2 baths, 3-car side entry garage
- Basement, crawl space or slab foundation, please specify when ordering

Total Living Area: 5,826 sq. ft.

Width: 101'-4"
Depth: 92'-6"

First Floor
3,631 sq. ft.

Second Floor
2,195 sq. ft.

Plan Features

- The master bedroom, family and living rooms enjoy access onto the patio
- The second floor gameroom and loft area access a relaxing balcony
- A comfortable living area is created with the adjoining family room, nook and kitchen
- Bonus rooms above the garages have an additional 822 square feet of living area
- 5 bedrooms, 6 1/2 baths, two 2-car side entry garages
- Slab foundation

Total Living Area: 1,929 sq. ft.

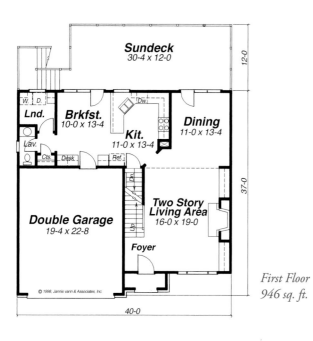

Sundeck
30-4 x 12-0

12-0

Lnd.

W. **D.**

Brkfst.
10-0 x 13-4

Lav.

Cts. **Desk**

Kit.
11-0 x 13-4

Dw.

Ref.

Dining
11-0 x 13-4

37-0

Double Garage
19-4 x 22-8

**Two Story
Living Area**
16-0 x 19-0

Foyer

© 1998, Jannis vann & Associates, Inc.

40-0

First Floor
946 sq. ft.

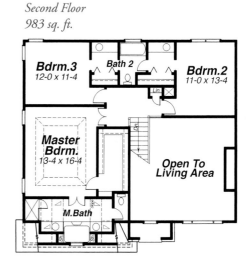

Second Floor
983 sq. ft.

Bdrm.3
12-0 x 11-4

Bath 2

Bdrm.2
11-0 x 13-4

Lin.

**Master
Bdrm.**
13-4 x 16-4

**Open To
Living Area**

M.Bath

Plan Features

- Luxurious master bath has an enormous spa tub with surrounding shelves and double vanities
- Spacious laundry room has counterspace for folding
- Breakfast area has a handy desk
- 3 bedrooms, 2 1/2 baths, 2-car garage
- Walk-out basement foundation

Total Living Area: 2,254 sq. ft.

© design basics inc.

DID YOU KNOW?

Clean off the countertops by storing mail, keys, and to-do lists in an organized built-in desk like the one designed in this home plan. This feature helps keep the kitchen the place for cooking and dining exclusively.

Plan Features

- Built-in hutch in the formal dining room has a custom feel
- See-through fireplace from the kitchen into the great room is warm and well designed
- Large master bath has a wonderful corner whirlpool tub
- 2 bedrooms, 2 baths, 3-car side entry garage
- Basement foundation

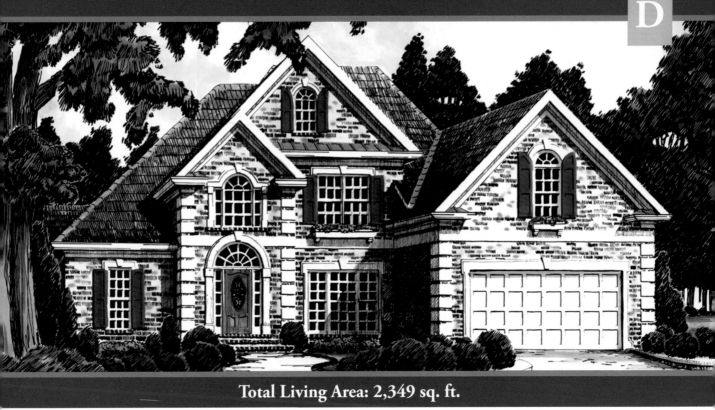

Total Living Area: 2,349 sq. ft.

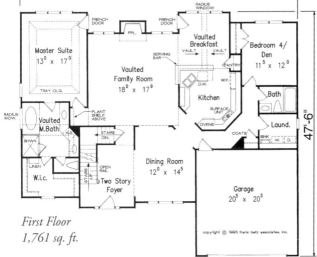

First Floor
1,761 sq. ft.

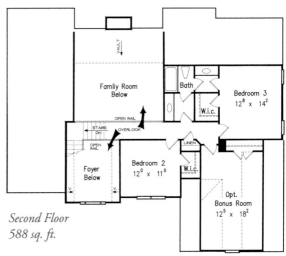

Second Floor
588 sq. ft.

Plan Features

- Open and airy home features a two-story foyer and family room
- Den is secluded from the rest of the home and is ideal as an office space
- Second floor bedrooms have walk-in closets and share a bath
- Optional bonus room has an additional 276 square feet of living area
- 4 bedrooms, 3 baths, 2-car garage
- Walk-out basement, slab or crawl space foundation, please specify when ordering

Total Living Area: 1,927 sq. ft.

First Floor
1,927 sq. ft.

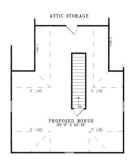

Optional
Second Floor

Plan Features

- Bedrooms are secluded on one side of the home
- The kitchen includes a wrap-around counter with seating and opens to the dining room and breakfast room
- Optional second floor has an additional 909 square feet of living space
- 3 bedrooms, 2 baths, 2-car rear entry garage
- Slab, crawl space, basement or walk-out basement foundation, please specify when ordering

Total Living Area: 2,340 sq. ft.

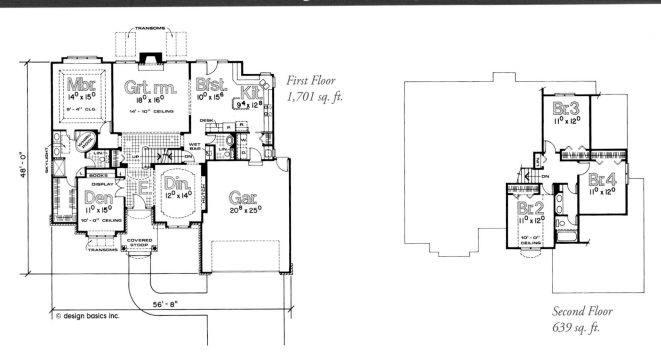

First Floor
1,701 sq. ft.

Second Floor
639 sq. ft.

Plan Features

- Box-bay windows in the front of home add interest in the dining room and den
- Master bedroom features a one-of-a-kind whirlpool tub
- Kitchen has lots of counterspace and cabinetry stretching into the breakfast area
- Centrally located wet bar for entertaining
- 4 bedrooms, 2 1/2 baths, 2-car garage
- Basement foundation

Total Living Area: 2,505 sq. ft.

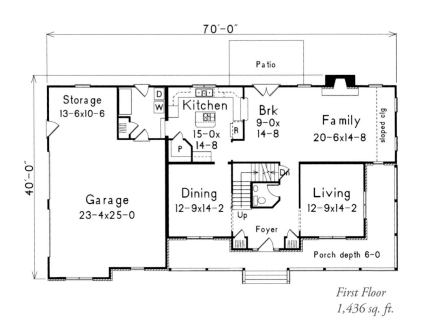

70'-0"

Patio

Storage
13-6x10-6

Kitchen
15-0x
14-8

Brk
9-0x
14-8

Family
20-6x14-8

sloped clg

40'-0"

Garage
23-4x25-0

Dining
12-9x14-2

Up

Dn

Living
12-9x14-2

Foyer

Porch depth 6-0

First Floor
1,436 sq. ft.

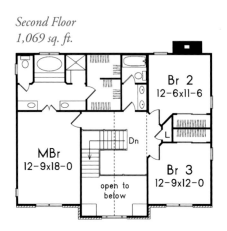

Second Floor
1,069 sq. ft.

Br 2
12-6x11-6

MBr
12-9x18-0

Dn

L

open to
below

Br 3
12-9x12-0

Plan Features

- The garage features extra storage area and ample workspace
- Laundry room is accessible from the garage and the outdoors
- Deluxe raised tub and immense walk-in closet grace the master bath
- 3 bedrooms, 2 1/2 baths, 2-car side entry garage
- Basement foundation, drawings also include crawl space foundation

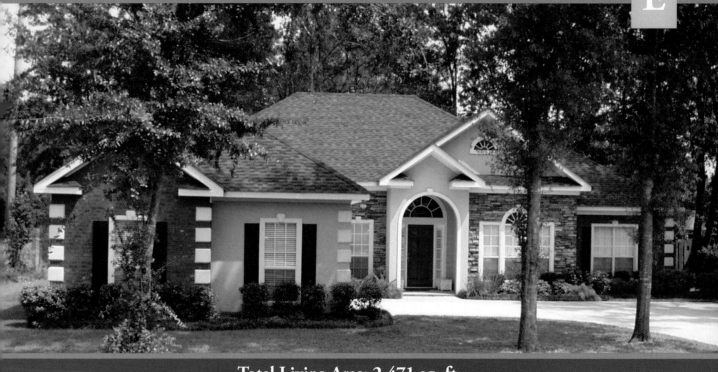

Total Living Area: 2,471 sq. ft.

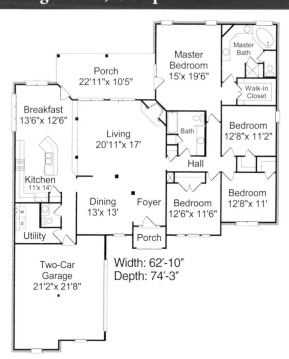

Porch
22'11"x 10'5"

Master Bedroom
15'x 19'6"

Master Bath

Walk-In Closet

Breakfast
13'6"x 12'6"

Living
20'11"x 17'

Bath

Bedroom
12'8"x 11'2"

Kitchen
11'x 14'

Hall

Dining
13'x 13'

Foyer

Bedroom
12'6"x 11'6"

Bedroom
12'8"x 11'

Utility

Porch

Two-Car Garage
21'2"x 21'8"

Width: 62'-10"
Depth: 74'-3"

Plan Features

- Decorative columns define the formal dining room
- The spacious living room enjoys a warm fireplace and porch access
- The kitchen and breakfast area combine and maintain openness with the living room
- The right side of the home is for relaxing with all the bedrooms situated together
- 4 bedrooms, 2 1/2 baths, 2-car side entry garage
- Slab foundation

Total Living Area: 1,763 sq. ft.

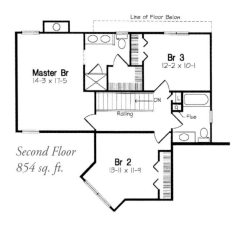

First Floor
909 sq. ft.

48'-0"

Deck

DN

Brkfst
10-4 x 9-6

Kitchen
10-9 x 12-5

DW

Living Rm
14-0 x 17-5

Pant.   Ref.

UP   DN

Flue

44'-0"

Clg Reveal

Dining Rm
11-8 x 14-0

Garage
21-5 x 21-9

Covered Porch

Second Floor
854 sq. ft.

Line of Floor Below

Master Br
14-3 x 17-5

Br 3
12-2 x 10-1

Railing

DN

Flue

Br 2
13-11 x 11-9

Plan Features

- Dining room has a large box-bay window and a recessed ceiling
- Living room includes a large fireplace
- Kitchen has plenty of workspace, a pantry and a double sink overlooking the deck
- Master bedroom features a large bath with walk-in closet
- 3 bedrooms, 2 1/2 baths, 2-car garage
- Basement foundation

Rear View

Total Living Area: 2,421 sq. ft.

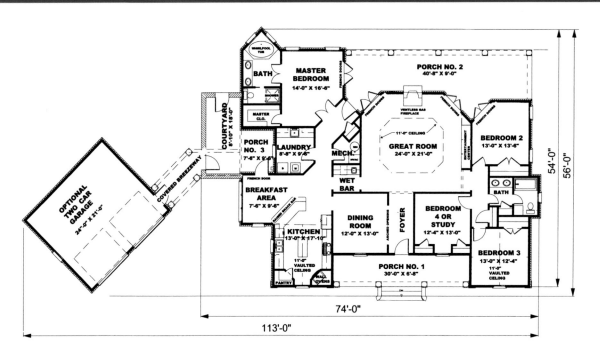

Plan Features

- Charming courtyard on the side of the home easily accesses the porch leading into the breakfast area
- French doors throughout home create a sunny atmosphere
- Master bedroom accesses the covered porch
- 4 bedrooms, 2 baths, optional 2-car detached garage
- Crawl space or slab foundation, please specify when ordering

Total Living Area: 2,029 sq. ft.

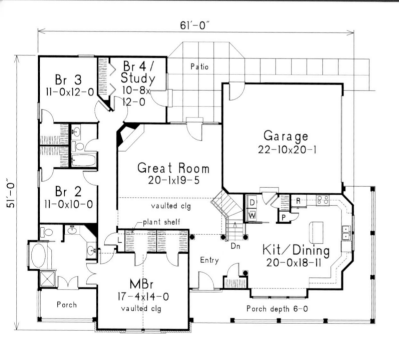

DID YOU KNOW?

The hearth generally refers to the space in front of the firebox, but most people use it loosely to refer to the entire fireplace.

Plan Features

- Stonework, gables, roof dormer and double porches create a country flavor
- Kitchen has an island snack bar, built-in pantry and cheery dining area with multiple tall windows
- Master bedroom boasts two walk-in closets, a private bath with double-door entry and a secluded porch
- 4 bedrooms, 2 baths, 2-car side entry garage
- Basement foundation, drawings also include crawl space and slab foundations

Total Living Area: 1,855 sq. ft.

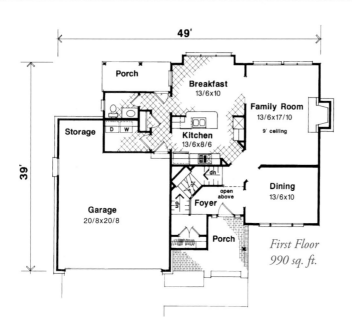

49'

39'

Porch

Breakfast
13/6x10

Family Room
13/6x17/10
9' ceiling

Storage

Kitchen
13/6x8/6

D W

Garage
20/8x20/8

sp

open
above

dn.

Foyer

Dining
13/6x10

Porch

First Floor
990 sq. ft.

Master
13/6x17/10

Br.#3
10 x13/6

Attic Storage

dn.

foyer below

Br.#2
11x11/2

Second Floor
865 sq. ft.

Plan Features

- Angled stairs add character to the two-story foyer
- Secluded dining area is formal and elegant
- Sunny master bedroom has all the luxuries
- A half bath is conveniently located off the kitchen and breakfast area
- 3 bedrooms, 2 1/2 baths, 2-car garage
- Basement foundation

Total Living Area: 2,449 sq. ft.

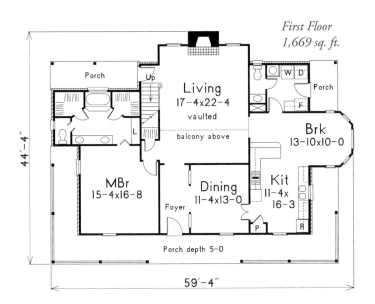

First Floor
1,669 sq. ft.

Porch

Up

Living
17-4x22-4
vaulted

W D

Porch

F

balcony above

Brk
13-10x10-0

L

MBr
15-4x16-8

Dining
11-4x13-0

Kit
11-4x
16-3

Foyer

P

R

Porch depth 5-0

44'-4"

59'-4"

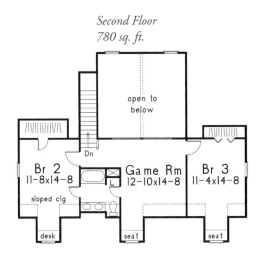

Second Floor
780 sq. ft.

open to
below

Dn

Br 2
11-8x14-8

Game Rm
12-10x14-8

Br 3
11-4x14-8

L

sloped clg

desk

seat

seat

Plan Features

- Striking living area features fireplace flanked with windows, cathedral ceiling and balcony
- First floor master bedroom has twin walk-in closets and large linen storage
- Dormers add space for desks or seats
- 3 bedrooms, 2 1/2 baths, 2-car detached garage
- Slab foundation, drawings also include crawl space foundation

D

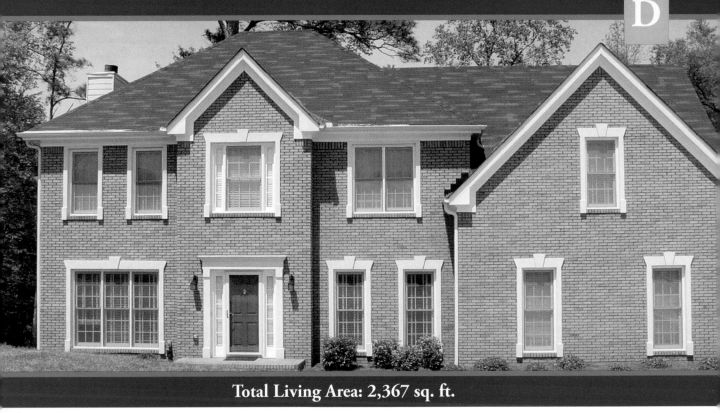

Total Living Area: 2,367 sq. ft.

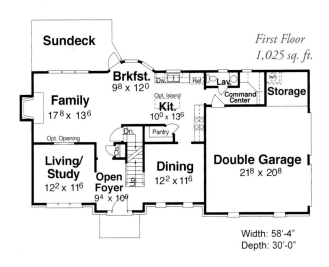

First Floor
1,025 sq. ft.

Sundeck

Brkfst.
9⁸ x 12⁰

Family
17⁸ x 13⁶

Lav.

Command Center

Storage

Kit.
10⁰ x 13⁶

Opt. Island

Living/Study
12² x 11⁶

Open Foyer
9⁴ x 10⁰

Dining
12² x 11⁶

Double Garage
21⁸ x 20⁸

Pantry

Width: 58'-4"
Depth: 30'-0"

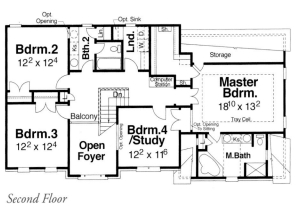

Bdrm.2
12² x 12⁴

Bth.2

Lnd.

Storage

Computer Station

Master Bdrm.
18¹⁰ x 13²

Balcony

Bdrm.3
12² x 12⁴

Open Foyer

Bdrm.4/Study
12² x 11⁶

M.Bath

Second Floor
1,342 sq. ft.

Plan Features

- Many optional features offer flexibility to this plan
- Bayed breakfast area features access to rear sundeck
- All bedrooms are located on the second floor with laundry room for convenience
- 4 bedrooms, 2 1/2 baths, 2-car side entry garage
- Walk-out basement foundation

Total Living Area: 2,874 sq. ft.

Second Floor
728 sq. ft.

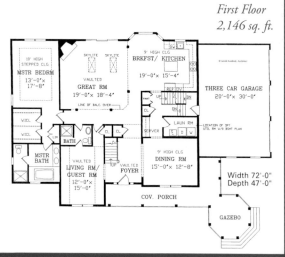

First Floor
2,146 sq. ft.

Width 72'-0"
Depth 47'-0"

Plan Features

- Openness characterizes the casual areas
- The kitchen is separated from the bayed breakfast nook by an island workspace
- Stunning great room has dramatic vaulted ceiling and a corner fireplace
- Unfinished loft on the second floor has an additional 300 square feet of living area
- 4 bedrooms, 3 baths, 3-car side entry garage
- Basement, crawl space or slab foundation, please specify when ordering

Total Living Area: 1,600 sq. ft.

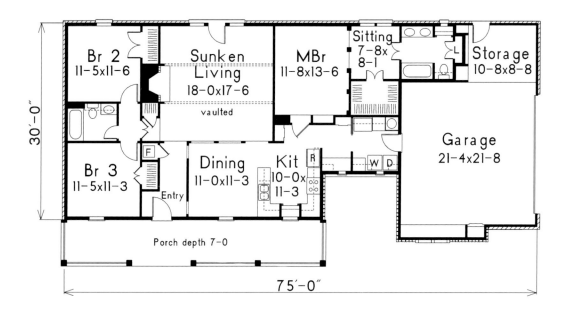

Br 2
11-5x11-6

Sunken Living
18-0x17-6
vaulted

MBr
11-8x13-6

Sitting
7-8x 8-1

Storage
10-8x8-8

Br 3
11-5x11-3

Entry

Dining
11-0x11-3

Kit
10-0x 11-3

R

W D

Garage
21-4x21-8

F

30'-0"

Porch depth 7-0

75'-0"

Plan Features

- Energy efficient home with 2" x 6" exterior walls
- Impressive sunken living room features a massive stone fireplace and 16' vaulted ceiling
- Special amenities include a sewing room, glass shelves in kitchen and master bath and a large utility area
- 3 bedrooms, 2 baths, 2-car side entry garage
- Slab foundation, drawings also include crawl space and basement foundations

Total Living Area: 1,965 sq. ft.

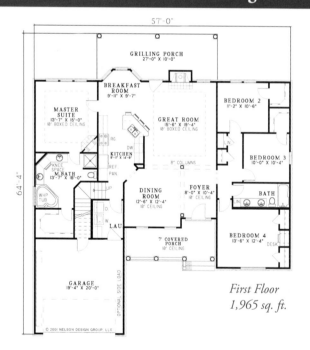

*First Floor
1,965 sq. ft.*

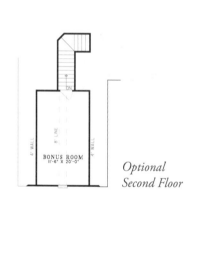

*Optional
Second Floor*

Plan Features

- Master bedroom has a cozy fireplace and a luxurious bath featuring a whirlpool tub, double vanities and a large walk-in closet
- Breakfast room has sunny bay windows
- Optional second floor has an additional 251 square feet of living area
- 4 bedrooms, 2 baths, 2-car garage
- Slab or crawl space foundation, please specify when ordering

Total Living Area: 3,160 sq. ft.

First Floor
1,868 sq. ft.

Second Floor
1,292 sq. ft.

Width: 55'-0"
Depth: 59'-4"

Plan Features

- Kitchen opens to family room with seating bar and connects with charming bayed nook
- The glorious master bedroom features a bayed sitting area, double-door access to covered patio and two walk-in closets
- Framing - only concrete block available
- 5 bedrooms, 3 1/2 baths, 2-car garage
- Slab foundation

Total Living Area: 2,531 sq. ft.

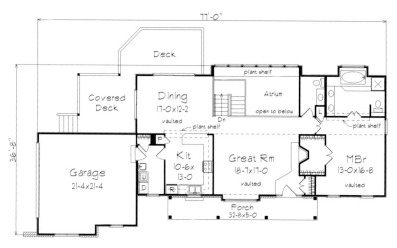

First Floor
1,297 sq. ft.

77'-0"

Deck

Covered Deck

Dining
17-0x12-2
vaulted

plant shelf

Atrium
open to below

plant shelf

plant shelf

36'-8"

Garage
21-4x21-4

Kit
10-6x
13-0

Great Rm
18-7x17-0
vaulted

MBr
13-0x16-8
vaulted

Porch
32-8x5-0

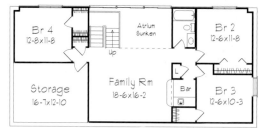

Lower Level
1,234 sq. ft.

Br 4
12-8x11-8

Atrium
Sunken

Br 2
12-6x11-8

Up

Storage
16-7x12-10

Family Rm
18-6x16-2

Bar

Br 3
12-6x10-3

Plan Features

- Charming porch with dormers leads into vaulted great room with atrium
- Well-designed kitchen and breakfast bar adjoin an extra-large laundry/mud room
- Double sinks, tub with window above and plant shelf complete vaulted master bath
- 4 bedrooms, 2 1/2 baths, 2-car side entry garage
- Walk-out basement foundation

Rear View

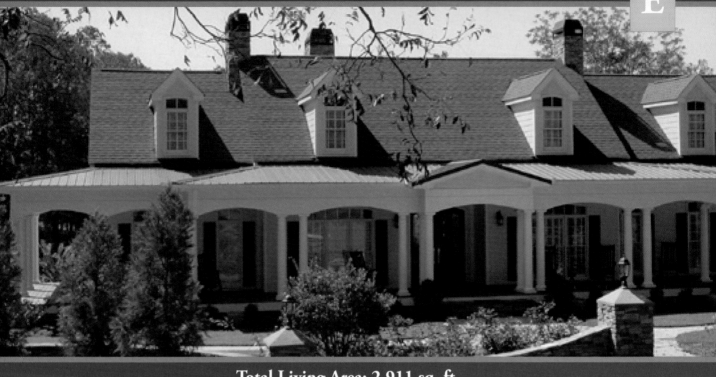

Total Living Area: 2,911 sq. ft.

DID YOU KNOW?

When planning a computer desk, you need a desk surface that is at least 24 inches deep unless you are using a laptop. But, keep in mind even more surface space will be welcomed for files and papers.

Rear View

Plan Features

- Wrap-around porch with double columns
- Optional living area above garage has an additional 512 square feet
- Beautiful master bath with corner tub, separate shower and large walk-in closet
- Large sundeck offers a great area to relax
- 3 bedrooms, 2 1/2 baths, 2-car side entry garage
- Partial basement/crawl space foundation

Total Living Area: 1,575 sq. ft.

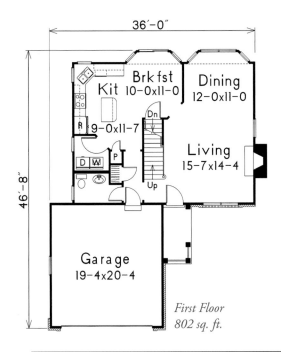

36'-0"

Brkfst
10-0x11-0

Kit
9-0x11-7

Dining
12-0x11-0

Living
15-7x14-4

Dn

Up

P

D W

R

46'-8"

Garage
19-4x20-4

First Floor
802 sq. ft.

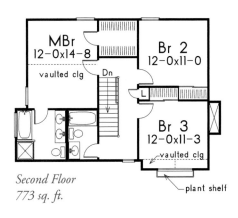

MBr
12-0x14-8
vaulted clg

Br 2
12-0x11-0

Dn

L

Br 3
12-0x11-3
vaulted clg

plant shelf

Second Floor
773 sq. ft.

Plan Features

- Inviting porch leads to spacious living and dining rooms
- Kitchen with corner windows features an island snack bar, attractive breakfast room bay, convenient laundry area and built-in pantry
- A luxury bath and walk-in closet adorn the master bedroom suite
- 3 bedrooms, 2 1/2 baths, 2-car garage
- Basement foundation, drawings also include crawl space and slab foundations

Total Living Area: 2,253 sq. ft.

First Floor
1,719 sq. ft.

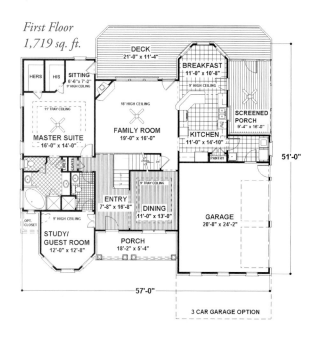

Second Floor
534 sq. ft.

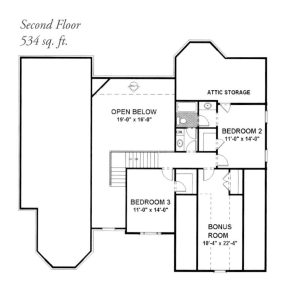

Plan Features

- Two bedrooms on the second floor share a bath
- Two walk-in closets, a private bath and a sitting area leading to an outdoor deck are all amenities of the master suite
- Bonus room on the second floor has an additional 247 square feet of living area
- 4 bedrooms, 3 baths, 2-car side entry garage
- Basement foundation

Plan #583-007D-0013

First Floor
760 sq. ft.

35'-0"

41'-8"

Deck

Brk
9-0x
11-0

Kit
10-9x14-6

Dining
12-0x9-4

Living
15-8x14-0

Up

Porch

Garage
19-4x21-4

Second Floor
732 sq. ft.

MBr
11-0x14-8

Dn.

Br 2
12-0x11-0

Br 3
12-0x9-9

raised
ceiling

Total Living Area: 1,492 sq. ft.

Plan Features

- Angled entry spills into the living and dining rooms which share warmth from the fireplace flanked by arched windows
- Master bedroom includes a double-door entry, huge walk-in closet, shower and bath with picture window
- Stucco and dutch-hipped roofs add warmth and charm
- 3 bedrooms, 2 1/2 baths, 2-car garage
- Basement foundation

Plan #583-024D-0041

Total Living Area: 1,401 sq. ft.

Plan Features

- This home is perfect for tackling a narrow lot
- The bedrooms share the right side of the home and are private from the living areas
- A corner fireplace in the family room also warms the adjoining kitchen and dining room
- Sliding glass doors lead to the relaxing rear porch
- 3 bedrooms, 2 baths
- Slab foundation

Porch

Extra Stor.

Master Bath

Walk-In Closet

Family Room
15'8"x 14'8"

Master Bedroom
13'4"x 15'2"

Kitchen
10'8"x 10'4"

Utility
9'4"x 5'4"

Bedroom
10'10"x 10'7"

Dining
10'8"x 10'6"

Bath

Width: 30'-0"
Depth: 59'-10"

Porch

Bedroom
10'10"x 10'6"

Total Living Area: 2,253 sq. ft.

57'-0"

First Floor
1,203 sq. ft.

GARAGE
22'-0" x 24'-0"

PORCH
DN

DINING ROOM
11'-0" x 14'-6"

GREAT ROOM
17'-6" x 15'-0"

POWDER ROOM

DN

KITCHEN
12'-6" x 12'-6"

BREAKFAST
10'-6" x 10'-6"

REF.

51'-8"

DN

UP

FOYER

PARLOR
15'-0" x 13'-0"

DN

PORCH
DN

Second Floor
1,050 sq. ft.

MASTER BEDROOM
16'-0" x 14'-4"

MASTER BATH

SLOPED CLG.

BATH

BEDROOM #2
14'-9" x 10'-6"

DN

LAUNDRY
W
D

BEDROOM #3
14'-6" x 13'-0"

OPEN TO FOYER BELOW

Plan Features

- Great room is joined by the rear covered porch
- Secluded parlor provides area for peace and quiet or a private office
- Sloped ceiling adds drama to the master bedroom
- Great room, kitchen and breakfast area combine for a large open living area
- 3 bedrooms, 2 1/2 baths, 2-car garage
- Basement foundation

Plan #583-016D-0055

Price Code: B

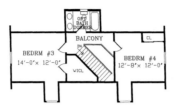

Optional Second Floor

Optional First Floor Design

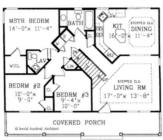

Width: 40'-0"
Depth: 26'-0"

First Floor 1,040 sq. ft.

Total Living Area: 1,040 sq. ft.

Plan Features

- A wide archway joins the formal living room to the dramatic angled kitchen and dining room
- Optional second floor has an additional 597 square feet of living area
- Optional first floor design has 2 bedrooms including a large master bedroom that enjoys a private luxury bath
- 3 bedrooms, 1 1/2 baths
- Basement, crawl space or slab foundation, please specify when ordering

---

Plan #583-011D-0002

Price Code: C

Total Living Area: 1,557 sq. ft.

Plan Features

- Vaulted dining room extends off the great room and features an eye-catching plant shelf above
- Double closets adorn the vaulted master bedroom which also features a private bath with tub and shower
- Bedroom #3/den has the option to add a double-door entry creating the feeling of a home office if needed
- 3 bedrooms, 2 baths, 2-car garage
- Crawl space foundation

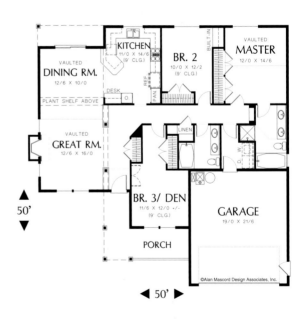

Total Living Area: 1,575 sq. ft.

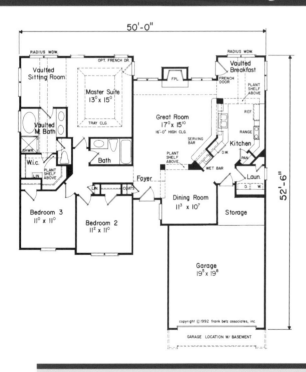

DID YOU KNOW?

Double your storage capacity in even the smallest of closets by adding two tiers of hanging rods instead of one. It's a simple and inexpensive way to increase your closet space. However, don't forget to leave a small portion for longer items so you don't loose that length entirely for storage.

Plan Features

- 9' ceilings throughout this home
- Plant shelves accent the vaulted breakfast room and dining room
- Enormous serving bar in great room is ideal for entertaining
- 3 bedrooms, 2 baths, 2-car garage
- Crawl space or walk-out basement foundation, please specify when ordering

Plan #583-035D-0039

Price Code: **D**

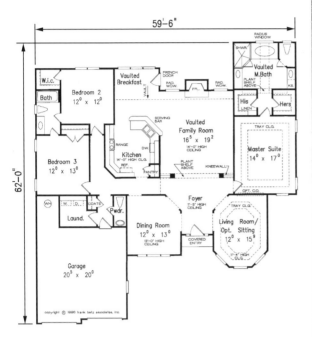

Total Living Area: 2,201 sq. ft.

Plan Features

- Open floor plan makes home feel airy and bright
- Beautiful living room has a cheerful bay window
- Master suite has two walk-in closets
- Family room, kitchen and breakfast area combine for added space
- 3 bedrooms, 2 1/2 baths, 2-car garage
- Walk-out basement, slab or crawl space foundation, please specify when ordering

---

Plan #583-017D-0007

Price Code: **C**

Total Living Area: 1,567 sq. ft.

Plan Features

- Living room flows into the dining room shaped by an angled pass-through into the kitchen
- Master bedroom is secluded for privacy
- Future area available on the second floor has an additional 338 square feet of living area
- 3 bedrooms, 2 baths, 2-car side entry garage
- Partial basement/crawl space foundation, drawings also include slab foundation

Optional Second Floor

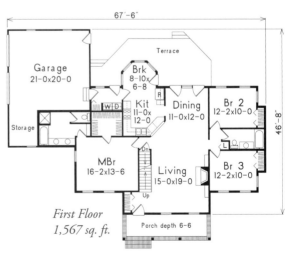

First Floor 1,567 sq. ft.

Total Living Area: 3,149 sq. ft.

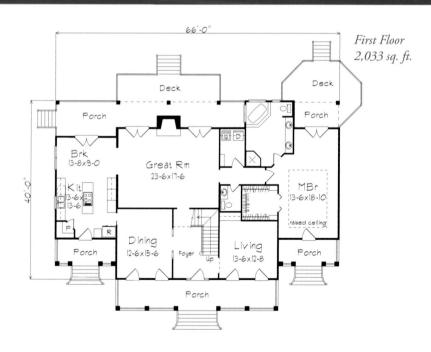

First Floor
2,033 sq. ft.

66'-0"

Deck

Deck

Porch

Porch

40'-0"

Brk
13-8x9-0

Great Rm
23-6x17-6

MBr
13-6x18-10

Kit
13-6x13-6

raised ceiling

P

R

Dining
12-6x15-6

Foyer

up

Living
13-6x12-8

Porch

Porch

Porch

Second Floor
1,116 sq. ft.

Br 4
13-6x12-0

Balcony

Br 2
12-6x13-6

Dn

open to below

Br 3
13-6x15-0

Rear View

Plan Features

- 10' ceilings on the first floor and 9' ceilings on the second floor
- All bedrooms include walk-in closets
- Formal living and dining rooms flank the two-story foyer
- 4 bedrooms, 3 1/2 baths, 2-car detached garage
- Slab foundation, drawings also include crawl space foundation

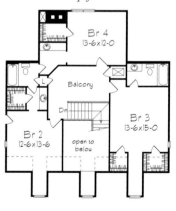

Total Living Area: 1,283 sq. ft.

DID YOU KNOW?

A compact kitchen can be efficient, but not when it lacks storage. One way to stretch the space without compromising design is to extend the cabinets to the ceiling. Although a harder reach, it is the perfect solution for items you rarely need.

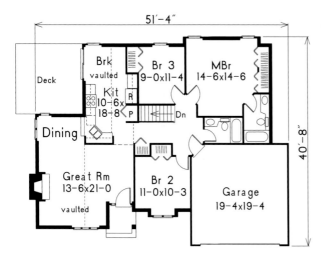

Plan Features

- Vaulted breakfast room has sliding doors that open onto deck
- Kitchen features convenient corner sink and pass-through to dining room
- Open living atmosphere in dining area and great room
- Vaulted great room features a fireplace
- 3 bedrooms, 2 baths, 2-car garage
- Basement foundation

Total Living Area: 1,992 sq. ft.

Plan Features

- Angled walls add drama to the family room, master bedroom and breakfast area
- Covered porch includes a spa and the outdoor kitchen with sink, refrigerator and cooktop
- Enter the majestic master bath to find a dramatic corner oversized tub
- 4 bedrooms, 3 baths, 2-car side entry garage
- Basement, crawl space or slab foundation, please specify when ordering

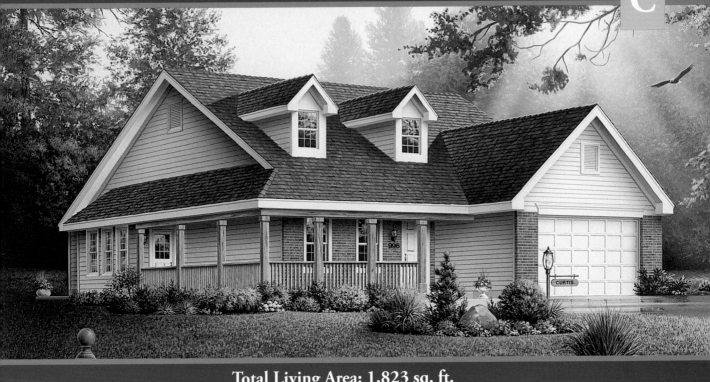

Total Living Area: 1,823 sq. ft.

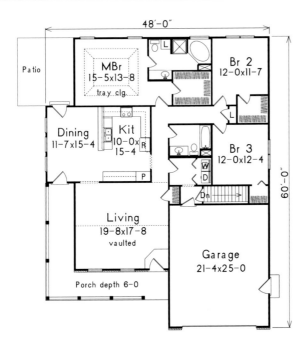

48'-0"

60'-0"

Patio

MBr
15-5x13-8
tray clg.

Br 2
12-0x11-7

Dining
11-7x15-4

Kit
10-0x
15-4

Br 3
12-0x12-4

W
D

Dn

Living
19-8x17-8
vaulted

Garage
21-4x25-0

Porch depth 6-0

DID YOU KNOW?

When making a bed, the top sheet or flat sheet always goes the "wrong" side up. This way when you fold back the top of the sheet the decorative or printed side will be seen.

Plan Features

- Vaulted living room is spacious and easily accesses the dining area
- The master bedroom boasts a tray ceiling, large walk-in closet and a private bath
- Cheerful dining area is convenient to the U-shaped kitchen and also enjoys patio access
- Centrally located laundry room connects the garage to the living areas
- 3 bedrooms, 2 baths, 2-car garage
- Basement foundation

Plan #583-055D-0016

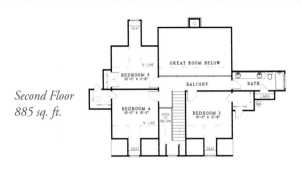

Second Floor
885 sq. ft.

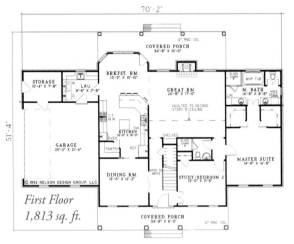

First Floor
1,813 sq. ft.

Total Living Area: 2,698 sq. ft.

Plan Features

- Great room feels spacious with a vaulted ceiling and windows overlooking the covered porch
- Master bath has a glass shower and whirlpool tub
- Laundry area includes counterspace and a sink
- 4 bedrooms, 3 baths, 2-car side entry garage
- Crawl space or slab foundation, please specify when ordering

Plan #583-020D-0005

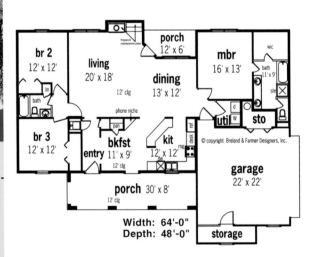

Total Living Area: 1,770 sq. ft.

Plan Features

- Open floor plan makes this home feel spacious
- 12' ceilings in kitchen, living, breakfast and dining areas
- Kitchen is the center of activity with views into all gathering places
- 3 bedrooms, 2 baths, 2-car side entry garage
- Slab foundation, drawings also include crawl space foundation

Total Living Area: 3,657 sq. ft.

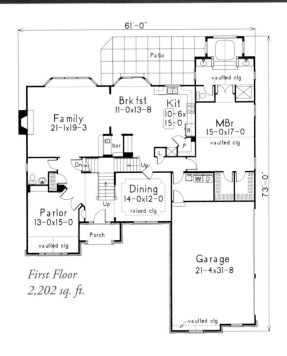

First Floor
2,202 sq. ft.

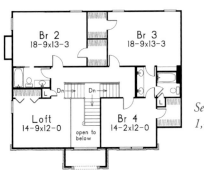

Second Floor
1,455 sq. ft.

Plan Features

- Dramatic two-story foyer has a stylish niche, a convenient powder room and French doors leading to parlor
- State-of-the-art kitchen includes a large walk-in pantry, breakfast island, computer center and 40' vista through family room with walk-in wet bar
- The master bath features marble steps, Roman columns and a whirlpool tub
- 4 bedrooms, 3 1/2 baths, 3-car side entry garage
- Basement foundation

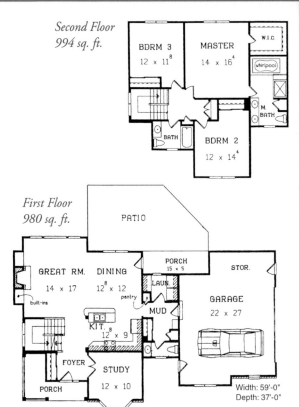

Second Floor
994 sq. ft.

BDRM 3
12 x 11⁸

MASTER
14 x 16⁴

W.I.C.

whirlpool

M. BATH

BATH

BDRM 2
12 x 14⁴

First Floor
980 sq. ft.

PATIO

GREAT RM.
14 x 17

DINING
12⁸ x 12

PORCH
15 x 5

STOR.

LAUN.

pantry

MUD

GARAGE
22 x 27

built-ins

KIT.
12⁸ x 9

FOYER

STUDY
12 x 10

PORCH

Width: 59'-0"
Depth: 37'-0"

Total Living Area: 1,974 sq. ft.

Plan Features

- Bayed study has a double-door entry
- Large mud room and laundry closet are perfect for family living
- Kitchen island has a sink and space for dining
- 3 bedrooms, 2 1/2 baths, 2-car side entry garage
- Basement foundation

Total Living Area: 1,994 sq. ft.

Plan Features

- Office/parlor/bedroom #4 has a double-door entry and is a very versatile space
- Sliding glass doors and many windows create a cheerful great room and breakfast room
- Double walk-in closets and vanity grace the master bath
- 3 bedrooms, 2 baths, optional 2-car side entry garage
- Basement, crawl space or slab foundation, please specify when ordering

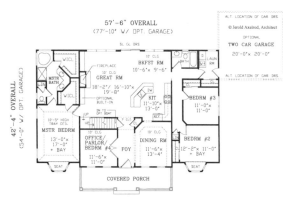

57'-6" OVERALL
(77'-10" W/ OPT. GARAGE)

© Jerold Axelrod, Architect

OPTIONAL
TWO CAR GARAGE
20'-0" x 20'-0"

ALT. LOCATION OF CAR DRS.

BKFST RM
10'-6" x 9'-6"

GREAT RM
18'-2" x 16'-10"
19'-8"

KIT
11'-10" x
13'-0"

BEDRM #3
11'-10" x
11'-0"

MSTR BATH

WICL
WICL

MSTR BEDRM
13'-0" x
17'-0"
+ BAY

OFFICE/
PARLOR/
BEDRM #4
11'-0" x
11'-0"

FOY

DINING RM
11'-6" x
13'-4"

BEDRM #2
12'-2" x 11'-0"
+ BAY

COVERED PORCH

42'-4" OVERALL
(54'-0" W/ OPT. GARAGE)

Total Living Area: 2,246 sq. ft.

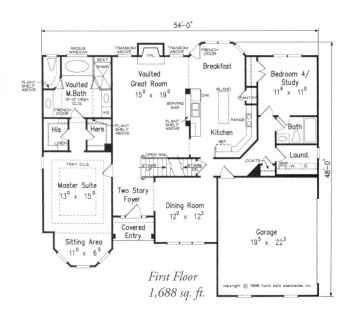

First Floor
1,688 sq. ft.

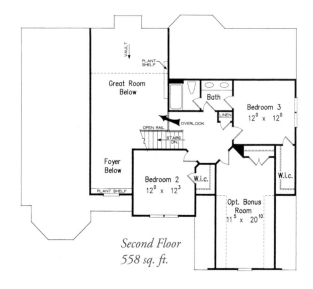

Second Floor
558 sq. ft.

Plan Features

- Master suite has a sitting area with bay window
- Breakfast area is near the kitchen
- Bedroom #4 easily converts to an office
- Optional bonus room has an additional 269 square feet of living area
- 4 bedrooms, 3 baths, 2-car side entry garage
- Walk-out basement, slab or crawl space foundation, please specify when ordering

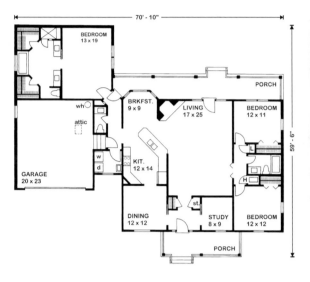

Total Living Area: 2,070 sq. ft.

Plan Features

- The immense living room features an 11' ceiling, corner fireplace and atrium doors leading to a large rear porch
- The kitchen includes a handy buffet bar and opens to the charming bayed breakfast area and formal living room
- A private bedroom, perfect for a master suite, features a bath, walk-in closets, two vanities and a whirlpool tub
- 3 bedrooms, 2 1/2 baths, 2-car garage
- Crawl space or slab foundation, please specify when ordering

Plan #583-033D-0012

Price Code:

C

Total Living Area: 1,546 sq. ft.

Plan Features

- Spacious, open rooms create a casual atmosphere
- Master bedroom is secluded for privacy
- Dining room features a large bay window
- Kitchen and dinette combine for added space and include access to the outdoors
- Large laundry room includes a convenient sink
- 3 bedrooms, 2 baths, 2-car garage
- Basement foundation

Total Living Area: 2,198 sq. ft.

Second Floor
997 sq. ft.

First Floor
1,201 sq. ft.

Plan Features

- Great room features a warm fireplace flanked by bookshelves for storage
- Double French doors connect the formal dining room to the kitchen
- An oversized laundry room has extra counterspace
- The second floor bonus room has an additional 385 square feet of living area
- 4 bedrooms, 2 1/2 baths, 2-car side entry garage with shop/storage
- Basement, crawl space or slab foundation, please specify when ordering

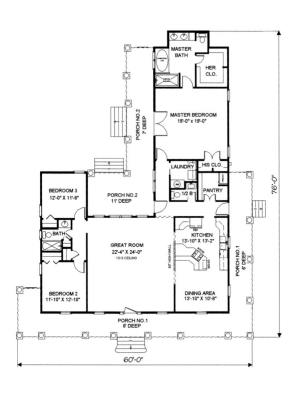

Total Living Area: 2,123 sq. ft.

Plan Features

- L-shaped porch extends the entire length of this home creating lots of extra space for outdoor living
- Master bedroom is secluded for privacy and has two closets, double vanity in bath and a double-door entry onto covered porch
- Efficiently designed kitchen
- 3 bedrooms, 2 1/2 baths
- Crawl space or slab foundation, please specify when ordering

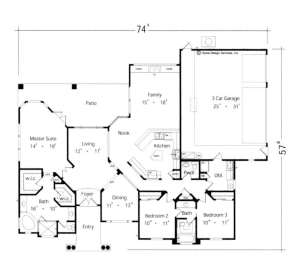

Total Living Area: 2,173 sq. ft.

Plan Features

- Enormous family room off kitchen has a fireplace surrounded by media shelves for state-of-the-art living
- The master bath has double walk-in closets as well as an oversized shower and whirlpool tub
- An arched entry graces the formal dining room
- 3 bedrooms, 2 1/2 baths, 3-car side entry garage
- Slab foundation

Total Living Area: 2,125 sq. ft.

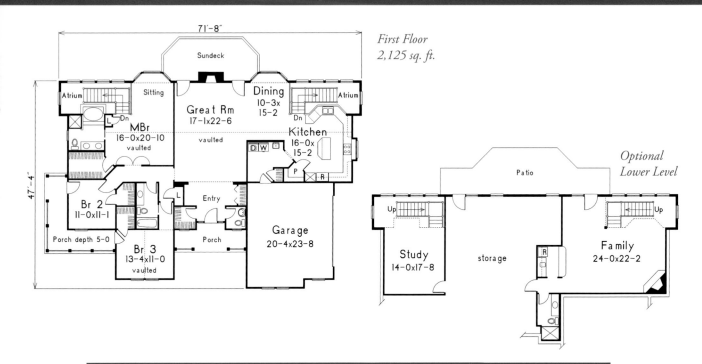

First Floor
2,125 sq. ft.

Optional
Lower Level

Plan Features

- A cozy porch leads to the vaulted great room with fireplace through the entry which has a walk-in closet and bath
- Master bedroom boasts a sitting room, large walk-in closet and bath with garden tub
- 1,047 square feet of optional living area on the lower level featuring a study and family room with walk-in bar and full bath below the kitchen
- 3 bedrooms, 2 1/2 baths, 2-car side entry garage
- Walk-out basement foundation

Plan #583-013D-0012

Second Floor
359 sq. ft.

LOFT
23'-1" x 15'-6"

40" KNEE WALL

OPEN BELOW
22' HIGH CEILING

VAULT

First Floor
1,288 sq. ft.

BEDROOM 1
11'-10" x 10'-0"

BEDROOM 2
11'-4" x 10'-0"

COATS

PANTRY

LINEN

46'-0"
+ PORCH

GREAT ROOM
27'-4" x 29'-5"
22' HIGH CEILING

VAULT   VAULT

DECK/PATIO
11'-6" x 18'-8"

DECK
7'-6" x 36'-0"

PORCH
24'-4" x 7'-6"

28'-0"
+ DECK/PATIO

Total Living Area: 1,647 sq. ft.

Plan Features

- Enormous great room boasts a vaulted ceiling
- Located in the great room is an open kitchen with an island and breakfast bar
- Stunning loft overlooks the great room
- 2 bedrooms, 1 bath
- Slab foundation

Plan #583-008D-0010

Total Living Area: 1,440 sq. ft.

Plan Features

- Foyer adjoins massive-sized great room with sloping ceiling and tall masonry fireplace
- The kitchen connects to the spacious dining room and features a pass-through to the breakfast bar
- An oversized two-car side entry garage offers plenty of storage for bicycles, lawn equipment, etc.
- 3 bedrooms, 2 baths, 2-car side entry garage
- Basement foundation, drawings also include crawl space and slab foundations

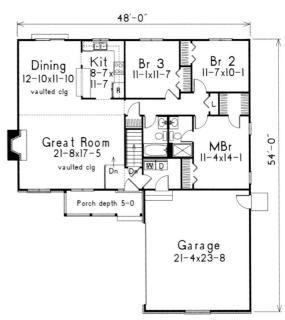

48'-0"

Dining
12-10x11-10
vaulted clg

Kit
8-7x
11-7

Br 3
11-1x11-7

Br 2
11-7x10-1

L

Great Room
21-8x17-5
vaulted clg

MBr
11-4x14-1

W D

Dn   Dn

Porch depth 5-0

54'-0"

Garage
21-4x23-8

Total Living Area: 3,570 sq. ft.

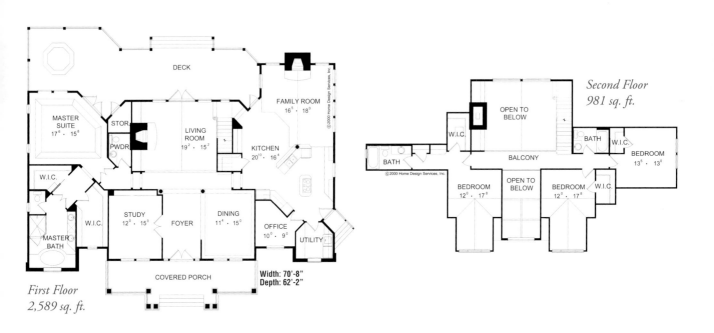

First Floor
2,589 sq. ft.

Second Floor
981 sq. ft.

Width: 70'-8"
Depth: 62'-2"

Plan Features

- The vaulted living room with fireplace features double-door access onto the rear deck
- A formal study and dining room flank the foyer for an elegant entrance into the home
- A large utility room and a private office are located off the kitchen for convenience
- The master suite pampers with two walk-in closets, a deluxe bath and access to the deck
- 4 bedrooms, 3 1/2 baths
- Crawl space foundation

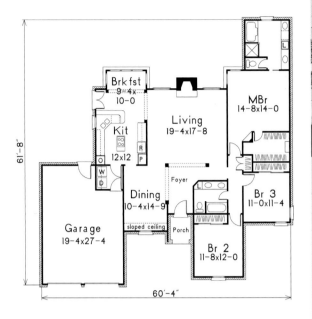

Total Living Area: 1,846 sq. ft.

Plan Features

- Enormous living area combines with the dining and breakfast rooms that are both complemented by extensive windows and high ceilings
- Secondary bedrooms share a bath and feature large closet space and a corner window
- Oversized two-car garage has plenty of storage
- 3 bedrooms, 2 baths, 2-car garage
- Slab foundation

Total Living Area: 1,380 sq. ft.

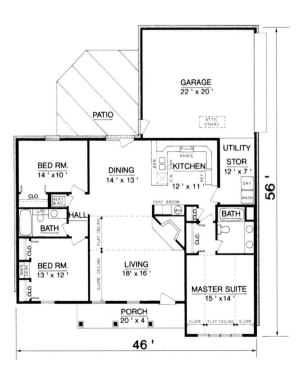

Plan Features

- Living room has a sloped ceiling and corner fireplace
- Kitchen features a breakfast bar overlooking the dining room
- Master suite is separate from other bedrooms for privacy
- Large utility/storage area
- 3 bedrooms, 2 baths, 2-car side entry garage
- Slab foundation, drawings also include crawl space foundation

Total Living Area: 2,523 sq. ft.

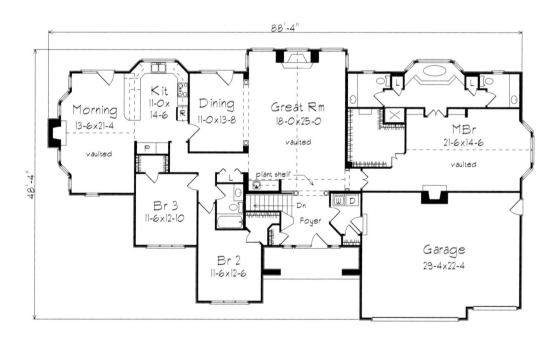

Rear View

Plan Features

- Entry with high ceiling leads to massive vaulted great room with wet bar, plant shelves, pillars and fireplace with a harmonious window trio
- Elaborate kitchen with bay and breakfast bar adjoins morning room with fireplace
- Vaulted master bedroom features fireplace, book and plant shelves, large walk-in closet and double baths
- 3 bedrooms, 2 baths, 3-car garage
- Basement foundation

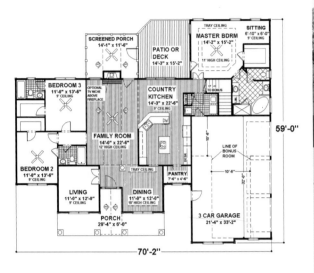

Total Living Area: 2,097 sq. ft.

Plan Features

- Angled kitchen, family room and eating area add interest to this home
- Sumptuous master bedroom includes a sitting area, double walk-in closet and a full bath with double vanities
- Bonus room above garage has an additional 452 square feet of living area
- 3 bedrooms, 3 baths, 3-car side entry garage
- Crawl space or slab foundation, please specify when ordering

Total Living Area: 2,450 sq. ft.

Plan Features

- Computer room is situated between bedrooms for easy access
- Two covered porches; one in front and one in rear of home
- Master bedroom includes bath with double walk-in closets and a luxurious step-up tub
- 4 bedrooms, 2 1/2 baths, 2-car side entry garage
- Slab foundation

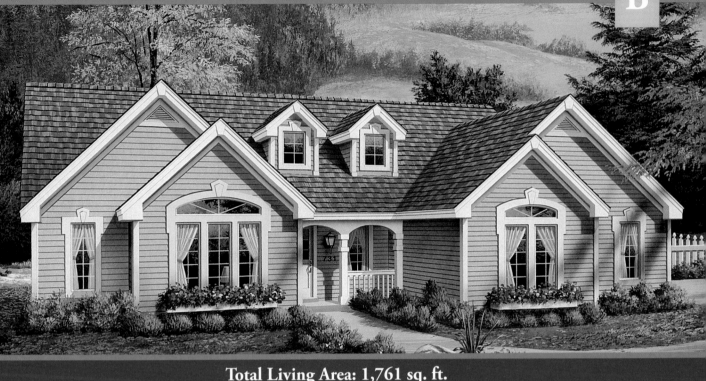

Total Living Area: 1,761 sq. ft.

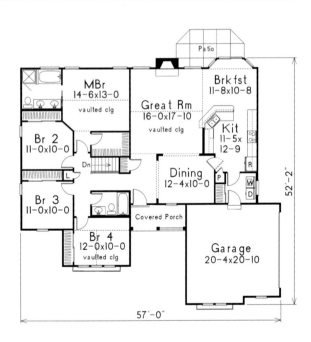

DID YOU KNOW?

The best and most efficient way to clean mini-blinds is to use a lamb's wool duster. Close the blinds and gently sweep the entire surface starting at the top. If this is done regularly, there is no need to do anything more involved.

Plan Features

- Exterior window dressing, roof dormers and planter boxes provide visual warmth and charm
- Great room boasts a vaulted ceiling, fireplace and opens to a pass-through kitchen
- The vaulted master bedroom includes a luxury bath and walk-in closet
- 4 bedrooms, 2 baths, 2-car side entry garage
- Basement foundation

Plan #583-039D-0012

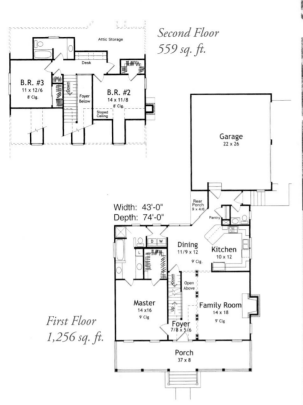

Second Floor
559 sq. ft.

B.R. #3
11 x 12/6
8' Clg.

B.R. #2
14 x 11/8
8' Clg.

Attic Storage

Desk

Foyer Below

Sloped Ceiling

Garage
22 x 26

Width: 43'-0"
Depth: 74'-0"

Rear Porch
9 x 4/6

Pantry

Dining
11/9 x 12
9' Clg

Kitchen
10 x 12

Master
14 x16
9' Clg

Open Above

Family Room
14 x 18
9' Clg

Foyer
7/8 x 5/6

First Floor
1,256 sq. ft.

Porch
37 x 8

Total Living Area: 1,815 sq. ft.

Plan Features

- Second floor has a built-in desk in the hall that is ideal as a computer work station or mini office area
- Two doors into the laundry area make it handy from the master bedroom and the rest of the home
- Inviting covered porch
- Lots of counterspace and cabinetry in kitchen
- 3 bedrooms, 2 1/2 baths, 2-car side entry garage
- Basement foundation

Plan #583-021D-0011

Total Living Area: 1,800 sq. ft.

Plan Features

- Energy efficient home with 2"x 6" exterior walls
- 12' ceilings in the kitchen, breakfast area, dining and living rooms
- Private master bedroom features an expansive bath
- Pillared styling with brick and stucco exterior finish
- 3 bedrooms, 2 baths, 2-car side entry garage
- Crawl space foundation, drawings also include slab foundation

66'-0"

54'-0"

MBr
13-4x14-4

Brm

Stor.

Stor.

D W P

Garage
21-8x25-2

Up

Brk
10-0x8-0

Porch

Br 3
10-8x11-8

Kit
13-2x11-0

skylt

Living
16-0x17-0

R

Dining
13-2x11-4

Br 2
10-8x 13-2

Porch depth 6-0

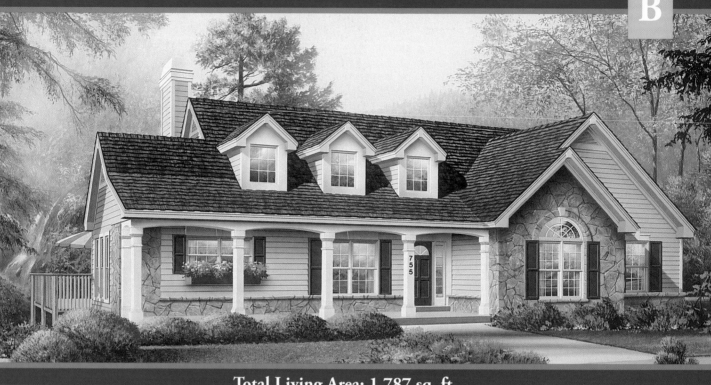

Total Living Area: 1,787 sq. ft.

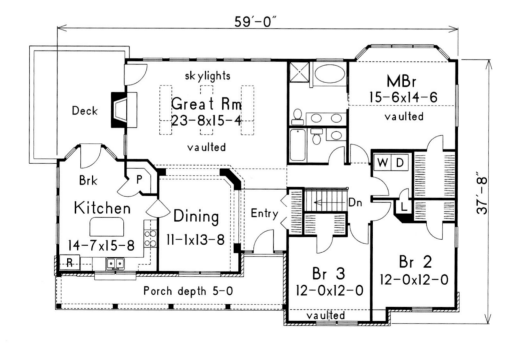

Plan Features

- Large great room with fireplace and vaulted ceiling features three large skylights and windows galore
- The L-shaped kitchen includes a bayed breakfast area with access to the rear deck
- 415 square feet of optional living area available on the lower level
- 3 bedrooms, 2 baths, 2-car drive under garage
- Walk-out basement foundation

Plan #583-029D-0002

Second Floor
360 sq. ft.

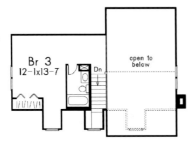

First Floor
1,259 sq. ft.

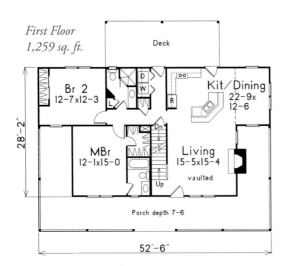

Total Living Area: 1,619 sq. ft.

Plan Features

- Private second floor bedroom and bath
- Kitchen features a snack bar and adjacent dining area
- Master bedroom has a private bath
- Centrally located washer and dryer
- 3 bedrooms, 3 baths
- Basement foundation, drawings also include crawl space and slab foundations

Plan #583-013D-0027

Total Living Area: 2,184 sq. ft.

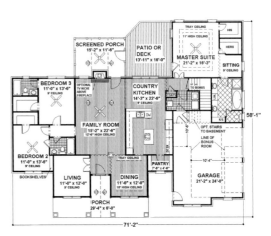

Plan Features

- Delightful family room has access to the screened porch for enjoyable outdoor living
- Secluded master suite is complete with a sitting area and luxurious bath
- Formal living room has a double-door entry easily converting it to a study or home office
- 3 bedrooms, 3 baths, 2-car side entry garage
- Basement, crawl space or slab foundation, please specify when ordering

Total Living Area: 3,398 sq. ft.

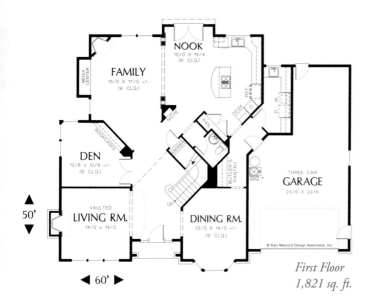

First Floor
1,821 sq. ft.

◀ 60' ▶

50'

Second Floor
1,577 sq. ft.

Plan Features

- Large built-in media center in the family room is perfect for relaxing
- Large and luxurious master bedroom features a beautiful bath
- Second floor library nook is a quiet retreat
- 4 bedrooms, 2 1/2 baths, 3-car garage
- Crawl space foundation

Plan #583-032D-0051

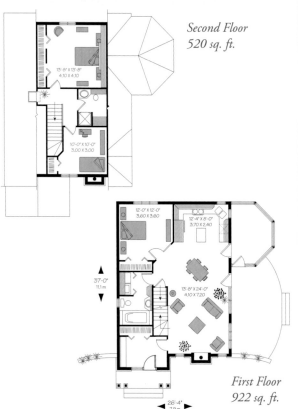

Second Floor
520 sq. ft.

13'-8" X 13'-8"
4.10 X 4.10

10'-0" X 10'-0"
3.00 X 3.00

12'-0" X 12'-0"
3.60 X 3.60

12'-4" X 8'-0"
3.70 X 2.40

37'-0"
11.1 m

13'-8" X 24'-0"
4.10 X 7.20

First Floor
922 sq. ft.

26'-4"
7.9 m

Total Living Area: 1,442 sq. ft.

Plan Features

- Energy efficient home with 2"x 6" exterior walls
- Kitchen accesses bayed area and porch which provide a cozy atmosphere
- Open living area makes relaxing a breeze
- 3 bedrooms, 2 baths
- Basement foundation

Plan #583-008D-0045

B

Total Living Area: 1,540 sq. ft.

Plan Features

- Porch entrance into foyer leads to an impressive dining area with a full window and a half-circle window above
- Great room with cathedral ceiling and exposed beams is accessible from the foyer
- Master bedroom includes a full bath and walk-in closet
- 3 bedrooms, 2 baths, 2-car garage
- Basement foundation, drawings also include crawl space and slab foundations

66'-0"

Great Room
22-8x14-11
vaulted clg

Br 2
14-9x10-0

Br 3
11-4x10-0

Garage
21-8x21-4

38'-0"

Foyer

Kit/Brk
13-4x19-1
vaulted clg

Porch

MBr
14-9x12-0
skylt

Total Living Area: 2,420 sq. ft.

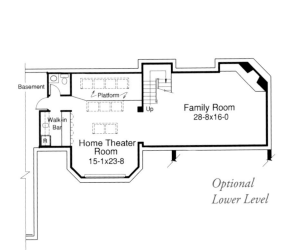

Optional Lower Level

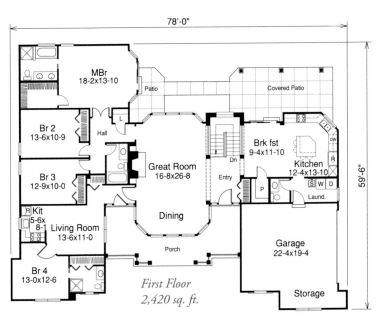

First Floor 2,420 sq. ft.

Plan Features

- The great room has a fireplace with flanking shelves, a bay window and dining area
- Many excellent features adorn the kitchen including a corner window sink, island snack bar, walk-in pantry and breakfast area with adjoining covered patio
- 1,014 square feet of optional living area on the lower level
- 4 bedrooms, 3 1/2 baths, 2-car side entry garage
- Basement foundation

Plan #583-037D-0002

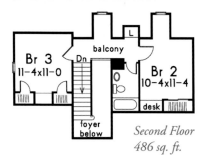

Second Floor
486 sq. ft.

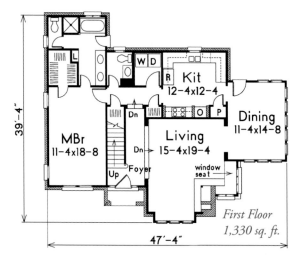

First Floor
1,330 sq. ft.

Total Living Area: 1,816 sq. ft.

Plan Features

- The living room features a two-way fireplace with nearby window seat
- Wrap-around dining room windows create a sunroom appearance
- Master bedroom has abundant closet and storage space
- 3 bedrooms, 2 1/2 baths, 2-car detached garage
- Slab foundation, drawings also include crawl space foundation

Plan #583-026D-0145

Total Living Area: 2,526 sq. ft.

Plan Features

- A grand two-story living room has a cozy fireplace flanked by two doors to a large deck
- Central staircase is right where the action is located in the kitchen
- First floor master bedroom has access to the deck as well as a private bath and walk-in closet
- 3 bedrooms, 2 1/2 baths
- Basement foundation

Second Floor
876 sq. ft.

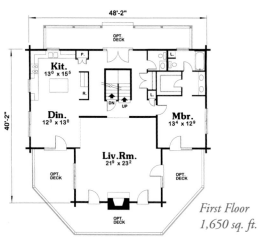

First Floor
1,650 sq. ft.

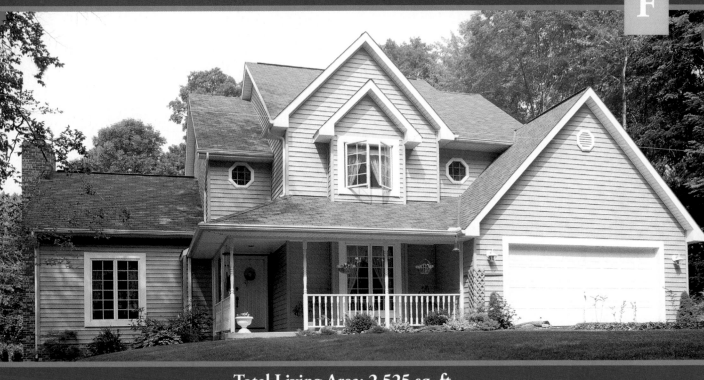

Total Living Area: 2,525 sq. ft.

First Floor
1,409 sq. ft.

Second Floor
1,116 sq. ft.

Rear View

Plan Features

- The living room has a 10' ceiling and a large fireplace
- The parlor is a perfect place for entertaining guests
- The bayed breakfast room is flooded with light and opens to the optional deck
- 3 bedrooms, 2 1/2 baths, 2-car garage
- Basement, crawl space or slab foundation, please specify when ordering

Total Living Area: 1,737 sq. ft.

Plan Features

- Cozy breakfast nook is located directly off kitchen
- Formal dining room has 10' vaulted ceiling and a view onto the front covered porch
- Laundry room is tucked away near activity areas
- 3 bedrooms, 2 baths, 2-car garage
- Basement, crawl space or slab foundation, please specify when ordering

Plan #583-055D-0030

Price Code:

C

Total Living Area: 2,107 sq. ft.

Plan Features

- Master bedroom is secluded for privacy
- Spacious breakfast room and kitchen include center island with eating space
- Centralized great room has fireplace and easy access to any area in the home
- 4 bedrooms, 2 1/2 baths, 2-car garage
- Crawl space, basement, walk-out basement or slab foundation, please specify when ordering

Total Living Area: 6,549 sq. ft.

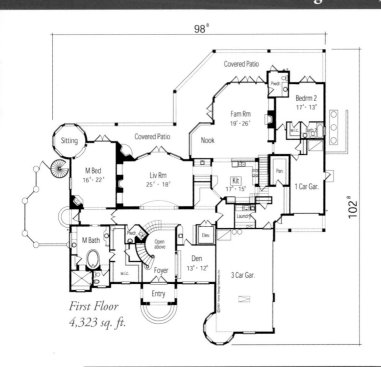

First Floor
4,323 sq. ft.

Second Floor
2,226 sq. ft.

Plan Features

- Master bedroom has an octagon-shaped sitting area as well as a cozy fireplace
- A butler's pantry/wet bar connects the living room to the kitchen
- Framing - only concrete block available
- Bonus room on the second floor has an additional 453 square feet of living area
- 5 bedrooms, 6 full baths, 2 half baths, 3-car side entry garage
- Slab foundation

Plan #583-039D-0002

A

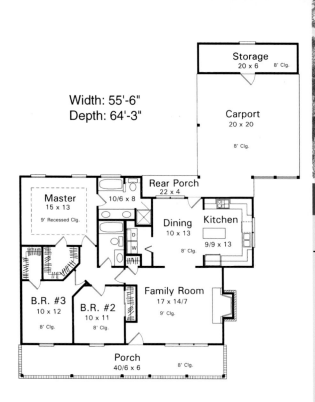

Width: 55'-6"
Depth: 64'-3"

Storage
20 x 6   8' Clg.

Carport
20 x 20
8' Clg.

Master
15 x 13
9' Recessed Clg.

Rear Porch
22 x 4

10/6 x 8

Dining
10 x 13
8' Clg.

Kitchen
9/9 x 13

D W

B.R. #3
10 x 12
8' Clg.

B.R. #2
10 x 11
8' Clg.

Family Room
17 x 14/7
9' Clg.

Porch
40/6 x 6   8' Clg.

Total Living Area: 1,333 sq. ft.

Plan Features

- Country charm with a covered front porch
- Dining area looks into the family room with fireplace
- Master suite has a walk-in closet and private bath
- 3 bedrooms, 2 baths, 2-car attached carport
- Slab or crawl space foundation, please specify when ordering

---

Plan #583-032D-0030

B

*Second Floor
454 sq. ft.*

14'-0" X 17'-4"
4,20 X 5,20

OPEN TO BELOW

*First Floor
1,062 sq. ft.*

9'-8" X 10'-4"
2,90 X 3,10

10'-8" X 13'-4"
3,20 X 4,00

9'-2" X 10'-0"
2,75 X 3,00

17'-4" X 13'-0"
5,20 X 3,90

8'-4" X 12'-8"
2,50 X 3,80

28'-0"
8,4 m

40'-0"
12,0 m

Total Living Area: 1,516 sq. ft.

Plan Features

- Energy efficient home with 2"x 6" exterior walls
- Warm fireplace adds coziness to living areas
- Dining area and kitchen are convenient to each other making entertaining easy
- 3 bedrooms, 2 baths
- Basement foundation

Total Living Area: 2,338 sq. ft.

First Floor
1,633 sq. ft.

Patio

Great Room
15'2" x 18'2"

Breakfast
11'10" x 9'10"

Laun.

Kitchen
11'10" x 11'11"

pantry

Bath

Dressing

Master
Bedroom
13' x 17'

Foyer

Dining Room
11' x 13'

Porch

Two Car
Garage
20' x 21'

58'6"

49'

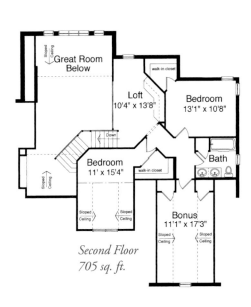

Great Room
Below

walk-in closet

Loft
10'4" x 13'8"

Bedroom
13'1" x 10'8"

Bedroom
11' x 15'4"

walk-in closet

Bath

Bonus
11'1" x 17'3"

Second Floor
705 sq. ft.

Plan Features

- The great room is illuminated by multiple windows and is warmed by a fireplace
- The spacious master bedroom enjoys a deluxe bath and large walk-in closet
- The charming breakfast room has French doors leading to the relaxing patio
- The second floor bonus room has an additional 203 square feet of living area
- 3 bedrooms, 2 1/2 baths, 2-car side entry garage
- Basement foundation

Plan #583-040D-0019

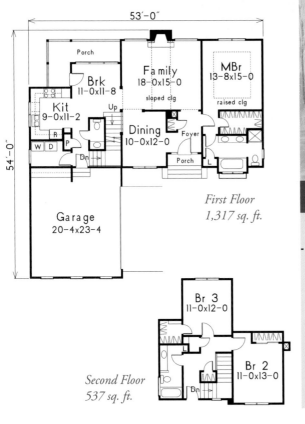

53'-0"

54'-0"

Porch

Brk
11-0x11-8

Kit
9-0x11-2

Family
18-0x15-0
sloped clg

MBr
13-8x15-0
raised clg

Up

Dining
10-0x12-0

Foyer

Porch

Dn

W D

R
P

Garage
20-4x23-4

First Floor
1,317 sq. ft.

Br 3
11-0x12-0

Br 2
11-0x13-0

Dn

Second Floor
537 sq. ft.

Total Living Area: 1,854 sq. ft.

Plan Features

- Front entrance is enhanced by arched transom windows
- The master bedroom includes a dressing area and walk-in closet
- Family room features a high sloped ceiling and a large fireplace
- Breakfast area accesses covered rear porch
- 3 bedrooms, 2 1/2 baths, 2-car side entry garage
- Basement foundation

Plan #583-047D-0077

Total Living Area: 2,326 sq. ft.

Plan Features

- A glorious sunroom with skylights brightens the home
- The kitchen serves the formal and informal dining areas with ease
- The bonus room above the garage has an additional 358 square feet of living area
- 3 bedrooms, 2 1/2 baths, 2-car side entry garage
- Basement, walk-out basement or slab foundation, please specify when ordering

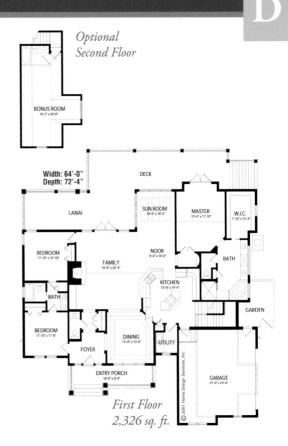

Optional Second Floor

BONUS ROOM
16'-2" x 26'-4"

Width: 64'-0"
Depth: 72'-4"

DECK

LANAI

SUN ROOM
10'-6" x 10'-2"

MASTER
13'-4" x 17'-10"

W.I.C.
7'-10" x 12'-4"

BEDROOM
11'-10" x 12'-10"

FAMILY
18'-8" x 20'-4"

NOOK
9'-4" x 10'-0"

BATH

KITCHEN
15'-8" x 14'-4"

BATH

BEDROOM
11'-10" x 11'-6"

DINING
12'-4" x 13'-8"

UTILITY

GARDEN

FOYER

ENTRY PORCH
18'-0" x 6'-0"

GARAGE
21'-0" x 24'-4"

First Floor
2,326 sq. ft.

Total Living Area: 3,688 sq. ft.

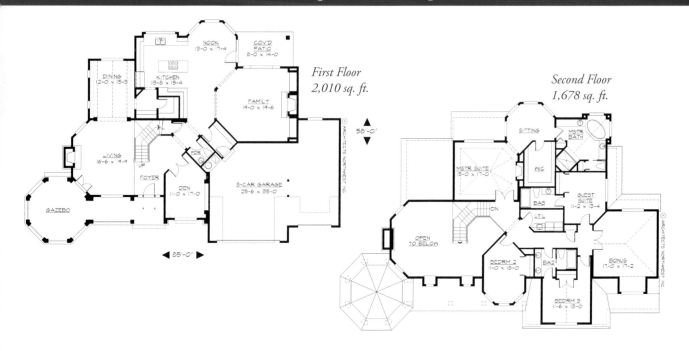

First Floor
2,010 sq. ft.

Second Floor
1,678 sq. ft.

Plan Features

- A bayed two-story living room connects directly to the gazebo for added living space
- A coffered ceiling, octagon-shaped sitting area and a fireplace add drama and luxury to the master suite
- Bonus room on the second floor has an additional 342 square feet of living area
- 4 bedrooms, 3 1/2 baths, 3-car garage
- Crawl space foundation

Plan #583-065D-0026

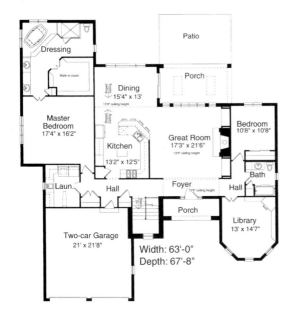

Total Living Area: 2,269 sq. ft.

Plan Features

- An open atmosphere encourages an easy flow of activities
- Grand windows and a covered porch offer a cozy atmosphere
- The master bedroom boasts a double vanity, whirlpool tub and spacious walk-in closet
- 3 bedrooms, 2 baths, 2-car garage
- Basement foundation

Plan #583-028D-0004

Total Living Area: 1,785 sq. ft.

Plan Features

- 9' ceilings throughout home
- Luxurious master bath includes a whirlpool tub and separate shower
- Cozy breakfast area is convenient to the kitchen
- 3 bedrooms, 3 baths, 2-car detached garage
- Basement, crawl space or slab foundation, please specify when ordering

Total Living Area: 2,403 sq. ft.

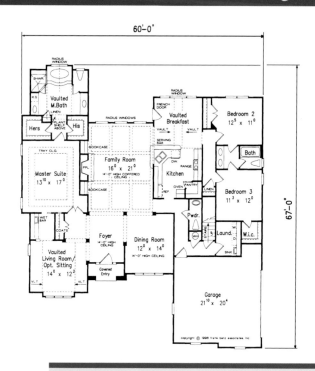

DID YOU KNOW?

Photography or artwork that is hanging in a high traffic area often bears the brunt of all the activity and becomes crooked and misaligned. A way to alleviate such a problem is to use Velcro® circles (available at hardware stores) on the back of the picture. Stick one side of the Velcro® on the picture and the other side on the wall remembering to keep them level. Now, your pictures will not move when that basketball goes bouncing down the hall.

Plan Features

- Cozy family room has a high coffered ceiling and a fireplace flanked by bookcases
- Vaulted breakfast room features a wall of windows
- Master suite has a private bath with double walk-in closets and access to a vaulted living room with wet bar
- 3 bedrooms, 2 1/2 baths, 2-car side entry garage
- Slab, crawl space, or walk-out basement foundation, please specify when ordering

---

MASTER
12/0 X 13/0

Second Floor
809 sq. ft.

LINEN

BR. 3
10/8 X 10/0

DN

FOYER
BELOW

BR. 2
11/0 X 11/8

DINING
10/0 X 10/0

GREAT RM.
15/0 X 13/0
(9' CLG.)

RANGE

REF

First Floor
655 sq. ft.

STOR

GARAGE
19/0 X 19/6 +

UP

42'

30'

©Alan Mascord Design Associates, Inc.

Total Living Area: 1,464 sq. ft.

Plan Features

- Contemporary styled home has a breathtaking two-story foyer and a lovely open staircase
- U-shaped kitchen is designed for efficiency
- Elegant great room has a cozy fireplace
- 3 bedrooms, 2 1/2 baths, 2-car garage
- Crawl space foundation

Total Living Area: 1,772 sq. ft.

Plan Features

- Bedroom #2 boasts a walk-in closet and built-in desk
- The centrally located kitchen serves the formal dining room and charming breakfast nook with ease
- A 10' ceiling adds spaciousness to the living room
- The garage includes a large shop area
- 3 bedrooms, 2 baths, 2-car garage
- Slab or crawl space foundation, please specify when ordering

75'-10"

BED RM.3
12'-0" X 11'-0"

PORCH
16'-0" X 9'-0"

NOOK
11'-0" X 9'-0"

MASTER SUITE
12'-0" X 15'-0"

BATH 1

SHOP AREA

B.2

STOR

RAISED BAR

MARBLE TUB

LINEN

10'-0" HIGH CEILING
LIVING RM.
15'-0" X 22'-6"

KITCH.
11' X 11'

WALK IN CLOSET

GARAGE
20'-0" X 20'-0"

38'-8"

BED RM.2
12'-0" X 11'-6"

W.I. CLOS.

DINING
11'-0" X 12'-0"

UTIL.
12' X 7'

PORCH
31'-6" X 7'-0"

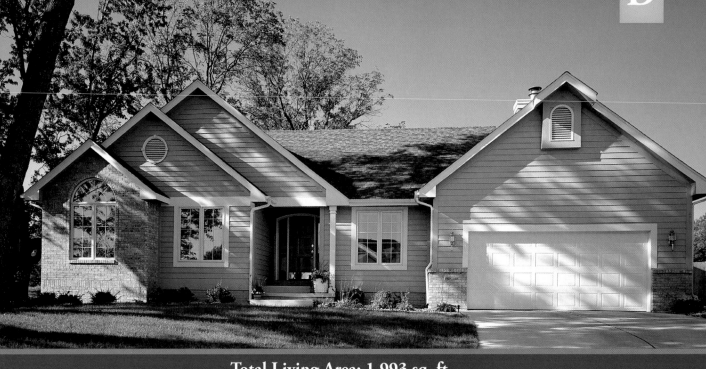

Total Living Area: 1,993 sq. ft.

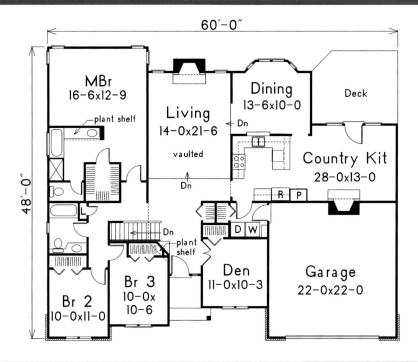

Plan Features

- Spacious country kitchen boasts a fireplace and plenty of natural light from windows
- Formal dining room features large bay window and steps down to the sunken living room
- Master bedroom features corner windows, plant shelves and a deluxe private bath
- 3 bedrooms, 2 baths, 2-car garage
- Basement foundation

Plan #583-028D-0016

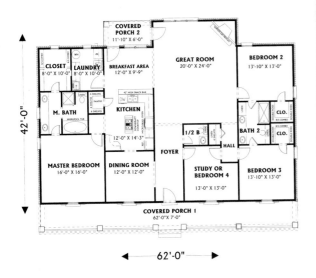

Total Living Area: 2,354 sq. ft.

Plan Features

- 9' ceilings throughout this home
- Dramatic corner fireplace in the great room can be viewed from a lovely breakfast area
- Master bedroom is separated from other bedrooms for privacy and quiet
- 4 bedrooms, 2 1/2 baths
- Crawl space or slab foundation, please specify when ordering

---

Plan #583-062D-0061

Price Code:

AA

Total Living Area: 1,092 sq. ft.

Plan Features

- Energy efficient home with 2"x 6" exterior walls
- The spacious vaulted great room is warmed by a grand fireplace
- The kitchen features a vaulted ceiling, pantry, dining area and access onto a covered porch
- 3 bedrooms, 1 bath
- Basement or crawl space foundation, please specify when ordering

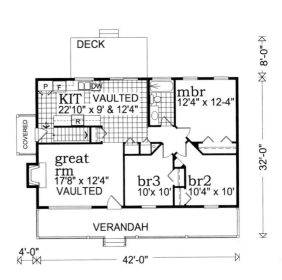

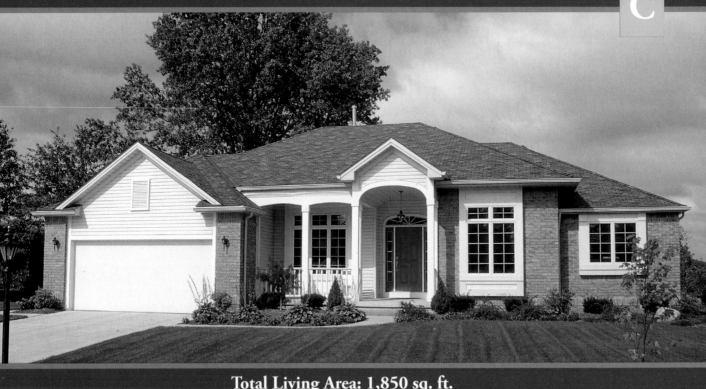

Total Living Area: 1,850 sq. ft.

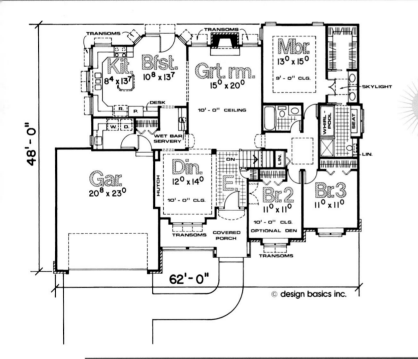

DID YOU KNOW?

Furnishing a covered porch or patio by mixing indoor and outdoor furniture and accessories is a terrific way to combine the interior and the exterior. Plus, it allows the decorating scheme to flow seamlessly from the indoor spaces into the more seasonal space without the two places looking disconnected.

Plan Features

- Oversized rooms throughout
- Great room spotlights fireplace with sunny windows on both sides
- Master bedroom has a private skylighted bath
- Interesting wet bar between kitchen and dining area is an added bonus for entertaining
- 3 bedrooms, 2 baths, 2-car garage
- Basement foundation

Plan #583-027D-0005

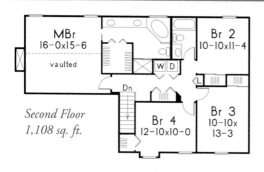

Second Floor
1,108 sq. ft.

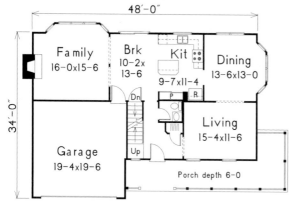

First Floor
1,027 sq. ft.

Total Living Area: 2,135 sq. ft.

Plan Features

- Family room features extra space, an impressive fireplace and full wall of windows that joins the breakfast room creating a spacious entertainment area
- Washer and dryer are conveniently located on the second floor near the bedrooms
- The kitchen features an island counter and pantry
- 4 bedrooms, 2 1/2 baths, 2-car garage
- Basement foundation

Plan #583-011D-0004

Price Code: **D**

Total Living Area: 1,997 sq. ft.

Plan Features

- Corner fireplace warms the vaulted family room located near the kitchen
- A spa tub and shower enhance the master bath
- Plenty of closet space throughout
- 4 bedrooms, 2 1/2 baths, 3-car garage
- Crawl space foundation

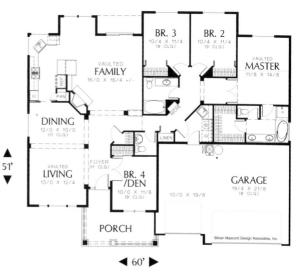

Total Living Area: 576 sq. ft.

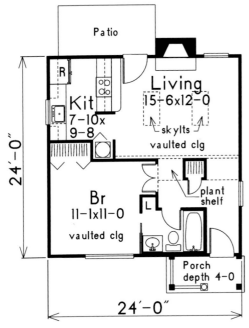

DID YOU KNOW?

Using hairspray to clean a countertop, wall or wallpaper works fabulously. Lightly spray the hairspray onto the surface to treat and let it sit for a few seconds. Then, just wipe away. Repeat if necessary.

Plan Features

- Perfect country retreat features vaulted living room and entry with skylights and a plant shelf above
- A double-door entry leads to the vaulted bedroom with bath access
- Kitchen offers generous storage and pass-through breakfast bar
- 1 bedroom, 1 bath
- Crawl space foundation

Plan #583-037D-0020

Price Code: D

Total Living Area: 1,994 sq. ft.

Plan Features

- Bedroom #2 features a 12' vaulted ceiling and the dining room boasts a 10' ceiling
- Master bedroom offers a full bath with an oversized tub, separate shower and walk-in closet
- Entry leads to the formal dining room and attractive living room with double French doors and fireplace
- 3 bedrooms, 2 baths, 2-car garage
- Slab foundation

Plan #583-025D-0021

Price Code: C

Total Living Area: 2,080 sq. ft.

Plan Features

- Gallery hall creates a grand entrance into the great room
- Computer nook located in the breakfast room is a functional living area near the center of activity
- Built-in entertainment center and bookshelves make relaxing a breeze in the great room
- 3 bedrooms, 2 baths, 2-car side entry garage
- Basement, crawl space or slab foundation, please specify when ordering

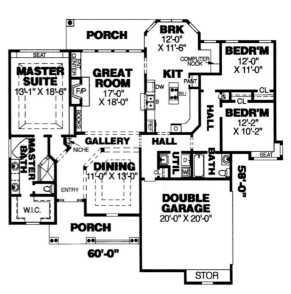

Total Living Area: 1,892 sq. ft.

First Floor
1,892 sq. ft.

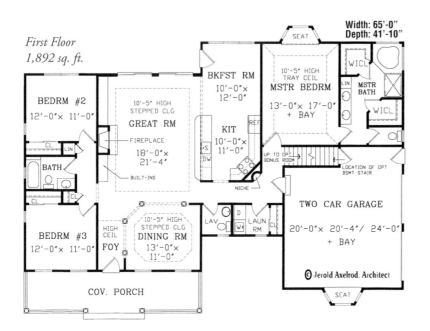

Width: 65'-0"
Depth: 41'-10"

BEDRM #2
12'-0" x 11'-0"

BKFST RM
10'-0" x
12'-0"

10'-5" HIGH
TRAY CEIL
MSTR BEDRM
13'-0" x 17'-0"
+ BAY

WICL

LIN MSTR
BATH

WICL

10'-5" HIGH
STEPPED CLG
GREAT RM
FIREPLACE
18'-0" x
21'-4"

KIT
10'-0" x
11'-0"

REF

CL LIN

BATH

UP TO OPT
BONUS ROOM

LOCATION OF OPT
BSMT STAIR

BUILT-INS

CL

NICHE

TWO CAR GARAGE
20'-0" x 20'-4"/ 24'-0"
+ BAY

BEDRM #3
12'-0" x 11'-0"

HIGH
CEIL
FOY

10'-5" HIGH
STEPPED CLG
DINING RM
13'-0" x
11'-0"

LAV

D

LAUN
RM

CL

W

© Jerold Axelrod, Architect

COV. PORCH

SEAT

Optional
Second Floor

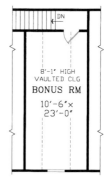

DN

8'-1" HIGH
VAULTED CLG
BONUS RM
10'-6" x
23'-0"

Plan Features

- This split bedroom plan places a lovely master bedroom on the opposite end of the other two bedrooms for privacy
- Central living and dining areas combine creating a great place for entertaining
- Bonus room on the second floor has an additional 285 square feet of living area
- 3 bedrooms, 2 1/2 baths, 2-car side entry garage
- Basement, crawl space or slab foundation, please specify when ordering

Plan #583-008D-0134

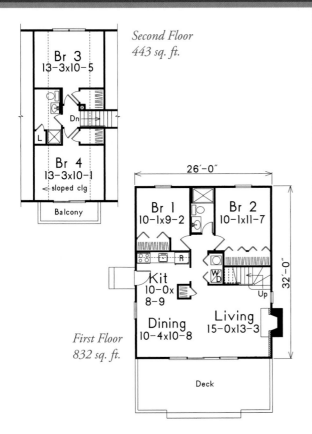

Second Floor
443 sq. ft.

Br 3
13-3x10-5

Dn

Br 4
13-3x10-1
← sloped clg

Balcony

26'-0"

Br 1
10-1x9-2

Br 2
10-1x11-7

R

W
D

Up

32'-0"

Kit
10-0x
8-9

Dining
10-4x10-8

Living
15-0x13-3

First Floor
832 sq. ft.

Deck

Total Living Area: 1,275 sq. ft.

Plan Features

- Wall shingles and stone veneer fireplace all fashion an irresistible rustic appeal
- Living area features a fireplace and opens to an efficient kitchen
- Two bedrooms on the second floor
- 4 bedrooms, 2 baths
- Basement foundation, drawings also include crawl space and slab foundations

---

Plan #583-011D-0049

Total Living Area: 2,079 sq. ft.

Plan Features

- A home office is convenient to the front entry making it very accessible for visitors
- Vaulted great room enjoys views of the dining room and kitchen
- The vaulted master bedroom has all the luxuries with an amenity-full bath
- 3 bedrooms, 2 1/2 baths, 3-car garage
- Crawl space foundation

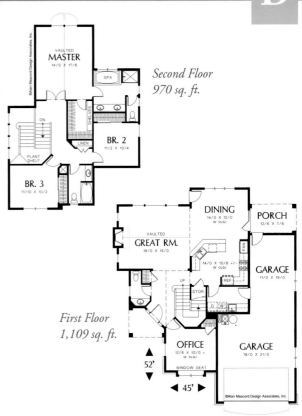

VAULTED
MASTER
14/0 X 17/6

SPA

Second Floor
970 sq. ft.

DN

SHELVES

LINEN

BR. 2
11/2 X 10/4

PLANT
SHELF

BR. 3
11/10 X 10/2

DINING
14/0 X 12/0
(9' CLG)

PORCH
12/6 X 7/6

VAULTED
GREAT RM.
18/0 X 15/0

14/0 X 10/8
(9' CLG)

PAN

GARAGE
11/0 X 19/0

UP

REF

STOR

First Floor
1,109 sq. ft.

OFFICE
12/6 X 10/0
(9' CLG)

GARAGE
19/0 X 21/0

WINDOW SEAT

52'

45'

©Alan Mascord Design Associates, Inc.

D

Total Living Area: 2,483 sq. ft.

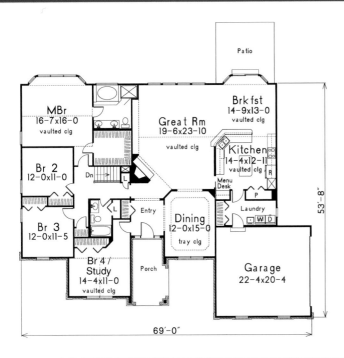

DID YOU KNOW?

Small details make big impressions when entertaining. Take cues from the season. Some creative and beautiful ideas for a place card when entertaining include a ripe pear or another fruit of the season, a pine cone or even beautiful fall leaves. Attach a paper name tag to the stem or on the plate beside the treasure and you'll have a memorable reminder of the gathering.

Plan Features

- A large entry porch with open brick arches and palladian door welcomes guests
- The vaulted great room features an entertainment center alcove
- A convenient kitchen with wrap-around counter, menu desk and pantry opens to the cozy breakfast area
- 4 bedrooms, 2 baths, 2-car side entry garage
- Basement foundation

Total Living Area: 2,401 sq. ft.

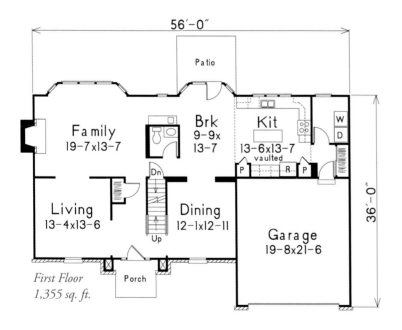

56'-0"

Patio

Family
19-7x13-7

Brk
9-9x
13-7

Kit
13-6x13-7
vaulted

W
D

P   R   P

Living
13-4x13-6

Dn

Dining
12-1x12-11

Up

Garage
19-8x21-6

36'-0"

First Floor
1,355 sq. ft.

Porch

Second Floor
1,046 sq. ft.

vaulted

Br 3
12-1x11-0

MBr
15-0x17-0

Dn

Br 2
12-1x10-4

Plan Features

- Master bedroom has two walk-in closets, dressing rooms, elegant double-door entry and deluxe bath
- Full bay windows located on both floors create a great view from the rear of this home
- Spacious kitchen features a studio ceiling, double pantry, and a large work island
- 3 bedrooms, 2 1/2 baths, 2-car garage
- Basement foundation, drawings also include slab and crawl space foundations

Total Living Area: 5,800 sq. ft.

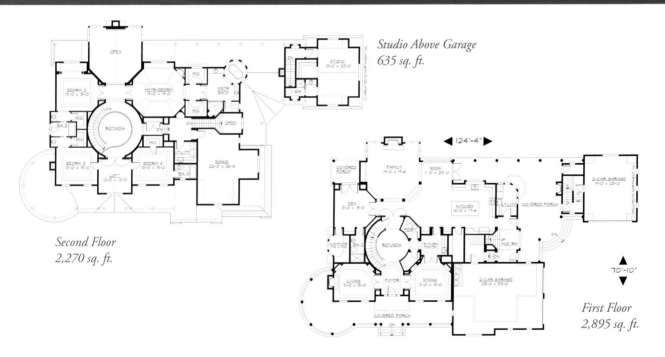

Studio Above Garage
635 sq. ft.

Second Floor
2,270 sq. ft.

First Floor
2,895 sq. ft.

Plan Features

- Covered porch accesses several rooms and features a cozy fireplace for outdoor living
- A spectacular foyer leads directly to a central rotunda with a circular stair
- Amenities on the first floor include a computer room, mud room and butler's pantry
- Bonus room on the second floor has an additional 500 square feet of living area
- 4 bedrooms, 5 1/2 baths, 2-car side entry garage and 2-car detached garage
- Crawl space foundation

Total Living Area: 1,708 sq. ft.

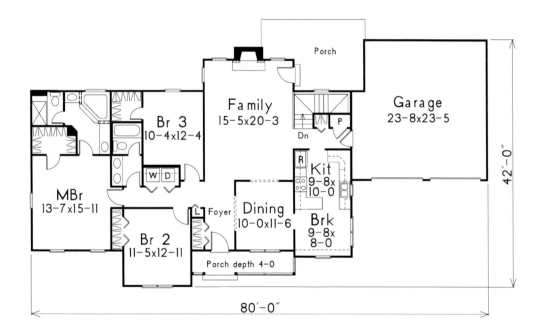

Plan Features

- Family room is enhanced with several windows, a fireplace and access to the porch
- Deluxe master bath is accented by a step-up corner tub flanked by double vanities
- Closets throughout maintain organized living
- Bedrooms are isolated from living areas
- 3 bedrooms, 2 baths, 2-car garage
- Basement foundation, drawings also include crawl space foundation

Total Living Area: 2,452 sq. ft.

DID YOU KNOW?

55 million people work from home in North America; 1/3 of them (18 million people) run home-based businesses.

Plan Features

- Delightful great room features a vaulted ceiling, fireplace, extra storage closets and patio doors to sundeck
- Extra-large kitchen features walk-in pantry, cooktop island and bay window
- Vaulted master bedroom includes transomed windows, walk-in closet and luxurious bath
- 3 bedrooms, 2 1/2 baths, 3-car garage
- Basement foundation

Total Living Area: 2,972 sq. ft.

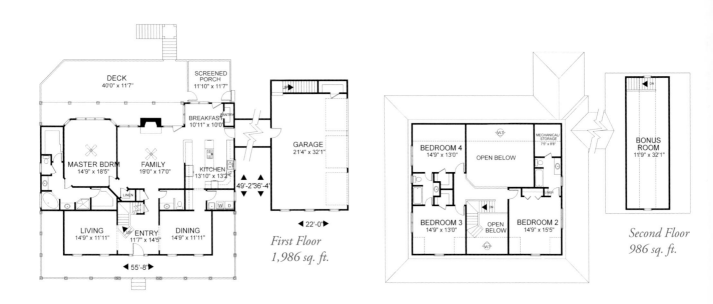

First Floor
1,986 sq. ft.

Second Floor
986 sq. ft.

Plan Features

- Extra storage available off the second floor bedroom
- Angled staircase in entry adds interest
- Charming screened porch is accessible from the breakfast room
- Bonus room above the garage has an additional 396 square feet of living area
- 4 bedrooms, 3 1/2 baths, 3-car side entry garage
- Basement foundation

Total Living Area: 2,196 sq. ft.

First Floor
1,658 sq. ft.

VAULTED
MASTER
13/6 X 16/6

NOOK
10/0 X 12/6
(9' CLG.)

3RD CAR
/SHOP
11/0 X 15/6

VAULTED
GREAT RM.
17/6 X 17/10

56'

GARAGE
20/0 X 19/6

STOR.

UP

BUILT-IN

VAULTED
FOYER

DINING
10/6 X 12/0
(9' CLG.)

DEN/BR. 4
11/0 X 10/6
(9' CLG.)

© Alan Mascord Design Associates, Inc.

◄ 50' ►

Second Floor
538 sq. ft.

BR. 2
10/0 X 12/2

ATTIC
STORAGE

OPEN TO
BELOW

LINEN

BONUS
20/2 X 23/0 +/-

DN.

ATTIC
STORAGE

OPEN TO
BELOW

BR. 3
10/6 X 12/0

Plan Features

- Built-in cabinet space in the formal dining room
- Sunny breakfast nook is adjacent to the kitchen
- Bonus room above the garage has an additional 496 square feet of living area and can easily be converted to a children's play area
- 4 bedrooms, 2 1/2 baths, 3-car garage
- Crawl space foundation

Total Living Area: 1,860 sq. ft.

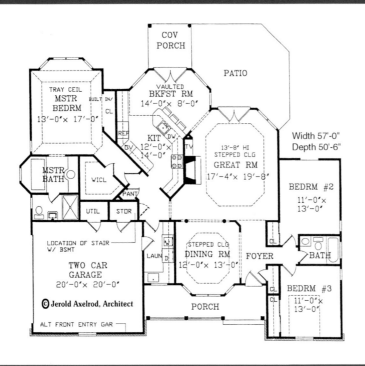

COV PORCH

PATIO

VAULTED BKFST RM
14'-0" x 8'-0"

TRAY CEIL MSTR BEDRM
13'-0" x 17'-0"

BUILT IN/CL

KIT
12'-0" x 14'-0"

13'-8" HI STEPPED CLG GREAT RM
17'-4" x 19'-8"

Width 57'-0"
Depth 50'-6"

MSTR BATH

WICL

PANT

BEDRM #2
11'-0" x 13'-0"

UTIL

STOR

LOCATION OF STAIR W/ BSMT

LAUN

STEPPED CLG DINING RM
12'-0" x 13'-0"

FOYER

BATH

TWO CAR GARAGE
20'-0" x 20'-0"

© Jerold Axelrod, Architect

PORCH

BEDRM #3
11'-0" x 13'-0"

ALT FRONT ENTRY GAR

Plan Features

- Dining room has an 11' stepped ceiling with a bay window creating a pleasant dining experience
- Breakfast room has a 12' sloped ceiling with French doors leading to a covered porch
- Great room has a columned arched entrance, a built-in media center and a fireplace
- 3 bedrooms, 2 baths, 2-car side entry garage
- Basement, crawl space or slab foundation, please specify when ordering

Total Living Area: 2,223 sq. ft.

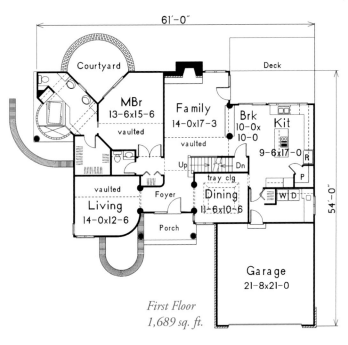

61'-0"

Courtyard

Deck

MBr
13-6x15-6
vaulted

Family
14-0x17-3
vaulted

Brk
10-0x
10-0

Kit
9-6x17-0

Up   Dn

tray clg

vaulted

Living
14-0x12-6

Foyer

Dining
11-6x10-6

Porch

54'-0"

W D

R

P

Garage
21-8x21-0

First Floor
1,689 sq. ft.

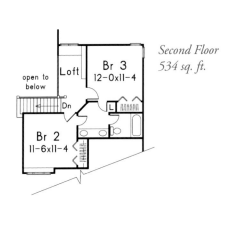

Second Floor
534 sq. ft.

open to
below

Loft

Br 3
12-0x11-4

Dn

Br 2
11-6x11-4

Plan Features

- Vaulted master bedroom opens to courtyard
- Master bath features curved glass block wall around tub and shower
- Vaulted family room combines with breakfast and kitchen to create a casual living area
- Second floor includes secondary bedrooms and a possible loft/office
- 3 bedrooms, 2 1/2 baths, 2-car garage
- Basement foundation

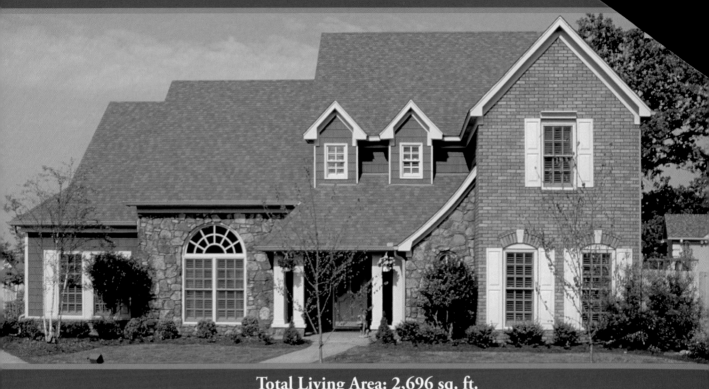

Total Living Area: 2,696 sq. ft.

First Floor
1,904 sq. ft.

Garage
21-0x21-0

Kit
12-4x13-2

Great Rm
17-4x17-4
12-0 ceiling

up

Covered
Porch

Brk
12-4x12-6

Dining
15-4x11-4

Foyer

MBr
16-8x14-8

Porch

Br 2
11-4x11-8

64'-0"

66'-10"

Second Floor
792 sq. ft.

Br 3
12-4x12-5

Balcony

Game Rm
17-4x13-8

open to
below

Dn

plant
shelf

Loft

Br 4
12-0x12-4

Plan Features

- Magnificent master bedroom with private covered porch and luxurious bath
- Second floor game room with balcony access and adjacent loft
- Well-planned kitchen includes walk-in pantry, island cooktop and nearby spacious breakfast room
- 4 bedrooms, 3 baths, 2-car side entry garage
- Slab foundation, drawings also include crawl space foundation

Total Living Area: 2,723 sq. ft.

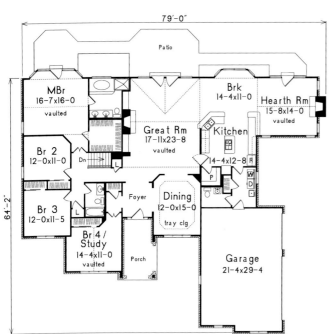

DID YOU KNOW?

Wood for burning requires at least 6 to 12 months to dry thoroughly. In order to be sure your firewood is ready, look for cracks along the cross-sectioned surfaces.

Plan Features

- A large porch invites you into an elegant foyer which accesses a vaulted study with private hall and coat closet
- Vaulted great room features a fireplace, built-in shelves and a 1 1/2 story window wall
- A spectacular hearth room with vaulted ceiling and masonry fireplace opens to an elaborate kitchen featuring two snack bars, a cooking island and walk-in pantry
- 4 bedrooms, 2 1/2 baths, 3-car side entry garage
- Basement foundation

To order call toll-free 1-800-DREAM HOME or visit www.houseplansandmore.com

Total Living Area: 2,433 sq. ft.

First Floor
1,590 sq. ft.

63'-0"

MSTR BATH (9' CLG)
SHWR
JACC
W.I.C.

GARAGE 21'-0"x27'-0" (9'-6" CLG)

STORAGE

COVERED PORCH 26'-10"x10'-6"

WORK BENCH

STORAGE

MASTER BEDROOM 14'-0"x19'-0" (10' TRAY CLG)

GREAT ROOM 22'-3"x14'-0" (9' CLG)

NOOK

KITCHEN 13'-0"x11'-8" (9' CLG)

LNDRY

OPTIONAL DOORS

OFFICE/GUEST/ BEDROOM #4 11'-8"x10'-1" (9' CLG)

FOYER (9' CLG)

FRENCH DOORS

FORMAL DINING 11'-8"x11'-0" (9' CLG)

PANTRY

PWDR

UP

COVERED PORCH 41'-6"x8'-0"

61'-0"

STEPS

Second Floor
843 sq. ft.

BEDROOM #2 11'-1"x11'-7" (8' CLG)

BATH

W.I.C.

LINEN STORAGE

TUB/SHWR

REC ROOM 21'-3"x12'-6" (VAULTED)

BEDROOM #3 11'-8"x16'-2" (VAULTED)

DN

SITTING AREA (VAULTED)

Plan Features

- Two second floor bedrooms share a Jack and Jill bath
- Terrific covered porch has access into master bedroom or great room
- Snack bar in kitchen provides additional seating for dining
- 3 bedrooms, 2 1/2 baths, 2-car side entry garage
- Basement, crawl space or slab foundation, please specify when ordering

Total Living Area: 1,724 sq. ft.

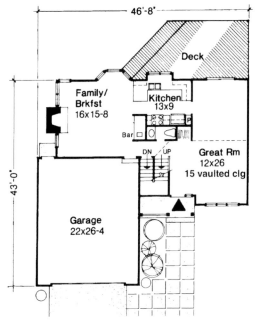

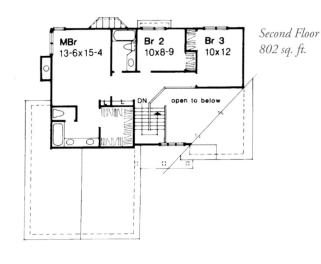

First Floor
922 sq. ft.

Second Floor
802 sq. ft.

46'-8"

43'-0"

Deck

Family/
Brkfst
16x15-8

Kitchen
13x9

Bar

DN UP

Great Rm
12x26
15 vaulted clg

Garage
22x26-4

MBr
13-6x15-4

Br 2
10x8-9

Br 3
10x12

DN

open to below

Plan Features

- Beautiful palladian windows enliven the two-story entry
- Sliding glass doors in the formal dining room connect to the large backyard deck
- Second floor master bedroom boasts corner windows, large walk-in closet and a split bath
- 3 bedrooms, 2 1/2 baths, 2-car garage
- Basement foundation

Total Living Area: 1,994 sq. ft.

First Floor
1,112 sq. ft.

43'

40'

©Alan Mascord Design Associates, Inc.

NOOK
11/0 X 9/0 +/-
(9' CLG.)

FAMILY
15/8 X 12/8
(9' CLG.)

DEN
9/8 X 10/4
(9' CLG.)

11/0 X 10/6 +/-

REF. P

DINING
11/0 X 10/0
(9' CLG.)

UP

GARAGE
19/0 X 19/6 +

VAULTED
LIVING
13/0 X 12/0

Second Floor
882 sq. ft.

VAULTED
MASTER
14/4 X 12/8

LINEN

BR. 2
11/4 X 10/0 +/-

W.
D.

DN.

PLANT
SHELF

VAULTED
BR. 3
10/0 X 11/0

Plan Features

- Breakfast nook overlooks the kitchen and great room creating an airy feeling
- A double-door entry off the family room leads to a cozy den ideal as a home office
- Master suite has a walk-in closet and private bath
- 3 bedrooms, 2 1/2 baths, 2-car garage
- Crawl space foundation

Total Living Area: 2,300 sq. ft.

First Floor
1,067 sq. ft.

Second Floor
1,233 sq. ft.

Plan Features

- Cozy fireplace in master suite
- 9' ceilings on the first floor
- Energy efficient home with 2"x 6" exterior walls
- 3 bedrooms, 2 1/2 baths, 2-car side entry garage
- Basement foundation

Total Living Area: 2,406 sq. ft.

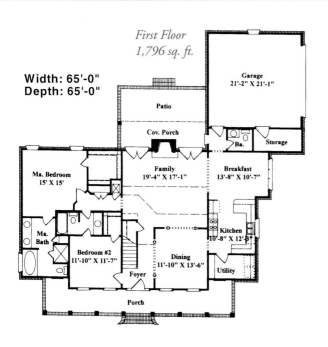

First Floor
1,796 sq. ft.

Width: 65'-0"
Depth: 65'-0"

Garage
21'-2" X 21'-1"

Patio

Cov. Porch

Ba.   Storage

Ma. Bedroom
15' X 15'

Family
19'-4" X 17'-1"

Breakfast
13'-8" X 10'-7"

Ma.
Bath

Bedroom #2
11'-10" X 11'-7"

Kitchen
10'-8" X 12'-8"

Dining
11'-10" X 13'-6"

Foyer

Utility

Porch

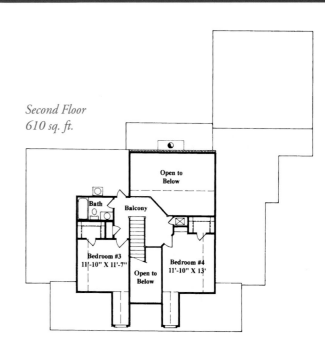

Second Floor
610 sq. ft.

Open to
Below

Bath   Balcony

Bedroom #3
11'-10" X 11'-7"

Open to
Below

Bedroom #4
11'-10" X 13'

Plan Features

- Beautiful family area with fireplace surrounded by double French doors
- Covered rear porch and patio
- Sunny breakfast room located off kitchen and adjacent to family area
- Plenty of closet space for a growing family
- 4 bedrooms, 3 1/2 baths, 2-car side entry garage
- Crawl space or slab foundation, please specify when ordering

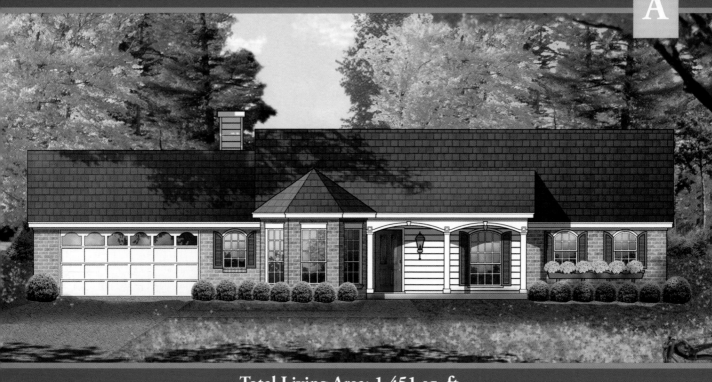

Total Living Area: 1,451 sq. ft.

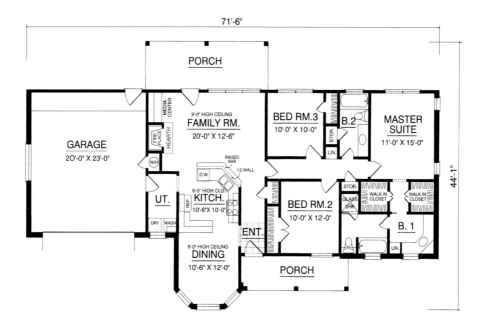

Plan Features

- Luxurious master suite boasts two walk-in closets and a large compartmented bath
- Large family room has a fireplace, built-in media center and access to the rear porch
- The charming kitchen includes a raised snack bar and easily serves the large formal dining room
- 3 bedrooms, 2 baths, 2-car garage
- Slab or crawl space foundation, please specify when ordering

Total Living Area: 1,220 sq. ft.

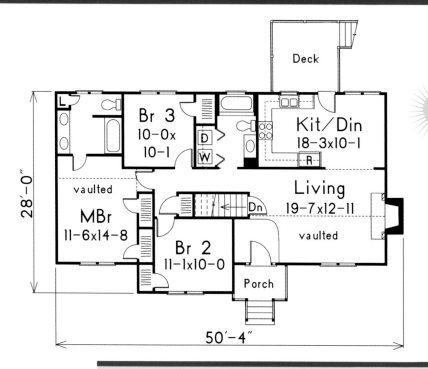

DID YOU KNOW?

Partitions help distinguish the edge of rooms within a home and can be flexible or fixed. They can take the form of walls, glass panels, doors or even fireplaces. Low partitions are especially appealing because they allow the overall space to remain open and airy.

Plan Features

- A vaulted ceiling adds luxury to the living room
- Living room is accented with a large fireplace and hearth
- Gracious dining area is adjacent to the convenient wrap-around kitchen
- Rear deck adjoins dining area
- 3 bedrooms, 2 baths, 2-car drive under garage
- Basement foundation

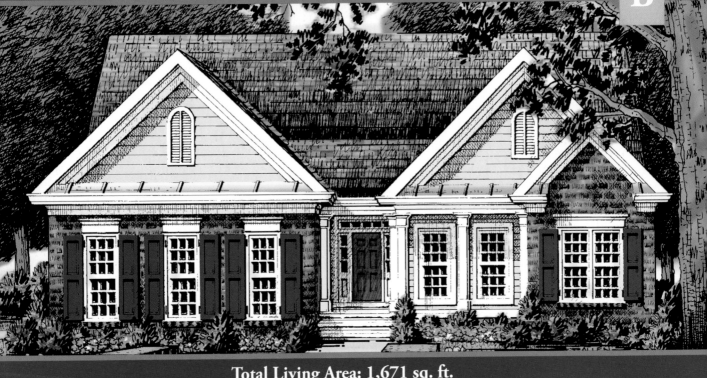

Total Living Area: 1,671 sq. ft.

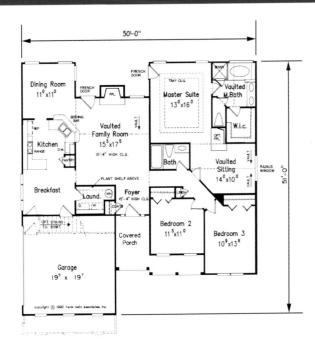

DID YOU KNOW?

To avoid scuffing wood, vinyl or linoleum floors when rearranging furniture pieces, slide a folded towel under each side of the piece of furniture you wish to move. Not only does this avoid scratches and scrapes, but it tends to make moving the piece a lot easier.

Plan Features

- Kitchen is conveniently located between the breakfast and dining rooms
- Vaulted family room is centrally located
- Laundry room is located near the garage for easy access
- 3 bedrooms, 2 baths, 2-car side entry garage
- Slab, crawl space or walk-out basement foundation, please specify when ordering

Total Living Area: 2,758 sq. ft.

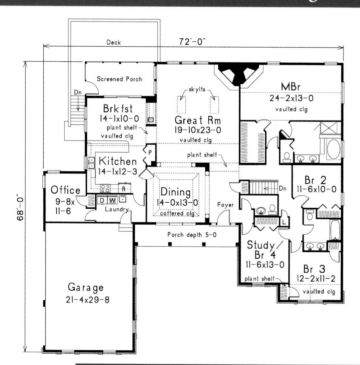

DID YOU KNOW?

Avoid using fabric or paper light shades in a kitchen as they are likely to harbor grease and cooking odors. Glass and metal fittings are more practical.

Plan Features

- Great room enjoys a fireplace, wet bar, and plant shelves
- Vaulted master bedroom has a fireplace, large bath and walk-in closet
- The kitchen and breakfast area adjoin the screened porch
- Convenient office near kitchen is perfect for hobby enthusiasts or fifth bedroom
- 4 bedrooms, 2 1/2 baths, 3-car side entry garage
- Basement foundation

Total Living Area: 3,176 sq. ft.

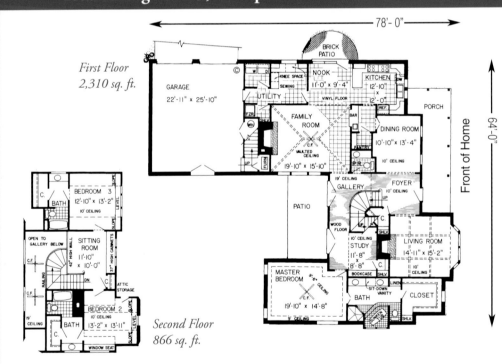

First Floor
2,310 sq. ft.

Second Floor
866 sq. ft.

Plan Features

- Varied ceiling heights throughout
- Beautifully designed foyer has a prominent center staircase and a lovely adjacent gallery space
- A casual sitting room connects the secondary bedrooms
- 3 bedrooms, 3 1/2 baths, 2-car rear entry garage
- Basement, crawl space or slab foundation, please specify when ordering

Total Living Area: 2,317 sq. ft.

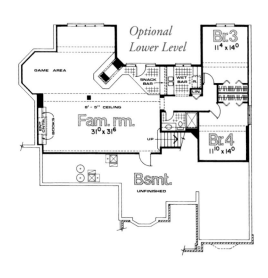

Optional Lower Level

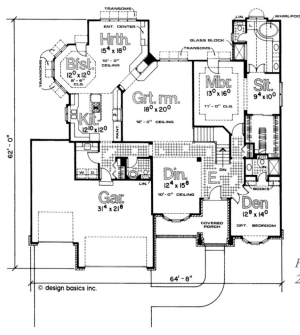

First Floor
2,317 sq. ft.

© design basics inc.

Plan Features

- Built-in bookshelves complete the private den
- Cheerful breakfast room is octagon-shaped and overlooks the cozy hearth room
- Optional lower level has an additional 1,475 square feet of living area
- 1 bedroom, 2 1/2 baths, 3-car garage
- Walk-out basement or basement foundation, please specify when ordering

Total Living Area: 1,187 sq. ft.

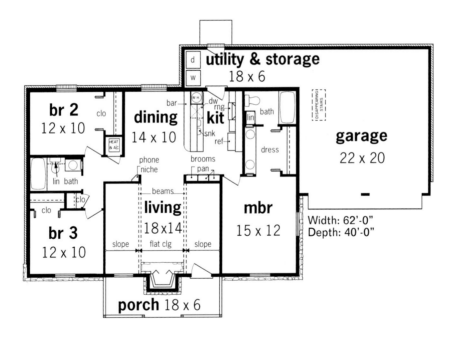

utility & storage
18 x 6

br 2
12 x 10

dining
14 x 10

kit

bath

garage
22 x 20

phone niche

brooms

dress

lin bath

living
18 x 14

mbr
15 x 12

br 3
12 x 10

slope   flat clg   slope

Width: 62'-0"
Depth: 40'-0"

porch 18 x 6

Plan Features

- Wood and stone were used to accent the facade of this farmhouse design
- The living room has a cathedral ceiling with exposed beams and a stone fireplace
- The kitchen and dining area amenities include a built-in phone niche and floor-to-ceiling built-in pantries
- 3 bedrooms, 2 baths, 2-car garage
- Slab foundation, drawings also include crawl space foundation

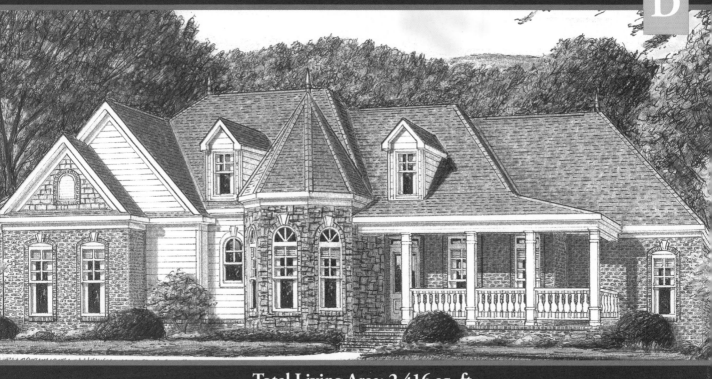

Total Living Area: 2,416 sq. ft.

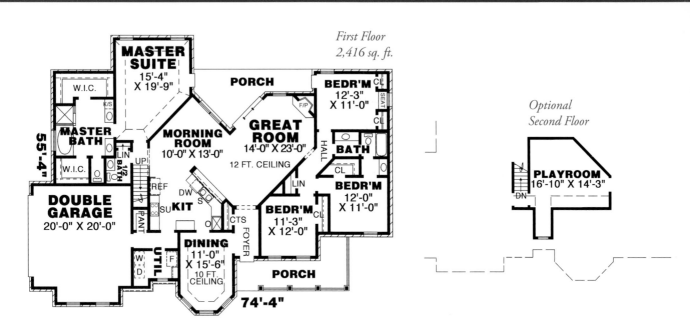

First Floor
2,416 sq. ft.

Optional
Second Floor

Plan Features

- Octagon-shaped formal dining room makes an impact on the exterior of this home
- Angled walls add interest to the floor plan throughout this home
- Future playroom on the second floor has an additional 207 square feet of living area
- 4 bedrooms, 2 1/2 baths, 2-car side entry garage
- Slab foundation

Total Living Area: 2,613 sq. ft.

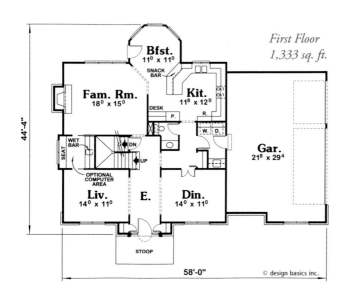

First Floor
1,333 sq. ft.

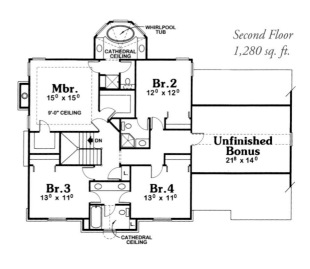

Second Floor
1,280 sq. ft.

Plan Features

- Traditional styling makes this home a favorite
- Well-designed living and family rooms connect with a pass-through wet bar
- Master bedroom includes a dramatic private bath
- Bonus room above garage has an additional 323 square feet of living area
- 4 bedrooms, 3 1/2 baths, 3-car side entry garage
- Basement foundation

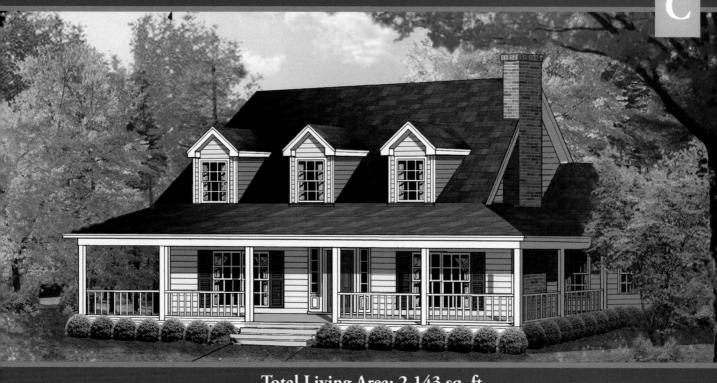

Total Living Area: 2,143 sq. ft.

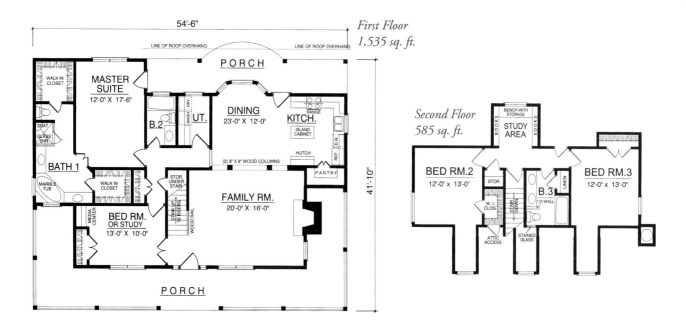

First Floor
1,535 sq. ft.

Second Floor
585 sq. ft.

Plan Features

- Enter the home into the expansive family room and view the bayed dining area defined by wood columns
- The kitchen includes an island, hutch, extra-large pantry and access to the rear porch
- A study area in a box-bay on the second floor includes built-in bookshelves and a bench
- 4 bedrooms, 3 baths
- Basement, slab or crawl space foundation, please specify when ordering

Total Living Area: 2,869 sq. ft.

First Floor
2,152 sq. ft.

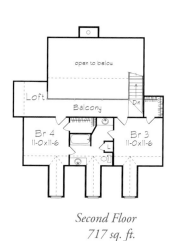

Second Floor
717 sq. ft.

Plan Features

- Foyer, flanked by columned living and dining rooms, leads to the vaulted family room with fireplace and twin sets of French doors
- 10' ceilings on the first floor and 9' ceilings on the second floor
- 4 bedrooms, 3 baths, 2-car rear entry garage
- Slab foundation, drawings also include crawl space foundation

Total Living Area: 2,007 sq. ft.

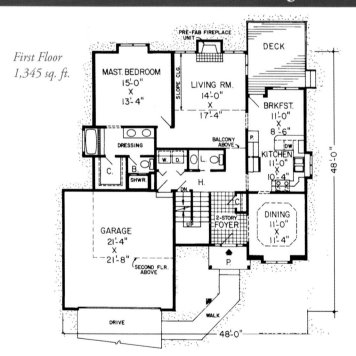

First Floor
1,345 sq. ft.

Second Floor
662 sq. ft.

Plan Features

- Energy efficient home with 2"x 6" exterior walls
- The two-story foyer opens into the living room which features a sloping ceiling and fireplace
- The centrally located kitchen serves the dining and breakfast areas with ease
- 3 bedrooms, 2 1/2 baths, 2-car garage
- Slab, crawl space or basement foundation, please specify when ordering

Total Living Area: 3,268 sq. ft.

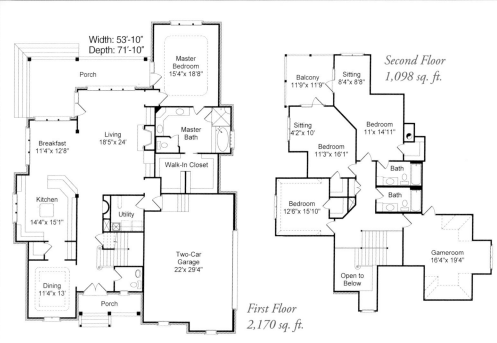

Width: 53'-10"
Depth: 71'-10"

Porch

Master Bedroom
15'4"x 18'8"

Master Bath

Breakfast
11'4"x 12'8"

Living
18'5"x 24'

Walk-In Closet

Kitchen
14'4"x 15'1"

Utility

Dining
11'4"x 13'

Porch

Two-Car Garage
22'x 29'4"

First Floor
2,170 sq. ft.

Second Floor
1,098 sq. ft.

Balcony
11'9"x 11'9"

Sitting
8'4"x 8'8"

Sitting
4'2"x 10'

Bedroom
11'x 14'11"

Bedroom
11'3"x 16'1"

Bath

Bath

Bedroom
12'6"x 15'10"

Gameroom
16'4"x 19'4"

Open to Below

Plan Features

- Stucco and brick combine to create a beautiful facade
- A grand entrance greets guests with an elegant staircase and formal dining room
- Two second floor bedrooms open to the balcony and include their own sitting areas
- The future gameroom has an additional 323 square feet of living space
- 4 bedrooms, 3 1/2 baths, 2-car side entry garage
- Slab foundation

Total Living Area: 3,291 sq. ft.

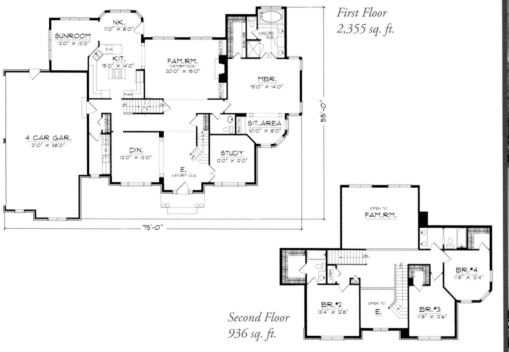

First Floor
2,355 sq. ft.

Second Floor
936 sq. ft.

Plan Features

- The two-story family room boasts a grand fireplace flanked by built-in shelves
- The sunroom connects with the bayed nook and kitchen
- The vaulted master bedroom features a bayed sitting area and a deluxe bath
- All secondary bedrooms enjoy walk-in closets
- 4 bedrooms, 3 1/2 baths, 4-car side entry garage
- Basement foundation

Total Living Area: 1,392 sq. ft.

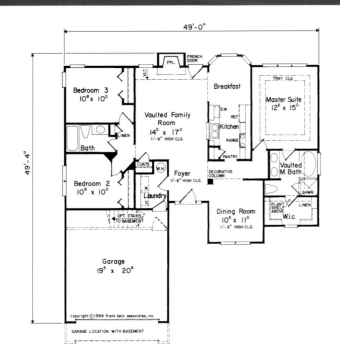

DID YOU KNOW?

Studies show a home near or on a park can increase the property value as much as 20%.

Plan Features

- Bay windows give the breakfast room a warm and inviting feel
- Master suite has privacy from the rest of the home and includes a large vaulted bath
- 9' ceilings throughout home
- 3 bedrooms, 2 baths, 2-car garage
- Crawl space, slab or walk-out basement foundation, please specify when ordering

Plan #583-007D-0066

Price Code: D

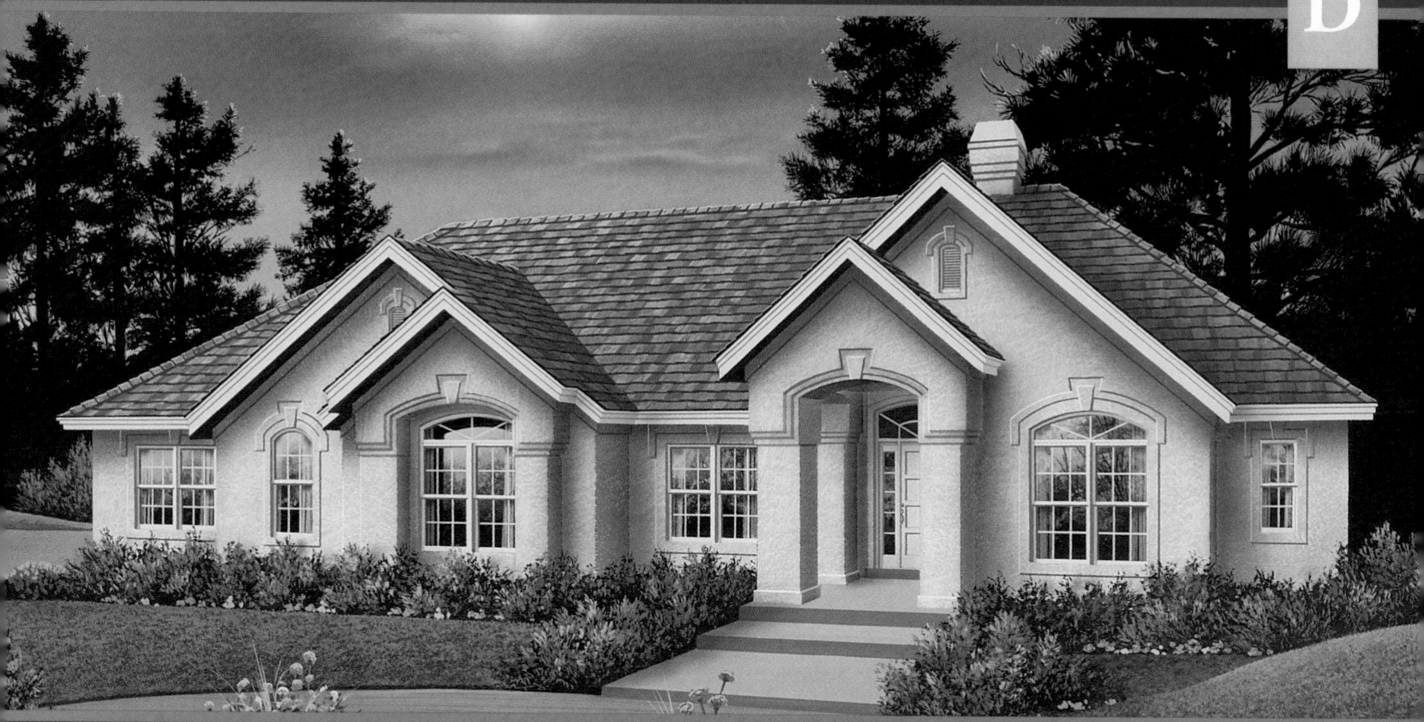

Total Living Area: 2,408 sq. ft.

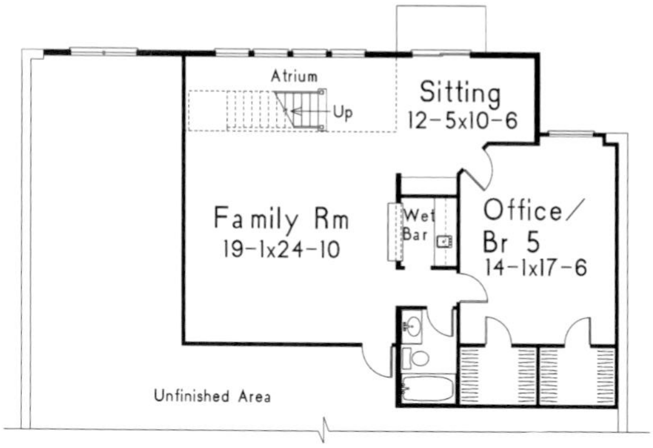
Atrium
Up
Sitting
12-5x10-6
Family Rm
19-1x24-10
Wet Bar
Office/
Br 5
14-1x17-6
Unfinished Area

Optional Lower Level

First Floor
2,408 sq. ft.

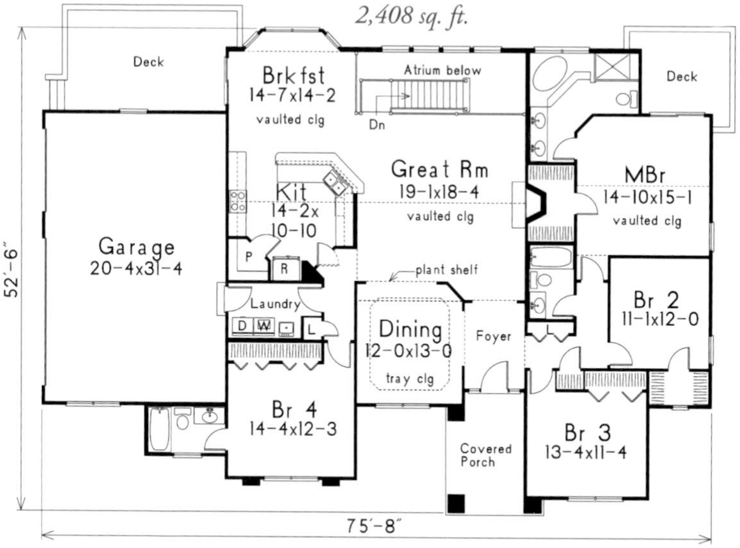
Deck
Brkfst
14-7x14-2
vaulted clg
Atrium below
Dn
Deck
Garage
20-4x31-4
Kit
14-2x
10-10
Great Rm
19-1x18-4
vaulted clg
MBr
14-10x15-1
vaulted clg
P
R
plant shelf
Laundry
D
W
L
Dining
12-0x13-0
tray clg
Foyer
Br 2
11-1x12-0
Br 4
14-4x12-3
Covered Porch
Br 3
13-4x11-4
52'-6"
75'-8"

Plan Features

- Large vaulted great room overlooks atrium and window wall, adjoins dining room, spacious breakfast room with bay and pass-through kitchen
- A special private bedroom with bath, separate from other bedrooms, is perfect for a mother-in-law suite or children home from college
- Atrium opens to 1,100 square feet of optional living area below
- 4 bedrooms, 3 baths, 3-car side entry garage
- Walk-out basement foundation

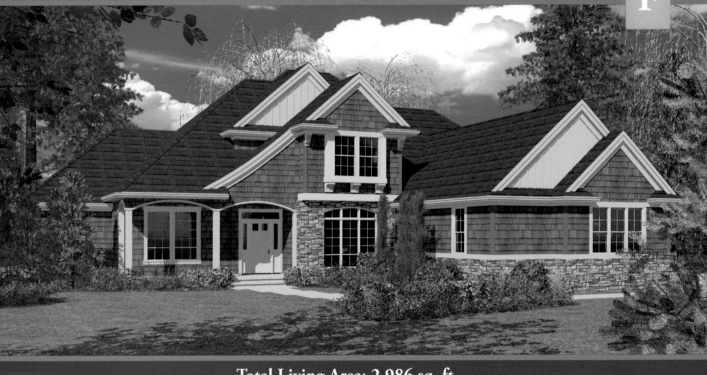

Total Living Area: 2,986 sq. ft.

PATIO

NOOK
12/0 X 11/0
(9' CLG.)

MASTER
13/2 X 16/0
(10'-8" CLG.)

TWO STORY
GREAT RM.
19/0 X 19/8

DEN
14/2 X 12/0
(9' - 10' CLG.)

BUTLER'S PANTRY   PANTRY

DINING
12/6 X 15/4
(9' CLG.)

GARAGE
22/0 X 29/0

◄ 67' ►

68'

First Floor
2,162 sq. ft.

GREAT RM.
BELOW

BR. 2
12/0 X 10/8

LIBRARY
12/6 X 8/8 +/-

LINEN

BR. 3
12/6 X 11/0

GAMES RM.
12/6 X 11/0

Second Floor
824 sq. ft.

Plan Features

- Large laundry room has lots of storage and a convenient sink
- A second floor library connects to a game room
- Master bedroom is close to a private den, ideal for a home office
- 3 bedrooms, 2 1/2 baths, 3-car side entry garage
- Crawl space foundation

Total Living Area: 2,147 sq. ft.

DID YOU KNOW?

Clutter can really detract from an open floor plan. When planning your living area, make a list of all of the items that will need to be stored. Everything from media equipment to children's toy bins should be considered. Also, don't forget to list books and collectibles. Often times when rooms are designed there is not enough storage for all of the everyday living items and rooms pile up with unwanted clutter. Designing a room initially with these needs in mind will not compromise the overall beauty of the space once all of your belongings are in place.

Plan Features

- The foyer opens to the great room which features a 10' ceiling and grand fireplace
- The centrally located kitchen adjoins the formal dining room and relaxing bayed breakfast room
- The master suite is a luxurious retreat with a deluxe bath and access to the covered porch
- 4 bedrooms, 2 1/2 baths, 2-car side entry garage
- Slab or crawl space foundation, please specify when ordering

Total Living Area: 3,312 sq. ft.

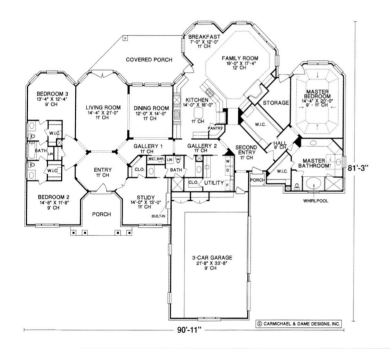

DID YOU KNOW?

Never use disinfectants to clean a refrigerator. The food inside will pick up the taste and odor of the cleaning solution. Warm soapy water works well and is a less harmful choice.

Plan Features

- Front entry commands attention with an enormous living room straight ahead
- A casual family room and breakfast area combine to create a terrific gathering place just off the kitchen
- A second entry near the master bedroom is a convenient way into the home directly from the garage
- 3 bedrooms, 2 1/2 baths, 3-car side entry garage
- Slab foundation

Plan #583-051D-0116

Price Code: G

Total Living Area: 3,511 sq. ft.

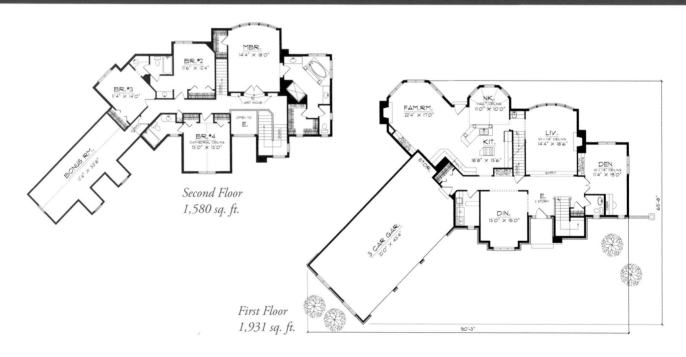

Second Floor
1,580 sq. ft.

First Floor
1,931 sq. ft.

Plan Features

- The grand living room features a bowed window and cozy fireplace
- The bayed nook and family room create a relaxing area
- All bedrooms are located on the second floor for additional privacy
- The second floor bonus room has an additional 440 square feet of living area
- 4 bedrooms, 3 1/2 baths, 3-car side entry garage
- Basement foundation

Total Living Area: 2,491 sq. ft.

DID YOU KNOW?

The word porch is used freely to mean any sort of covered area that attaches to a home. Other variations include breezeway, veranda, portico or even a sleeping porch. Each different term typically is popularized depending on the region of the country you reside.

Plan Features

- Impressive master suite has an enormous sitting room with fireplace and access outdoors
- Vaulted family room is cozy with fireplace and conveniently located near breakfast room
- Handy bath between secondary bedrooms is easily accessible
- Optional bonus room above the garage has an additional 588 square feet of living area
- 3 bedrooms, 2 1/2 baths, 2-car side entry garage
- Crawl space, slab or walk-out basement foundation, please specify when ordering

Total Living Area: 3,222 sq. ft.

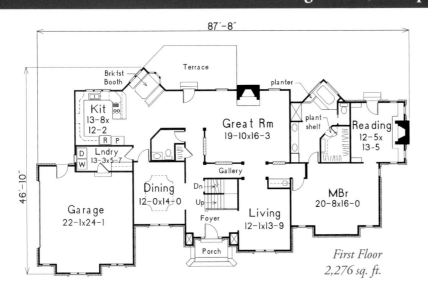

First Floor 2,276 sq. ft.

Second Floor 946 sq. ft.

Plan Features

- The two-story foyer, dining and living rooms all have views to the second floor
- Built-in breakfast booth is surrounded by windows
- Two-story great room features a large fireplace and arched openings to the second floor
- Elegant master bedroom has separate reading room with bookshelves and fireplace
- 4 bedrooms, 3 1/2 baths, 2-car side entry garage
- Basement foundation, drawings also include crawl space and slab foundations

Total Living Area: 1,080 sq. ft.

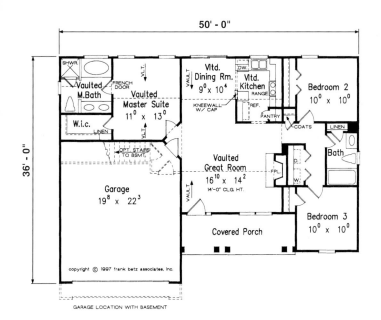

GARAGE LOCATION WITH BASEMENT

DID YOU KNOW?

A dining room table's style and shape affects the look of a room. As a general rule, many designers suggest buying a table that mimics the shape of your room for clean lines that are appealing to the eye.

Plan Features

- Secondary bedrooms are separate from master suite allowing privacy
- Compact kitchen is well organized
- The laundry closet is conveniently located next to the secondary bedrooms
- 3 bedrooms, 2 baths, 2-car garage
- Walk-out basement or crawl space foundation, please specify when ordering

Total Living Area: 2,838 sq. ft.

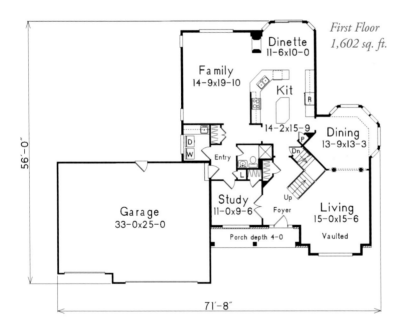

First Floor
1,602 sq. ft.

Dinette
11-6x10-0

Family
14-9x19-10

Kit
14-2x15-9

Dining
13-9x13-3

Entry

Study
11-0x9-6

Foyer

Living
15-0x15-6
Vaulted

Dn
Up

Garage
33-0x25-0

Porch depth 4-0

56'-0"

71'-8"

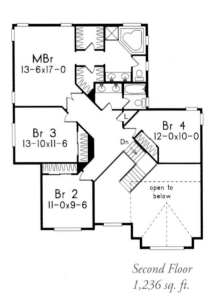

MBr
13-6x17-0

Br 3
13-10x11-6

Br 4
12-0x10-0

Br 2
11-0x9-6

Dn

open to
below

Second Floor
1,236 sq. ft.

Plan Features

- 10' ceilings throughout the first floor
- Dining room is enhanced with large corner bay windows
- Master bath boasts a double-bowl vanity and an oversized tub
- Kitchen features an island and double sink which overlooks dinette and family room
- 4 bedrooms, 2 1/2 baths, 3-car garage
- Basement foundation

E

Total Living Area: 3,013 sq. ft.

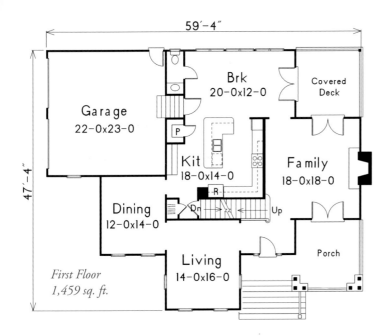

Garage
22-0x23-0

Brk
20-0x12-0

Covered
Deck

Kit
18-0x14-0

Family
18-0x18-0

Dining
12-0x14-0

Dn   Up

Living
14-0x16-0

Porch

59'-4"

47'-4"

P

R

*First Floor
1,459 sq. ft.*

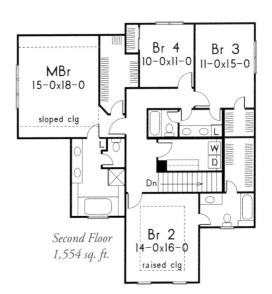

MBr
15-0x18-0

sloped clg

Br 4
10-0x11-0

Br 3
11-0x15-0

L

W
D

Dn

Br 2
14-0x16-0

raised clg

*Second Floor
1,554 sq. ft.*

Plan Features

- Oversized rooms throughout
- Kitchen features an island sink, large pantry and opens into the sunny breakfast room
- Large family room with fireplace accesses the rear deck and front porch
- Master bedroom includes a large walk-in closet and private deluxe bath
- 4 bedrooms, 3 1/2 baths, 2-car side entry garage
- Basement foundation

Total Living Area: 1,269 sq. ft.

Lower Level
42 sq. ft.

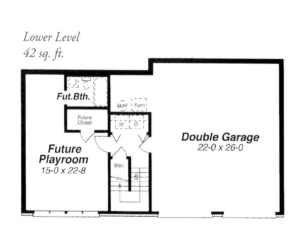

First Floor
1,227 sq. ft.

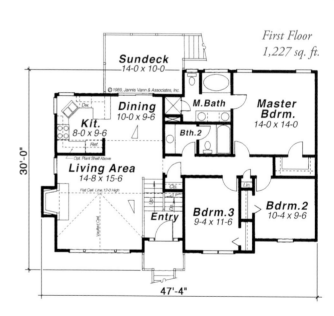

Plan Features

- Dining area has sliding glass doors to outdoor sundeck
- Compact, yet efficient kitchen
- Vaulted living room adds appeal
- The lower level includes 463 square feet of optional living area
- 3 bedrooms, 2 baths, 2-car garage
- Walk-out basement foundation

Total Living Area: 1,631 sq. ft.

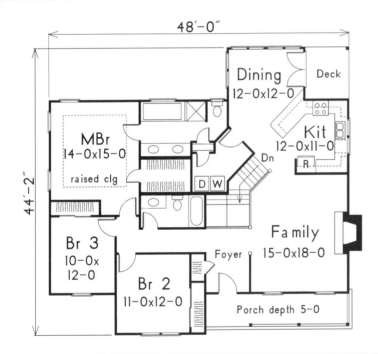

48'-0"

44'-2"

Dining
12-0x12-0

Deck

MBr
14-0x15-0

raised clg

Kit
12-0x11-0

Dn

D W

R

Family
15-0x18-0

Br 3
10-0x
12-0

Foyer

Br 2
11-0x12-0

Porch depth 5-0

DID YOU KNOW?

Learn the "rule of threes" and apply to your home decorating projects. Overall, odd numbers of objects when decorating are more eye-catching and interesting than even numbers.

Plan Features

- 9' ceilings throughout this home
- Utility room is conveniently located near the kitchen
- Roomy kitchen and dining area boast a breakfast bar and deck access
- Raised ceiling accents master bedroom
- 3 bedrooms, 2 baths, 2-car drive under garage
- Basement foundation

Total Living Area: 2,352 sq. ft.

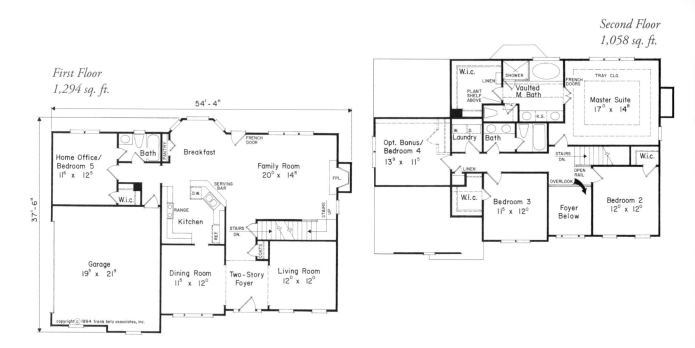

Second Floor
1,058 sq. ft.

First Floor
1,294 sq. ft.

Plan Features

- All bedrooms are located on the second floor for privacy
- Kitchen and breakfast area flow into the family room with fireplace
- Two-story foyer is open and airy
- Optional bonus room has an additional 168 square feet of living area
- 4 bedrooms, 3 baths, 2-car side entry garage
- Walk-out basement or crawl space foundation, please specify when ordering

Total Living Area: 1,624 sq. ft.

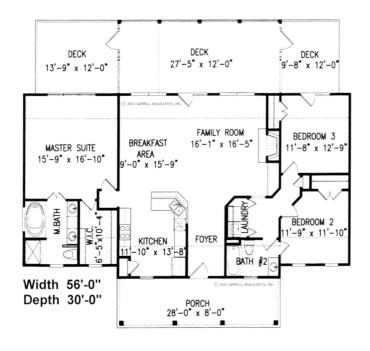

DECK
13'-9" x 12'-0"

DECK
27'-5" x 12'-0"

DECK
9'-8" x 12'-0"

© 2003 GARRELL ASSOCIATES, INC.

FAMILY ROOM
16'-1" x 16'-5"

BEDROOM 3
11'-8" x 12'-9"

MASTER SUITE
15'-9" x 16'-10"

BREAKFAST
AREA
9'-0" x 15'-9"

M.BATH

W.I.C.
6'-5"x10'-4"

KITCHEN
11'-10" x 13'-8"

FOYER

LAUNDRY

BEDROOM 2
11'-9" x 11'-10"

BATH #2

Width 56'-0"
Depth 30'-0"

© 2003 GARRELL ASSOCIATES, INC.

PORCH
28'-0" x 8'-0"

DID YOU KNOW?

The size of the American yard continues to shrink; currently it is only 9,000 square feet.

Plan Features

- Large covered deck leads to two uncovered decks accessible by the master bedroom and bedroom #3
- Well-organized kitchen overlooks into the breakfast area and family room
- Laundry closet is located near the secondary bedrooms
- 3 bedrooms, 2 baths
- Crawl space or slab foundation, please specify when ordering

Total Living Area: 2,311 sq. ft.

First Floor
2,311 sq. ft.

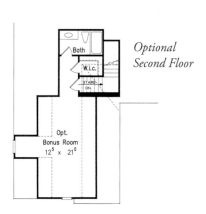

Optional
Second Floor

Plan Features

- Fireplaces warm the master suite and family room
- Vaulted breakfast room is adjacent to the kitchen
- Formal living room is near the dining room
- Optional bonus room on the second floor has an additional 425 square feet of living area
- 3 bedrooms, 2 1/2 baths, 2-car side entry garage
- Walk-out basement, slab or crawl space foundation, please specify when ordering

Total Living Area: 2,082 sq. ft.

First Floor
1,524 sq. ft.

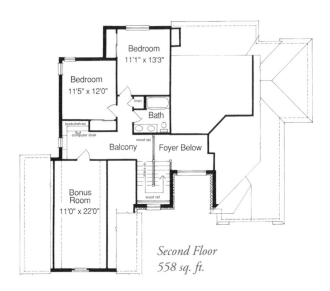

Second Floor
558 sq. ft.

Plan Features

- Master bedroom boasts a deluxe bath and a large walk-in closet
- Natural light floods the breakfast room through numerous windows
- Great room features a 12' ceiling, cozy fireplace and stylish French doors
- Bonus room on the second floor has an additional 267 square feet of living area
- 3 bedrooms, 2 1/2 baths, 2-car garage
- Basement foundation

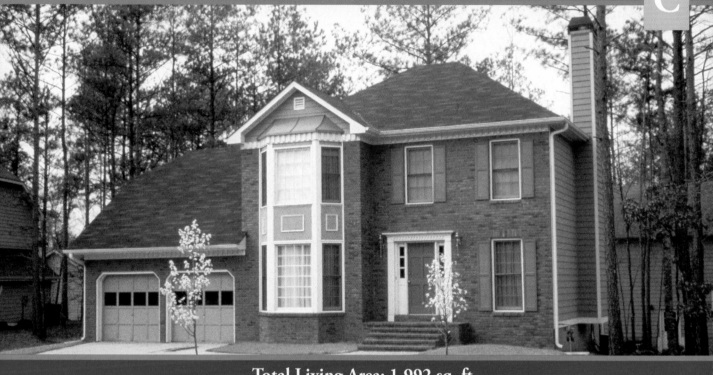

Total Living Area: 1,992 sq. ft.

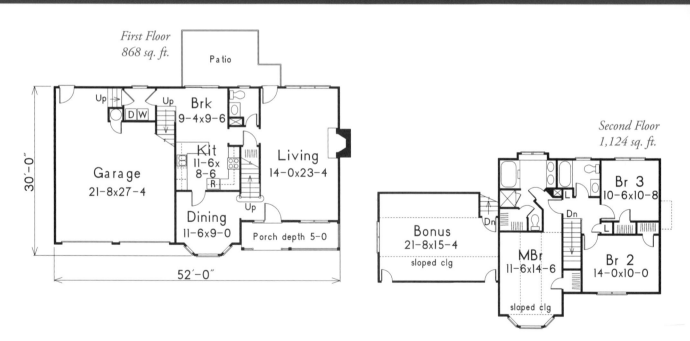

First Floor
868 sq. ft.

Second Floor
1,124 sq. ft.

Plan Features

- Distinct living, dining and breakfast areas
- Master bedroom boasts a full-end bay window and a cathedral ceiling
- Storage and laundry area are located adjacent to the garage
- Bonus room over the garage is included in the square footage
- 3 bedrooms, 2 1/2 baths, 2-car garage
- Crawl space foundation, drawings also include basement foundation

D

Total Living Area: 2,272 sq. ft.

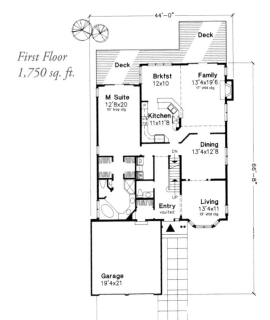

First Floor
1,750 sq. ft.

44'-0"

Deck

Deck

Brkfst
12x10

Family
13'4x19'6
17' vltd clg

M Suite
12'8x20
10' tray clg

Kitchen
11x11'8

Dining
13'4x12'8

DN

UP

Entry
vaulted

Living
13'4x11
13' vltd clg

Garage
19'4x21

66'-8"

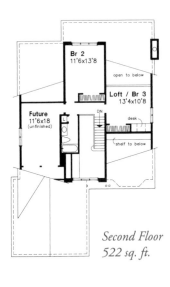

Second Floor
522 sq. ft.

Br 2
11'6x13'8

open to below

Loft / Br 3
13'4x10'8

Future
11'6x18
(unfinished)

DN

desk

shelf to below

Rear View

Plan Features

- Defined yet joined, these formal spaces can handle many entertaining needs
- A vaulted ceiling crowns the family room which includes a fireplace and access onto the deck
- The master suite boasts its own deck access along with a private bath
- 3 bedrooms, 2 1/2 baths
- Basement foundation

Total Living Area: 2,967 sq. ft.

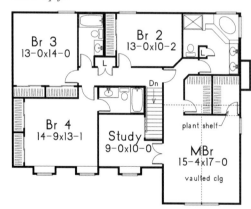

Second Floor
1,517 sq. ft.

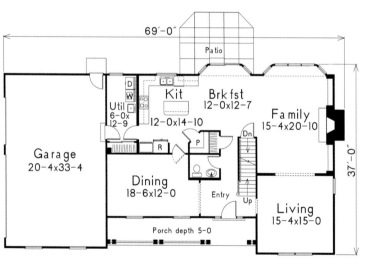

First Floor
1,450 sq. ft.

Plan Features

- An exterior with charm graced with country porch and multiple arched projected box windows
- Dining area is oversized and adjoins a fully equipped kitchen with walk-in pantry
- Two bay windows light up the enormous informal living area to the rear
- 4 bedrooms, 3 1/2 baths, 3-car side entry garage
- Basement foundation

Total Living Area: 1,467 sq. ft.

First Floor
1,001 sq. ft.

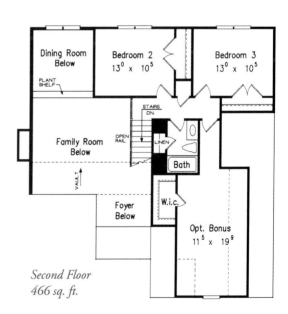

Second Floor
466 sq. ft.

Plan Features

- 9' ceilings throughout this home
- Two-story family and dining rooms are open and airy
- Bonus room above the garage has an additional 292 square feet of living area
- 3 bedrooms, 2 1/2 baths, 2-car garage
- Walk-out basement, slab or crawl space foundation, please specify when ordering

Total Living Area: 2,900 sq. ft.

*Optional
Lower Level*

*First Floor
2,900 sq. ft.*

Plan Features

- The great room offers a vaulted ceiling, palladian windows and an 8' brick fireplace
- A smartly designed built-in-a-bay kitchen features a picture window above sink, huge pantry, cooktop island and is open to a large morning room with 12' of cabinetry
- 1,018 square feet of optional living area on the lower level with family room, walk-in bar and a fifth bedroom with a bath
- 4 bedrooms, 2 1/2 baths, 3-car side entry garage
- Walk-out basement foundation

Total Living Area: 1,324 sq. ft.

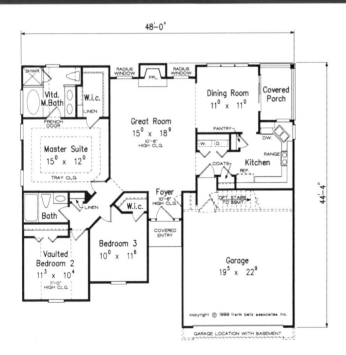

DID YOU KNOW?

For centuries beeswax candles were used to light the homes of European nobility. Beeswax, considered to be a precious material during these times, was typically only cultivated by the noblemen themselves on their own land in fear that the wax would be stolen or sold.

Plan Features

- Appealing French door in the master suite leads to a private bath with oversized tub and separate shower
- Corner sink in the kitchen has surrounding windows creating a cheerful atmosphere
- Enormous great room is centrally located and features a fireplace flanked by windows
- 3 bedrooms, 2 baths, 2-car garage
- Crawl space, slab or walk-out basement foundation, please specify when ordering

Total Living Area: 2,420 sq. ft.

First Floor 1,252 sq. ft.

DEN/BR. 4
10/6 x 11/0 +
(9' CLG.)

GREAT RM.
15/8 X 13/4
(9' CLG.)

NOOK
8/6 X 9/4 +/-
(9' CLG.)

DESK

BUILT-IN

11/8 X 11/10 +/-
(9' CLG.)

W D

PAN REF

GARAGE
19/6 X 19/6 +

UP

VAULTED
LIV/DIN
15/2 X 20/6 +/-

©Alan Mascord Design Associates, Inc.

51'

40'

PORCH

SPA

VAULTED
MASTER
15/0 X 14/8

BR. 2
12/0 X 10/0

LINEN

NICHE

LINEN

SHLVS.

NICHE

DN.

BR. 3
10/10 X 10/8

OPEN TO
BELOW

VAULTED
BONUS
14/0 X 13/0 +/-

©Alan Mascord Design Associates, Inc.

Second Floor 1,168 sq. ft.

Plan Features

- Master suite has a double-door entry, spacious bath with spa tub and a walk-in closet
- Den/bedroom #4 has easy access to a full bath and is secluded from other bedrooms
- Central living areas combine for maximum living space
- Second floor bonus room is included in the square footage
- 3 bedrooms, 2 1/2 baths, 2-car garage
- Crawl space foundation

Total Living Area: 2,560 sq. ft.

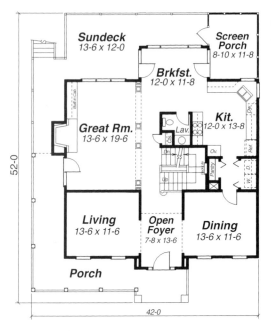

First Floor
1,250 sq. ft.

Sundeck 13-6 x 12-0
Screen Porch 8-10 x 11-8
Brkfst. 12-0 x 11-8
Great Rm. 13-6 x 19-6
Kit. 12-0 x 13-8
Lav.
Living 13-6 x 11-6
Open Foyer 7-8 x 13-6
Dining 13-6 x 11-6
Porch
52-0
42-0

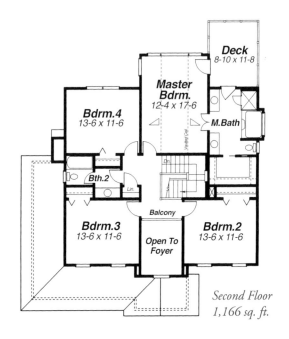

Second Floor
1,166 sq. ft.

Deck 8-10 x 11-8
Master Bdrm. 12-4 x 17-6
M.Bath
Bdrm.4 13-6 x 11-6
Bth.2
Bdrm.3 13-6 x 11-6
Open To Foyer
Balcony
Bdrm.2 13-6 x 11-6

Plan Features

- Open two-story foyer adds charm to this elegant home
- Large great room features a fireplace, built-in cabinet and access to porch and sundeck
- Breakfast area has windows on all exterior walls with access to porch and screen porch
- 144 square feet on the lower level
- 4 bedrooms, 2 1/2 baths, 2-car drive under garage
- Basement foundation

Plan #583-065D-0043

Price Code: F

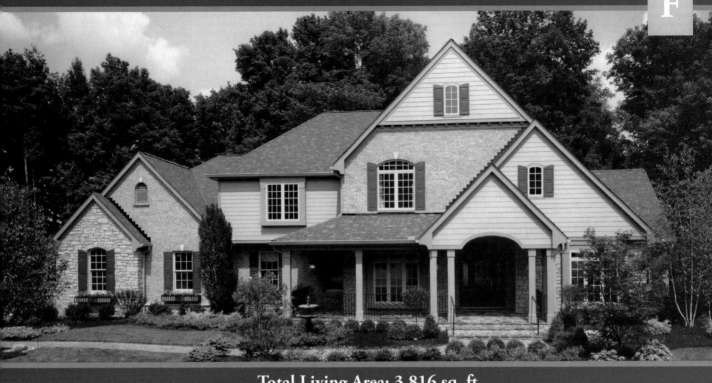

Total Living Area: 3,816 sq. ft.

First Floor
2,725 sq. ft.

Second Floor
1,091 sq. ft.

Plan Features

- The master bedroom enjoys a lavish dressing area as well as access to the library
- Second floor computer loft is centrally located and includes plenty of counterspace
- The two-story great room has an impressive arched opening and a beamed ceiling
- The outdoor covered deck has a popular fireplace
- 4 bedrooms, 3 1/2 baths, 3-car side entry garage
- Basement foundation

Total Living Area: 1,124 sq. ft.

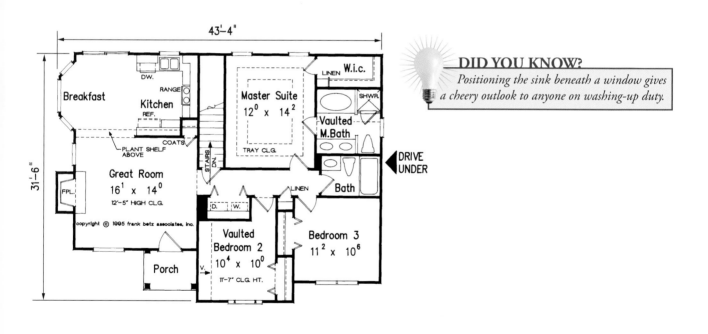

DID YOU KNOW?
Positioning the sink beneath a window gives a cheery outlook to anyone on washing-up duty.

Plan Features

- Varied ceiling heights throughout this home
- Enormous bayed breakfast room overlooks the great room with fireplace
- The washer and dryer closet are conveniently located
- 3 bedrooms, 2 baths, 2-car drive under garage
- Walk-out basement foundation

Total Living Area: 2,373 sq. ft.

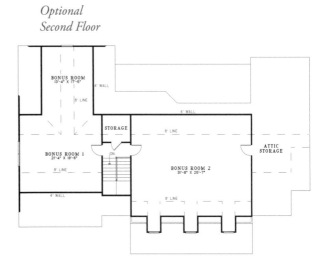

First Floor
2,373 sq. ft.

Optional
Second Floor

Plan Features

- The grilling porch extends dining opportunities to the outdoors
- Fireplace in great room also warms the adjoining kitchen and breakfast room
- The relaxing master suite enjoys a deluxe bath with whirlpool tub and walk-in closet
- The optional second floor has an additional 1,672 square feet of living space
- 4 bedrooms, 3 baths, 2-car side entry garage
- Slab or crawl space foundation, please specify when ordering

Total Living Area: 2,111 sq. ft.

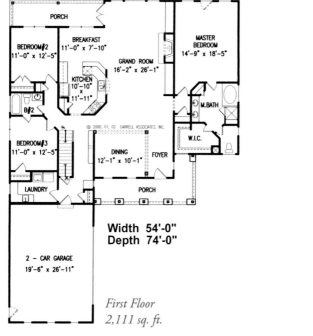

First Floor
2,111 sq. ft.

Width 54'-0"
Depth 74'-0"

Optional
Second Floor

Plan Features

- 9' ceilings throughout first floor
- The spacious formal dining room has decorative columns maintaining an open feel
- Master bedroom has privacy from other bedrooms
- Bonus room on the second floor has an additional 345 square feet of living area
- 3 bedrooms, 2 baths, 2-car side entry garage
- Basement foundation

C

Total Living Area: 2,059 sq. ft.

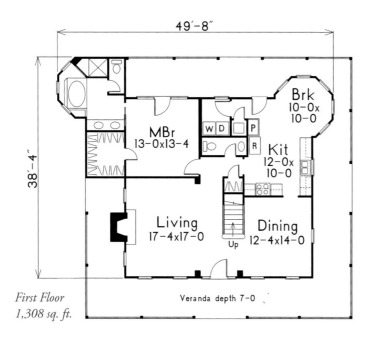

49'-8"

38'-4"

First Floor
1,308 sq. ft.

Veranda depth 7-0

Brk
10-0x
10-0

MBr
13-0x13-4

W D
P
R

Kit
12-0x
10-0

Living
17-4x17-0

Up

Dining
12-4x14-0

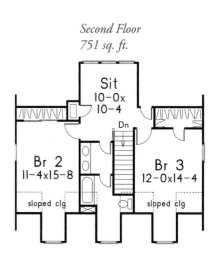

Second Floor
751 sq. ft.

Sit
10-0x
10-4

Dn

Br 2
11-4x15-8

Br 3
12-0x14-4

sloped clg

sloped clg

Plan Features

- Octagon-shaped breakfast room offers plenty of windows and a view to the veranda
- First floor master bedroom has a large walk-in closet and deluxe bath
- 9' ceilings throughout the home
- Secondary bedrooms and bath feature dormers and are adjacent to the cozy sitting area
- 3 bedrooms, 2 1/2 baths, 2-car detached garage
- Slab foundation, drawings also include basement and crawl space foundations

Total Living Area: 5,250 sq. ft.

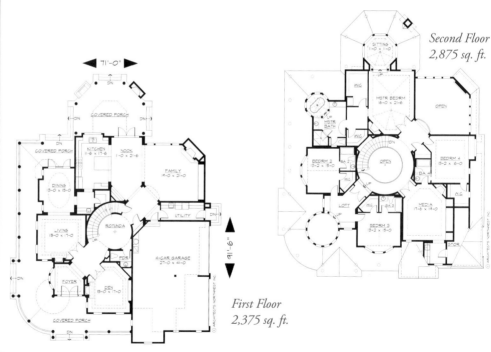

Second Floor
2,875 sq. ft.

First Floor
2,375 sq. ft.

Plan Features

- Wrap-around covered porch features an outdoor fireplace and built-in barbecue grill
- Each bedroom has its own bath and walk-in closet
- Dramatic circular staircase is highlighted in rotunda with 27' ceiling
- Master bath showcases an octagon-shaped space featuring a whirlpool tub
- 4 bedrooms, 4 1/2 baths, 4-car side entry garage
- Crawl space foundation

Total Living Area: 2,261 sq. ft.

First Floor
2,261 sq. ft.

Optional
Second Floor

Plan Features

- Efficiently designed kitchen with work island and snack bar
- Master bath has a double vanity, whirlpool tub and two walk-in closets
- Spacious laundry room includes ironing board space
- Optional second floor has an additional 367 square feet of living area
- 4 bedrooms, 3 1/2 baths, 2-car side entry garage
- Slab or crawl space foundation, please specify when ordering foundation

---

Price Code:

C

Total Living Area: 2,128 sq. ft.

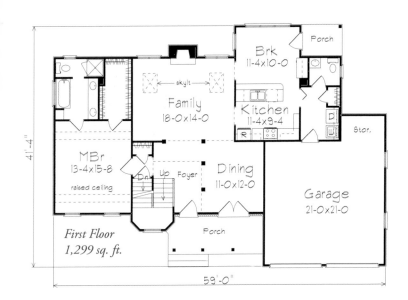

First Floor
1,299 sq. ft.

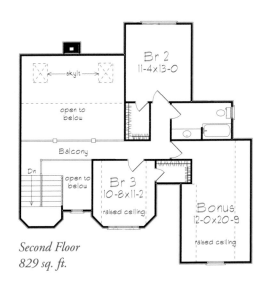

Second Floor
829 sq. ft.

Plan Features

- Large bonus room offers many possibilities and is included in the second floor square footage
- Convenient laundry room is located near the kitchen
- Private master bath features a raised ceiling, large walk-in closet and deluxe bath
- 3 bedrooms, 2 1/2 baths, 2-car garage
- Basement foundation

Total Living Area: 2,750 sq. ft.

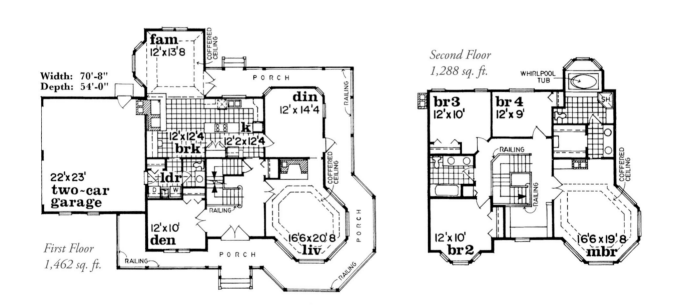

Width: 70'-8"
Depth: 54'-0"

First Floor
1,462 sq. ft.

Second Floor
1,288 sq. ft.

Plan Features

- Spacious dining room is connected to the kitchen for ease and also has access onto the wrap-around porch
- A double-door entry leads into the master bedroom enhanced with a spacious walk-in closet and a private bath with whirlpool tub
- Secluded den is an ideal place for a home office
- 4 bedrooms, 2 1/2 baths, 2-car side entry garage
- Basement or crawl space foundation, please specify when ordering

Total Living Area: 3,570 sq. ft.

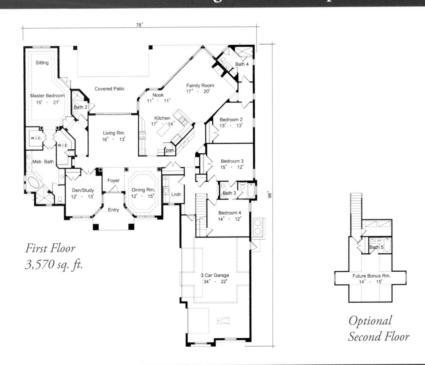

First Floor
3,570 sq. ft.

Optional
Second Floor

Plan Features

- Casual living areas combine creating lots of space for living
- Spacious master bedroom includes sitting area and an oversized bath
- Framing - only concrete block available
- Bonus room on the second floor has an additional 430 square feet of living area
- 4 bedrooms, 4 baths, 3-car side entry garage
- Slab foundation

To order call toll-free 1-800-DREAM HOME or visit www.houseplansandmore.com

C

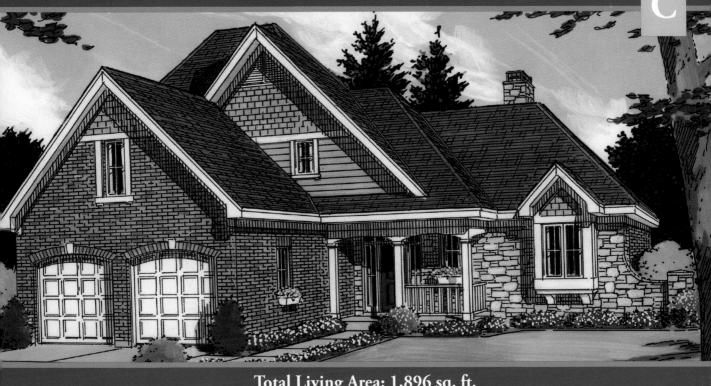

Total Living Area: 1,896 sq. ft.

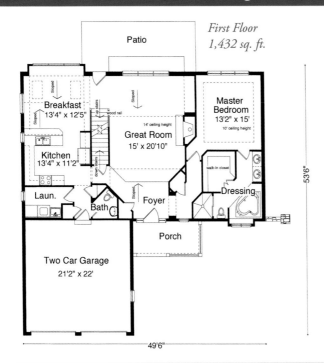

First Floor
1,432 sq. ft.

Patio

Breakfast
13'4" x 12'5"

Master
Bedroom
13'2" x 15'
10' ceiling height

Great Room
15' x 20'10"
14' ceiling height

Kitchen
13'4" x 11'2"

walk-in closet

Laun.

Dressing

Bath

Foyer

Porch

Two Car Garage
21'2" x 22'

49'6"

53'6"

Second Floor
464 sq. ft.

skylights

Bedroom
13'4" x 10'6"

stairs down

Bath

Bedroom
11'1" x 10'8"

Bonus
Room
11' x 15'2"
sloped   sloped

Plan Features

- The kitchen opens to the breakfast area which enjoys warmth from skylights
- The spacious great room boasts a sloped 14' ceiling and a grand fireplace
- The master bedroom enjoys a deluxe bath with double-bowl vanity and whirlpool tub
- The second floor bonus room has an additional 153 square feet of living area
- 3 bedrooms, 2 1/2 baths, 2-car garage
- Basement foundation

Total Living Area: 2,282 sq. ft.

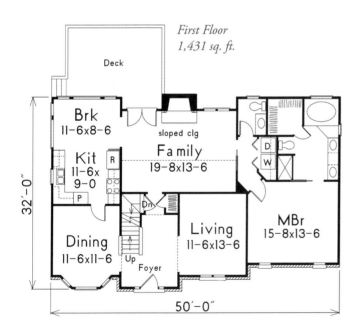

First Floor
1,431 sq. ft.

Deck

Brk
11-6x8-6

sloped clg

Kit
11-6x
9-0

Family
19-8x13-6

R

D

W

P

Dn

Dining
11-6x11-6

Up

Living
11-6x13-6

MBr
15-8x13-6

Foyer

32'-0"

50'-0"

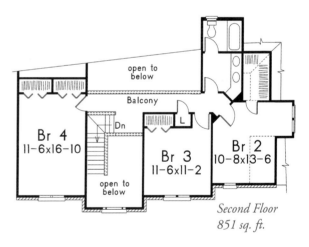

open to below

Balcony

Br 4
11-6x16-10

Dn

L

Br 3
11-6x11-2

Br 2
10-8x13-6

open to below

Second Floor
851 sq. ft.

Plan Features

- Balcony and two-story foyer add spaciousness to this compact plan
- First floor master bedroom has a corner tub in its large private bath
- Out-of-the-way kitchen is open to the full-windowed breakfast room
- 4 bedrooms, 2 1/2 baths, 2-car drive under garage
- Basement foundation

Plan #583-065D-0024

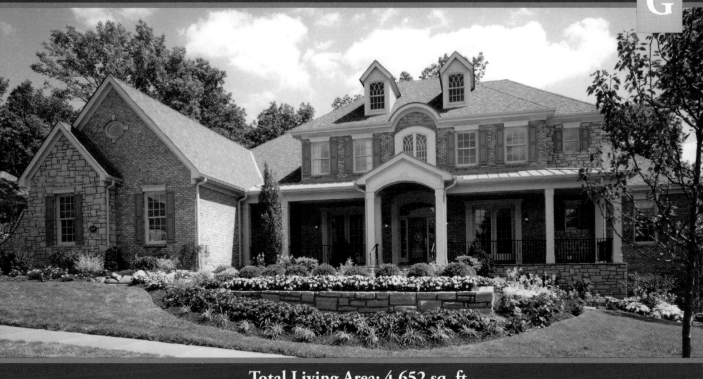

Total Living Area: 4,652 sq. ft.

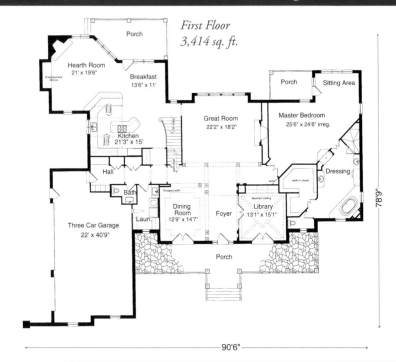

First Floor
3,414 sq. ft.

Porch

Hearth Room
21' x 19'6"

Breakfast
13'6" x 11'

Entertainment Alcove

Porch

Sitting Area

Kitchen
21'3" x 15'

Great Room
22'2" x 18'2"

Master Bedroom
25'6" x 24'6" irreg.

Hall

Dressing

Bath

Dropped soffit

Library
13'1" x 15'1"

walk-in closet

Dining Room
12'9" x 14'7"

Foyer

Three Car Garage
22' x 40'9"

Laun.

Beamed Ceiling

Porch

78'9"

90'6"

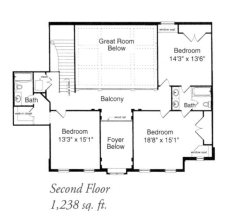

Second Floor
1,238 sq. ft.

Great Room Below

Bedroom
14'3" x 13'6"

Bath

Balcony

Bath

walk-in closet

Bedroom
13'3" x 15'1"

Foyer Below

Bedroom
18'8" x 15'1"

window seat

mech.

wood rail

Plan Features

- A grand foyer introduces a formal dining room and library with beamed ceiling
- Covered porches at the rear of the home offer splendid views
- The master bedroom has a 10' ceiling, sitting area and dressing room with walk-in closet
- Secondary bedrooms have window seats, large closets and private bath access
- 4 bedrooms, 3 1/2 baths, 3-car side entry garage
- Walk-out basement foundation

Total Living Area: 2,215 sq. ft.

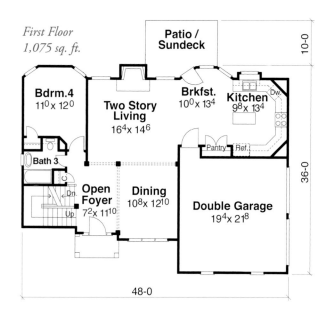

First Floor
1,075 sq. ft.

Patio / Sundeck

10-0

Bdrm.4
11⁰ x 12⁰

Two Story Living
16⁴x 14⁶

Brkfst.
10⁰x 13⁴

Kitchen
9⁸x 13⁴

Dw.

Bath 3

Pantry   Ref.

Open Foyer
7²x 11¹⁰

Dining
10⁸x 12¹⁰

Double Garage
19⁴x 21⁸

36-0

Dn.   Up

48-0

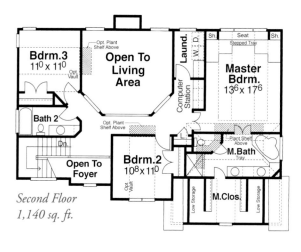

Bdrm.3
11⁰ x 11⁰

Opt. Plant Shelf Above

Opt. Vault

Open To Living Area

Laund.

Computer Station

W. D.

Sh.   Seat   Sh.
Stepped Tray

Master Bdrm.
13⁶ x 17⁶

Bath 2

Opt. Plant Shelf Above

Plant Shelf Above

M.Bath
Tray

Dn.

Open To Foyer

Bdrm.2
10⁸x 11⁰

Opt. Vault

Low Storage   M.Clos.   Low Storage

Second Floor
1,140 sq. ft.

Plan Features

- Two-story living room is open to the dining room and combined breakfast area and kitchen for an open feel
- Master bedroom has a window seat and includes a bath with large tub, double vanity and separate shower
- Laundry room is located on the second floor for added convenience
- 4 bedrooms, 3 baths, 2-car side entry garage
- Walk-out basement foundation

Total Living Area: 3,623 sq. ft.

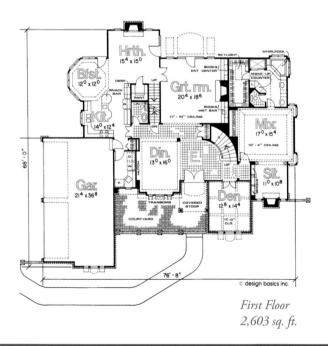

First Floor
2,603 sq. ft.

Second Floor
1,020 sq. ft.

© design basics inc.

Plan Features

- Exquisite master bedroom includes sitting area with built-in bookcases and fireplace
- The spacious great room features a fireplace wall with entertainment center, bookcases and a wet bar
- Each secondary bedroom includes a walk-in closet, built-in desk and private bath
- 4 bedrooms, 4 1/2 baths, 4-car side entry garage
- Basement foundation

Rear View

Total Living Area: 2,287 sq. ft.

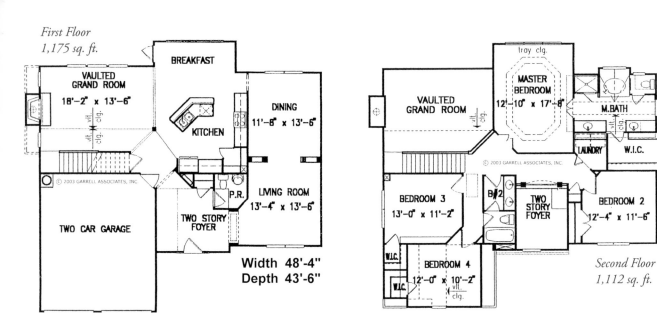

First Floor
1,175 sq. ft.

BREAKFAST

VAULTED GRAND ROOM
18'-2" x 13'-6"

DINING
11'-8" x 13'-6"

KITCHEN

© 2003 GARRELL ASSOCIATES, INC.

LIVING ROOM
13'-4" x 13'-6"

P.R.

TWO STORY FOYER

TWO CAR GARAGE

Width 48'-4"
Depth 43'-6"

tray clg.

MASTER BEDROOM
12'-10" x 17'-8"

M.BATH

VAULTED GRAND ROOM

LAUNDRY   W.I.C.

© 2003 GARRELL ASSOCIATES, INC.

BEDROOM 3
13'-0" x 11'-2"

B#2

TWO STORY FOYER

BEDROOM 2
12'-4" x 11'-6"

W.I.C.

BEDROOM 4
12'-0" x 10'-2"

W.I.C.

vlt. clg.

Second Floor
1,112 sq. ft.

Plan Features

- 9' ceilings throughout the first floor
- Two-story grand room has a fireplace for warmth
- Columns separate the formal dining and living rooms keeping an open feel
- All bedrooms are on the second floor for privacy
- 4 bedrooms, 2 1/2 baths, 2-car garage
- Basement or slab foundation, please specify when ordering

Total Living Area: 5,463 sq. ft.

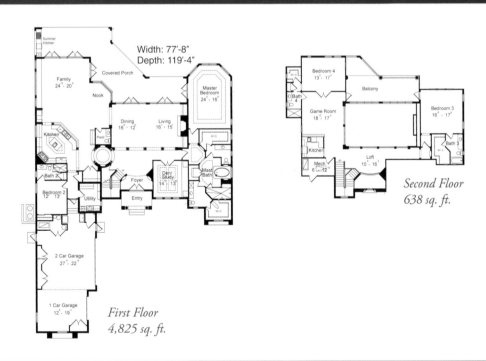

Width: 77'-8"
Depth: 119'-4"

First Floor
4,825 sq. ft.

Second Floor
638 sq. ft.

Plan Features

- Covered porch includes a summer kitchen and can be accessed from the master bedroom, family, dining and living rooms
- The second floor can be used as separate living quarters with two bedrooms, two baths, kitchen, game room and balcony access
- Framing - only concrete block available
- 4 bedrooms, 4 1/2 baths, 3-car side entry garage
- Slab foundation

Total Living Area: 1,161 sq. ft.

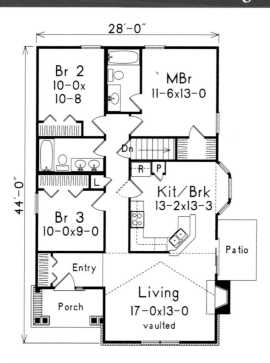

28'-0"

44'-0"

Br 2
10-0x
10-8

MBr
11-6x13-0

Dn

R P

Kit/Brk
13-2x13-3

Br 3
10-0x9-0

Patio

Entry

Living
17-0x13-0
vaulted

Porch

DID YOU KNOW?

A single shelf or a collection of corner shelves are surprisingly appealing offering an opportunity to show off collectibles in an exciting new way. Plus, they also work well in more compact homes with smaller rooms.

Plan Features

- Brickwork and feature window add elegance to this home for a narrow lot
- Living room enjoys a vaulted ceiling, fireplace and opens to the kitchen
- U-shaped kitchen offers a breakfast area with bay window, snack bar and built-in pantry
- 3 bedrooms, 2 baths
- Basement foundation

Total Living Area: 2,770 sq. ft.

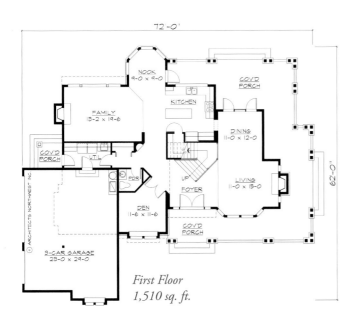

First Floor
1,510 sq. ft.

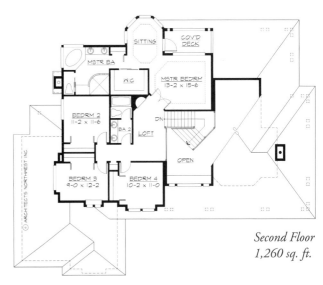

Second Floor
1,260 sq. ft.

Plan Features

- Formal living and dining areas combine for optimal entertaining possibilities including access outdoors and a fireplace
- The cheerful family and breakfast rooms connect for added spaciousness
- A double-door entry into the master bedroom leads to a private covered deck, sitting area and luxurious bath
- 4 bedrooms, 2 1/2 baths, 3-car side entry garage
- Crawl space foundation

Total Living Area: 2,583 sq. ft.

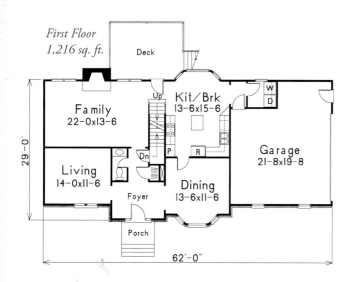

First Floor
1,216 sq. ft.

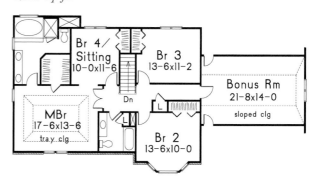

Second Floor
1,367 sq. ft.

Plan Features

- Prominent double bay windows add dimension and light
- Bonus room above the garage, which is included in the square footage, converts to a fifth bedroom or an activity center
- Master bedroom offers a corner tub, walk-in closet and coffered ceiling
- 4 bedrooms, 2 1/2 baths, 2-car side entry garage
- Basement foundation

Total Living Area: 2,240 sq. ft.

Width: 71'-10"
Depth: 66'-10"

Deck
31'x 10'

Porch
18'2"x 10'

Breakfast
11'10"x 11'

Ma.
Bath

Master
Bedroom
14'6"x 18'4"

Walk-In
Closet

Living
22'x 17'

Kitchen
11'10"x 12'

Utility

Bath

WIC

Bedroom
11'8"x 12'6"

Foyer

Dining
13'8"x 12'

Pantry

1/2
Bath

Bedroom
11'4"x 13'

Porch

Three-Car
Garage
21'2"x 34'8"

Courtyard

Plan Features

- All four bedrooms are located on the left side of the home remaining private from the more active living areas
- The breakfast area is bright and cheery with an abundance of windows
- The master bedroom and living area access the porch and deck for outdoor living
- 3 bedrooms, 2 1/2 baths, 3-car side entry garage
- Crawl space or basement foundation, please specify when ordering

Total Living Area: 3,570 sq. ft.

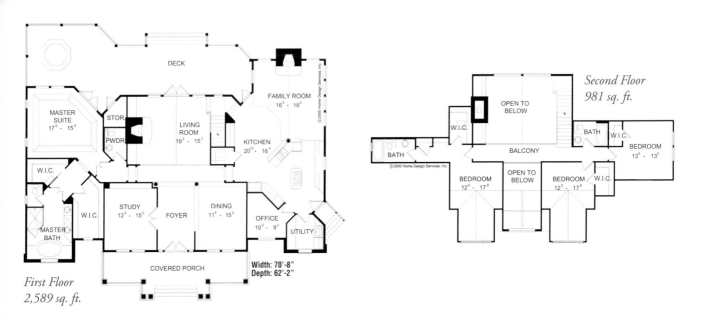

First Floor
2,589 sq. ft.

Second Floor
981 sq. ft.

Width: 70'-8"
Depth: 62'-2"

Plan Features

- View the formal areas of the living and dining rooms upon entering the home
- The family room and kitchen with cooktop island create a spacious informal living area
- The large deck provides a wonderful space for outdoor entertaining
- Three bedrooms and two baths comprise the spacious second floor
- 4 bedrooms, 3 1/2 baths
- Crawl space foundation

D

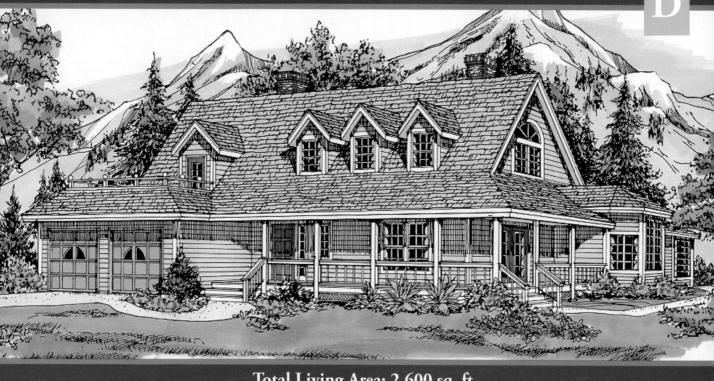

Total Living Area: 2,600 sq. ft.

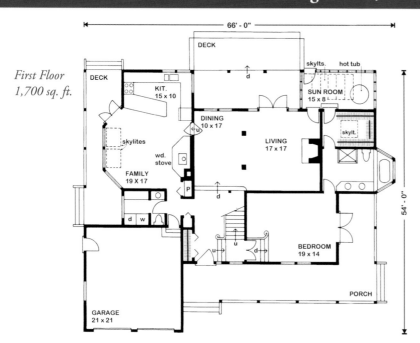

First Floor
1,700 sq. ft.

Second Floor
900 sq. ft.

Plan Features

- All first floor rooms feature French doors for easy access to the great outdoors
- The large family room features a bay window, skylights and a woodstove
- A unique stairway landing creates a sunken master suite
- The private sunroom has space for a hot tub creating a relaxing atmosphere
- 4 bedrooms, 2 1/2 baths, 2-car garage
- Crawl space foundation

Total Living Area: 1,230 sq. ft.

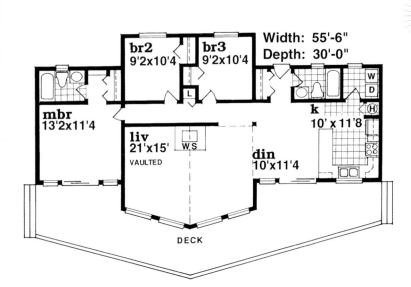

Width: 55'-6"
Depth: 30'-0"

br2 9'2x10'4

br3 9'2x10'4

mbr 13'2x11'4

k 10' x 11'8

liv 21'x15' VAULTED

din 10'x11'4

W.S

DECK

DID YOU KNOW?

Plant deciduous trees (the type that lose their leaves in winter) on the south side of your house. They will provide summer shade without blocking winter sun. Plant evergreens on the north to shield your home from cold winter winds.

Plan Features

- Full-width deck creates plenty of outdoor living area
- The master bedroom accesses the deck through sliding glass doors and features a private bath
- Vaulted living room has a woodstove
- 3 bedrooms, 2 baths
- Crawl space or basement foundation, please specify when ordering

Total Living Area: 1,787 sq. ft.

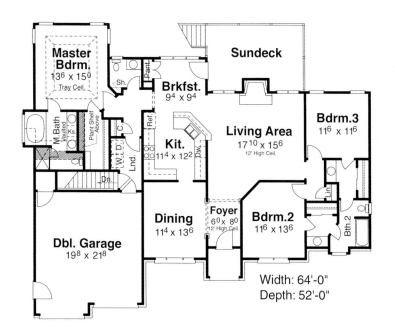

Width: 64'-0"
Depth: 52'-0"

DID YOU KNOW?

According to the techniques of feng shui, it is a good idea to keep a bowl or arrangement of fruit on your dining room table. This represents continuous sustenance for your family. Add a mirror on the west or northwest wall of the dining room to double the food on your table.

Plan Features

- Private master bedroom features an enormous tub, walk-in closet and close proximity to the laundry room
- A Jack and Jill style bath is shared by bedrooms #2 and #3
- 12' ceiling in foyer makes a dramatic entrance
- 3 bedrooms, 2 1/2 baths, 2-car garage
- Walk-out basement foundation

Total Living Area: 2,088 sq. ft.

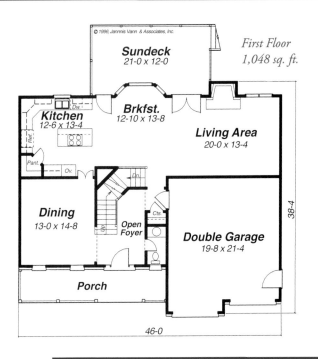

© 1996, Jannnis Vann & Associates, Inc.

First Floor
1,048 sq. ft.

Sundeck
21-0 x 12-0

Kitchen
12-6 x 13-4

Brkfst.
12-10 x 13-8

Living Area
20-0 x 13-4

Dining
13-0 x 14-8

Open Foyer

Double Garage
19-8 x 21-4

Porch

38-4

46-0

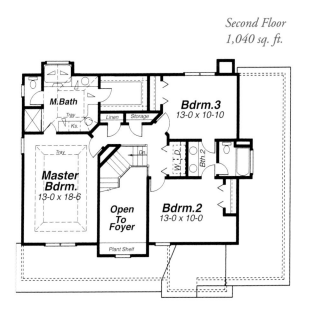

Second Floor
1,040 sq. ft.

M.Bath

Bdrm.3
13-0 x 10-10

Linen   Storage

Master Bdrm.
13-0 x 18-6

Open To Foyer

Bdrm.2
13-0 x 10-0

Bth.2

Plant Shelf

Plan Features

- A large and open foyer makes a welcoming entry into this home
- Vaulted master bath and a tray ceiling in the master bedroom add distinction
- A sunny bayed breakfast room is sure to be a popular place
- 3 bedrooms, 2 1/2 baths, 2-car garage
- Walk-out basement foundation

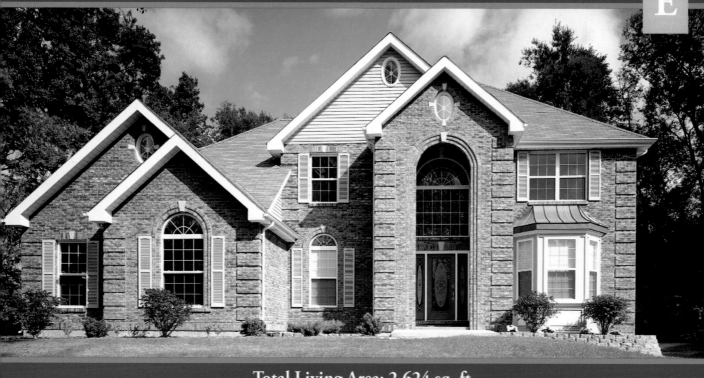

Total Living Area: 2,624 sq. ft.

69'-8"

46'-0"

MBr
17-0x17-8
vaulted
plant shelf

Great Rm
20-6x15-10

Brk
14-10x10-0

Kitchen
14-10x10-6

Dining
14-10x12-4

Foyer

Dn

Up

Garage
21-4x20-4

First Floor
1,774 sq. ft.

Br 4
12-6x12-0

open to below

Br 2
11-8x10-4

open to below

Br 3
12-6x12-0

Dn

Second Floor
850 sq. ft.

Plan Features

- Dramatic two-story entry opens to a bayed dining room through a classic colonnade
- Magnificent great room with 18' ceiling is brightly lit with three palladian windows
- Master bedroom includes bay window, walk-in closets, plant shelves and sunken bath
- 4 bedrooms, 2 1/2 baths, 2-car side entry garage
- Basement foundation

Interior View -
Master Bath

Total Living Area: 1,924 sq. ft.

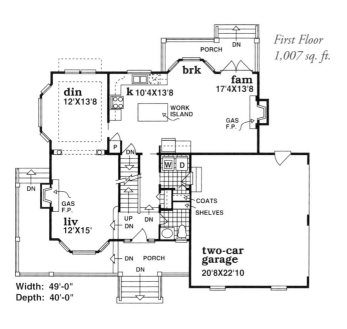

First Floor
1,007 sq. ft.

PORCH

DN

brk

fam
17'4X13'8

din
12'X13'8

k 10'4X13'8

WORK
ISLAND

GAS
F.P.

P

DN

liv
12'X15'

GAS
F.P.

DN

W D

COATS
SHELVES

UP
DN

DN

DN

DN

PORCH

DN

two-car
garage
20'8X22'10

Width: 49'-0"
Depth: 40'-0"

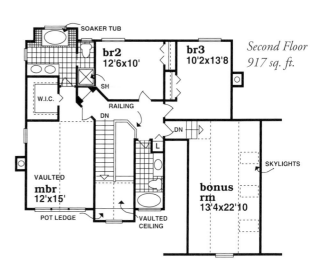

SOAKER TUB

br2
12'6x10'

br3
10'2x13'8

Second Floor
917 sq. ft.

W.I.C.

SH

RAILING

DN

DN

L

SKYLIGHTS

VAULTED
mbr
12'x15'

POT LEDGE

VAULTED
CEILING

bonus
rm
13'4x22'10

Plan Features

- Gourmet kitchen has a work island and a bayed breakfast area
- A fireplace warms the family room which opens to a rear porch through French doors
- Bonus room on the second floor has an additional 325 square feet of living area
- 3 bedrooms, 2 1/2 baths, 2-car side entry garage
- Basement or crawl space foundation, please specify when ordering

Plan #583-055D-0029

Price Code:

D

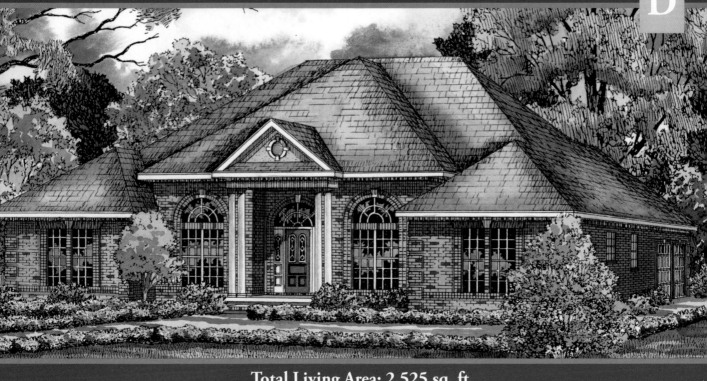

Total Living Area: 2,525 sq. ft.

DID YOU KNOW?

A colored ceiling can make a room much more interesting. If the walls have been painted, but the ceiling is still white, the eye is drawn to the white ceiling because of the contrast. Why not make the contrast an unexpected color to complement the space creating an element of surprise?

Plan Features

- Glorious sun room off great room has French doors leading to the outdoors
- Enormous laundry room includes a sink and loads of counterspace to make chores much easier
- Formal living/study as well as the dining room are accented with decorative columns
- 3 bedrooms, 2 1/2 baths, 2-car side entry garage
- Basement or walk-out basement foundation, please specify when ordering

Total Living Area: 1,601 sq. ft.

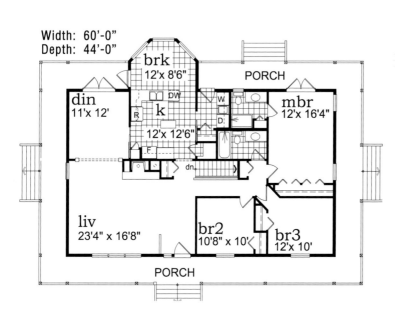

Width: 60'-0"
Depth: 44'-0"

brk
12'x 8'6"

PORCH

din
11'x 12'

k
12'x 12'6"

mbr
12'x 16'4"

liv
23'4" x 16'8"

br2
10'8" x 10'

br3
12'x 10'

PORCH

DID YOU KNOW?

If a natural disaster should happen to occur causing damage to your home or possessions, homeowners should contact their insurance carrier as soon as possible to begin the claims process. However, keep in mind that standard homeowner policies do not cover flood damage so be sure to inquire about such coverage if you live in a flood prone area.

Plan Features

- Energy efficient home with 2" x 6" exterior walls
- The wrap-around porch offers a wonderful place for relaxing
- The bayed breakfast area will brighten any morning
- The expansive living area has plenty of space and opens to a formal dining room
- 3 bedrooms, 2 baths
- Basement or crawl space foundation, please specify when ordering

Total Living Area: 2,587 sq. ft.

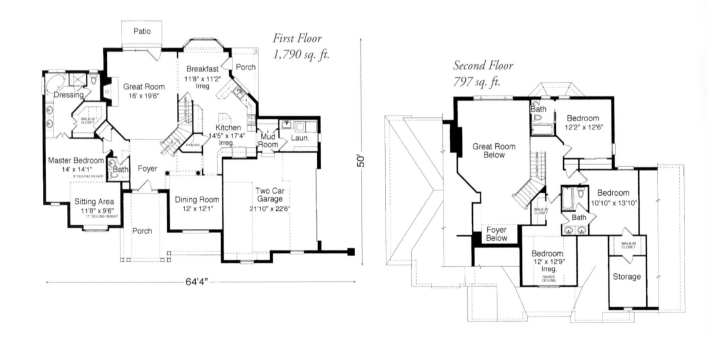

First Floor
1,790 sq. ft.

Second Floor
797 sq. ft.

64'4"

50'

Plan Features

- High windows above French doors in the great room create a spectacular view
- The spacious kitchen serves the breakfast and dining rooms with ease
- The second floor offers plenty of space with three bedrooms and a storage area
- 4 bedrooms, 3 1/2 baths, 2-car side entry garage
- Basement foundation

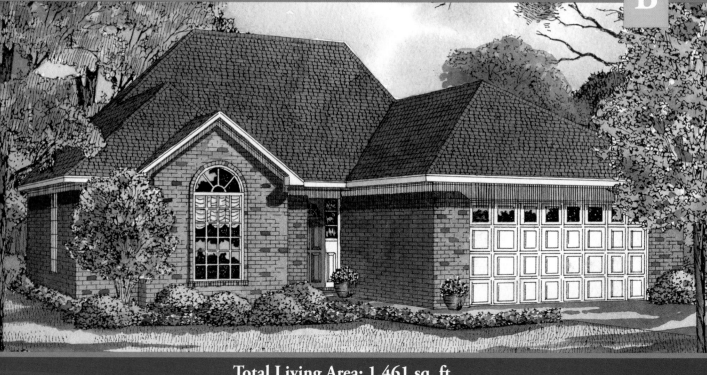

Total Living Area: 1,461 sq. ft.

DID YOU KNOW?

An all brick home has many advantages. While easy to maintain, it offers beauty and a variety of colors perfect for creative design choices while building.

Plan Features

- The kitchen features a bar which is sure to see many quick meals
- The elegant great room has a 9' boxed ceiling and a handsome fireplace
- The bayed dining room is full of natural light
- 3 bedrooms, 2 baths, 2-car garage
- Slab, crawl space, basement or walk-out basement foundation, please specify when ordering

Plan #583-065D-0045

Total Living Area: 2,085 sq. ft.

First Floor
935 sq. ft.

Second Floor
1,150 sq. ft.

Plan Features

- All bedrooms located on the second floor for privacy
- The master bedroom showcases a raised ceiling and dressing area with a whirlpool tub and two walk-in closets
- The kitchen offers an abundance of counterspace, cabinets and a pantry for added storage
- 4 bedrooms, 2 1/2 baths, 2-car side entry garage
- Basement foundation

To order call toll-free 1-800-DREAM HOME or visit www.houseplansandmore.com

Plan #583-072D-0010

Total Living Area: 2,198 sq. ft.

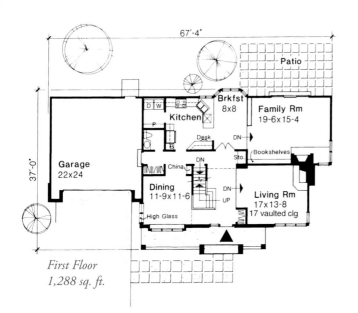

First Floor
1,288 sq. ft.

67'-4"

37'-0"

Garage
22x24

Kitchen

Dining
11-9x11-6

Brkfst
8x8

Family Rm
19-6x15-4

Living Rm
17x13-8
17 vaulted clg

Patio

Desk

Bookshelves

Sto.

China

High Glass

DW

P

DN

UP

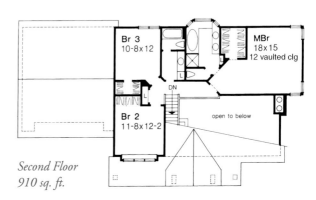

Second Floor
910 sq. ft.

Br 3
10-8x12

MBr
18x15
12 vaulted clg

Br 2
11-8x12-2

open to below

DN

Plan Features

- Sunken living room has a vaulted ceiling, a corner fireplace and eye-catching windows with transoms
- A china hutch services the quiet dining room
- Well-planned and stylish, the kitchen offers a snack bar and a built-in desk
- 3 bedrooms, 2 1/2 baths, 2-car garage
- Basement foundation

Total Living Area: 3,556 sq. ft.

First Floor
2,553 sq. ft.

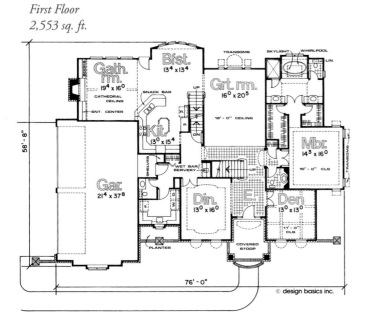

Second Floor
1,001 sq. ft.

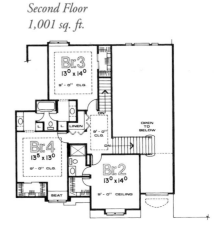

Plan Features

- Gathering room boasts a bright wall of windows and a fireplace
- Dining and great rooms feature 13' ceilings
- Kitchen with wrap-around counter and snack bar opens to a bayed breakfast area
- Each second floor bedroom enjoys a walk-in closet and bath access
- 4 bedrooms, 3 1/2 baths, 4-car side entry garage
- Basement foundation

Rear View

Total Living Area: 2,773 sq. ft.

First Floor
1,498 sq. ft.

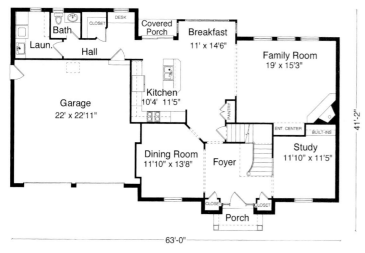

Bath
Laun.
CLOSET
DESK
Hall
Covered Porch
Breakfast 11' x 14'6"
Family Room 19' x 15'3"
Garage 22' x 22'11"
Kitchen 10'4' 11'5"
PANTRY
ENT. CENTER
BUILT-INS
Dining Room 11'10" x 13'8"
Foyer
Study 11'10" x 11'5"
CLOSET
CLOSET
Porch
63'-0"
41'-2"

Second Floor
1,275 sq. ft.

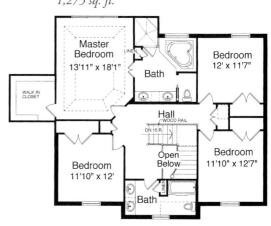

Master Bedroom 13'11" x 18'1"
LINEN
Bath
Bedroom 12' x 11'7"
WALK IN CLOSET
Hall
WOOD RAIL
DN 15 R
Open Below
Bedroom 11'10" x 12'7"
Bedroom 11'10" x 12'
LINEN
Bath

Plan Features

- A private study has an alcove for built-ins and provides a quiet space to relax
- Entry from the garage introduces a spectacular work area with large laundry room, half bath, walk-in closet and built-in desk
- The spacious kitchen includes a center island with sink and snack bar and opens to the bright breakfast nook
- 4 bedrooms, 2 1/2 baths, 2-car garage
- Basement foundation

Total Living Area: 2,742 sq. ft.

First Floor
2,742 sq. ft.

Optional Second Floor

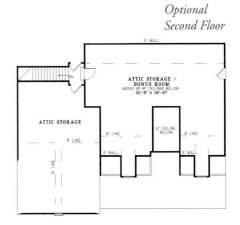

Plan Features

- The great room features a fireplace, media center and French doors to the sun room
- A charming screened porch is accessed by the sun room, breakfast room and master suite
- The optional second floor has an additional 916 square feet of living space
- 4 bedrooms, 2 1/2 baths, 2-car side entry garage
- Slab, crawl space, basement or walk-out basement foundation, please specify when ordering

Total Living Area: 1,741 sq. ft.

52'-4"

Patio

Patio

Din
11-0x12-0

Br 2
10-10x10-0

Kit
13-1x10-0

Great Room
14-0x20-9
vaulted

Mbr
15-0x13-0
vaulted

54'-8"

Study
10-0x11-0

Br 3
10-1x11-3

Br 4
10-0x11-3

vaulted

Entry

Porch

Garage
19-4x20-4

DID YOU KNOW?
Distressed cabinetry or flooring has become a popular trend in recent years. Artificially antiquing the wood by adding deliberate marks of wear and tear creates the feeling of timeless appeal and a custom look as well.

Plan Features

- Handsome exterior has multiple gables and elegant brickwork
- The great room offers a fireplace, vaulted ceiling and is open to the bayed dining area and kitchen with breakfast bar
- The master bedroom boasts a vaulted ceiling, large walk-in closet, luxury bath and enjoys a nearby room perfect for a study, nursery or fifth bedroom
- 4 bedrooms, 2 baths, 2-car garage
- Crawl space foundation, drawings also include slab and basement foundations

Total Living Area: 2,327 sq. ft.

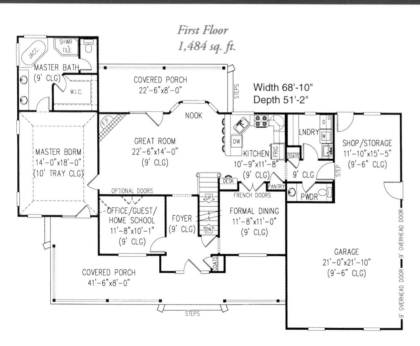

First Floor
1,484 sq. ft.

Width 68'-10"
Depth 51'-2"

Second Floor
843 sq. ft.

Plan Features

- Bayed nook nestled between the great room and kitchen provides ample area for dining
- Vaulted second floor recreation room is an ideal place for casual family living
- Room off the entry has the ability to become an office, guest bedroom or an area for home schooling if needed
- 4 bedrooms, 2 1/2 baths, 2-car side entry garage with shop/storage
- Basement, crawl space or slab foundation, please specify when ordering

Total Living Area: 1,379 sq. ft.

DID YOU KNOW?

Use decorative medallions and other ornamental period style moulding to add visual interest to a plain mantel facing. Stain or finish the added details to match the existing fireplace and suddenly a new, somewhat bland fireplace has the look of an old-world antique treasure.

Plan Features

- The pass-through laundry area connects the garage and the kitchen and includes a pantry
- The bright breakfast room and master suite feature access to the rear covered porch
- A gas fireplace in the great room warms the entire living area
- 3 bedrooms, 2 baths, 2-car garage
- Slab or crawl space foundation, please specify when ordering

Total Living Area: 2,428 sq. ft.

Utility

Porch
24'x 8'

Width: 45'-10"
Depth: 48'-5"

Breakfast
9'2"x 9'11"

Living
18'8"x 15'

Kitchen
11'6"x 12'

Dining
12'8"x 11'6"

Foyer
8'8"x 6'6"

Master
Bedroom
14'10"x 13'

First Floor
1,533 sq. ft.

Porch
35'10"x 5'

Second Floor
895 sq. ft.

Bedroom
13'7"x 11'9"

Open to
Below

Bedroom
15'x 11'11"

Bedroom
11'11"x 11'4"

Plan Features

- The formal dining room defined by elegant columns will grab your eye as you enter this inviting home
- The corner fireplace adds to the warm ambiance of the living room
- Two secondary bedrooms enjoy the unique space created by the charming dormers
- 4 bedrooms, 2 1/2 baths
- Basement foundation

Total Living Area: 3,108 sq. ft.

First Floor
2,107 sq. ft.

Second Floor
1,001 sq. ft.

Plan Features

- The two-story great room features French doors to the rear deck
- The kitchen and breakfast room combine and include a cooktop island, walk-in pantry and TV cabinet
- Second floor bonus rooms provide an additional 485 square feet of living space
- 3 bedrooms, 2 1/2 baths, 3-car side entry garage
- Slab or crawl space foundation, please specify when ordering

Total Living Area: 2,083 sq. ft.

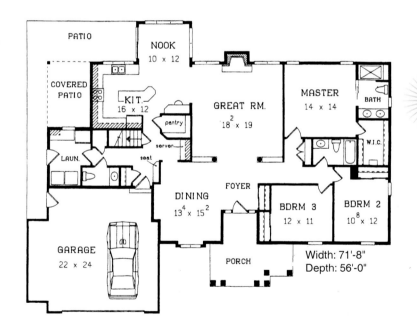

DID YOU KNOW?

Many house plants thrive in the steamy and humid atmosphere of a kitchen, so use their lush foliage to enhance a country scheme or liven up a windowsill.

Plan Features

- A handy server counter located between the kitchen and formal dining room is ideal for entertaining
- Decorative columns grace the entrance into the great room
- A large island in the kitchen aids in food preparation
- 3 bedrooms, 2 1/2 baths, 2-car garage
- Basement foundation

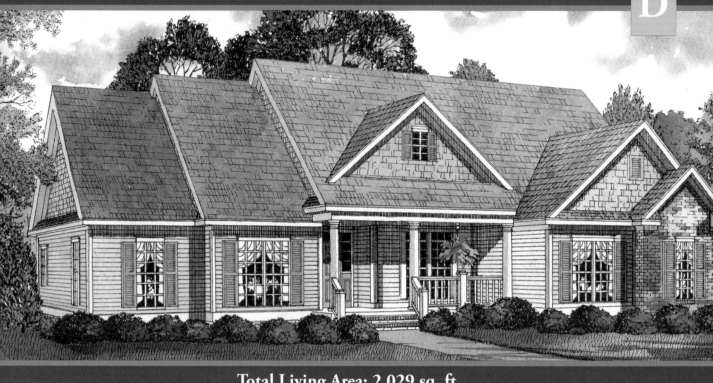

Total Living Area: 2,029 sq. ft.

First Floor
2,029 sq. ft.

Optional
Second Floor

Plan Features

- The bedrooms are located together and away from main living areas to maintain privacy
- Fireplaces in the great room and hearth room warm the entire home
- The optional second floor has an additional 754 square feet of living area
- 3 bedrooms, 2 baths, 2-car side entry garage
- Slab, crawl space, basement or walk-out basement foundation, please specify when ordering

Total Living Area: 4,650 sq. ft.

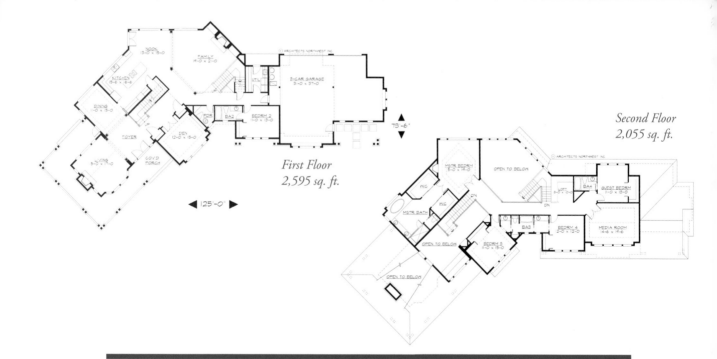

First Floor
2,595 sq. ft.

◀ 125'-0" ▶

Second Floor
2,055 sq. ft.

Plan Features

- Two-story foyer, living and family rooms create a sense of spaciousness throughout the first floor
- Double walk-in closets create plenty of storage in the master bath
- The second floor media room is sure to be a gathering place near the bedrooms
- 5 bedrooms, 4 1/2 baths, 3-car rear entry garage
- Crawl space foundation

Total Living Area: 2,837 sq. ft.

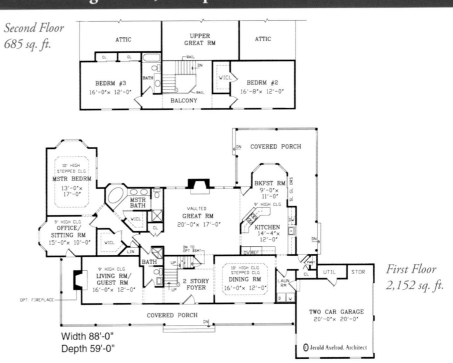

Second Floor
685 sq. ft.

ATTIC

UPPER GREAT RM

ATTIC

CL CL

BATH

BEDRM #3
16'-0"× 12'-0"

WICL

BEDRM #2
16'-8"× 12'-0"

BALCONY

10' HIGH STEPPED CLG
MSTR BEDRM
13'-0"× 17'-0"

MSTR BATH

WICL

COVERED PORCH

BKFST RM
9'-0"× 11'-0"

9' HIGH CLG

9' HIGH CLG
OFFICE/
SITTING RM
15'-0"× 10'-0"

WICL

CL

VAULTED
GREAT RM
20'-0"× 17'-0"

KITCHEN
14'-4"× 12'-0"

LIN

BATH

DN TO OPT BSMT

9' HIGH CLG
LIVING RM/
GUEST RM
16'-0"× 12'-0"

UP

2 STORY
FOYER

UP

10' HIGH STEPPED CLG
DINING RM
16'-0"× 12'-0"

LAUN RM

UTIL STOR

OPT. FIREPLACE

First Floor
2,152 sq. ft.

COVERED PORCH

DN

TWO CAR GARAGE
20'-0"× 20'-0"

Width 88'-0"
Depth 59'-0"

© Jerold Axelrod, Architect

Plan Features

- Office/sitting room directly off the master bedroom is perfect for a home office or quiet place to relax
- Living room/guest room offers a cozy fireplace adding a memorable touch
- A covered porch wraps around the sunny bayed breakfast room
- 3 bedrooms, 3 baths, 2-car side entry garage
- Basement, crawl space or slab foundation, please specify when ordering

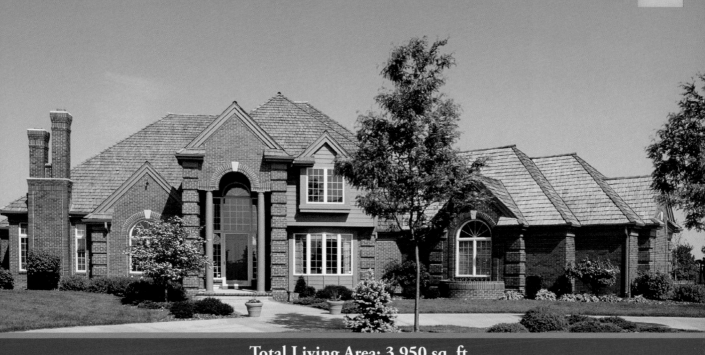

Total Living Area: 3,950 sq. ft.

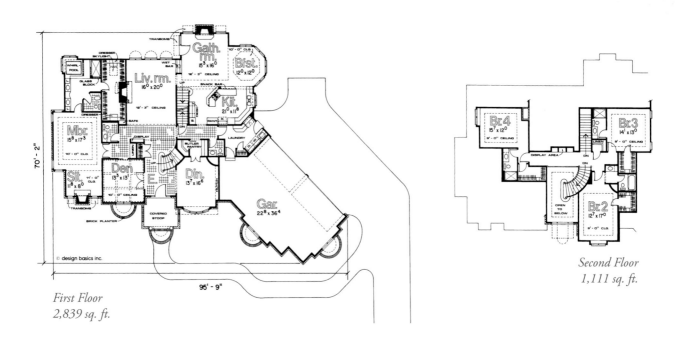

First Floor
2,839 sq. ft.

Second Floor
1,111 sq. ft.

Plan Features

- All bedrooms include a private bath and walk-in closet
- The formal dining room boasts a bay window and a butler's pantry
- The living and gathering rooms feature 12' ceilings, fireplaces and connect with a wet bar
- 4 bedrooms, 3 1/2 baths, 4-car rear entry garage
- Basement foundation

Total Living Area: 1,761 sq. ft.

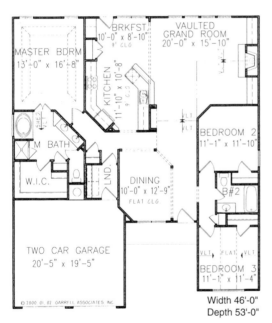

Width 46'-0"
Depth 53'-0"

DID YOU KNOW?

Listening to music, watching a movie or even having a conversation can be very unpleasant in a room with too many parallel hard surfaces. Adding texture and soft surfaces like carpet and cozy seating can create a fuller sound to acoustics and make movie watching or listening to music much more enjoyable.

Plan Features

- 9' ceilings throughout this home
- Vaulted grand room has a beautiful fireplace surrounded by bookshelves
- Secondary bedrooms are separated from the master bedroom for privacy
- Kitchen includes counter for extra dining space
- 3 bedrooms, 2 baths, 2-car garage
- Slab foundation

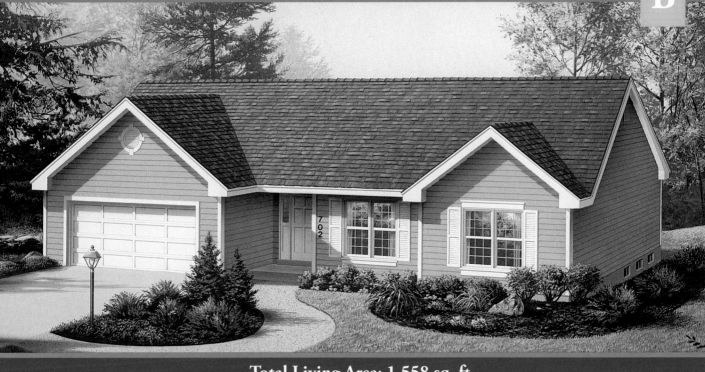

Total Living Area: 1,558 sq. ft.

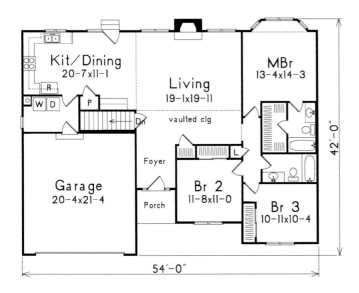

DID YOU KNOW?

A few simple precautions can go a long way toward protecting your home from termites. Fixing all leaks, cleaning overflowing gutters and using splash blocks to divert water from the foundation will keep your house dry and uninviting for the pests. Isolating wood from concrete or masonry, trimming shrubbery and keeping wood mulch away from your house will also keep termites at bay. Also, make sure all firewood is stored off the ground at least 15 feet from the house and that there are no tree stumps or scrap wood in close vicinity.

Plan Features

- The utility room is located conveniently between the garage and kitchen/dining area
- Bedrooms are separated from the living area by hallway
- The living area with fireplace and vaulted ceiling opens to the kitchen and dining area
- Master bedroom is enhanced with a large bay window, walk-in closet and private bath
- 3 bedrooms, 2 baths, 2-car garage
- Basement foundation

Total Living Area: 2,136 sq. ft.

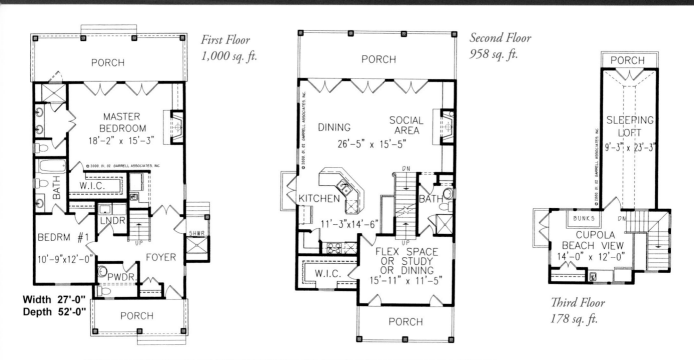

First Floor
1,000 sq. ft.

PORCH

MASTER
BEDROOM
18'-2" x 15'-3"

© 2000, 01, 02 GARRELL ASSOCIATES, INC.

BATH

W.I.C.

LNDR

BEDRM #1
10'-9"x12'-0"

FOYER

SHWR.

PWDR.

UP

Width 27'-0"
Depth 52'-0"

PORCH

Second Floor
958 sq. ft.

PORCH

DINING   SOCIAL
AREA
26'-5" x 15'-5"

KITCHEN
11'-3"x14'-6"

BATH

DN

UP

FLEX SPACE
OR STUDY
OR DINING
15'-11" x 11'-5"

W.I.C.

PORCH

Third Floor
178 sq. ft.

PORCH

SLEEPING
LOFT
9'-3" x 23'-3"

© 2000, 01, 02 GARRELL ASSOCIATES, INC.

BUNKS

CUPOLA
BEACH VIEW
14'-0" x 12'-0"

DN

Plan Features

- 9' ceilings on the first and third floors and 10' ceilings on the second floor
- Unique third floor loft has space for sleeping as well as a balcony for enjoying views
- Open living areas allow plenty of space for entertaining
- Terrific master bedroom has a private bath, cozy fireplace and two sets of double doors
- 2 bedrooms, 3 1/2 baths
- Crawl space foundation

Total Living Area: 2,516 sq. ft.

Width: 62-6"
Depth: 42'-6"

fam 13'x16'
GAS F.P.

brk 11'x10'
BAR
RAILING

k 12'9x11'6

din 10'5x12'
BUFFET

20'x23'
two~car garage

D W

TRAY CEILING
11'x11'
den

FOYER

TRAY CEILING

12'11x14'8
liv

RAILING

VERANDA

First Floor 1,324 sq. ft.

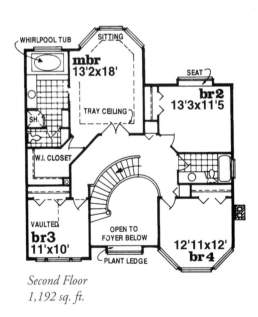

WHIRLPOOL TUB   SITTING

mbr 13'2x18'
TRAY CEILING

SEAT
br2 13'3x11'5

SH.

W.I. CLOSET

VAULTED
br3 11'x10'

OPEN TO
FOYER BELOW

PLANT LEDGE

12'11x12'
br4

Second Floor 1,192 sq. ft.

Plan Features

- Living room has a fireplace, while the formal dining room has a buffet alcove and access to the veranda
- A cozy sitting area and tray ceiling accent the master bedroom
- Spacious bedrooms make this a wonderful family home
- 4 bedrooms, 2 1/2 baths, 2-car side entry garage
- Basement or crawl space foundation, please specify when ordering

Total Living Area: 2,797 sq. ft.

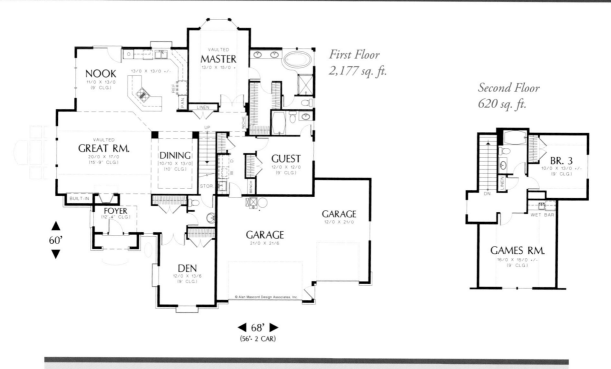

First Floor
2,177 sq. ft.

Second Floor
620 sq. ft.

Plan Features

- Second floor game room has a wet bar perfect for entertaining
- A private guest room with its own bath is situated near the garage
- Formal dining room has decorative corner columns
- 3 bedrooms, 3 1/2 baths, 3-car garage
- Crawl space foundation

Total Living Area: 2,503 sq. ft.

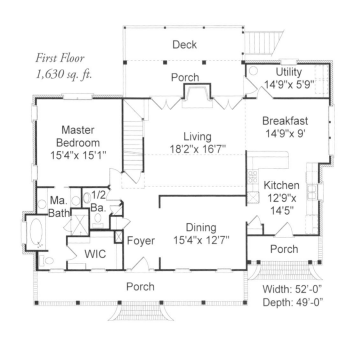

First Floor
1,630 sq. ft.

Deck

Porch

Utility
14'9" x 5'9"

Master
Bedroom
15'4" x 15'1"

Living
18'2" x 16'7"

Breakfast
14'9" x 9'

Kitchen
12'9" x 14'5"

Ma.
Bath

1/2
Ba.

WIC

Foyer

Dining
15'4" x 12'7"

Porch

Porch

Width: 52'-0"
Depth: 49'-0"

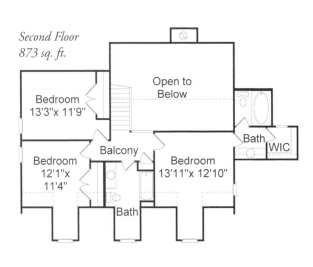

Second Floor
873 sq. ft.

Open to
Below

Bedroom
13'3" x 11'9"

Bath

WIC

Balcony

Bedroom
12'1" x 11'4"

Bedroom
13'11" x 12'10"

Bath

Plan Features

- 10' ceilings throughout the first floor
- A secondary entrance into the kitchen is convenient and casual
- First floor master bedroom has its own bath and walk-in closet
- The living room features a fireplace flanked by doors leading to the rear porch
- 4 bedrooms, 3 1/2 baths, 2-car drive under garage
- Walk-out basement foundation

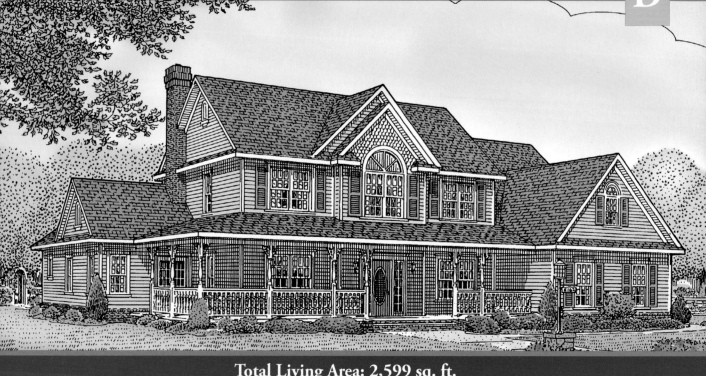

Total Living Area: 2,599 sq. ft.

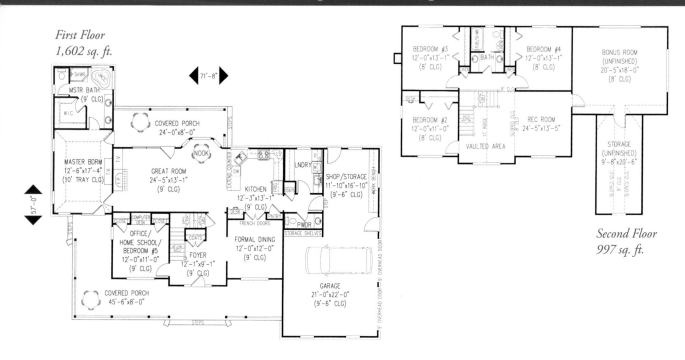

First Floor
1,602 sq. ft.

Second Floor
997 sq. ft.

Plan Features

- Office/home school room could easily be converted to a fifth bedroom
- Recreation room on the second floor would make a great casual living area or play room
- Large shop/storage has an oversized work bench for hobbies or projects
- Bonus room on the second floor has an additional 385 square feet of living area
- 4 bedrooms, 2 1/2 baths, 2-car garage with shop/storage
- Basement, crawl space or slab foundation, please specify when ordering

Total Living Area: 2,716 sq. ft.

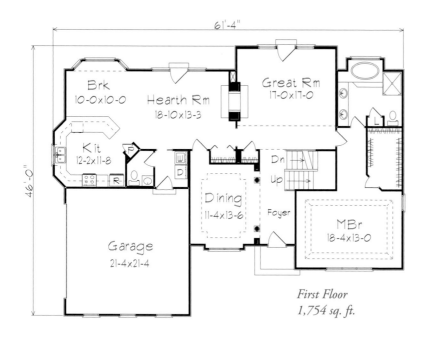

First Floor
1,754 sq. ft.

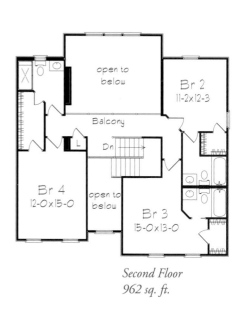

Second Floor
962 sq. ft.

Plan Features

- 9' ceilings throughout first floor
- All bedrooms boast walk-in closets
- Great room and hearth room share a see-through fireplace
- Balcony overlooks large great room
- 4 bedrooms, 4 1/2 baths, 2-car side entry garage
- Basement foundation

Total Living Area: 2,618 sq. ft.

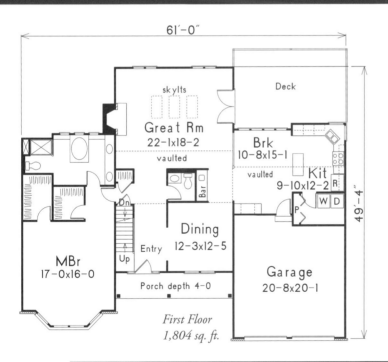

61'-0"

49'-4"

sk ylts

Deck

Great Rm
22-1x18-2
vaulted

Brk
10-8x15-1
vaulted

Kit
9-10x12-2

Bar

Dn

Dining
12-3x12-5

Entry

Up

MBr
17-0x16-0

Porch depth 4-0

Garage
20-8x20-1

First Floor
1,804 sq. ft.

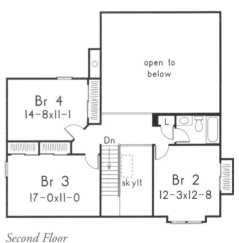

open to
below

Br 4
14-8x11-1

Dn

sk ylt

Br 3
17-0x11-0

Br 2
12-3x12-8

Second Floor
814 sq. ft.

Plan Features

- Great room features vaulted ceiling, skylights and large fireplace
- Master bedroom and bath have two large walk-in closets, separate oversized tub and shower, first floor convenience and privacy
- Kitchen overlooks the deck and features circle-top windows and corner window view
- 4 bedrooms, 2 1/2 baths, 2-car garage
- Basement foundation, drawings also include slab and crawl space foundations

Total Living Area: 3,006 sq. ft.

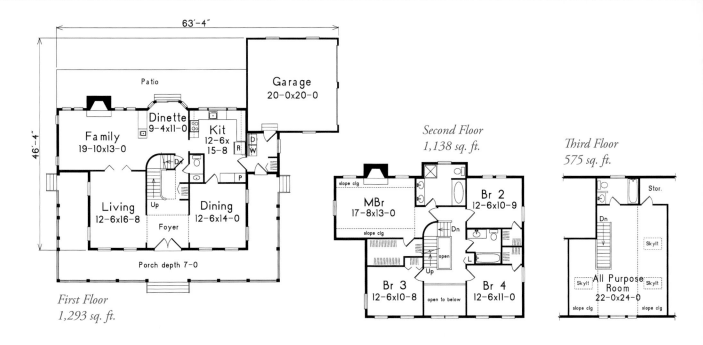

First Floor
1,293 sq. ft.

Second Floor
1,138 sq. ft.

Third Floor
575 sq. ft.

Plan Features

- Energy efficient home with 2"x 6" exterior walls
- Large all-purpose room and bath on third floor
- Efficient U-shaped kitchen includes a pantry and adjacent planning desk
- 4 bedrooms, 3 1/2 baths, 2-car side entry garage
- Basement foundation, drawings also include slab foundation

Total Living Area: 2,092 sq. ft.

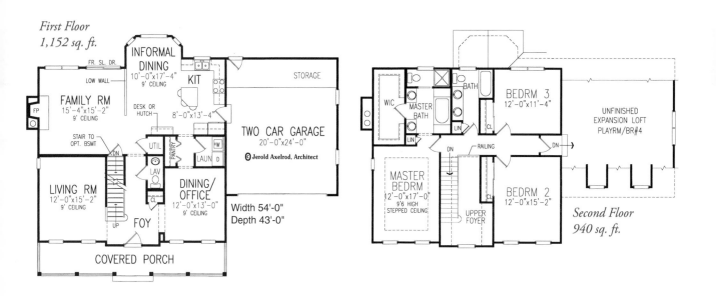

First Floor
1,152 sq. ft.

FR. SL. DR.

INFORMAL DINING
10'-0"x17'-4"
9' CEILING

LOW WALL

KIT
8'-0"x13'-4"

STORAGE

FAMILY RM
15'-4"x15'-2"
9' CEILING

FP

DESK OR HUTCH

TWO CAR GARAGE
20'-0"x24'-0"

STAIR TO OPT. BSMT

UTIL

PANTRY

W

DN

LAUN D

© Jerold Axelrod, Architect

LIVING RM
12'-0"x15'-2"
9' CEILING

LAV

CL

DINING/ OFFICE
12'-0"x13'-0"
9' CEILING

Width 54'-0"
Depth 43'-0"

UP

FOY

COVERED PORCH

Second Floor
940 sq. ft.

WIC

BATH

MASTER BATH

LIN

LIN

BEDRM 3
12'-0"x11'-4"

CL

UNFINISHED EXPANSION LOFT PLAYRM/BR#4

DN

RAILING

DN

MASTER BEDRM
12'-0"x17'-0"
9'6 HIGH STEPPED CEILING

CL

BEDRM 2
12'-0"x15'-2"

UPPER FOYER

Plan Features

- Dining room can used as an office or den
- Living room can be converted to a guest room
- Expansion loft is ideal for a playroom or a fourth bedroom and includes an additional 300 square feet of living area
- 3 bedrooms, 2 1/2 baths, 2-car garage
- Basement, crawl space or slab foundation, please specify when ordering

To order call toll-free 1-800-DREAM HOME or visit www.houseplansandmore.com

Plan #583-020D-0011

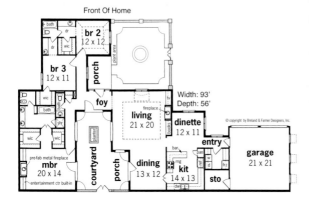

Front Of Home

Width: 93'
Depth: 56'

© copyright by Breland & Farmer Designers, Inc.

Total Living Area: 2,259 sq. ft.

Plan Features

- The courtyard accesses home through the dining room, living room or master bedroom
- Fireplace in the master bedroom warms surroundings
- Extra storage area is provided off the garage
- 3 bedrooms, 2 1/2 baths, 2-car garage
- Slab foundation, drawings also include crawl space foundation

---

Plan #583-003D-0002

Total Living Area: 1,676 sq. ft.

Plan Features

- The living area skylights and large breakfast room with bay window provide plenty of sunlight
- The master bedroom has a walk-in closet and both the secondary bedrooms have large closets
- Vaulted ceilings, plant shelving and a fireplace provide a quality living area
- 3 bedrooms, 2 baths, 2-car garage
- Basement foundation, drawings also include crawl space and slab foundations

Total Living Area: 2,182 sq. ft.

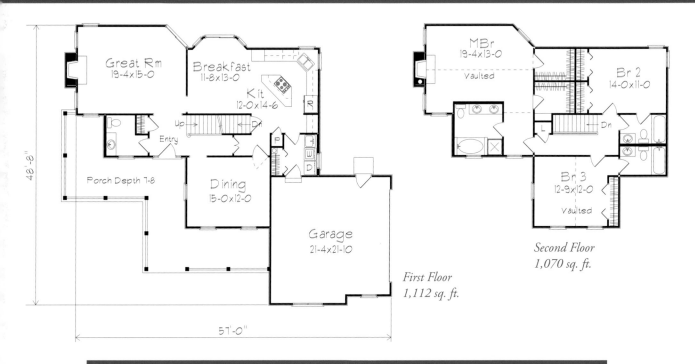

First Floor
1,112 sq. ft.

Second Floor
1,070 sq. ft.

Plan Features

- Meandering porch creates an inviting look
- Generous great room has four double-hung windows and sliding doors to exterior
- Functional kitchen features island/breakfast bar, menu desk and convenient pantry
- Each secondary bedroom includes generous closet space and a private bath
- 3 bedrooms, 3 1/2 baths, 2-car side entry garage
- Basement foundation, drawings also include crawl space and slab foundations

Plan #583-001D-0031

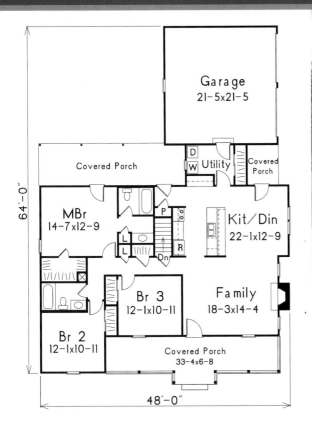

Total Living Area: 1,501 sq. ft.

Plan Features

- Spacious kitchen with dining area is open to the outdoors
- Convenient utility room is adjacent to garage
- Master bedroom features a private bath, dressing area and access to the large covered porch
- Large family room creates openness
- 3 bedrooms, 2 baths, 2-car side entry garage
- Basement foundation, drawings also include crawl space and slab foundations

Plan #583-013D-0021

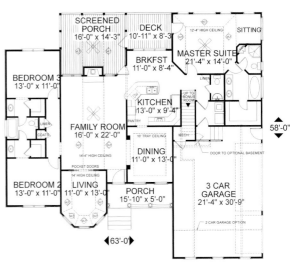

Total Living Area: 1,982 sq. ft.

Plan Features

- Large screened porch creates a great casual living area and connects to a covered deck leading into the master suite
- Dramatic formal living room has a sunny bay window and high ceilings
- Master suite has a private sitting area as well as a private luxury-filled bath
- 3 bedrooms, 2 1/2 baths, 3-car side entry garage
- Basement, crawl space or slab foundation, please specify when ordering

Total Living Area: 2,050 sq. ft.

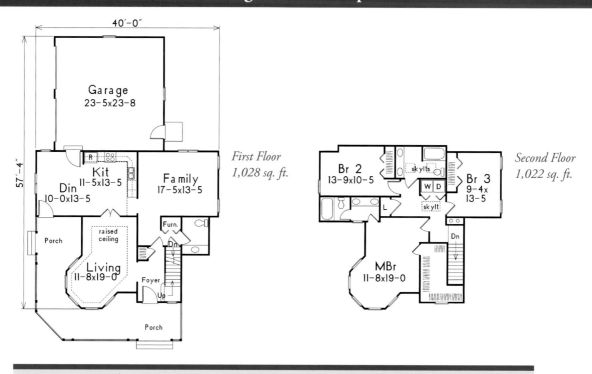

First Floor
1,028 sq. ft.

Second Floor
1,022 sq. ft.

Plan Features

- Large kitchen and dining area have access to garage and porch
- Master bedroom features a unique turret design, private bath and large walk-in closet
- Laundry facilities are conveniently located near the bedrooms
- 3 bedrooms, 2 1/2 baths, 2-car side entry garage
- Basement foundation, drawings also include crawl space and slab foundations

Plan #583-065D-0039

B

First Floor
1,794 sq. ft.

Optional
Lower Level

Total Living Area: 1,794 sq. ft.

Plan Features

- The great room with sloped ceiling and a fireplace connects with the kitchen and dining area for an open atmosphere
- Seating at the snack bar, angled walls and French doors to a covered porch form the dining area
- Optional lower level has an additional 1,130 square feet of living area
- 3 bedrooms, 2 baths, 2-car side entry garage
- Walk-out basement foundation

Plan #583-007D-0017

C

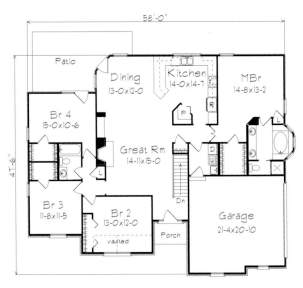

Total Living Area: 1,882 sq. ft.

Plan Features

- Spacious great room and dining area combination is brightened by unique corner windows and patio access
- Well-designed kitchen incorporates a breakfast bar peninsula, sweeping casement window above sink and a walk-in pantry island
- Master bedroom features a large walk-in closet and private bath with bay window
- 4 bedrooms, 2 baths, 2-car side entry garage
- Basement foundation

Total Living Area: 2,277 sq. ft.

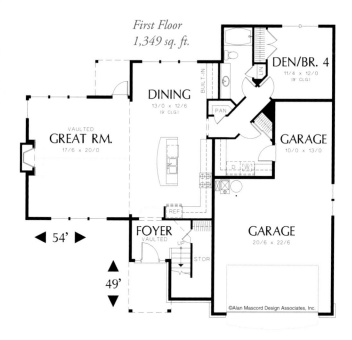

First Floor
1,349 sq. ft.

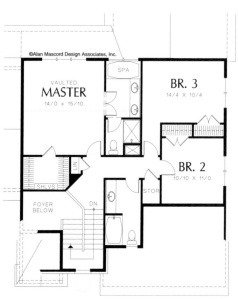

Second Floor
928 sq. ft.

Plan Features

- Lots of windows in the great room create an inviting feeling
- First floor den/bedroom #4 would make an ideal home office
- Enormous dining area and kitchen combine to create a large gathering area overlooking into the great room
- 4 bedrooms, 3 baths, 2-car garage
- Crawl space foundation

Plan #583-001D-0013

58'-8"

MBr 15-0x14-4 vaulted	Great Rm 24-0x17-0 vaulted	Dining 11-8x12-0	covered porch

Kit 12-6x12-0

Brk 11-6x9-0

Br 3 11-0x11-3

Br 2 12-0x11-5

Foyer

Porch

Garage 20-0x20-7

51'-2"

Total Living Area: 1,882 sq. ft.

Plan Features

- Living and dining areas are conveniently joined but still allow privacy
- Private covered porch extends breakfast area
- Practical passageway runs through the laundry room from the garage to the kitchen
- Vaulted ceiling in master bedroom
- 3 bedrooms, 2 baths, 2-car garage
- Basement foundation

Plan #583-021D-0001

Total Living Area: 2,396 sq. ft.

Plan Features

- Central living area with a 12' ceiling and large fireplace
- Kitchen is secluded, yet has easy access to the living, dining and breakfast areas
- Master bath has a walk-in closet, oversized tub, shower and other amenities
- Energy efficient home with 2"x 6" exterior walls
- 4 bedrooms, 2 baths, 2-car garage
- Slab foundation, drawings also include basement and crawl space foundations

MBr 16-0x15-0

Patio

skylt

Porch

Br 2 16-0x11-0

Brk 10-0x10-0

storage

Br 3 12-0x12-0

Living 20-0x20-0

Kit 14-0x 10-0

Garage 22-0x22-0

Entry

Br 4 14-0x12-0

Porch

Dining 17-0x14-0

72'-0"

60'-0"

Total Living Area: 1,980 sq. ft.

50'-8"

ACTIVITY AREA
21'-4" x 12'-0"

WET BAR

LIVING ROOM
13'-0" x 11'-6"

UP

DN.

UP

KITCHEN
D.W. 13'-0" x 14'-0"

REF.

MASTER BEDROOM
15'-0" x 13'-8"

L.

D.
W.

LAUN.

P.R.

BATH

47'-0"

First Floor
1,337 sq. ft.

UP

GARAGE
22'-0" x 21'-6"

Second Floor
643 sq. ft.

BEDROOM
11'-9" x 13'-2"

SITTING
ROOM
8'-6" x 17'-5"

DN.

OPEN BELOW
TO FOYER

L.

BATH

BEDROOM
14'-2" x 10'-5"

ATTIC STORAGE SPACE

Plan Features

- Step down into magnificent living and activity rooms sharing a cozy fireplace, wet bar, pass-through to kitchen and lots of glass area
- The kitchen features plenty of storage space and an eat-in area
- A delightful sitting room accesses the second floor bedrooms and offers a view to the step-up foyer below
- 3 bedrooms, 2 1/2 baths, 2-car garage
- Basement foundation

Plan #583-007D-0031

AA

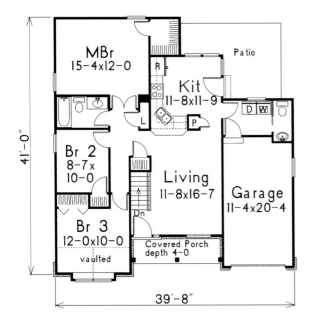

Total Living Area: 1,092 sq. ft.

Plan Features

- Box window and inviting porch with dormers create a charming facade
- Eat-in kitchen offers a pass-through breakfast bar, corner window wall to patio, pantry and convenient laundry with half bath
- Master bedroom features a double-door entry and walk-in closet
- 3 bedrooms, 1 1/2 baths, 1-car garage
- Basement foundation

Plan #583-025D-0009

Price Code:

B

Total Living Area: 1,680 sq. ft.

Plan Features

- Vaulted great room has a wet bar making it an ideal space for entertaining
- Spacious dining area features an eating bar for additional seating
- Fourth bedroom could easily be converted to a study
- 4 bedrooms, 2 baths, 2-car garage
- Slab foundation

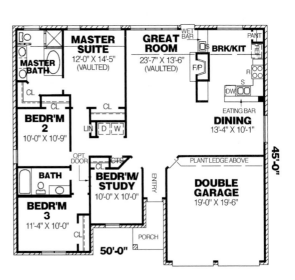

Total Living Area: 2,197 sq. ft.

DID YOU KNOW?

Draperies are getting longer and longer. One of the best ways to add height to any room is to place window treatments just below the ceiling line. Use this designer trick in any room that could use a little lift.

Plan Features

- Centrally located great room opens to the kitchen, breakfast nook and private backyard
- Den located off entry is ideal for a home office
- Vaulted master bath has a spa tub, shower and double vanity
- 3 bedrooms, 2 1/2 baths, 3-car garage
- Crawl space foundation

Width: 65'-1"
Depth: 69'-0"

Total Living Area: 2,158 sq. ft.

Plan Features

- Private master suite has a walk-in closet and bath
- Sloped ceiling in family room adds drama
- Secondary bedrooms include 9' ceilings and walk-in closets
- Covered porch adds a charming touch
- 4 bedrooms, 3 baths, 2-car side entry garage
- Crawl space or slab foundation, please specify when ordering

---

Total Living Area: 2,334 sq. ft.

Plan Features

- Roomy front porch gives home a country flavor
- Vaulted great room boasts a fireplace, TV alcove, pass-through snack bar to kitchen and atrium featuring bayed window wall and an ascending stair to family room
- Oversized master bedroom features a vaulted ceiling, double-door entry and large walk-in closet
- 3 bedrooms, 2 baths, 2-car garage
- Walk-out basement foundation

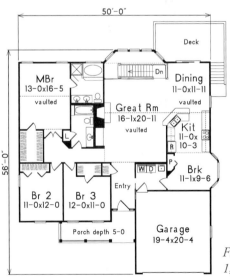

First Floor
1,777 sq. ft.

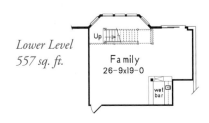

Lower Level
557 sq. ft.

Total Living Area: 2,484 sq. ft.

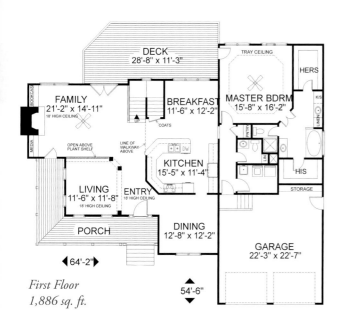

First Floor
1,886 sq. ft.

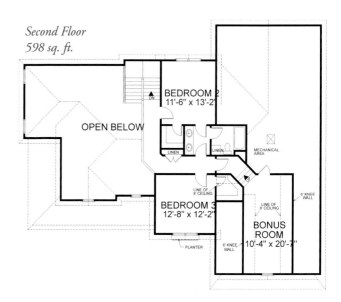

Second Floor
598 sq. ft.

Plan Features

- The master bedroom has two walk-in closets and a dramatic bath with whirlpool tub
- Living room has an 18' ceiling, decorative columns and a plant shelf
- Family room includes built-in bookcases and French doors leading to an outdoor deck
- Bonus room has an additional 262 square feet of living area on the second floor
- 3 bedrooms, 2 1/2 baths, 2-car garage
- Crawl space foundation

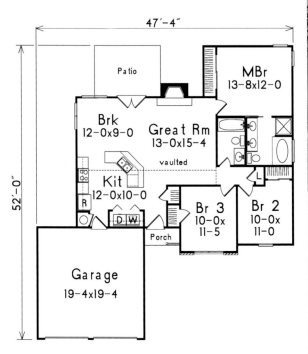

Total Living Area: 1,170 sq. ft.

Plan Features

- Master bedroom enjoys privacy at the rear of this home
- Kitchen has an angled bar that overlooks the great room and breakfast area
- Living areas combine to create a greater sense of spaciousness
- Great room has a cozy fireplace
- 3 bedrooms, 2 baths, 2-car garage
- Slab foundation

Plan #583-038D-0040

Price Code:

B

Total Living Area: 1,642 sq. ft.

Plan Features

- Built-in cabinet in dining room adds a custom feel
- Secondary bedrooms share an oversized bath
- Master bedroom includes private bath with dressing table
- 3 bedrooms, 2 baths, 2-car garage
- Crawl space foundation

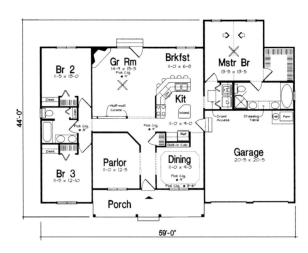

Total Living Area: 2,347 sq. ft.

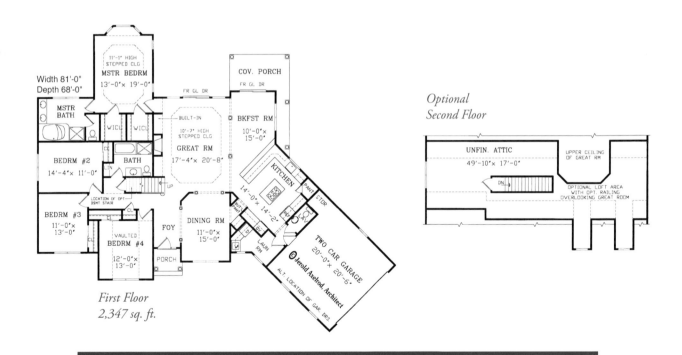

Width 81'-0"
Depth 68'-0"

11'-1" HIGH STEPPED CLG
MSTR BEDRM
13'-0" x 19'-0"

MSTR BATH

WIC/U WIC/U

FR GL DR

BUILT-IN
10'-7" HIGH STEPPED CLG
GREAT RM
17'-4" x 20'-8"

COV. PORCH
FR GL DR

BKFST RM
10'-0" x 15'-0"

BEDRM #2
14'-4" x 11'-0"

BATH

LIN

KITCHEN
14'-0" x 14'-2"

PANT STOR

LOCATION OF OPT BSMT STAIR

UP

BEDRM #3
11'-0" x 13'-0"

FOY

DINING RM
11'-0" x 15'-0"

LAUN RM

© Jerold Axelrod, Architect

TWO CAR GARAGE
20'-0" x 20'-6"

VAULTED BEDRM #4
12'-0" x 13'-0"

PORCH

ALT LOCATION OF GAR. DRS.

First Floor
2,347 sq. ft.

Optional
Second Floor

UNFIN. ATTIC
49'-10" x 17'-0"

UPPER CEILING OF GREAT RM

DN.

OPTIONAL LOFT AREA WITH OPT. RAILING OVERLOOKING GREAT ROOM

Plan Features

- Bedroom #4 could easily double as a home office or study
- A spacious rear-facing great room is the focal point of the living area with high stepped ceiling, fireplace and space for built-ins
- Optional second floor has an additional 823 square feet of living area
- 4 bedrooms, 2 1/2 baths, 2-car side entry garage
- Basement, crawl space or slab foundation, please specify when ordering

Plan #583-040D-0011

Price Code: B

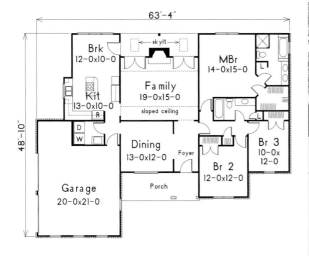

Total Living Area: 1,739 sq. ft.

Plan Features

- Vaulted ceiling lends drama to the family room with fireplace and double French doors
- Island kitchen is enhanced by adjoining breakfast area with access to the patio
- Formal dining room features a 10' ceiling
- Private hallway separates bedrooms from the living area
- 3 bedrooms, 2 baths, 2-car side entry garage
- Slab foundation

Plan #583-011D-0008

Price Code: C

Total Living Area: 1,728 sq. ft.

Plan Features

- Kitchen includes extras such as a large pantry, wall niche, built-in desk and a wrap-around counter for dining
- Vaulted great room features an oversized fireplace and a built-in wall for a media center
- Master bath enjoys a spa tub as well as a large shower
- 2 bedrooms, 2 baths, 3-car garage
- Crawl space foundation

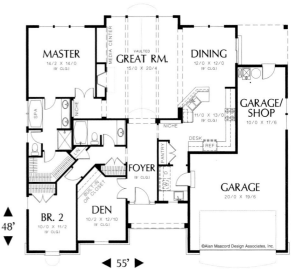

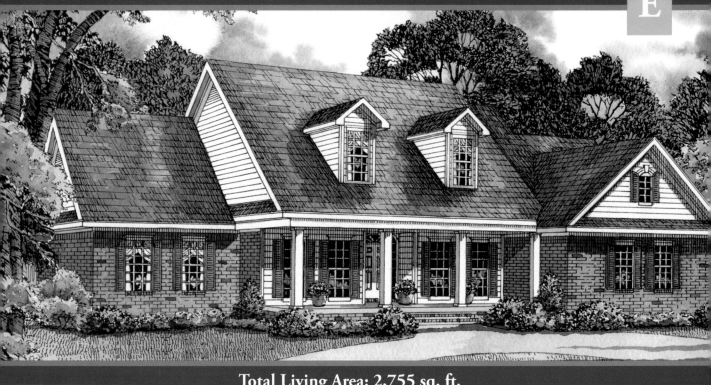

Total Living Area: 2,755 sq. ft.

First Floor
2,406 sq. ft.

Second Floor
349 sq. ft.

Plan Features

- The breakfast room boasts a two-story vaulted ceiling
- Each bedroom has a private bath
- The 10' covered porch has plenty of space for eating outdoors or just relaxing
- 4 bedrooms, 3 1/2 baths, 3-car side entry garage
- Slab, crawl space, basement or walk-out basement foundation, please specify when ordering

Plan #583-007D-0123

A

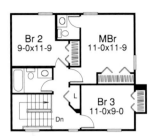

Second Floor
638 sq. ft.

Br 2
9-0x11-9

MBr
11-0x11-9

Br 3
11-0x9-0

Dn

L

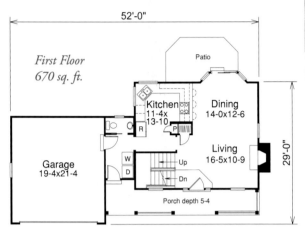

52'-0"

First Floor
670 sq. ft.

Patio

Kitchen
11-4x
13-10

Dining
14-0x12-6

R

P

Living
16-5x10-9

Garage
19-4x21-4

W
D

Up

Dn

29'-0"

Porch depth 5-4

Total Living Area: 1,308 sq. ft.

Plan Features

- Multi-gabled facade and elongated porch create a pleasing country appeal
- Large dining room with bay window and view to rear patio opens to a full-functional kitchen with snack bar
- An attractive U-shaped stair with hall overlook leads to the second floor
- 3 bedrooms, 1 full bath, 2 half baths, 2-car garage
- Basement foundation

Plan #583-032D-0047

C

Total Living Area: 2,129 sq. ft.

Plan Features

- Energy efficient home with 2"x 6" exterior walls
- Home office has a double-door entry and is secluded from other living areas
- Corner fireplace in living area is a nice focal point
- Bonus room above the garage has an additional 407 square feet of living area
- 3 bedrooms, 2 1/2 baths, 2-car side entry garage
- Basement foundation

13'-0" X 14'-4"
3.90 X 4.30

10'-8" X 12'-0"
3.20 X 3.60

21'-4" X 16'-0"
6.40 X 4.80

12'-0" X 11'-0"
3.60 X 3.30

Second Floor
993 sq. ft.

19'-0" X 13'-4"
5.70 X 4.00

13'-4" X 11'-0"
4.00 X 3.30

13'-4" X 15'-4"
4.00 X 4.60

21'-4" X 24'-8"
6.40 X 7.40

12'-0" X 13'-4"
3.60 X 4.00

38'-0"
11.4 m

First Floor
1,136 sq. ft.

56'-0"
16.8 m

Total Living Area: 1,484 sq. ft.

Second Floor
576 sq. ft.

14'-4" X 11'-0"
4,30 X 3,30

14'-4" X 12'-8"
4,30 X 3,80

10'-0" X 11'-0"
3,00 X 3,30

36'-0"
10,8 m

14'-4" X 10'-0"
4,30 X 3,00

12'-0" X 12'-8"
3,60 X 3,80

12'-8" X 11'-8"
3,80 X 3,50

14'-0" X 11'-8"
4,20 X 3,50

First Floor
908 sq. ft.

26'-0"
7,8 m

Plan Features

- Energy efficient home with 2"x 6" exterior walls
- Useful screened porch is ideal for dining and relaxing
- Corner fireplace warms the living room
- Snack bar adds extra counterspace in kitchen
- 3 bedrooms, 2 baths
- Basement foundation

Plan #583-047D-0075

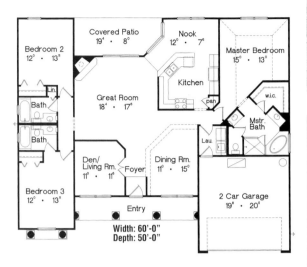

Width: 60'-0"
Depth: 50'-0"

Total Living Area: 2,052 sq. ft.

Plan Features

- The kitchen features a wrap-around counter with extra seating which opens to the charming nook area
- Sliding glass doors that access the covered patio and a corner fireplace enhance the great room
- The master bedroom is separate from the secondary bedrooms and enjoys a private bath with walk-in closet and whirlpool tub
- 3 bedrooms, 3 baths, 2-car garage
- Slab foundation

Plan #583-037D-0006

Total Living Area: 1,772 sq. ft.

Plan Features

- Extended porches in front and rear add charm
- Large bay windows lend distinction to the dining room and bedroom #3
- Master bedroom includes two walk-in closets
- Full corner fireplace in family room
- 3 bedrooms, 2 baths, 2-car detached garage
- Slab foundation, drawings also include crawl space foundation

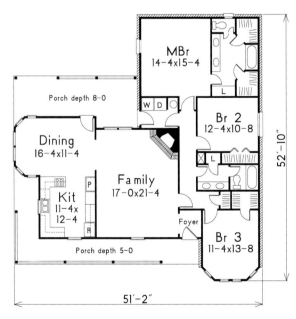

Total Living Area: 2,781 sq. ft.

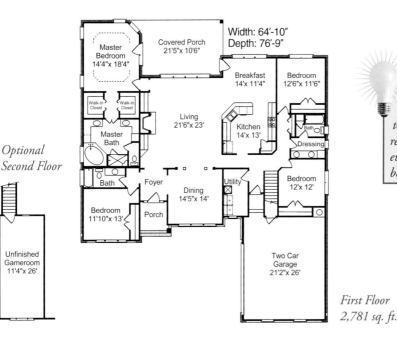

Width: 64'-10"
Depth: 76'-9"

Optional Second Floor

First Floor 2,781 sq. ft.

DID YOU KNOW?

If you are planning a new kitchen, don't miss the chance to build in space - creating touches such as a drawer-front that pulls out to reveal a useful extra work surface. Some ranges even incorporate drawers into the base area below the cabinets.

Plan Features

- The foyer features a 12' ceiling and opens to the formal dining room and living room
- The living room has a great view of the backyard with a full wall of transom windows
- A snack bar and walk-in pantry add efficiency to the kitchen
- Optional second floor has an additional 318 square feet of living area
- 4 bedrooms, 3 baths, 2-car side entry garage
- Slab or crawl space foundation, please specify when ordering

Plan #583-007D-0038

Price Code: B

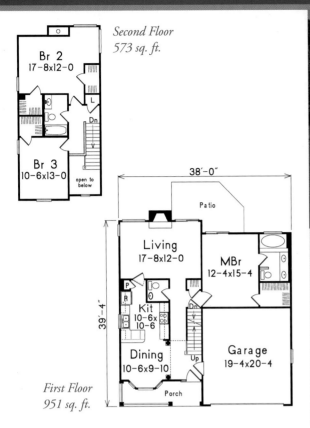

Second Floor
573 sq. ft.

Br 2
17-8x12-0

Br 3
10-6x13-0

open to below

Dn

38'-0"

Patio

Living
17-8x12-0

MBr
12-4x15-4

Kit
10-6x
10-6

Dining
10-6x9-10

Garage
19-4x20-4

Up

Porch

39'-4"

First Floor
951 sq. ft.

Total Living Area: 1,524 sq. ft.

Plan Features

- Delightful balcony overlooks two-story entry illuminated by oval window
- Roomy first floor master bedroom offers quiet privacy
- All bedrooms feature one or more walk-in closets
- 3 bedrooms, 2 1/2 baths, 2-car garage
- Basement foundation, drawings also include crawl space and slab foundations

---

Plan #583-026D-0130

Price Code: A

Total Living Area: 1,479 sq. ft.

Plan Features

- Centrally located great room is enhanced with fireplace
- Den can easily convert to a third bedroom
- Master bedroom has private bath with large walk-in closet
- Sunny kitchen/breakfast room enjoys view into great room
- 2 bedrooms, 2 baths, 2-car garage
- Basement foundation

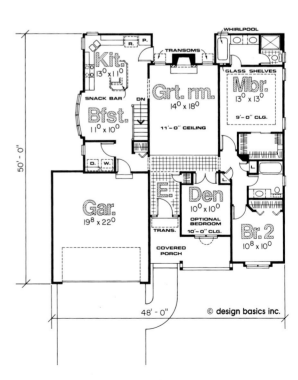

WHIRLPOOL

Kit.
13⁰ x 11⁰

SNACK BAR

TRANSOMS

GLASS SHELVES

Mbr.
13⁰ x 13⁰

9'-0" CLG.

Bfst.
11⁰ x 10⁰

Grt. rm.
14⁰ x 18⁰

11'-0" CEILING

D. W.

Gar.
19⁸ x 22⁰

DN

E.

Den
10⁰ x 10⁰

OPTIONAL BEDROOM
10'-0" CLG.

L

Br. 2
10⁸ x 10⁰

TRANS.

COVERED PORCH

50'-0"

48'-0"

© design basics inc.

Total Living Area: 2,322 sq. ft.

DID YOU KNOW?

Flexible lighting is essential for a living room. Aim to include three different types of light source: ambient, for general illumination; task lamps to focus on activities such as reading or sewing; and decorative lighting, which gives you the chance to introduce unusual and attractive fittings or interesting effects.

Plan Features

- Vaulted family room has a fireplace and access to the kitchen
- Decorative columns and arched openings surround dining area
- Master suite has a sitting room and grand-scale bath
- Kitchen includes an island with serving bar
- 3 bedrooms, 2 1/2 baths, 2-car side entry garage
- Walk-out basement, crawl space or slab foundation, please specify when ordering

Plan #583-055D-0026

Total Living Area: 1,538 sq. ft.

Plan Features

- Dining and great rooms are highlighted in this design
- Master suite has many amenities
- Kitchen and laundry room are accessible from any room in the house
- 3 bedrooms, 2 baths, 2-car garage
- Walk-out basement, basement, crawl space or slab foundation, please specify when ordering

Plan #583-039D-0014

Total Living Area: 1,849 sq. ft.

Plan Features

- Open floor plan creates an airy feeling
- Kitchen and breakfast area include center island, pantry and built-in desk
- Master bedroom has a private entrance off the breakfast area and a view of the vaulted porch
- 3 bedrooms, 2 baths, 2-car garage
- Crawl space or slab foundation, please specify when ordering

Width: 66'-5"
Depth: 60'-0"

Total Living Area: 3,359 sq. ft.

First Floor
3,359 sq. ft.

Optional
Second Floor

DID YOU KNOW?

Have you ever wondered how long perishable food items will keep in the refrigerator or freezer if you happen to lose electricity? Remember that items in a full freezer will stay frozen for about two days with the door kept closed and in a half-full freezer for about a day. Refrigerated foods can keep up to four hours. Discard any perishable refrigerated foods that have been above 40 degrees for more than two hours.

Plan Features

- A covered patio wraps around the rear of the home providing extra outdoor living area
- Master suite is separated from other bedrooms for privacy
- Optional second floor has an additional 459 square feet of living area
- Framing - only concrete block available
- 4 bedrooms, 3 1/2 baths, 3-car side entry garage
- Slab foundation

Plan #583-056D-0004

Second Floor
1,057 sq. ft.

First Floor
1,260 sq. ft.

Width 35'-0"
Depth 56'-0"

Total Living Area: 2,317 sq. ft.

Plan Features

- 10' ceilings throughout the first floor and 9' ceilings on the second floor
- Second floor covered balcony is accessible to everyone
- Cozy breakfast room leads to a covered porch
- Master suite on the first floor has privacy and luxury
- 5 bedrooms, 2 1/2 baths, 2-car rear entry garage
- Slab foundation

Plan #583-048D-0005

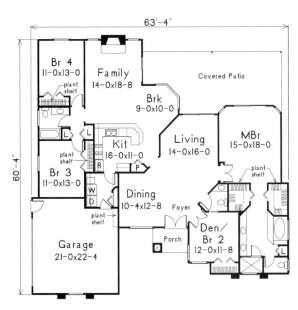

Total Living Area: 2,287 sq. ft.

Plan Features

- A double-door entry leads into an impressive master bedroom which accesses the covered porch and features a deluxe bath with double closets and a step-up tub
- Kitchen easily serves formal and informal areas of home
- The spacious foyer opens into formal dining and living rooms
- 4 bedrooms, 2 1/2 baths, 2-car side entry garage
- Slab foundation

Total Living Area: 1,636 sq. ft.

DID YOU KNOW?

Hanging light and fan fixtures can be a nuisance when painting a ceiling. A simple solution to save the fixture from paint splatter without taking it down is to slip a large plastic trash bag over the light and seal it closed with a twist tie. Do the same to seal out dust and dirt during demolition and renovation projects. Just be sure to keep the light off while it's sealed so heat from the bulbs won't melt or ignite the plastic bag.

Plan Features

- The grilling porch is large enough for outdoor cooking and entertaining
- The bar with seating in the kitchen is great for serving snacks
- Columns separate the dining room from the rest of the house without enclosing it
- 3 bedrooms, 2 baths, 2-car side entry garage
- Slab or crawl space foundation, please specify when ordering

Plan #583-062D-0033

A

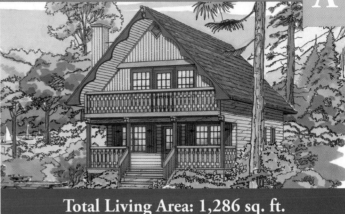

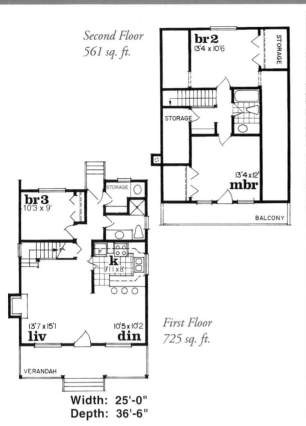

Second Floor
561 sq. ft.

br2
13'4 x 10'6

STORAGE

STORAGE

13'4 x 12'
mbr

BALCONY

br3
10'3 x 9'

STORAGE

k
9'11 x 8'

First Floor
725 sq. ft.

13'7 x 15'1
liv

10'5 x 10'2
din

VERANDAH

Width: 25'-0"
Depth: 36'-6"

Total Living Area: 1,286 sq. ft.

Plan Features

- Living room has a warm fireplace and a dining room with a snack bar counter through to the kitchen
- U-shaped kitchen has a window sink
- The master bedroom has private access to a balcony
- Lots of storage throughout this home
- 3 bedrooms, 2 baths
- Crawl space foundation

Plan #583-055D-0032

D

Total Living Area: 2,439 sq. ft.

Plan Features

- Enter columned gallery area just before reaching the family room with a see-through fireplace
- Master bath has a corner whirlpool tub
- Double-door entrance leads into the study
- 4 bedrooms, 3 baths, 2-car garage
- Slab, crawl space, basement or walk-out basement foundation, please specify when ordering

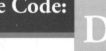

65' 8"

M. BATH

COVERED PORCH
14'-10" X 5'-8"

BREAKFAST ROOM
13'-0" X 12'-0"

MASTER SUITE
16'-0" X 13'-0"
10' PAN CEILING

FAMILY ROOM
17'-10" X 16'-0"

PASS-THRU FIREPLACE

COMP. DESK

KITCHEN
13'-0" X 12'-0"

BEDROOM 2
14'-10" X 11'-0"

BATH

GALLERY

8" BOXED COLUMNS

BATH

FRENCH DOORS

FOYER
10' CEILING

LAU

BEDROOM 3
13'-0" X 11'-0"

BEDROOM 4
11'-0" X 10'-8"

STUDY
11'-6" X 15'-0"

DINING ROOM
11'-0" X 13'-6"
10' BOXED CEILING

PORCH

GARAGE
23'-0" X 22'-0"

Total Living Area: 2,292 sq. ft.

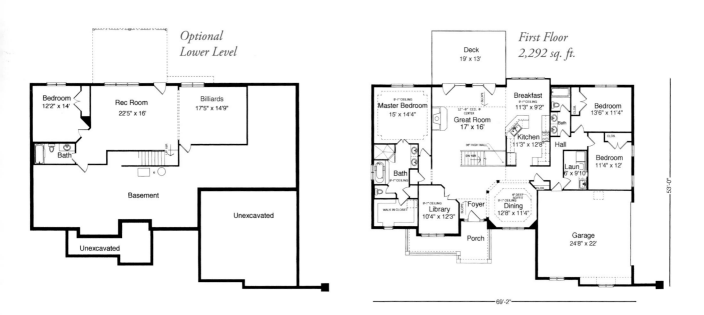

Optional Lower Level

- Bedroom 12'2" x 14'
- Rec Room 22'5" x 16'
- Billiards 17'5" x 14'9"
- Bath
- Basement
- Unexcavated
- Unexcavated

First Floor 2,292 sq. ft.

- Deck 19' x 13'
- Master Bedroom 15' x 14'4"
- Great Room 17' x 16'
- Breakfast 11'3" x 9'2"
- Kitchen 11'3" x 12'8"
- Bedroom 13'6" x 11'4"
- Bath
- Hall
- Bath
- Laun 6' x 9'10"
- Bedroom 11'4" x 12'
- Library 10'4" x 12'3"
- Foyer
- Dining 12'8" x 11'4"
- Porch
- Garage 24'8" x 22'
- Walk In Closet

69'-2"
53'-0"

Plan Features

- Brick and stone exterior showcase a spectacular curb appeal
- A great room with 12' ceiling, informal dining and a kitchen with snack bar combine to form the family activity center
- Optional lower level has 964 square feet of additional living space
- 3 bedrooms, 2 baths, 2-car side entry garage
- Walk-out basement foundation

Plan #583-007D-0110

Price Code: AA

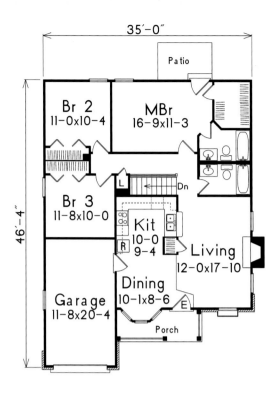

35'-0"

Patio

Br 2
11-0x10-4

MBr
16-9x11-3

46'-4"

Br 3
11-8x10-0

Kit
10-0
9-4

Living
12-0x17-10

Dn
L

Garage
11-8x20-4

Dining
10-1x8-6

E

Porch

Total Living Area: 1,169 sq. ft.

Plan Features

- Living room enjoys a wood-burning fireplace and pass-through to kitchen
- A stylish U-shaped kitchen offers an abundance of cabinet and counterspace with view to living room
- A large walk-in closet, access to rear patio and private bath are many features of the master bedroom
- 3 bedrooms, 2 baths, 1-car garage
- Basement foundation

Plan #583-062D-0041

Price Code: B

DID YOU KNOW?

Flowers of one type in a vase will last longer than a bouquet of mixed varieties. Also, a single bloom will survive longer than many blossoms of the same type.

Total Living Area: 1,541 sq. ft.

Plan Features

- Dining area offers access to a screened porch for outdoor dining and entertaining
- Country kitchen features a center island and a breakfast bay for casual meals
- Great room is warmed by a woodstove
- 3 bedrooms, 2 baths, 2-car garage
- Basement or crawl space foundation, please specify when ordering

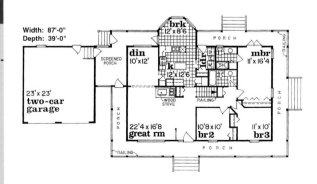

Width: 87'-0"
Depth: 39'-0"

brk
12'x8'6

din
10'x12'

k
12'x12'6

mbr
11'x16'4

SCREENED
PORCH

PORCH

23' x 23'
two-car
garage

WOOD
STOVE

RAILING

RAILING

PORCH

22'4 x 16'8
great rm

10'8 x 10'
br2

11'x10'
br3

RAILING

PORCH

Total Living Area: 2,695 sq. ft.

First Floor
1,315 sq. ft.

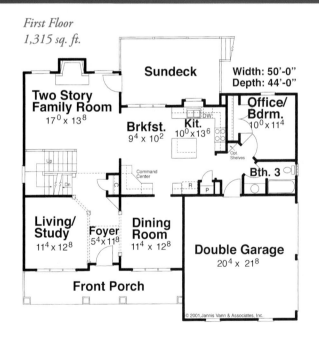

Sundeck

Width: 50'-0"
Depth: 44'-0"

Two Story Family Room 17⁰ x 13⁸

Office/ Bdrm. 10⁰ x 11⁴

Brkfst. 9⁴ x 10²

Kit. 10⁰ x 13⁶

Opt. Shelves

Bth. 3

Command Center

Living/ Study 11⁴ x 12⁸

Foyer 5⁴ x 11⁸

Dining Room 11⁴ x 12⁸

Double Garage 20⁴ x 21⁸

Front Porch

© 2001 Jannis Vann & Associates, Inc.

Second Floor
1,380 sq. ft.

Open To Family Room

Bdrm. 2 10⁶ x 11⁶

Master Bdrm. 13⁶ x 17⁶

Stepped Ceiling

Sh. Seat Sh.

Bth. 2

Plant Shelf Above

Balcony

Plant Shelf Above

Comp. Station

Bdrm. 3 11¹⁰ x 10⁶

Master Bth.

Bdrm. 4 11⁴ x 11⁴

Open To Foyer

Lnd.

Plant Shelf Above

Master Closet

Dn

Plan Features

- The view from the front door to the family room's two-story fireplace wall is amazing
- The expansive kitchen and breakfast area feature a perfect place for the family computer
- The master bedroom features a window seat dramatized by a stepped ceiling
- The second floor laundry area and computer desk complete this well-appointed design
- 5 bedrooms, 3 baths, 2-car side entry garage
- Walk-out basement foundation

Plan #583-027D-0006

Price Code:

Total Living Area: 2,076 sq. ft.

Plan Features

- Vaulted great room has a fireplace flanked by windows and skylights that welcome the sun
- Kitchen leads to the vaulted breakfast room and rear deck
- Study located off the foyer provides a great location for a home office
- Large bay windows grace the master bedroom and bath
- 3 bedrooms, 2 baths, 2-car garage
- Basement foundation

Plan #583-007D-0088

Price Code:

Total Living Area: 1,299 sq. ft.

Plan Features

- Large porch for enjoying relaxing evenings
- First floor master bedroom has a bay window, walk-in closet and roomy bath
- Two generous bedrooms with lots of closet space, a hall bath, linen closet and balcony overlook comprise second floor
- 3 bedrooms, 2 1/2 baths
- Basement foundation

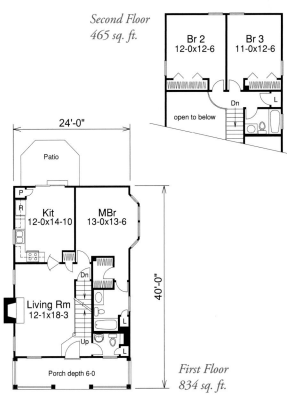

Second Floor
465 sq. ft.

First Floor
834 sq. ft.

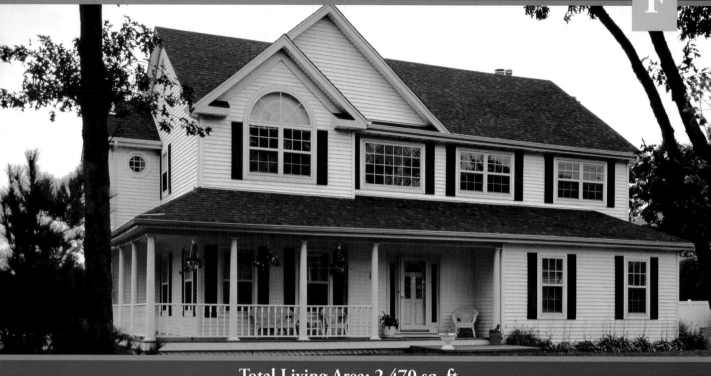

Total Living Area: 2,470 sq. ft.

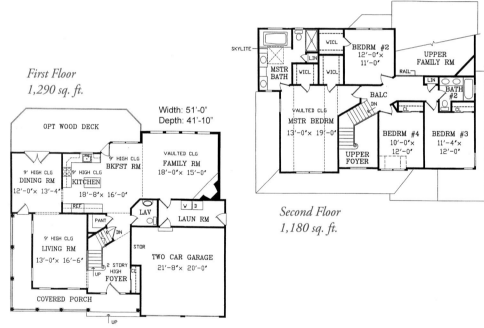

First Floor
1,290 sq. ft.

Width: 51'-0"
Depth: 41'-10"

OPT WOOD DECK

9' HIGH CLG
BKFST RM

VAULTED CLG
FAMILY RM
18'-0" x 15'-0"

9' HIGH CLG
DINING RM
12'-0" x 13'-4"

9' HIGH CLG
KITCHEN
18'-8" x 16'-0"

REF

PANT

LAV

LAUN RM

W D

9' HIGH CLG
LIVING RM
13'-0" x 16'-6"

DN

STOR

TWO CAR GARAGE
21'-8" x 20'-0"

UP

2 STORY
HIGH
FOYER

CL

COVERED PORCH

UP

SKYLITE

WICL

MSTR
BATH

WICL

WICL WICL

LIN

BEDRM #2
12'-0" x
11'-0"

UPPER
FAMILY RM

RAIL

LIN

BATH
#2

VAULTED CLG
MSTR BEDRM
13'-0" x 19'-0"

BALC

DN

UPPER
FOYER

CL

CL

BEDRM #4
10'-0" x
12'-0"

BEDRM #3
11'-4" x
12'-0"

Second Floor
1,180 sq. ft.

Plan Features

- All bedrooms are located on the second floor for privacy
- The U-shaped kitchen with island opens into the breakfast and family rooms
- The vaulted master bedroom features two walk-in closets and a private bath
- 4 bedrooms, 2 1/2 baths, 2-car garage
- Basement, walk-out basement, crawl space or slab foundation, please specify when ordering

Plan #583-077D-0001

Total Living Area: 1,638 sq. ft.

WIDTH: 72'-10"
DEPTH: 41'-0"

Plan Features

- Great room features a fireplace with flanking doors that access the covered porch
- The centrally located kitchen serves the breakfast and dining areas with ease
- Plenty of storage area is located in the garage
- 3 bedrooms, 2 baths, 2-car side entry garage
- Basement, crawl space or slab foundation, please specify when ordering

Plan #583-072D-0003

Total Living Area: 1,317 sq. ft.

Plan Features

- A large window topped by a clerestory window gives the living room a bright, airy feel
- A three-way fireplace defines the space between the living and dining rooms
- An efficient kitchen neatly serves the dining room
- 3 bedrooms, 2 baths, 2-car garage
- Basement foundation

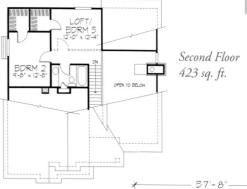

Second Floor 423 sq. ft.

First Floor 894 sq. ft.

C

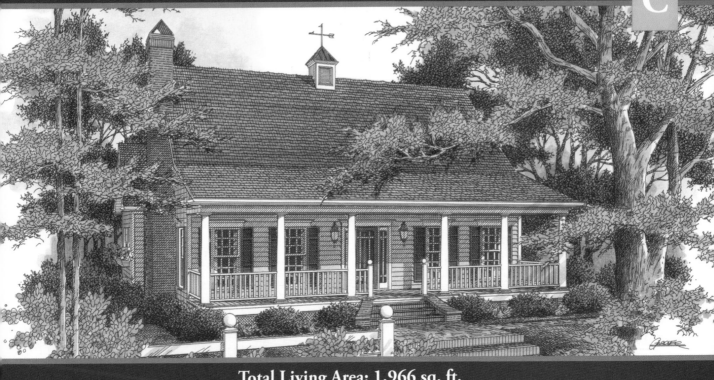

Total Living Area: 1,966 sq. ft.

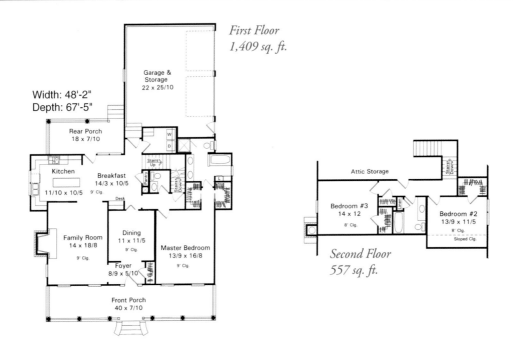

First Floor
1,409 sq. ft.

Width: 48'-2"
Depth: 67'-5"

Garage & Storage
22 x 25/10

Rear Porch
18 x 7/10

Kitchen
11/10 x 10/5

Breakfast
14/3 x 10/5
9' Clg.

Stairs Up

Stairs Down

Desk

Family Room
14 x 18/8
9' Clg.

Dining
11 x 11/5
9' Clg.

Master Bedroom
13/9 x 16/8
9' Clg.

Foyer
8/9 x 5/10

Front Porch
40 x 7/10

Attic Storage

Stairs Down

Bedroom #3
14 x 12
8' Clg.

Linen

Bedroom #2
13/9 x 11/5
8' Clg.
Sloped Clg.

Second Floor
557 sq. ft.

Plan Features

- Private dining room remains the focal point when entering the home
- Kitchen and breakfast room join to create a functional area
- Lots of closet space in the second floor bedrooms
- 3 bedrooms, 2 1/2 baths, 2-car side entry garage
- Basement foundation

Plan #583-028D-0013

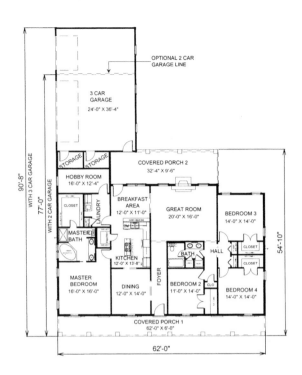

Total Living Area: 2,423 sq. ft.

Plan Features

- All bedrooms have large walk-in closets
- Unique hobby room located off the laundry area is a nice workshop area
- Kitchen boasts a walk-in pantry and snack bar open to the breakfast area
- 4 bedrooms, 2 baths, 3-car side entry garage
- Crawl space or slab foundation, please specify when ordering

---

Plan #583-007D-0046

Total Living Area: 1,712 sq. ft.

Plan Features

- Stylish stucco exterior enhances curb appeal
- Sunken great room offers corner fireplace flanked by 9' wide patio doors
- Well-designed kitchen features ideal view of the great room and fireplace through breakfast bar opening
- 3 bedrooms, 2 1/2 baths, 2-car garage
- Crawl space foundation

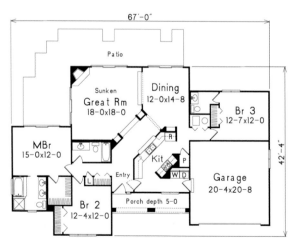

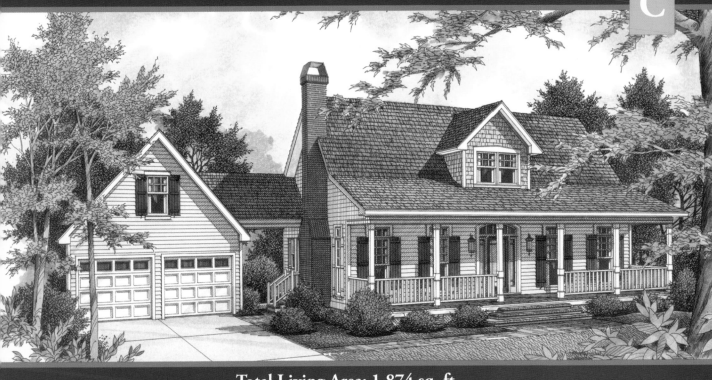

Total Living Area: 1,874 sq. ft.

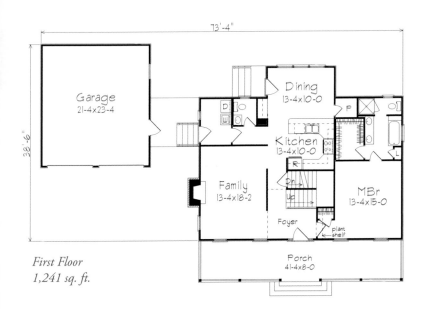

First Floor
1,241 sq. ft.

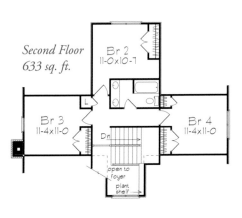

Plan Features

- 9' ceilings throughout the first floor
- Two-story foyer opens into the large family room with fireplace
- First floor master bedroom includes a private bath with tub and shower
- 4 bedrooms, 2 1/2 baths, 2-car garage
- Basement foundation, drawings also include slab foundation

Plan #583-038D-0039

Price Code:

B

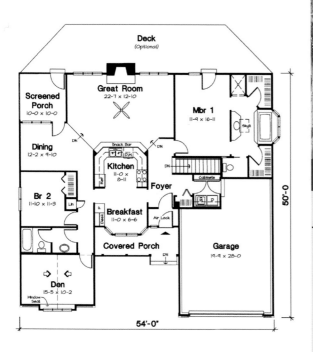

Total Living Area: 1,771 sq. ft.

Plan Features

- Den has a sloped ceiling and charming window seat
- Private master bedroom has access to the outdoors
- Central kitchen allows for convenient access when entertaining
- 2 bedrooms, 2 baths, 2-car garage
- Basement, crawl space or slab foundation, please specify when ordering

---

Plan #583-058D-0002

Price Code:

C

Total Living Area: 2,059 sq. ft.

Plan Features

- Large desk and pantry add to the breakfast room
- Laundry is located on the second floor near bedrooms
- Vaulted ceiling in the master bedroom
- Mud room is conveniently located near the garage
- 3 bedrooms, 2 1/2 baths, 2-car garage
- Basement foundation

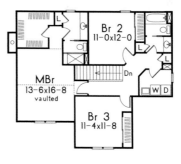

Second Floor 1,016 sq. ft.

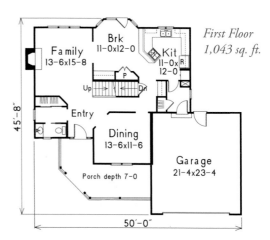

First Floor 1,043 sq. ft.

Total Living Area: 2,232 sq. ft.

First Floor
1,944 sq. ft.

Patio

Porch
17'10"x 8'

WIC

WIC

Bedroom
12'x 11'6"

Living
18'6"x 17'

Breakfast
11'6"x 11'

Ma.
Bath

Bath

Master
Bedroom
13'x 16'4"

Kitchen
11'6"x 11'8"

Foyer

Dining
10'9"x 13'3"

Bedroom
12'2"x 11'6"

Porch

Width: 57'-5"
Depth: 62'-10"

Two Car
Garage
20'4"x 24'

Second Floor
288 sq. ft.

Gameroom
21'8"x 16'

Plan Features

- The master bedroom, living and dining rooms feature raised tray ceilings
- Kitchen includes a pantry and snack bar that is open to the breakfast area
- The master bedroom enjoys a deluxe bath with a garden tub, double-bowl vanity and two walk-in closets
- 3 bedrooms, 3 baths, 2-car side entry garage
- Slab foundation

Plan #583-056D-0007

Price Code: G

Optional Second Floor

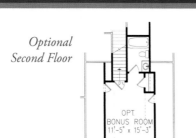

First Floor 1,985 sq. ft.

Width 54'-0"
Depth 54'-0"
© 2003 GARRELL ASSOCIATES, INC.

Total Living Area: 1,985 sq. ft.

Plan Features

- 9' ceilings throughout home
- Master suite has direct access into the sunroom
- Sunny breakfast room features a bay window
- Bonus room on the second floor has an additional 191 square feet of living area
- 3 bedrooms, 3 baths, 2-car side entry garage
- Slab foundation

Plan #583-007D-0044

Price Code: B

Total Living Area: 1,516 sq. ft.

Plan Features

- Spacious great room is open to dining area with a bay and unique stair location
- Attractive and well-planned kitchen offers breakfast bar and built-in pantry
- Smartly designed master bedroom enjoys patio view
- 3 bedrooms, 2 baths, 2-car garage
- Basement foundation

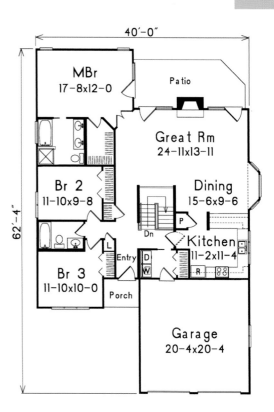

Total Living Area: 2,696 sq. ft.

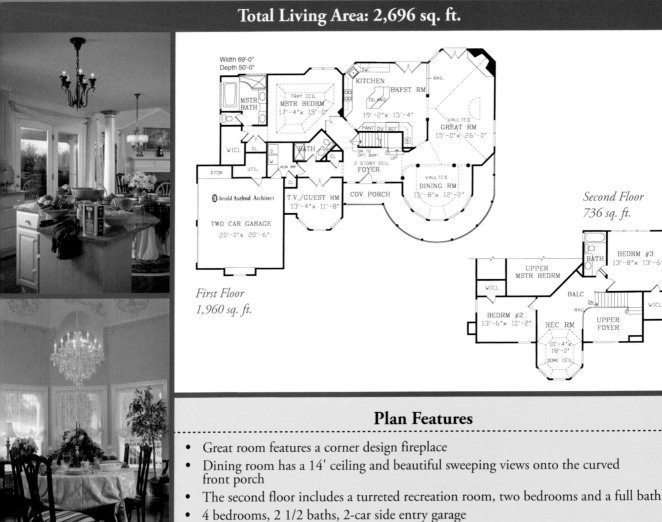

Width 69'-0"
Depth 50'-0"

MSTR BATH

TRAY CEIL
MSTR BEDRM
17'-4" x 15'-0"

KITCHEN

BKFST RM
19'-2" x 15'-4"

RAIL

GREAT RM
15'-0" x 26'-0"
VAULTED

WICL   CL   BATH   PANT   OV   REF

STOR   UTIL   LAUN RM   CL   DN TO OPT BSMT   UP   S

2 STORY CEIL
FOYER

VAULTED
DINING RM
15'-8" x 12'-2"

Jerold Axelrod, Architect

TWO CAR GARAGE
20'-0" x 20'-6"

T.V./GUEST RM
13'-4" x 11'-8"

COV PORCH

First Floor
1,960 sq. ft.

Second Floor
736 sq. ft.

BATH   BEDRM #3
13'-8" x 13'-6"

UPPER
MSTR BEDRM

WICL   BALC   DN RAIL   WICL

BEDRM #2
13'-6" x 10'-2"   REC RM
10'-4" x 18'-0"
DOME CEIL   UPPER
FOYER

Plan Features

- Great room features a corner design fireplace
- Dining room has a 14' ceiling and beautiful sweeping views onto the curved front porch
- The second floor includes a turreted recreation room, two bedrooms and a full bath
- 4 bedrooms, 2 1/2 baths, 2-car side entry garage
- Basement, crawl space or slab foundation, please specify when ordering

Plan #583-052D-0070

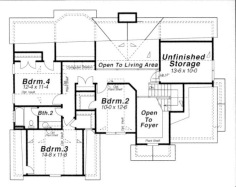

Second Floor 907 sq. ft.

First Floor 1,382 sq. ft.

Total Living Area: 2,289 sq. ft.

Plan Features

- Lots of storage and extra space throughout this plan including a command center near kitchen and extra storage on the second floor
- Beautiful master bedroom with sunny bay window
- Second floor computer center is perfect for students
- 4 bedrooms, 2 1/2 baths, 2-car garage
- Walk-out basement foundation

Plan #583-038D-0033

Total Living Area: 1,312 sq. ft.

Plan Features

- A beamed ceiling and fireplace create an exciting feel to the living room
- Box window behind double sink in kitchen is a nice added feature
- Private bath and generous closet space in the master bedroom
- 3 bedrooms, 2 baths, 2-car garage
- Basement or crawl space foundation, please specify when ordering

Total Living Area: 2,871 sq. ft.

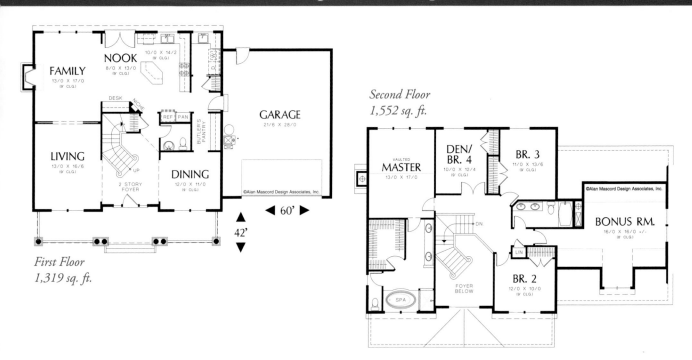

First Floor
1,319 sq. ft.

Second Floor
1,552 sq. ft.

Plan Features

- A grand two-story foyer greets guests upon entering the home
- A handy butler's pantry connects the kitchen and the formal dining room
- Luxurious master bedroom has a gorgeous bath with spa tub and a double vanity
- Bonus room above the garage is included in the square footage
- 4 bedrooms, 2 1/2 baths, 2-car garage
- Crawl space foundation

Plan #583-062D-0053

DID YOU KNOW?

A long island has the ability to separate the kitchen from the living area while providing additional lower cabinet storage plus a great place to serve meals buffet-style.

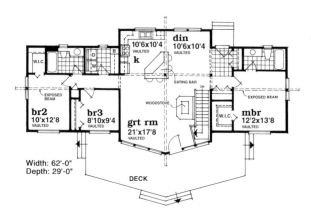

Width: 62'-0"
Depth: 29'-0"

Total Living Area: 1,405 sq. ft.

Plan Features

- An expansive wall of glass gives a spectacular view to the great room and accentuates the high vaulted ceilings throughout the design
- Great room is warmed by a woodstove and is open to the dining room and L-shaped kitchen
- Triangular snack bar graces the kitchen
- 3 bedrooms, 2 baths
- Basement or crawl space foundation, please specify when ordering

---

Plan #583-001D-0034

Total Living Area: 1,642 sq. ft.

Plan Features

- Walk-through kitchen boasts a vaulted ceiling and corner sink overlooking the family room
- Vaulted family room features a cozy fireplace and access to the rear patio
- Master bedroom includes a sloped ceiling, walk-in closet and private bath
- 3 bedrooms, 2 baths, 2-car garage
- Basement foundation, drawings also include slab and crawl space foundations

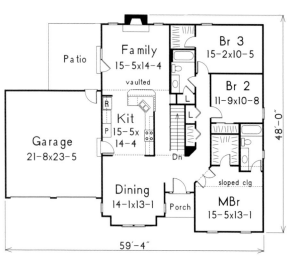

A

Total Living Area: 1,403 sq. ft.

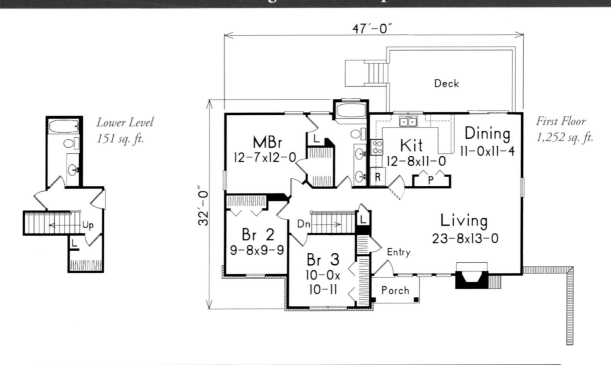

47'-0"

Deck

Lower Level
151 sq. ft.

First Floor
1,252 sq. ft.

32'-0"

MBr
12-7x12-0

Kit
12-8x11-0

Dining
11-0x11-4

L

P

R

Up

L

Br 2
9-8x9-9

Dn

L

Living
23-8x13-0

Br 3
10-0x
10-11

Entry

Porch

Plan Features

- Impressive living areas for a modest-sized home
- Special master/hall bath has linen storage, step-up tub and lots of window light
- Spacious closets everywhere you look
- 3 bedrooms, 2 baths, 2-car drive under garage
- Basement foundation

Plan #583-065D-0042

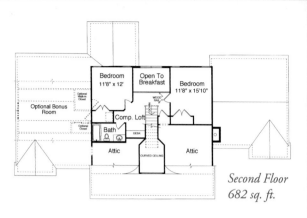

Second Floor
682 sq. ft.

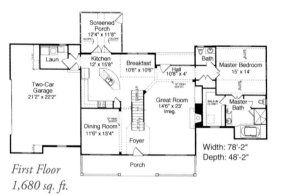

First Floor
1,680 sq. ft.

Total Living Area: 2,362 sq. ft.

Plan Features

- A spacious kitchen with an oversized island, breakfast area and delightful screened porch combine for family enjoyment
- The second floor offers a computer area in addition to the two bedrooms
- Bonus room on the second floor has an additional 271 square feet of living area
- 3 bedrooms, 2 1/2 baths, 2-car side entry garage
- Basement foundation

Plan #583-035D-0052

Total Living Area: 2,072 sq. ft.

Plan Features

- Master suite has a large bay sitting area, private vaulted bath and an enormous walk-in closet
- Tray ceilings in the breakfast and dining rooms are charming touches
- Great room has a centered fireplace and a French door leading outdoors
- 3 bedrooms, 2 1/2 baths, 2-car side entry garage
- Walk-out basement, slab or crawl space foundation, please specify when ordering

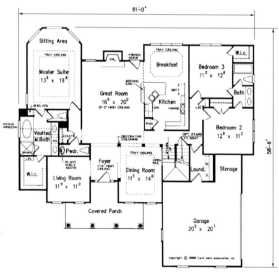

Total Living Area: 1,868 sq. ft.

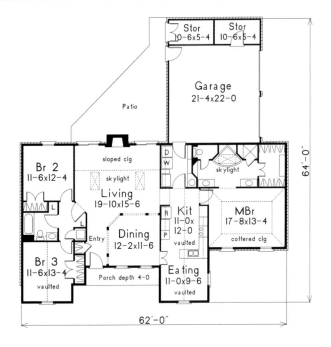

DID YOU KNOW?

Before a major cleaning session, take stock of your cleaning supplies. Don't wait until you're about to clean the oven to find out you don't have any oven cleaner left. Have everything you need on hand and ready to go for a smooth time.

Plan Features

- Luxurious master bath boasts an angled quarter-circle tub and separate vanities
- Energy efficient home with 2"x 6" exterior walls
- Dining room is surrounded by a series of arched openings which create an open feel
- Living room has a 12' ceiling accented by skylights and a large fireplace
- 3 bedrooms, 2 baths, 2-car side entry garage
- Slab foundation, drawings also include crawl space foundation

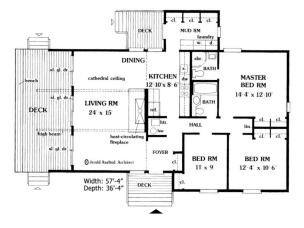

Total Living Area: 1,207 sq. ft.

Plan Features

- Triple sets of sliding glass doors leading to the deck brighten the living room
- Oversized mud room has lots of extra closet space for convenience
- Centrally located heat circulating fireplace creates a focal point while warming the home
- 3 bedrooms, 2 baths
- Basement or crawl space foundation, please specify when ordering

Total Living Area: 1,598 sq. ft.

Plan Features

- Family room features a large bay window and a cozy fireplace
- Impressive master bedroom has a vaulted ceiling, a large bay window and private bath with separate vanities
- Large storage area located off the garage
- 3 bedrooms, 2 1/2 baths, 2-car garage
- Crawl space or slab foundation, please specify when ordering

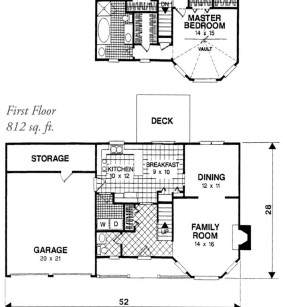

Second Floor
786 sq. ft.

First Floor
812 sq. ft.

D-0016

Price Code:

E

Total Living Area: 2,847 sq. ft.

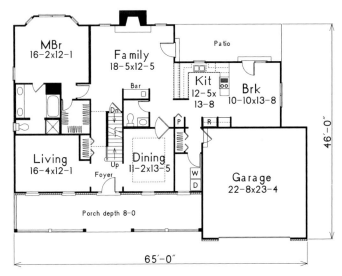

First Floor
1,745 sq. ft.

MBr
16-2x12-1

Family
18-5x12-5

Patio

Kit
12-5x
13-8

Brk
10-10x13-8

Bar

Living
16-4x12-1

Dn

Up

Dining
11-2x13-5

Foyer

P

R

W
D

Garage
22-8x23-4

46'-0"

Porch depth 8-0

65'-0"

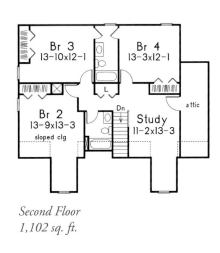

Second Floor
1,102 sq. ft.

Br 3
13-10x12-1

Br 4
13-3x12-1

L

Br 2
13-9x13-3
sloped clg

Dn

Study
11-2x13-3

attic

Plan Features

- Secluded first floor master bedroom includes an oversized window and a walk-in closet
- Extensive attic storage and closet space
- Spacious second floor bedrooms, two of which share a private bath
- Great starter home with option to finish the second floor as needed
- 4 bedrooms, 3 1/2 baths, 2-car garage
- Basement foundation, drawings also include slab and crawl space foundations

Total Living Area: 1,721 sq. ft.

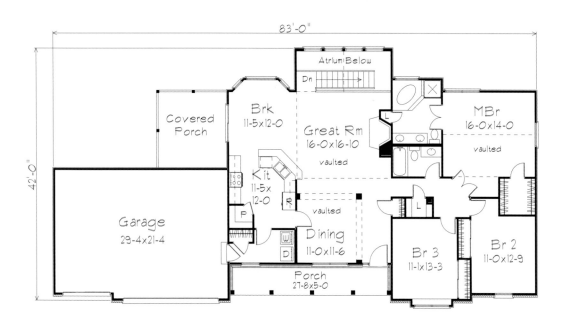

```
                        83'-0"
     Covered          Brk
     Porch          11-5x12-0      Atrium Below
                                    Dn

                              Great Rm       MBr
                              16-0x16-10    16-0x14-0
                               vaulted       vaulted
              Kit
             11-5x
42'-0"        12-0
                    R    vaulted
             P
   Garage
  29-4x21-4                Dining         Br 3        Br 2
             W            11-0x11-6      11-1x13-3   11-0x12-9
             D
                          Porch
                         27-8x5-0
```

Plan Features

- Vaulted dining and great rooms are immersed in light from the atrium window wall
- Breakfast room opens onto the covered porch
- 1,604 square feet on the first floor and 117 square feet on the lower level atrium
- 3 bedrooms, 2 baths, 3-car garage
- Walk-out basement foundation, drawings also include crawl space and slab foundations

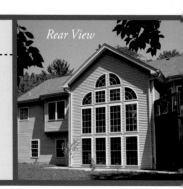

Rear View

Total Living Area: 1,525 sq. ft.

DID YOU KNOW?

Mulch comes in a variety of forms and is a great material for holding moisture in the soil and reducing weed infestations. Over time mulch can lose color making it somewhat less desirable in decorative planting areas. Aged pine bark mulch holds a great, uniform brown color for an entire season. Straight compost, which is black, will do the same. Light-colored mulch, such as cedar and hemlock, loses its color quickly.

Plan Features

- The kitchen is enhanced with an open bar that connects the great room
- A corner gas fireplace warms the entire living area
- The master suite features a whirlpool tub flanked by walk-in closets
- 3 bedrooms, 2 baths, 2-car garage
- Slab, crawl space, basement or walk-out basement foundation, please specify when ordering

Total Living Area: 1,345 sq. ft.

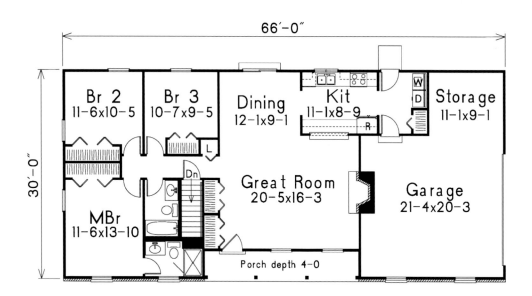

Plan Features

- Brick front details add a touch of elegance
- Master bedroom has a private full bath
- Great room combines with the dining area creating a sense of spaciousness
- Garage includes a handy storage area which could easily convert to a workshop space
- 3 bedrooms, 2 baths, 2-car side entry garage
- Basement foundation, drawings also include crawl space and slab foundations

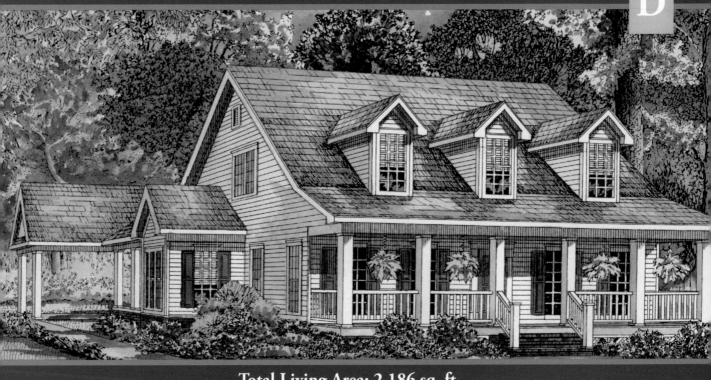

Total Living Area: 2,186 sq. ft.

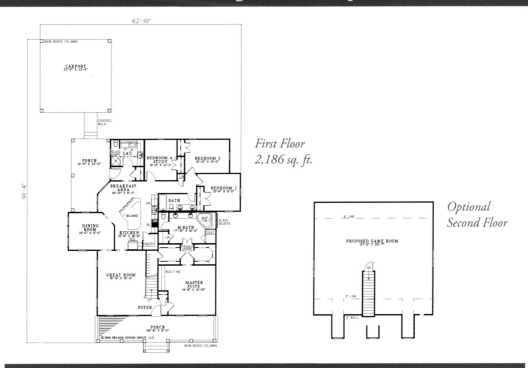

*First Floor
2,186 sq. ft.*

*Optional
Second Floor*

Plan Features

- A covered walkway leads from the carport to the rear of the home
- Plenty of dining space is provided with the breakfast room, formal dining room and extra-large island
- The optional second floor has an additional 1,283 square feet of living space
- 3 bedrooms, 4 baths, 2-car carport
- Crawl space, slab, basement or walk-out basement foundation, please specify when ordering

Total Living Area: 2,826 sq. ft.

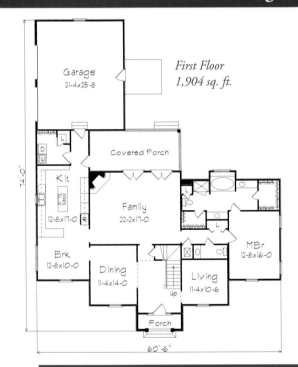

First Floor
1,904 sq. ft.

Second Floor
922 sq. ft.

Plan Features

- 9' ceilings throughout
- Fully appointed master bedroom with luxurious bath
- Second floor bedrooms include private dressing areas and walk-in closets
- Large, well-planned kitchen features a center island
- 4 bedrooms, 3 1/2 baths, 2-car side entry garage
- Slab foundation, drawings also include crawl space foundation

Code: **F**

Total Living Area: 3,118 sq. ft.

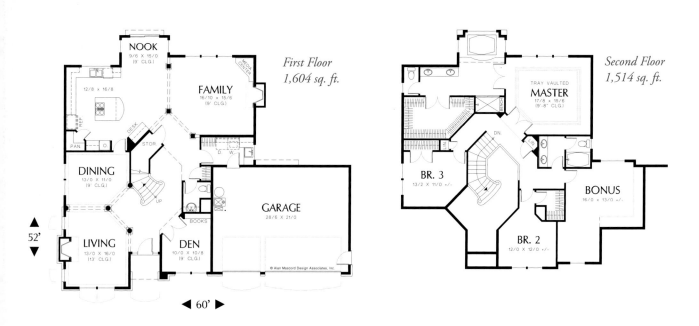

First Floor 1,604 sq. ft.

NOOK
9/6 X 15/0
(9' CLG.)

FAMILY
16/10 x 15/6
(9' CLG.)

12/8 x 16/8

DINING
13/0 X 11/0
(9' CLG.)

LIVING
13/0 X 16/0
(13' CLG.)

DEN
10/0 X 10/8
(9' CLG.)

GARAGE
28/6 X 21/0

© Alan Mascord Design Associates, Inc

52'

60'

Second Floor 1,514 sq. ft.

TRAY VAULTED
MASTER
17/8 x 15/6
(9'-8" CLG.)

BR. 3
13/2 X 11/0 +/-

BR. 2
12/0 X 12/0 +/-

BONUS
16/0 x 13/0 +/-

Plan Features

- Secluded den has a double-door entry and a built-in bookcase perfect for a home office
- Spacious master bedroom has a lovely bath with a whirlpool tub and walk-in closet
- An oversized island in the kitchen has enough room for dining
- Bonus room on the second floor is included in the square footage
- 3 bedrooms, 2 1/2 baths, 3-car garage
- Crawl space foundation

Total Living Area: 2,455 sq. ft.

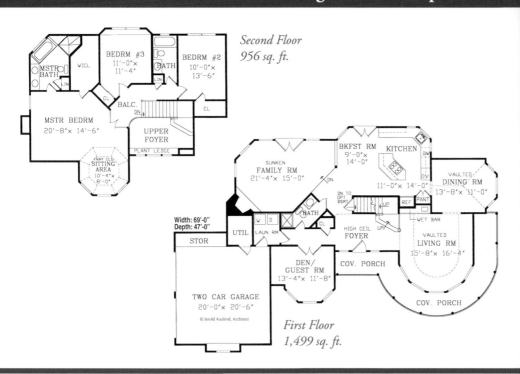

Second Floor
956 sq. ft.

MSTR BATH

WICL

BEDRM #3
11'-0" x
11'-4"

BATH

BEDRM #2
10'-0" x
13'-6"

LIN

LIN

BALC.

CL

CL

MSTR BEDRM
20'-8" x 14'-6"

DN

UPPER FOYER

PLANT LEDGE

BAYED SITTING AREA
10'-4" x 8'-0"

BKFST RM
9'-0" x
14'-0"

KITCHEN

DW

SUNKEN FAMILY RM
21'-4" x 15'-0"

DN

OV

11'-0" x 14'-0"

VAULTED DINING RM
13'-8" x 11'-0"

REF

PANT

DN TO OPT. BSMT

UP

BATH

CL

WET BAR

Width: 69'-0"
Depth: 47'-0"

W D

HIGH CEIL

FOYER

VAULTED LIVING RM
15'-8" x 16'-4"

UTIL

LAUN RM

STOR

DEN/ GUEST RM
13'-4" x 11'-8"

COV. PORCH

TWO CAR GARAGE
20'-0" x 20'-6"

COV. PORCH

© Jerold Axelrod, Architect

First Floor
1,499 sq. ft.

Plan Features

- The foyer is two stories high and opens to the living room
- 13' ceiling in the living room
- Master bedroom includes bayed sitting area ideal for relaxing
- 4 bedrooms, 3 baths, 2-car side entry garage
- Basement, crawl space or slab foundation, please specify when ordering

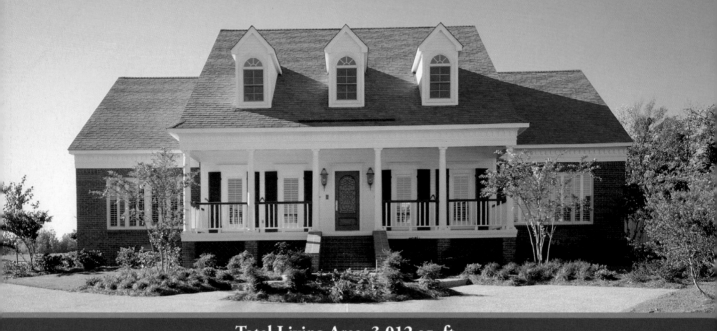

Total Living Area: 3,012 sq. ft.

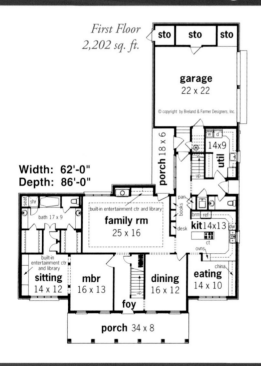

First Floor
2,202 sq. ft.

Width: 62'-0"
Depth: 86'-0"

sto sto sto

garage
22 x 22

© copyright by Breland & Farmer Designers, Inc.

porch 18 x 6

util

14x9

bath 17 x 9

built-in entertainment ctr and library

family rm
25 x 16

kit 14x13

built-in entertainment ctr and library

sitting
14 x 12

mbr
16 x 13

dining
16 x 12

eating
14 x 10

foy

porch 34 x 8

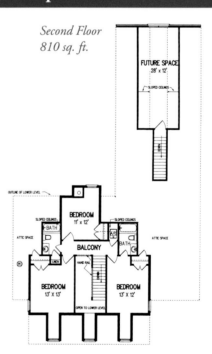

Second Floor
810 sq. ft.

FUTURE SPACE
28' x 12'

SLOPED CEILINGS

OUTLINE OF LOWER LEVEL

BEDROOM
11' x 12'

SLOPED CEILINGS

BATH

ATTIC SPACE

SLOPED CEILINGS

BATH

ATTIC SPACE

BALCONY

LINEN

HAND RAIL

BEDROOM
13' x 13'

OPEN TO LOWER LEVEL

BEDROOM
13' x 12'

Plan Features

- Master bedroom has a sitting area with an entertainment center/library
- Utility room has a sink and includes lots of storage and counterspace
- Future space above garage has an additional 336 square feet of living area
- 4 bedrooms, 3 1/2 baths, 2-car side entry garage
- Crawl space foundation, drawings also include slab and basement foundations

Total Living Area: 2,567 sq. ft.

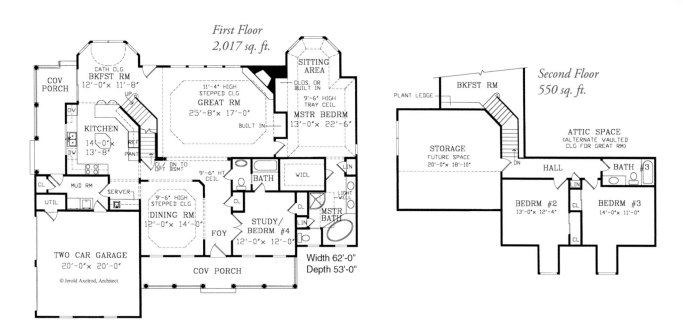

First Floor
2,017 sq. ft.

COV PORCH

CATH CLG
BKFST RM
12'-0" x 11'-8"

11'-4" HIGH
STEPPED CLG
GREAT RM
25'-8" x 17'-0"

BUILT IN

SITTING AREA

CLOS. OR BUILT IN

9'-6" HIGH
TRAY CEIL
MSTR BEDRM
13'-0" x 22'-6"

KITCHEN
14'-0" x 13'-8"

REF
PANT

CL/ DN TO
OPT BSMT

9'-6" HT CEIL

BATH

WICL

LIN

CL

MUD RM

SERVER

UTIL

CL

9'-6" HIGH
STEPPED CLG
DINING RM
12'-0" x 14'-0"

FOY

STUDY/
BEDRM #4
12'-0" x 12'-0"

CL

LIN

LIGHT WELL

LIGHT WELL

MSTR BATH

TWO CAR GARAGE
20'-0" x 20'-0"

© Jerold Axelrod, Architect

COV PORCH

Width 62'-0"
Depth 53'-0"

Second Floor
550 sq. ft.

PLANT LEDGE

BKFST RM

STORAGE
FUTURE SPACE
20'-0" x 18'-10"

ATTIC SPACE
(ALTERNATE VAULTED
CLG FOR GREAT RM)

DN

HALL

BATH #3

LIN

BEDRM #2
13'-0" x 12'-4"

CL

BEDRM #3
14'-0" x 11'-0"

CL

Plan Features

- Breakfast room has a 12' cathedral ceiling and a bayed area full of windows
- Great room has a stepped ceiling, built-in media center and a corner fireplace
- Bonus room on the second floor has an additional 300 square feet of living area
- 4 bedrooms, 3 baths, 2-car side entry garage
- Basement, crawl space or slab foundation, please specify when ordering

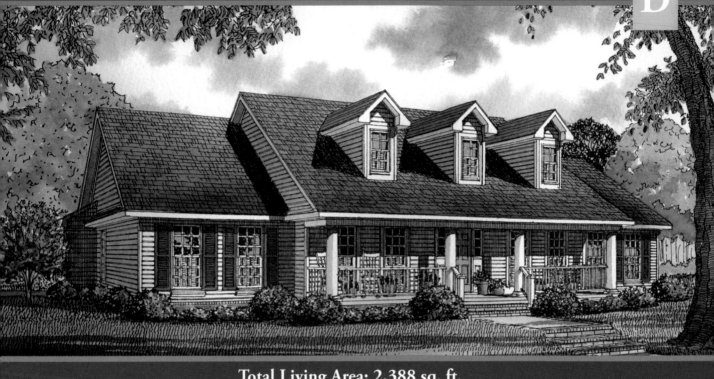

Total Living Area: 2,388 sq. ft.

DID YOU KNOW?

For a good sense of feng shui, don't place all of your furniture against the walls, which accentuates the straight lines of a room and creates a boxy feel. Try arranging your furniture at 45-degree angles to the walls along with a rug for a fresh look.

Plan Features

- The foyer opens into the great room which features a gas fireplace, media center and access to the rear porch
- Formal dining room, breakfast room with access to the porch and kitchen counter with seating provide plenty of dining space
- The master suite enjoys two walk-in closets, a deluxe bath and a whirlpool tub
- 4 bedrooms, 2 1/2 baths, 2-car side entry garage
- Slab or crawl space foundation, please specify when ordering

Total Living Area: 3,850 sq. ft.

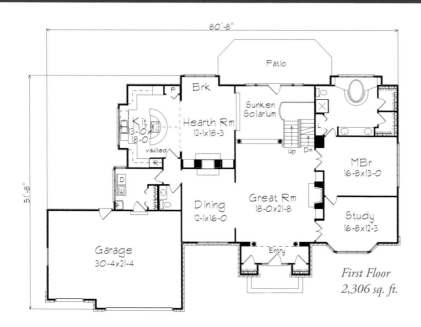

80'-8"

51'-8"

Patio

Brk

Kit
13-10x
18-0
vaulted

Hearth Rm
12-1x18-3

Sunken
Solarium

Dining
12-1x16-0

Great Rm
18-0x21-8

MBr
16-8x13-0

Study
16-8x12-3

Garage
30-4x21-4

Entry

*First Floor
2,306 sq. ft.*

Br 5
12-1x14-3

Sunken
Solarium
Below

Br 2
13-11x15-9

Loft

Br 4
12-1x12-0

Library
15-8x9-8

Br 3
15-5x12-0

open to below

*Second Floor
1,544 sq. ft.*

Plan Features

- Entry, with balcony above, leads into a splendid great room with sunken solarium
- Kitchen layout boasts a half-circle bar and cooktop island with banquet-sized area
- Solarium features U-shaped stairs with balcony and an arched window
- Master bedroom includes a luxurious bath and large study with bay window
- 5 bedrooms, 3 1/2 baths, 3-car garage
- Basement foundation

Interior View

Total Living Area: 2,135 sq. ft.

First Floor
1,050 sq. ft.

Second Floor
1,085 sq. ft.

Plan Features

- All bedrooms on second floor for privacy
- 9' ceilings on the first floor
- Energy efficient home with 2"x 6" exterior walls
- 4 bedrooms, 2 1/2 baths, 2-car side entry garage
- Basement foundation

Total Living Area: 2,460 sq. ft.

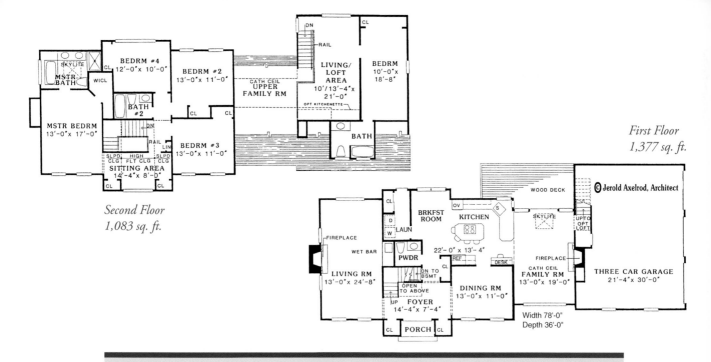

Second Floor
1,083 sq. ft.

First Floor
1,377 sq. ft.

© Jerold Axelrod, Architect

Width 78'-0"
Depth 36'-0"

Plan Features

- Living room has windows on three sides
- Kitchen contains island cooktop and built-in desk
- Enjoy a fireplace and a skylight in the spacious family room
- Bonus room on the second floor has an additional 597 square feet of living area
- 4 bedrooms, 2 1/2 baths, 3-car side entry garage
- Basement, crawl space or slab foundation, please specify when ordering

Total Living Area: 1,428 sq. ft.

First Floor
1,013 sq. ft.

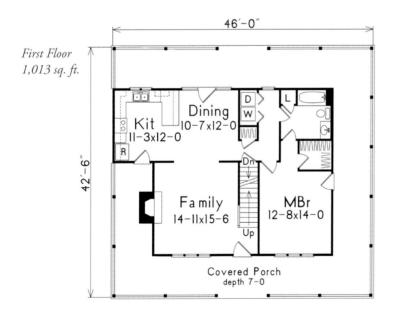

46'-0"

42'-6"

Kit
11-3x12-0

Dining
10-7x12-0

D
W

L

Family
14-11x15-6

Dn

Up

MBr
12-8x14-0

Covered Porch
depth 7-0

Second Floor
415 sq. ft.

Loft/
Br 3
10-7x11-11

L

Open To Below

Dn

Br 2
12-8x10-0

Plan Features

- Large vaulted family room opens to dining area and kitchen with breakfast bar
- First floor master bedroom offers large bath, walk-in closet and nearby laundry facilities
- A spacious loft/bedroom #3 overlooking the family room and an additional bedroom and bath complement the second floor
- 3 bedrooms, 2 baths
- Basement foundation

Total Living Area: 2,287 sq. ft.

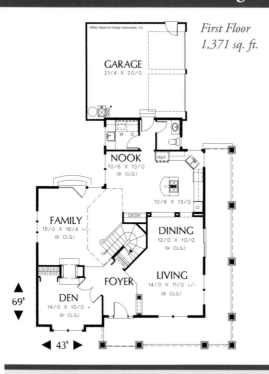

First Floor
1,371 sq. ft.

Second Floor
916 sq. ft.

Plan Features

- Wrap-around porch creates an inviting feeling
- First floor windows have transom windows above
- Den has see-through fireplace into the family area
- 3 bedrooms, 2 1/2 baths, 2-car side entry garage
- Crawl space foundation

Plan #583-041D-0006

Price Code:

AA

Total Living Area: 1,189 sq. ft.

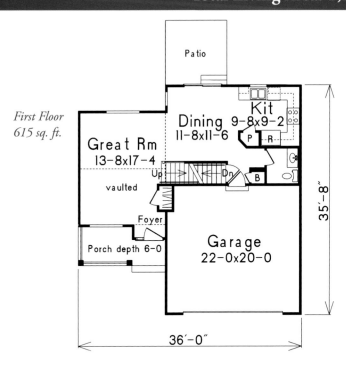

First Floor
615 sq. ft.

Patio

Kit
9-8x9-2

Dining
11-8x11-6

P   R

Great Rm
13-8x17-4

vaulted

Up   Dn   B

Foyer

Porch depth 6-0

Garage
22-0x20-0

35'-8"

36'-0"

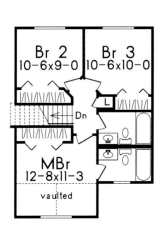

Second Floor
574 sq. ft.

Br 2
10-6x9-0

Br 3
10-6x10-0

L

Dn

MBr
12-8x11-3

vaulted

Plan Features

- All bedrooms are located on the second floor
- Dining room and kitchen both have views of the patio
- Convenient half bath is located near the kitchen
- Master bedroom has a private bath
- 3 bedrooms, 2 1/2 baths, 2-car garage
- Basement foundation

Total Living Area: 1,768 sq. ft.

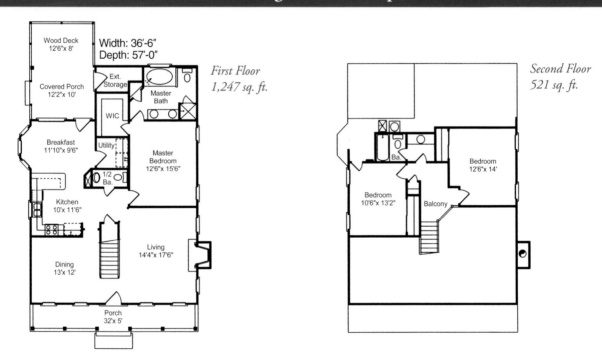

Width: 36'-6"
Depth: 57'-0"

First Floor
1,247 sq. ft.

Second Floor
521 sq. ft.

Plan Features

- Upon entering you will get a feeling of spaciousness with the two-story living and dining rooms
- The bayed breakfast area is a refreshing place to start the day
- The covered porch off the breakfast area extends the dining to the outdoors
- 3 bedrooms, 2 1/2 baths
- Slab or crawl space foundation, please specify when ordering

D

Total Living Area: 2,403 sq. ft.

First Floor
1,710 sq. ft.

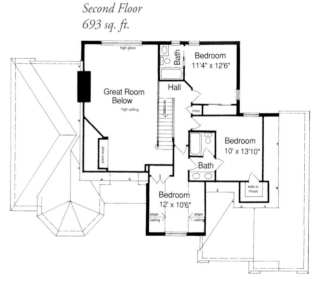

Second Floor
693 sq. ft.

Plan Features

- The master bedroom has a 9' ceiling that raises to 11' in the octagon-shaped sitting area
- Kitchen is enhanced by a bar area, center island and extra-large pantry
- Multiple windows in the breakfast area create a cheerful environment
- 4 bedrooms, 3 1/2 baths, 2-car side entry garage
- Basement or slab foundation, please specify when ordering

Total Living Area: 1,783 sq. ft.

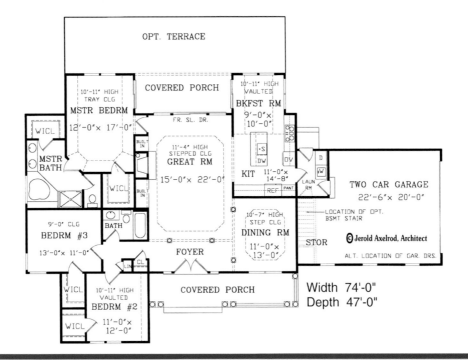

OPT. TERRACE

COVERED PORCH

10'-11" HIGH TRAY CLG

MSTR BEDRM
12'-0" x 17'-0"

WICL

MSTR BATH

10'-11" HIGH VAULTED
BKFST RM
9'-0" x 10'-0"

FR. SL. DR.

BUILT IN

11'-4" HIGH STEPPED CLG
GREAT RM
15'-0" x 22'-0"

WICL

BUILT IN

KIT 11'-0" x 14'-8"

DW

DV

REF

PANT

LAUN RM

D

W

TWO CAR GARAGE
22'-6" x 20'-0"

LOCATION OF OPT. BSMT STAIR

© Jerold Axelrod, Architect

ALT. LOCATION OF GAR. DRS.

9'-0" CLG
BEDRM #3
13'-0" x 11'-0"

BATH

10'-7" HIGH STEP CLG
DINING RM
11'-0" x 13'-0"

STOR

FOYER

LIN CL

WICL

10'-11" HIGH VAULTED
BEDRM #2
11'-0" x 12'-0"

WICL

COVERED PORCH

Width 74'-0"
Depth 47'-0"

Plan Features

- The flow of the great room, with built-ins on one side is a furnishing delight
- Bedrooms are all quietly zoned on one side
- The master bedroom is separated for privacy
- Every bedroom features a walk-in closet
- 3 bedrooms, 2 baths, 2-car side entry garage
- Basement, crawl space or slab foundation, please specify when ordering

Total Living Area: 3,689 sq. ft.

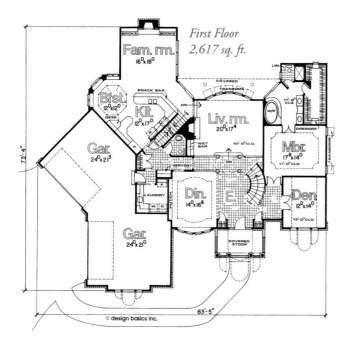

First Floor
2,617 sq. ft.

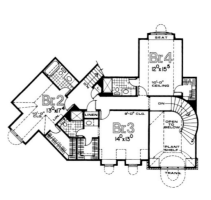

Second Floor
1,072 sq. ft.

© design basics inc.

Plan Features

- The formal living room creates an elegant entertaining space with a 10' ceiling, large bay window, fireplace and wet bar
- A serving station outside the formal dining room provides convenience
- The kitchen, breakfast and family rooms combine for a relaxing, open living space
- 4 bedrooms, 3 1/2 baths, 3-car side entry garage
- Basement foundation

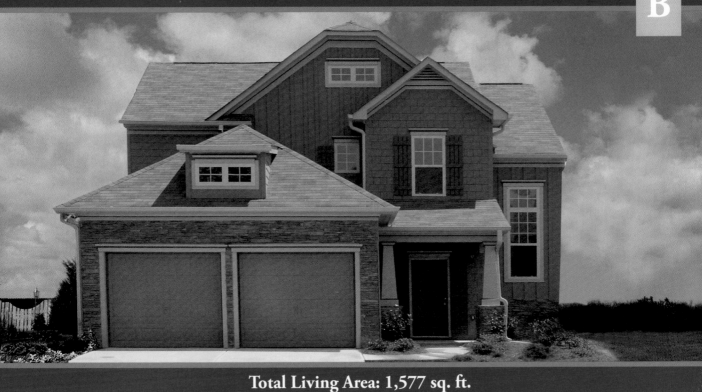

Total Living Area: 1,577 sq. ft.

First Floor 737 sq. ft.

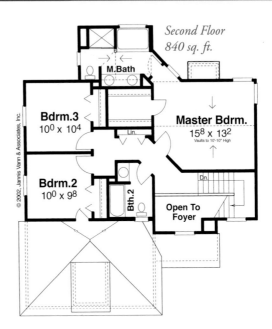

Second Floor 840 sq. ft.

Plan Features

- A well-organized kitchen has a conveniently located laundry room and work desk
- A bright and cheerful living room has lots of windows and a cozy fireplace
- Vaulted master bedroom has a walk-in closet as well as a private bath
- 3 bedrooms, 2 1/2 baths, 2-car garage
- Basement or slab foundation, please specify when ordering

Total Living Area: 2,571 sq. ft.

First Floor
1,658 sq. ft.

Second Floor
913 sq. ft.

GARAGE
21'-0"x27'-0"
(9'-6" CLG)

STORAGE

COVERED PORCH
26'-10"x10'-6"

MSTR BATH
(9' CLG)

W.I.C.

STORAGE

WORK BENCH

NOOK

KITCHEN
13'-0"x11'-8"
(9' CLG)

GREAT ROOM
22'-3"x16'-0"
(9' CLG)

MASTER BEDROOM
14'-0"x19'-0"
(10' TRAY CLG)

LNDRY

PWDR

FORMAL DINING
13'-0"x13'-0"
(9' CLG)

FOYER
(9' CLG)

OFFICE/GUEST/
BEDROOM #5
10'-8"x10'-1"
(9' CLG)

FRENCH DOORS

OPTIONAL DOORS

COVERED PORCH
41'-6"x8'-0"

STEPS

63'-0"

BEDROOM #3
11'-0"x11'-2"
(8' CLG)

BATH

BEDROOM #2
12'-2"x11'-2"
(8' CLG)

BEDROOM #4
13'-0"x12'-6"
(8' CLG)

REC. ROOM
19'-11"x12'-6"
(VAULTED)

SITTING AREA
(VAULTED)

Plan Features

- 9' ceilings throughout the first floor
- Room off foyer adds versatility and can serve as a home office, guest room or fifth bedroom
- Elegant French doors lead from the kitchen into the formal dining area
- 4 bedrooms, 2 1/2 baths, 2-car side entry garage
- Basement, crawl space or slab foundation, please specify when ordering

Total Living Area: 2,243 sq. ft.

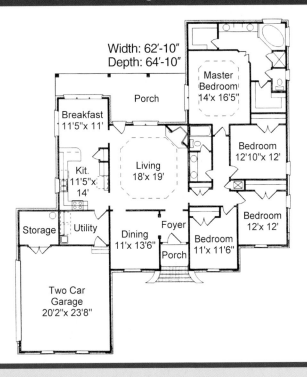

Width: 62'-10"
Depth: 64'-10"

Master Bedroom
14' x 16'5"

Porch

Breakfast
11'5" x 11'

Bedroom
12'10" x 12'

Kit.
11'5" x 14'

Living
18' x 19'

Storage   Utility

Dining
11' x 13'6"

Foyer

Bedroom
11' x 11'6"

Bedroom
12' x 12'

Porch

Two Car Garage
20'2" x 23'8"

Plan Features

- The formal dining room and spacious living room create an elegant first impression upon entering the home
- The master bedroom is a lavish retreat, yet easily accesses all secondary bedrooms
- A convenient storage area is located in the garage
- 4 bedrooms, 2 baths, 2-car side entry garage
- Slab or crawl space foundation, please specify when ordering

Total Living Area: 1,896 sq. ft.

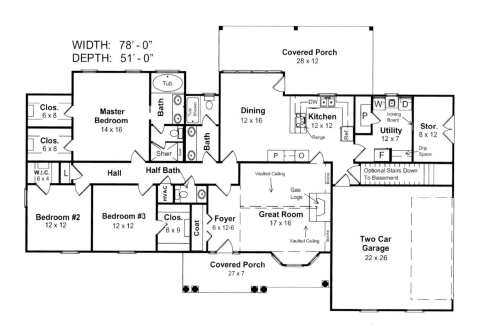

WIDTH: 78' - 0"
DEPTH: 51' - 0"

Plan Features

- The vaulted great room features a grand fireplace flanked by built-in bookshelves
- U-shaped kitchen opens to the dining area which enjoys access onto the covered porch
- The large utility room includes a sink and walk-in pantry
- Plenty of storage throughout with a walk-in closet in each bedroom
- 3 bedrooms, 2 1/2 baths, 2-car side entry garage
- Basement, crawl space or slab foundation, please specify when ordering

Total Living Area: 3,000 sq. ft.

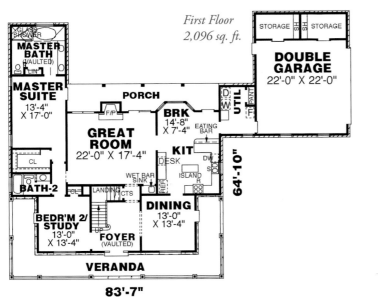

First Floor
2,096 sq. ft.

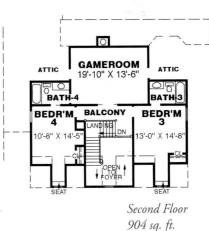

Second Floor
904 sq. ft.

Plan Features

- Sliding pocket doors on the second floor lead to a spacious gameroom
- First floor master suite has direct access onto the porch, a vaulted private bath and walk-in closet
- Secondary bedrooms each have private baths and unique window seats
- 4 bedrooms, 4 baths, 2-car side entry garage
- Basement or slab foundation, please specify when ordering

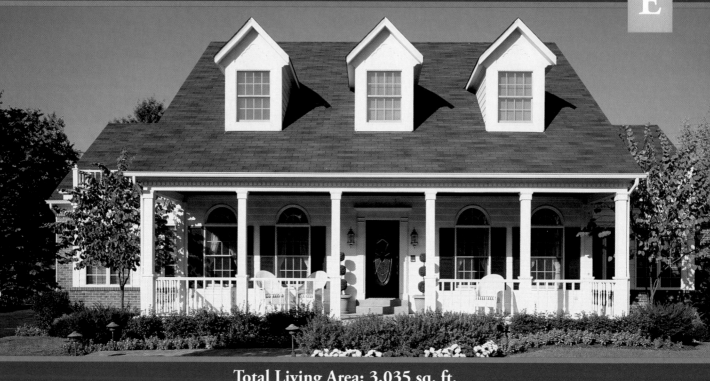

Total Living Area: 3,035 sq. ft.

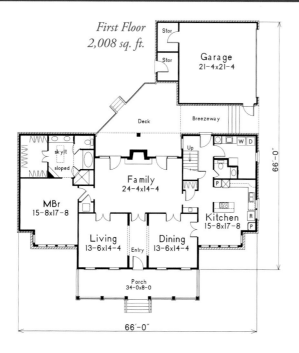

First Floor
2,008 sq. ft.

Stor
Stor

Garage
21-4x21-4

Deck

Breezeway

Up
W D

skylt
sloped

Family
24-4x14-4

MBr
15-8x17-8

Kitchen
15-8x17-8

Living
13-6x14-4

Dining
13-6x14-4

Entry

Porch
34-0x8-0

66'-0"

66'-0"

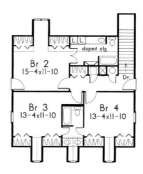

Second Floor
1,027 sq. ft.

sloped clg

Br 2
15-4x11-10

Dn

Br 3
13-4x11-10

Br 4
13-4x11-10

Plan Features

- Front facade includes large porch
- Master bedroom has a windowed sitting area, walk-in closet, sloped ceiling and skylight
- Formal living and dining rooms adjoin the family room through attractive French doors
- Energy efficient home with 2"x 6" exterior walls
- 4 bedrooms, 3 1/2 baths, 2-car detached side entry garage
- Crawl space foundation, drawings also include slab and basement foundations

A

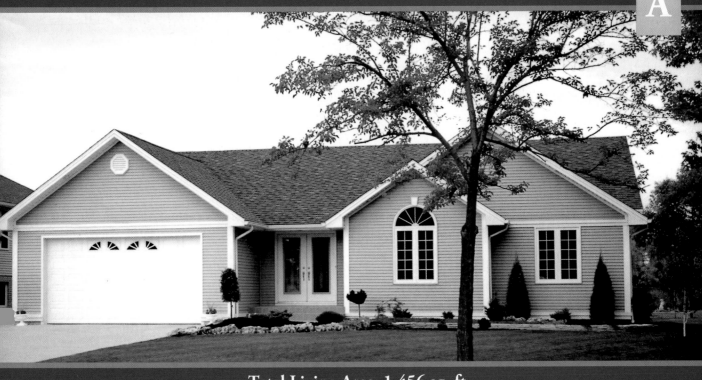

Total Living Area: 1,456 sq. ft.

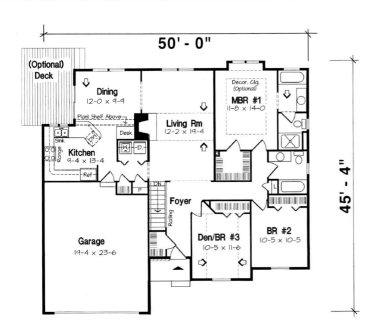

50' - 0"

45' - 4"

(Optional) Deck

Dining
12-0 x 9-9

Decor. Clg. (Optional)

MBR #1
11-8 x 14-0

Plant Shelf Above

Living Rm
12-2 x 19-4

Desk

Kitchen
9-4 x 13-4

Sink

Range

Ref.

P

DN

Foyer

Railing

Garage
19-4 x 23-6

Den/BR #3
10-5 x 11-6

BR #2
10-5 x 10-5

DID YOU KNOW?

Café curtains are short curtains hung from a rod suspended halfway across a window, as in some French cafés. This sort of curtaining is sometimes hung in a double tier and is a useful treatment for windows that open inward or face directly onto a street since the tier system allows privacy with a minimal loss of light.

Plan Features

- Energy efficient home with 2"x 6" exterior walls
- Master bath is compartmentalized with shower and toilet separated from sink and tub
- Convenient desk located near dining area and kitchen
- 3 bedrooms, 2 baths, 2-car garage
- Slab, basement or crawl space foundation, please specify when ordering

Rear View

Total Living Area: 1,833 sq. ft.

First Floor
1,288 sq. ft.

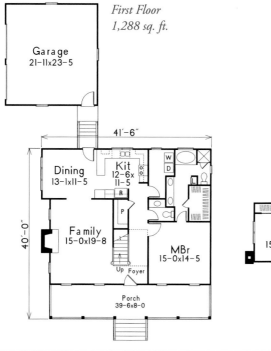

Garage
21-11x23-5

41'-6"

40'-0"

Dining
13-1x11-5

Kit
12-6x
11-5

W
D

Family
15-0x19-8

MBr
15-0x14-5

Up Foyer

Porch
39-6x8-0

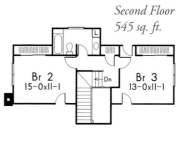

Second Floor
545 sq. ft.

Br 2
15-0x11-1

Dn

Br 3
13-0x11-1

Plan Features

- Large master bedroom includes a spacious bath with garden tub, separate shower and large walk-in closet
- The spacious kitchen and dining area are brightened by large windows and patio access
- Detached two-car garage with walkway leading to house adds charm to this home
- 3 bedrooms, 2 1/2 baths, 2-car detached side entry garage
- Crawl space foundation, drawings also include slab foundation

Total Living Area: 1,359 sq. ft.

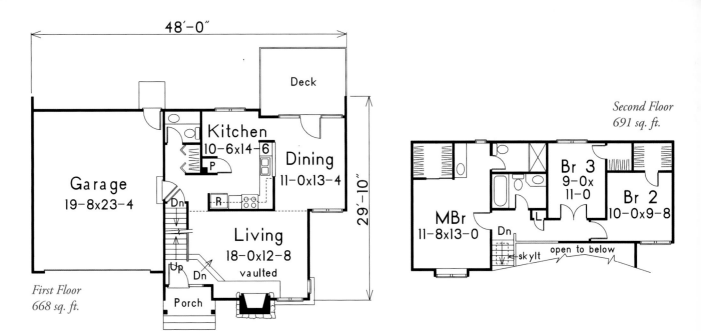

Second Floor
691 sq. ft.

First Floor
668 sq. ft.

Plan Features

- Covered porch, stone chimney and abundant windows lend an outdoor appeal
- Spacious and bright kitchen has pass-through to formal dining room
- Large walk-in closets in all bedrooms
- Extensive deck expands dining and entertaining areas
- 3 bedrooms, 2 1/2 baths, 2-car garage
- Basement foundation

Total Living Area: 2,243 sq. ft.

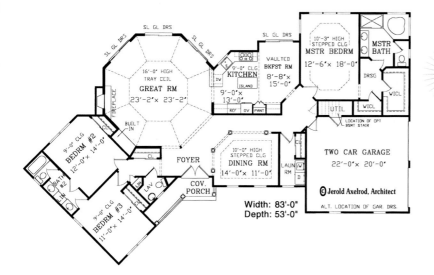

Width: 83'-0"
Depth: 53'-0"

© Jerold Axelrod, Architect

ALT. LOCATION OF GAR. DRS.

DID YOU KNOW?

To distress wooden furniture, first paint it a light color. When dry, rub a candle on areas where natural wear might occur, such as panel edges. Paint with a deeper color. When dry, rub the waxed areas with steel wool to expose patches of the base coat.

Plan Features

- An angled floor plan allows for flexible placement on any lot
- Great room has a 16' high tray ceiling, a fireplace and an entertainment center
- The luxurious master bedroom is separated for privacy
- The secondary bedrooms are in a private wing and share a common bath
- 3 bedrooms, 2 1/2 baths, 2-car side entry garage
- Basement, crawl space or slab foundation, please specify when ordering

Total Living Area: 2,521 sq. ft.

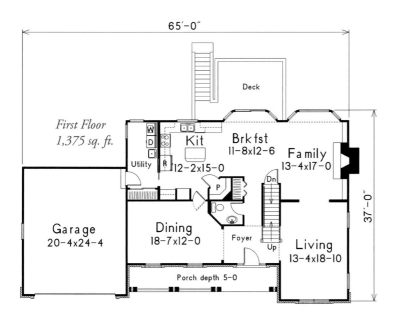

First Floor
1,375 sq. ft.

65'-0"

Deck

W
D

Kit

Utility

Brk fst
11-8x12-6

Family
13-4x17-0

Garage
20-4x24-4

Dining
18-7x12-0

Foyer

Living
13-4x18-10

Dn

Up

P

37'-0"

Porch depth 5-0

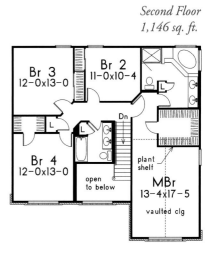

Second Floor
1,146 sq. ft.

Br 3
12-0x13-0

Br 2
11-0x10-4

Br 4
12-0x13-0

Dn

open
to below

plant
shelf

MBr
13-4x17-5

vaulted clg

Plan Features

- Large living and dining rooms are perfect for formal entertaining or large family gatherings
- Informal kitchen, breakfast and family rooms feature a 37' vista and double bay windows
- Generously sized master bedroom and three secondary bedrooms grace the second floor
- 4 bedrooms, 2 1/2 baths, 2-car garage
- Basement foundation

Total Living Area: 3,765 sq. ft.

First Floor
2,804 sq. ft.

Second Floor
961 sq. ft.

Rear View

Plan Features

- Ascending the grand staircase, French doors access the elevated den complete with bookcases and a bay window
- The kitchen adjoins the bayed breakfast area and sunroom with a raised hearth fireplace
- The lavish master bedroom features a double-door entry, sitting area and deluxe bath with access onto a private covered deck
- 4 bedrooms, 3 1/2 baths, 3-car side entry garage
- Basement foundation

Total Living Area: 2,262 sq. ft.

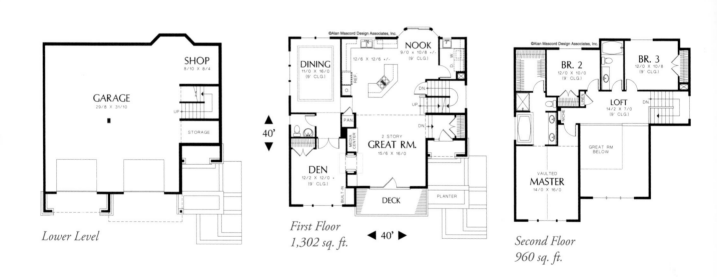

Lower Level

First Floor
1,302 sq. ft.

Second Floor
960 sq. ft.

Plan Features

- All bedrooms are located on the second floor for privacy
- Formal dining room is cheerful and sunny with two walls of windows
- Great room has access to a deck
- 3 bedrooms, 2 1/2 baths, 2-car drive under garage
- Basement foundation

Total Living Area: 1,556 sq. ft.

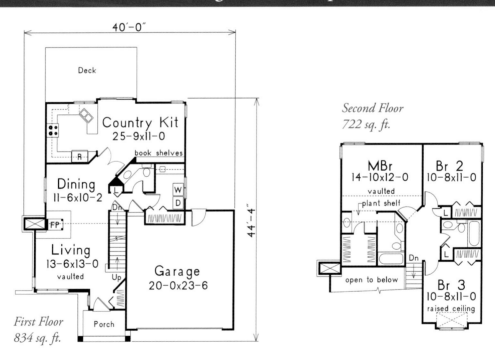

Second Floor
722 sq. ft.

First Floor
834 sq. ft.

Plan Features

- A compact home with all the amenities
- Kitchen combines practicality with access to other areas for eating and entertaining
- Two-way fireplace joins the dining and living areas
- Plant shelf and vaulted ceiling highlight the master bedroom
- 3 bedrooms, 2 1/2 baths, 2-car garage
- Basement foundation

Total Living Area: 1,532 sq. ft.

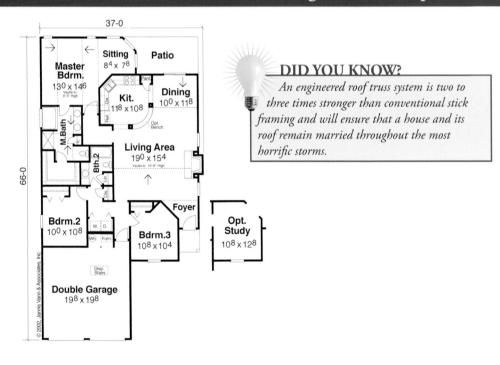

DID YOU KNOW?

An engineered roof truss system is two to three times stronger than conventional stick framing and will ensure that a house and its roof remain married throughout the most horrific storms.

Plan Features

- Master bedroom features a private bath with walk-in closet and a sunny sitting area
- Bedroom #3 can easily be converted to a study with an entrance near the foyer
- The kitchen design includes an option for a curved bench creating more space for dining if needed
- 3 bedrooms, 2 baths, 2-car garage
- Basement or slab foundation, please specify when ordering

Total Living Area: 2,397 sq. ft.

Optional Lower Level

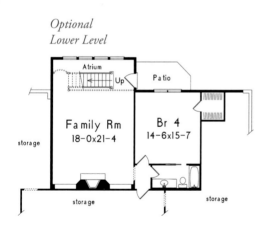

Atrium

Up

Patio

Family Rm
18-0x21-4

Br 4
14-6x15-7

storage

storage

storage

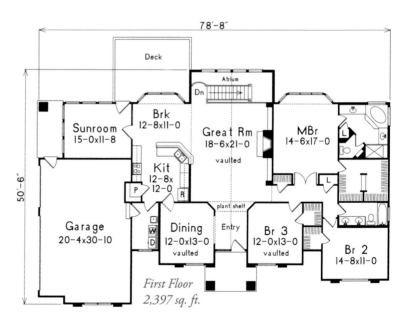

78'-8"

Deck

50'-6"

Atrium

Dn

Brk
12-8x11-0

Sunroom
15-0x11-8

Great Rm
18-6x21-0
vaulted

MBr
14-6x17-0

Kit
12-8x
12-0

Garage
20-4x30-10

P

R

L

L

plant shelf

Dining
12-0x13-0
vaulted

Entry

Br 3
12-0x13-0
vaulted

Br 2
14-8x11-0

W
D

First Floor
2,397 sq. ft.

Plan Features

- The great room enjoys a 12' vaulted ceiling, atrium featuring 2 1/2 story windows and fireplace with flanking bookshelves
- A conveniently located sunroom and side porch adjoin the breakfast room and garage
- 898 square feet of optional living area on the lower level
- 3 bedrooms, 2 baths, 3-car side entry garage
- Walk-out basement foundation

Total Living Area: 2,310 sq. ft.

First Floor
1,236 sq. ft.

Second Floor
1,074 sq. ft.

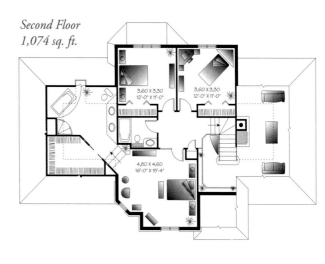

Plan Features

- Snack bar in kitchen provides eat-in dining
- Cathedral ceiling in the living room adds spaciousness
- Energy efficient home with 2"x 6" exterior walls
- 3 bedrooms, 2 1/2 baths, 2-car garage
- Basement foundation

Total Living Area: 1,650 sq. ft.

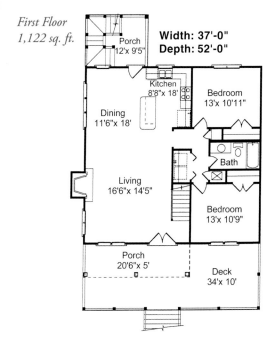

First Floor
1,122 sq. ft.

Width: 37'-0"
Depth: 52'-0"

Porch
12'x 9'5"

Kitchen
8'8"x 18'

Dining
11'6"x 18'

Bedroom
13'x 10'11"

Living
16'6"x 14'5"

Bath

Bedroom
13'x 10'9"

Porch
20'6"x 5'

Deck
34'x 10'

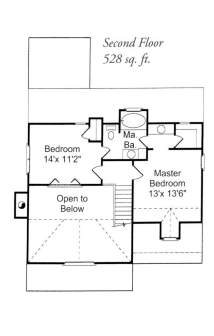

Second Floor
528 sq. ft.

Bedroom
14'x 11'2"

Ma.
Ba.

Master
Bedroom
13'x 13'6"

Open to
Below

Plan Features

- Master bedroom is located on the second floor for privacy
- Open living area connects to the dining area
- Two-story living area features lots of windows and a large fireplace
- Efficiently designed kitchen
- 4 bedrooms, 2 baths
- Pier foundation

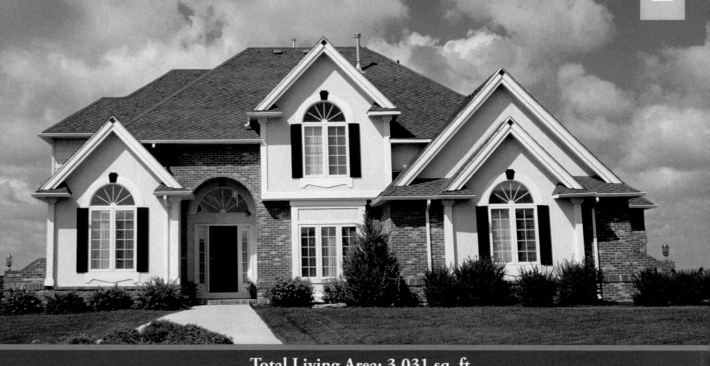

Total Living Area: 3,031 sq. ft.

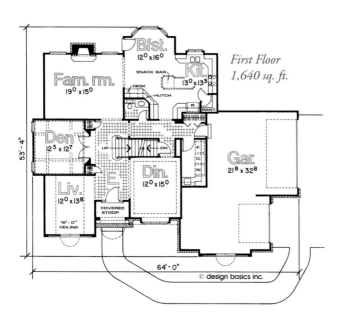

First Floor
1,640 sq. ft.

Fam. rm.
19⁰ x 15⁰

Bfst.
12⁰ x 16⁰

Kit.
13⁰ x 13³

SNACK BAR

DESK

HUTCH

PANT.

Den
12³ x 12⁷

Gar.
21⁸ x 32⁸

Liv.
12⁰ x 13⁸

12'-0" CEILING

Din.
12⁰ x 15⁰

COVERED STOOP

53'-4"

64'-0"

© design basics inc.

Second Floor
1,391 sq. ft.

Mbr.
17⁰ x 15¹⁰
10'-0" CEILING

BUILT-IN DRESSER

Br. 4
12⁰ x 13⁵

W/P

GLASS BLOCK

LIN.

LINEN

OPEN TO BELOW

Br. 2
13⁰ x 12⁰

Br. 3
12⁰ x 13⁰
10'-0" CEILING

17'-10" CEILING

DN

Plan Features

- Living and dining rooms flank the entry and are ideal for formal or cozy gatherings
- Superb family room with fireplace adjoins kitchen and bayed breakfast area
- Luxurious master bedroom features a French door entry, built-in dressers in a walk-in closet, double vanities and a whirlpool tub
- 4 bedrooms, 2 1/2 baths, 3-car side entry garage
- Basement foundation

Rear View

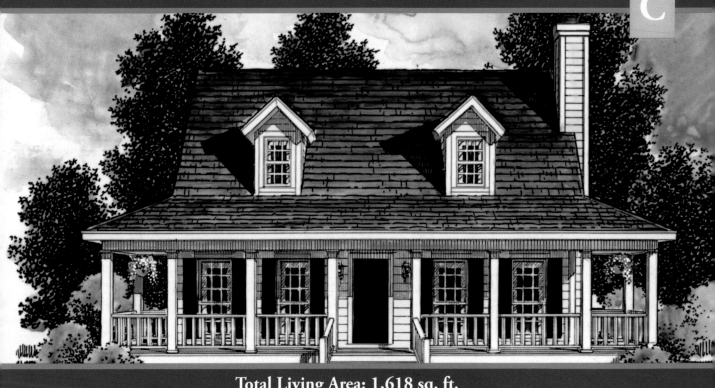

Total Living Area: 1,618 sq. ft.

First Floor
1,046 sq. ft.

Second Floor
572 sq. ft.

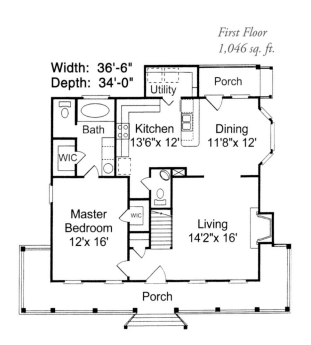

Width: 36'-6"
Depth: 34'-0"

Porch

Utility

Bath

Kitchen
13'6"x 12'

Dining
11'8"x 12'

WIC

Master
Bedroom
12'x 16'

WIC

Living
14'2"x 16'

Porch

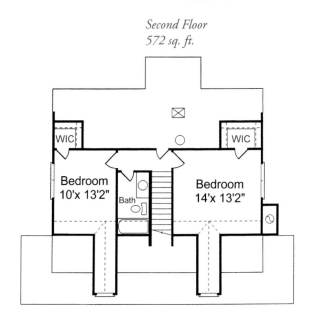

WIC

WIC

Bedroom
10'x 13'2"

Bath

Bedroom
14'x 13'2"

Plan Features

- Secondary bedrooms with walk-in closets are located on the second floor and share a bath
- Utility room is tucked away in the kitchen for convenience but is out of sight
- Dining area is brightened by a large bay window
- 3 bedrooms, 2 1/2 baths
- Slab or crawl space foundation, please specify when ordering

Total Living Area: 2,115 sq. ft.

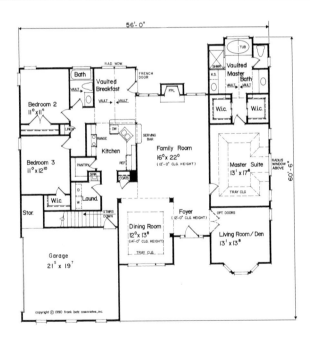

DID YOU KNOW?

Annual flowers germinate, grow and die within one year. Most produce a large number of flowers in one season, resulting in lots of seeds that help guarantee new plants the following year. Flowering quickly, they are ideal for impatient gardeners eager to experiment with color, texture and form.

Plan Features

- Cozy living room/den has a double-door entry and makes an ideal office space
- Kitchen has a serving bar which overlooks the vaulted breakfast area and family room
- Master suite has all the amenities
- 3 bedrooms, 2 baths, 2-car side entry garage
- Walk-out basement, crawl space or slab foundation, please specify when ordering

Total Living Area: 1,735 sq. ft.

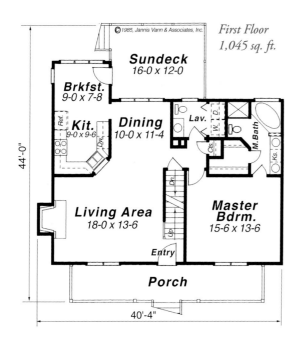

© 1985, Jannis Vann & Associates, Inc.

First Floor
1,045 sq. ft.

Sundeck
16-0 x 12-0

Brkfst.
9-0 x 7-8

Kit.
9-0 x 9-6

Ref.

Dining
10-0 x 11-4

Lav.

W. D.

Cls.

M.Bath

Ks.

Living Area
18-0 x 13-6

Master Bdrm.
15-6 x 13-6

Entry

Porch

44'-0"

40'-4"

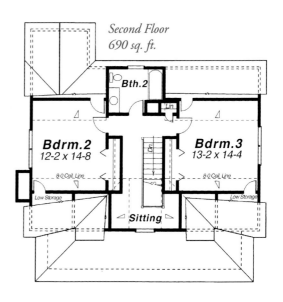

Second Floor
690 sq. ft.

Bth.2

Lin.

Bdrm.2
12-2 x 14-8

Bdrm.3
13-2 x 14-4

8-0 Ceil. Line

8-0 Ceil. Line

Low Storage

Low Storage

Sitting

Plan Features

- Angled kitchen wall expands space into the dining room
- Second floor has a cozy sitting area with cheerful window
- Two spacious bedrooms on the second floor share a bath
- 3 bedrooms, 2 1/2 baths, 2-car drive under garage
- Basement foundation

Total Living Area: 2,356 sq. ft.

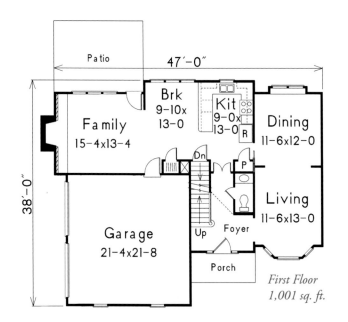

Patio

47'-0"

38'-0"

Brk
9-10x
13-0

Kit
9-0x
13-0

R

Dining
11-6x12-0

Family
15-4x13-4

Dn

P

Living
11-6x13-0

Up

Foyer

Garage
21-4x21-8

Porch

First Floor
1,001 sq. ft.

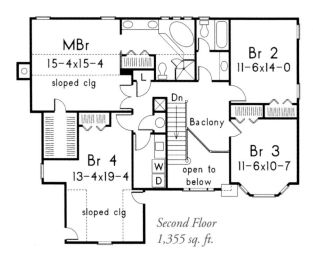

MBr
15-4x15-4
sloped clg

L

Br 2
11-6x14-0

Dn

Baclony

Br 4
13-4x19-4

W D

open to below

Br 3
11-6x10-7

sloped clg

Second Floor
1,355 sq. ft.

Plan Features

- Impressive arched and mullioned window treatment embellishes the entrance and foyer
- Bedroom #4 is located over the side entry garage
- A full-size laundry facility is located on the second floor for convenience
- Adjoining family room, breakfast area and kitchen form an extensive living area
- 4 bedrooms, 2 1/2 baths, 2-car side entry garage
- Basement foundation

C

Total Living Area: 2,089 sq. ft.

First Floor
1,441 sq. ft.

Second Floor
648 sq. ft.

Plan Features

- The living and dining rooms combine and open to the kitchen and breakfast nook
- The second floor boasts a unique study area and large bonus room
- A large utility room, walk-in pantry and half bath are conveniently located off the garage
- Second floor bonus room has an additional 270 square feet of living area
- 3 bedrooms, 2 1/2 baths, 2-car garage
- Slab or crawl space foundation, please specify when ordering

Price Code:

C

Total Living Area: 1,845 sq. ft.

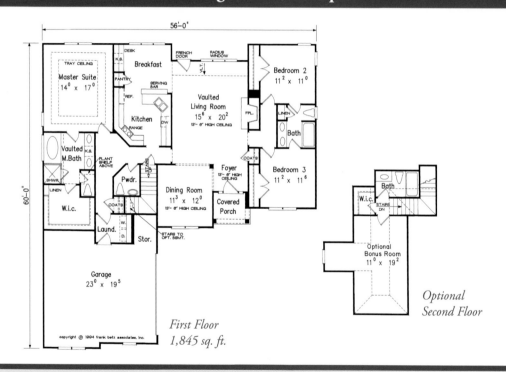

First Floor
1,845 sq. ft.

Optional Second Floor

Plan Features

- Vaulted living room has a cozy fireplace
- Breakfast area and kitchen are lovely gathering places
- Dining room overlooks the living room
- Optional second floor with bath has an additional 354 square feet of living area
- 3 bedrooms, 2 1/2 baths, 2-car side entry garage
- Walk-out basement or crawl space foundation, please specify when ordering

---

Total Living Area: 2,101 sq. ft.

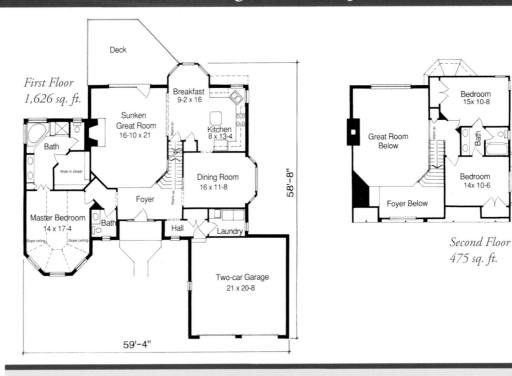

First Floor 1,626 sq. ft.

Deck

Breakfast
9-2 x 16

Sunken
Great Room
16-10 x 21

Kitchen
8 x 13-4

Bath

Walk-in closet

Dining Room
16 x 11-8

Foyer

Master Bedroom
14 x 17-4

Slope ceiling   Slope ceiling

Bath

Hall

Laundry

Two-car Garage
21 x 20-8

58'-8"

59'-4"

Second Floor 475 sq. ft.

Bedroom
15x 10-8

Great Room
Below

Bath

Bedroom
14x 10-6

Foyer Below

Plan Features

- Sunken great room has balcony above
- Octagon-shaped master bedroom is private
- Luxurious amenities in a modest size
- 3 bedrooms, 2 1/2 baths, 2-car garage
- Basement foundation

Total Living Area: 2,773 sq. ft.

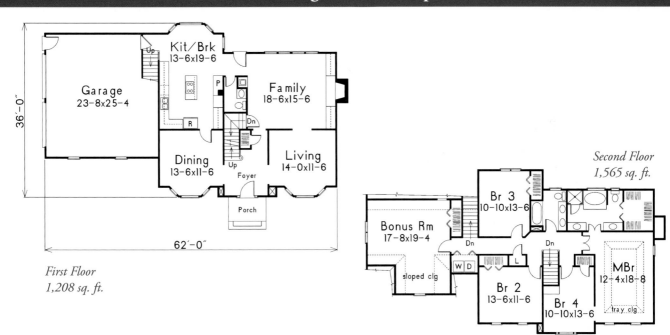

First Floor
1,208 sq. ft.

Second Floor
1,565 sq. ft.

Plan Features

- Extensive use of bay and other large windows front and rear adds brightness and space
- Master bedroom features double-door entrance, oversized walk-in closet and tray ceiling
- Rear stairway leads to both the bonus room, which is included in the square footage, and to the laundry area on the second floor
- 4 bedrooms, 2 1/2 baths, 2-car side entry garage
- Basement foundation

Total Living Area: 2,041 sq. ft.

Plan Features

- Great room accesses directly onto the covered rear deck with ceiling fan above
- Private master bedroom has a beautiful octagon-shaped sitting area that opens and brightens the space
- Two secondary bedrooms share a full bath
- 3 bedrooms, 2 baths, 2-car side entry garage
- Walk-out basement foundation

Total Living Area: 4,139 sq. ft.

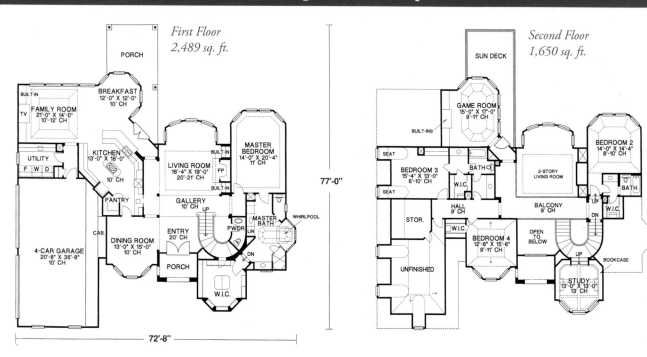

First Floor
2,489 sq. ft.

PORCH

BUILT-IN

FAMILY ROOM
21'-0" X 14'-0"
10'-12' CH

TV

BREAKFAST
12'-0" X 12'-0"
10' CH

UTILITY

F W D

KITCHEN
13'-0" X 18'-0"
10' CH

PANTRY

CAB.

4-CAR GARAGE
20'-8" X 36'-8"
10' CH

DINING ROOM
13'-0" X 15'-0"
10' CH

LIVING ROOM
16'-4" X 19'-0"
20'-21' CH

BUILT-IN

BUILT-IN

GALLERY
10' CH

UP

ENTRY
20' CH

PWDR

DN

LIN

MASTER BEDROOM
14'-0" X 20'-4"
11' CH

FP

MASTER BATH

WHIRLPOOL

PORCH

W.I.C.

72'-8"

77'-0"

Second Floor
1,650 sq. ft.

SUN DECK

GAME ROOM
15'-0" X 17'-0"
9'-11' CH

BUILT-INS

SEAT

SEAT

BEDROOM 3
15'-4" X 13'-0"
6'-10' CH

BATH

W.I.C.

HALL
9' CH

STOR.

W.I.C.

UNFINISHED

BEDROOM 4
12'-8" X 15'-6"
9'-11' CH

2-STORY LIVING ROOM

BALCONY
9' CH

OPEN TO BELOW

BEDROOM 2
14'-0" X 14'-4"
8'-10' CH

BATH

UP

W.I.C.

DN

UP

BOOKCASE

STUDY
13'-0" X 13'-0"
13' CH

Plan Features

- Second floor game room features an abundance of windows
- Elegant mid-level study enjoys built-in bookcases and a bay window
- The connecting kitchen, breakfast and family rooms offer an easy flow
- Master bedroom boasts a bay window, whirlpool tub and an extra-large walk-in closet
- 4 bedrooms, 3 1/2 baths, 4-car side entry garage
- Slab foundation

Rear View

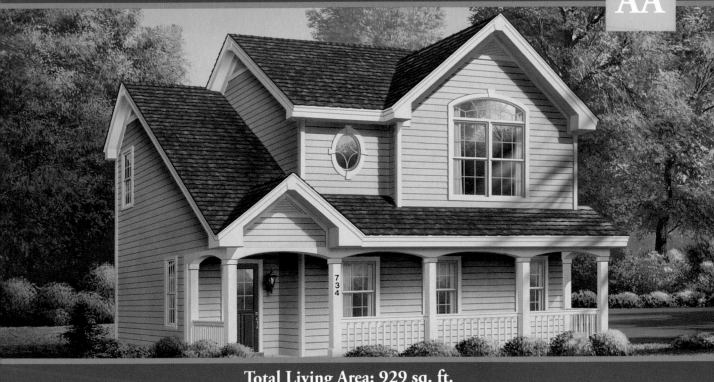

Total Living Area: 929 sq. ft.

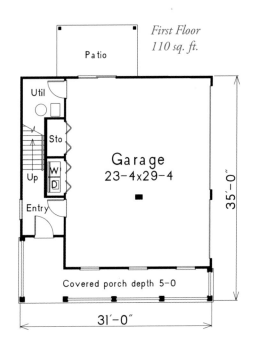

First Floor
110 sq. ft.

Patio

Util

Sto

W D

Up

Entry

Garage
23-4x29-4

35'-0"

Covered porch depth 5-0

31'-0"

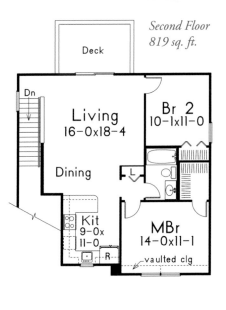

Second Floor
819 sq. ft.

Deck

Dn

Living
16-0x18-4

Br 2
10-1x11-0

Dining

L

Kit
9-0x
11-0

R

MBr
14-0x11-1

vaulted clg

Plan Features

- Living room with dining area has access to 8' x 12' deck through glass sliding doors
- U-shaped kitchen features a breakfast bar, oval window above sink and cabinet storage
- Master bedroom enjoys a walk-in closet and large elliptical feature window
- Laundry, storage closet and mechanical space are located off the first floor garage
- 2 bedrooms, 1 bath, 3-car side entry garage
- Slab foundation

Total Living Area: 2,624 sq. ft.

First Floor
2,624 sq. ft.

Optional
Second Floor

Plan Features

- Bedroom #2 is secluded and includes a private bath making it ideal for a guest suite
- The master suite features a 10' ceiling, porch access and a deluxe bath with two vanities and an extra-large walk-in closet
- The optional second floor has an additional 561 square feet of living space
- 4 bedrooms, 3 baths, 2-car side entry garage
- Slab or crawl space foundation, please specify when ordering

Total Living Area: 3,292 sq. ft.

Walk-In Closet

Bedroom
11'6"x 17'

Bath

Porch
19'x 6'

Breakfast
14'8"x 12'8"

Living
19'x 22'

Kitchen
12'5"x 13'

Master Bedroom
15'x 16'

Bedroom
13'x 11'

Bath

Foyer
9'8"x 8'6"

Dining
15'x 11'6"

1/2 Ba

Utility

Walk-In Closet

Bedroom
14'6"x 11'

Porch
9'8"x 5'8"

Office
8'11"x 10'7"

Master Bath

Walk-In Closet

Walk-In Closet

Width: 71'-4"
Depth: 74'-0"

Two-Car Garage
24'x 22'5"

First Floor
2,862 sq. ft.

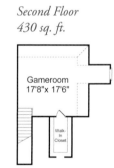

Second Floor
430 sq. ft.

Gameroom
17'8"x 17'6"

Walk-In Closet

Plan Features

- 10' ceilings throughout the first floor add to the spaciousness of this home
- The well-designed kitchen has lots of counterspace, an eating bar and a door to the rear porch from the breakfast area
- The office is perfect for a home business or a place for family members to retreat to for quiet time
- 4 bedrooms, 3 1/2 baths, 2-car side entry garage
- Slab foundation

Total Living Area: 2,560 sq. ft.

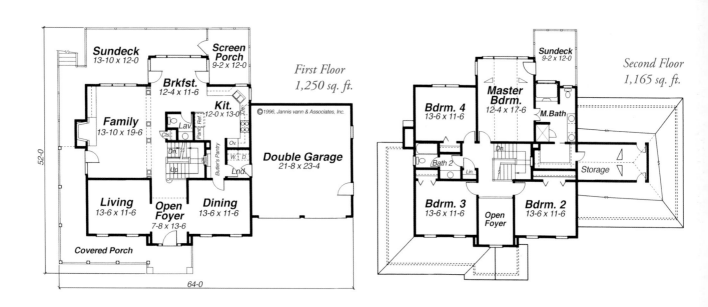

First Floor
1,250 sq. ft.

Sundeck
13-10 x 12-0

Screen Porch
9-2 x 12-0

Brkfst.
12-4 x 11-6

Kit.
12-0 x 13-0

© 1996, Jannis vann & Associates, Inc.

Family
13-10 x 19-6

Lav.

Pant. Ref.

Butler's Pantry

Ov.

W b

Dn

Up

Lnd.

Double Garage
21-8 x 23-4

52-0

Living
13-6 x 11-6

Open Foyer
7-8 x 13-6

Dining
13-6 x 11-6

Covered Porch

64-0

Second Floor
1,165 sq. ft.

Sundeck
9-2 x 12-0

Master Bdrm.
12-4 x 17-6

M.Bath

Bdrm. 4
13-6 x 11-6

Dn

Bath 2

Lin.

Storage

Bdrm. 3
13-6 x 11-6

Open Foyer

Bdrm. 2
13-6 x 11-6

Plan Features

- Large family room has fireplace, built-in cabinet and access to porch and sundeck
- Master bedroom with wonderful view accesses the second floor sundeck
- Breakfast area has windows on all exterior walls and access to the porch and screen porch
- 144 square feet on the lower level
- 4 bedrooms, 2 1/2 baths, 2-car garage
- Walk-out basement foundation

Total Living Area: 1,401 sq. ft.

Lower Level
52 sq. ft.

First Floor
1,349 sq. ft.

Plan Features

- Split-foyer design is ideal for family living
- Vaulted master suite and bath are all luxury
- Decorative plant shelf accents vaulted family room
- 3 bedrooms, 2 baths, 2-car drive under garage
- Walk-out basement foundation

Total Living Area: 2,850 sq. ft.

First Floor
1,464 sq. ft.

NOOK
10/0 X 11/4
(9' CLG)

©Alan Mascord Design Associates, Inc.

BR. 4
13/0 X 11/0
(9' CLG.)

9/6 X 13/10
(9' CLG.)

GREAT RM
19/0 X 15/0
2 STORY

12/10 X 11/0 +/-

NICHE

PAN

DESK

UP

STOR

GARAGE
21/0 X 19/6

DINING
11/0 X 13/2
(9' CLG.)

FOYER
(9' CLG)

BUILT-INS

DEN
10/5 X 13/3
(9' CLG.)

ALT GARAGE DR LOCATION

51'-6"

59'

Second Floor
1,386 sq. ft.

SPA

MASTER
19/2 X 13/0 +

OPEN TO
BELOW

©Alan Mascord Design Associates, Inc.

BONUS
11/0 X 23/0 +

DN.

LINEN

BR. 3
11/0 X 12/0

(8' CLG.)

BR. 2
13/0 X 10/0
(10' CLG.)

Plan Features

- A wrap-around porch surrounds the home on one side creating an outdoor living area
- A double-door entry leads to the master bedroom which features a private bath with spa
- Extra space in the garage allows for storage or work area
- Bonus room is included in the second floor square footage
- 3 bedrooms, 3 baths, 2-car side entry garage
- Crawl space foundation

Total Living Area: 1,856 sq. ft.

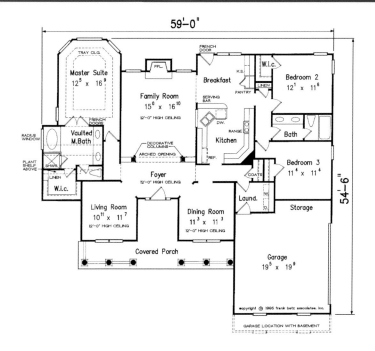

DID YOU KNOW?

Cedar is a light, reddish-brown, rather soft wood used from about 1750 for drawer linings, boxes, chests (inside and out), and wardrobes. It was and still is much valued for its moth and insect repelling qualities.

Plan Features

- Beautiful covered porch creates a Southern accent
- Kitchen has an organized feel with lots of cabinetry
- Large foyer has a grand entrance and leads into the family room through columns and an arched opening
- 3 bedrooms, 2 baths, 2-car side entry garage
- Walk-out basement, crawl space or slab foundation, please specify when ordering

Total Living Area: 1,292 sq. ft.

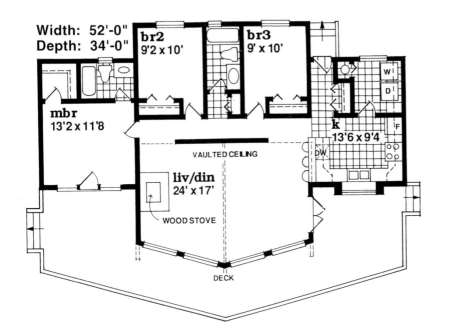

Width: 52'-0"
Depth: 34'-0"

br2 9'2 x 10'

br3 9' x 10'

mbr 13'2 x 11'8

k 13'6 x 9'4

VAULTED CEILING

liv/din 24' x 17'

WOOD STOVE

DECK

DID YOU KNOW?

Termites are the most destructive wood-destroying pest in the nation. At least 1% of housing in the United States each year requires treatment. Most termite species swarm in late summer or fall. The best way to determine is to look for evidence of tunneling in the wood. In most cases, it is best to hire a professional pest control company to carry out a routine regimen and keep the pests under control.

Plan Features

- Master bedroom features a walk-in closet, private bath and access to the outdoors onto an expansive deck
- Prominent woodstove enhances the vaulted living/dining area
- Kitchen has a convenient snack counter
- 3 bedrooms, 2 baths
- Crawl space foundation

Total Living Area: 3,421 sq. ft.

Optional
Lower Level

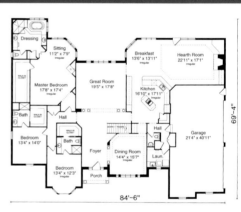

First Floor
3,421 sq. ft.

Plan Features

- The gourmet kitchen with island and snack bar combine with the spacious breakfast and hearth rooms to create a warm and friendly atmosphere
- The luxurious master bedroom has a sitting area, fireplace and deluxe bath
- The optional lower level has an additional 1,777 square feet of living area
- 3 bedrooms, 3 1/2 baths, 4-car side entry garage
- Basement foundation

Total Living Area: 1,880 sq. ft.

First Floor
1,244 sq. ft.

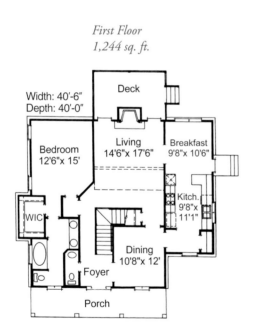

Width: 40'-6"
Depth: 40'-0"

Deck

Bedroom
12'6"x 15'

Living
14'6"x 17'6"

Breakfast
9'8"x 10'6"

WIC

Kitch.
9'8"x 11'1"

Foyer

Dining
10'8"x 12'

Porch

Open to Below

Bedroom
12'6"x 11"

Balcony

Bedroom
10'6"x 10'9"

Second Floor
636 sq. ft.

Plan Features

- The large front porch is a perfect spot to sit back and relax
- The first floor bedroom includes a private bath with double-bowl vanity and a walk-in closet, creating an ideal master suite
- The secondary bedrooms enjoy walk-in closets and share a Jack and Jill bath
- 3 bedrooms, 2 1/2 baths
- Crawl space foundation

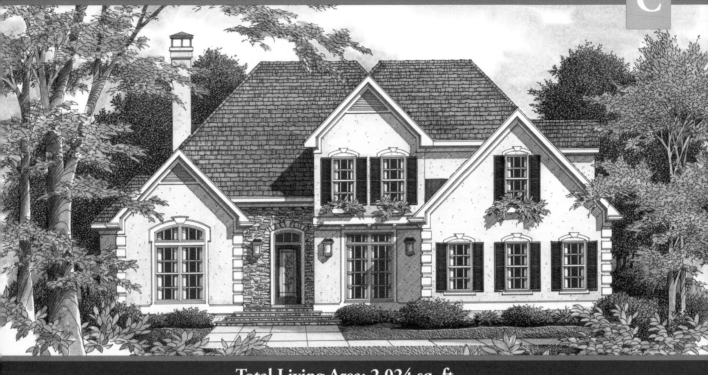

Total Living Area: 2,024 sq. ft.

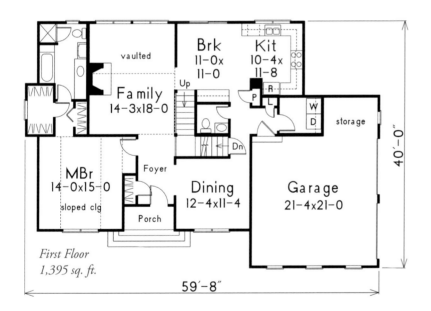

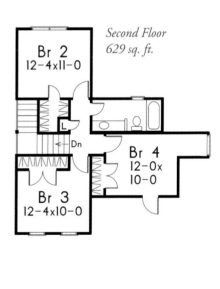

Second Floor 629 sq. ft.

First Floor 1,395 sq. ft.

Plan Features

- Impressive fireplace and sloped ceiling in the family room
- Master bedroom features a vaulted ceiling, separate dressing room and a walk-in closet
- Breakfast area includes a work desk and accesses the deck
- 4 bedrooms, 2 1/2 baths, 2-car side entry garage
- Basement foundation

Total Living Area: 1,749 sq. ft.

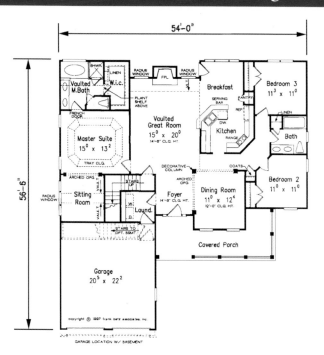

DID YOU KNOW?

Painting over mildew doesn't mean it's gone - the sturdy spores are quite capable of growing right through paint film. Shady spots outdoors are particularly susceptible to this fungal pest, which will root itself into a porous surface once the right temperature and enough moisture is available. To kill mildew, wash it with a mixture of 1 part household bleach to 3 parts water. Then rinse the area thoroughly.

Plan Features

- Tray ceiling in master suite
- A breakfast bar overlooks the vaulted great room
- Additional bedrooms are located away from the master suite for privacy
- Optional bonus room above the garage has an additional 308 square feet of living area
- 3 bedrooms, 2 baths, 2-car garage
- Slab, crawl space or walk-out basement foundation, please specify when ordering

Total Living Area: 2,890 sq. ft.

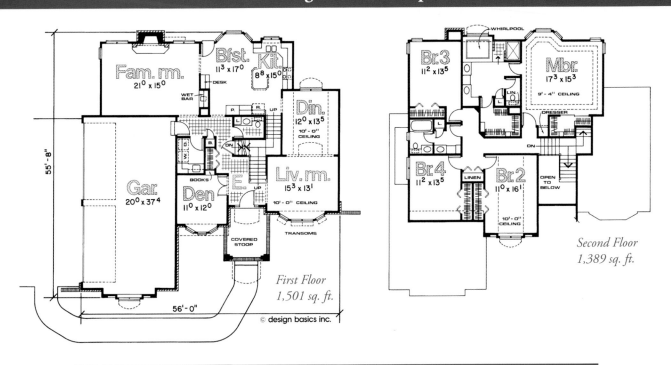

First Floor
1,501 sq. ft.

Second Floor
1,389 sq. ft.

© design basics inc.

Plan Features

- Centrally located kitchen serves the breakfast and dining rooms with ease
- The formal living and dining rooms feature 10' ceilings and a large bay window
- The expansive great room is relaxing with a cozy fireplace and wet bar
- 4 bedrooms, 2 1/2 baths, 4-car side entry garage
- Basement foundation

D

Total Living Area: 2,445 sq. ft.

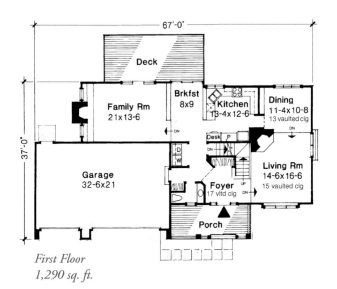

First Floor
1,290 sq. ft.

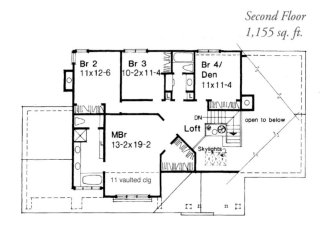

Second Floor
1,155 sq. ft.

Plan Features

- A dramatic, skylighted foyer preludes the formal, sunken living room, which includes a stunning corner fireplace
- A built-in desk and a pantry mark the smartly designed kitchen which opens to the breakfast room and beyond to the family room
- The family room features a fireplace plus French doors that open to a backyard deck
- 4 bedrooms, 2 1/2 baths, 3-car garage
- Basement foundation

A

Total Living Area: 1,318 sq. ft.

Lower Level
60 sq. ft.

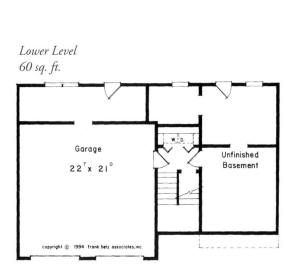

Garage
22⁷ x 21⁰

Unfinished Basement

W./D.

copyright © 1994 frank betz associates,inc.

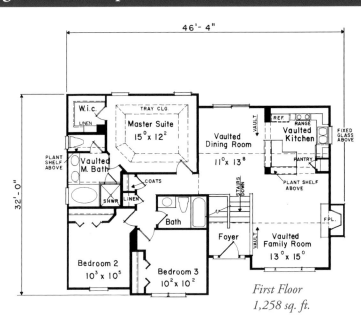

46'- 4"

32'- 0"

W.i.c.

LINEN

PLANT SHELF ABOVE

TRAY CLG

Master Suite
15⁰ x 12²

Vaulted M. Bath

COATS

LINEN

SHWR

VAULT

Vaulted Dining Room
11⁰ x 13⁸

REF.

RANGE

Vaulted Kitchen

FIXED GLASS ABOVE

PANTRY

PLANT SHELF ABOVE

Bath

STAIRS DOWN

Foyer

VAULT

FPL.

Vaulted Family Room
13⁰ x 15⁰

Bedroom 2
10³ x 10⁵

Bedroom 3
10² x 10²

First Floor
1,258 sq. ft.

Plan Features

- Vaulted kitchen, dining and family rooms create an open and dramatic feel
- Luxurious master suite has all the amenities
- Two secondary bedrooms share a hall bath
- 3 bedrooms, 2 baths, 2-car drive under garage
- Walk-out basement foundation

Plan #583-037D-0014

Total Living Area: 2,932 sq. ft.

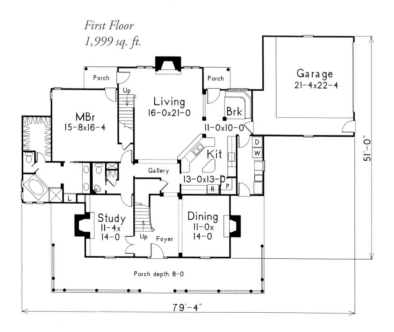

First Floor
1,999 sq. ft.

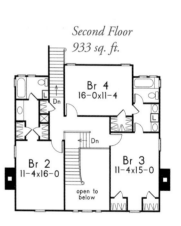

Second Floor
933 sq. ft.

Plan Features

- 9' ceilings throughout home
- Spacious kitchen has pass-through to the family room, a convenient island and pantry
- Cozy built-in table in breakfast area
- Secluded master bedroom has a luxurious bath and patio access
- 4 bedrooms, 3 1/2 baths, 2-car side entry garage
- Slab foundation

Total Living Area: 2,730 sq. ft.

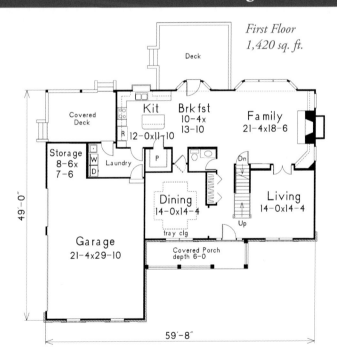

First Floor
1,420 sq. ft.

Deck

Covered Deck

Kit
12-0x11-10

Brk fst
10-4x
13-10

Family
21-4x18-6

Storage
8-6x
7-6

Laundry

P

Dining
14-0x14-4
tray clg

Living
14-0x14-4

Dn

Up

Garage
21-4x29-10

Covered Porch
depth 6-0

49'-0"

59'-8"

Second Floor
1,310 sq. ft.

vaulted clg

Br 4
11-4x11-8

Br 3
14-0x11-8

MBr
14-4x19-1
vaulted clg

Dn

Br 2
14-0x12-0

Rear View

Plan Features

- Spacious kitchen features an island and generous walk-in pantry
- Covered deck offers private retreat to the outdoors
- Large master bedroom has bath with whirlpool corner tub, separate shower and double walk-in closets
- 4 bedrooms, 2 1/2 baths, 3-car side entry garage with storage area
- Basement foundation

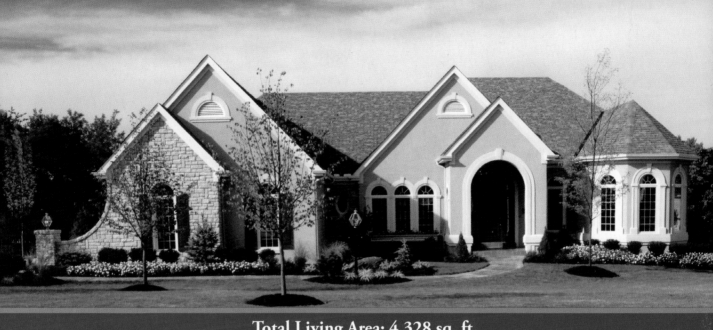

Total Living Area: 4,328 sq. ft.

Lower Level
1,746 sq. ft.

First Floor
2,582 sq. ft.

Plan Features

- The extra-large gourmet kitchen and breakfast room offer a spacious area and provide a striking view through the great room to the fireplace wall
- For convenience a butler's pantry is located in the hall leading to the dining room
- Lower level includes a media room, billiard room, exercise room and two bedrooms
- 3 bedrooms, 3 1/2 baths, 3-car side entry garage
- Basement foundation

Total Living Area: 2,826 sq. ft.

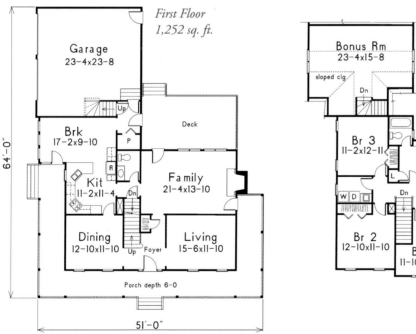

First Floor
1,252 sq. ft.

Garage
23-4x23-8

Brk
17-2x9-10

Deck

Kit
11-2x11-4

Family
21-4x13-10

Dining
12-10x11-10

Living
15-6x11-10

Foyer

Porch depth 6-0

64'-0"

51'-0"

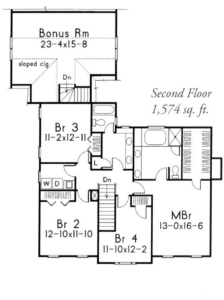

Bonus Rm
23-4x15-8

sloped clg.

Second Floor
1,574 sq. ft.

Br 3
11-2x12-11

Br 2
12-10x11-10

Br 4
11-10x12-2

MBr
13-0x16-6

Plan Features

- Wrap-around covered porch is accessible from the family and breakfast rooms in addition to front entrance
- Bonus room, which is included in the square footage, has a separate entrance and is suitable for an office or private accommodations
- Large, full-windowed breakfast room
- 4 bedrooms, 2 1/2 baths, 2-car side entry garage
- Basement foundation

C

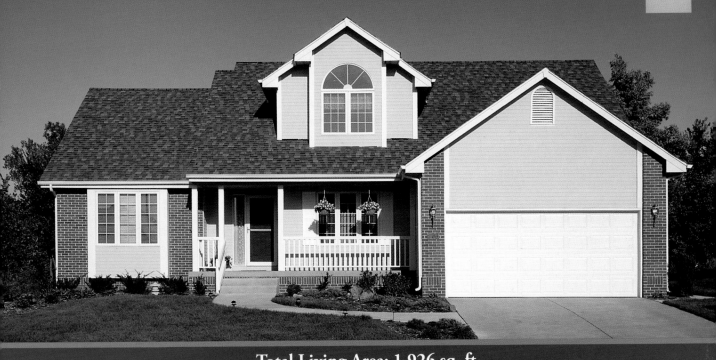

Total Living Area: 1,926 sq. ft.

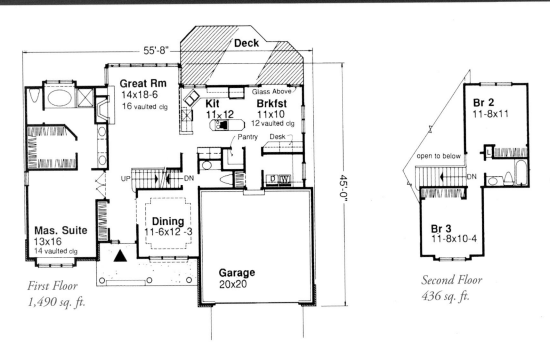

55'-8"

Deck

Great Rm
14x18-6
16 vaulted clg

Glass Above

Kit
11x12

Brkfst
11x10
12 vaulted clg

Pantry

Desk

UP

DN

45'-0"

Br 2
11-8x11

open to below

DN

Mas. Suite
13x16
14 vaulted clg

Dining
11-6x12 -3

D W

Garage
20x20

Br 3
11-8x10-4

First Floor
1,490 sq. ft.

Second Floor
436 sq. ft.

Plan Features

- A breathtaking wall of windows brightens the great room
- A double-door entry leads to the master suite which features a large bath and walk-in closet
- An island cooktop in the kitchen makes mealtime a breeze
- 3 bedrooms, 3 baths, 2-car garage
- Basement foundation

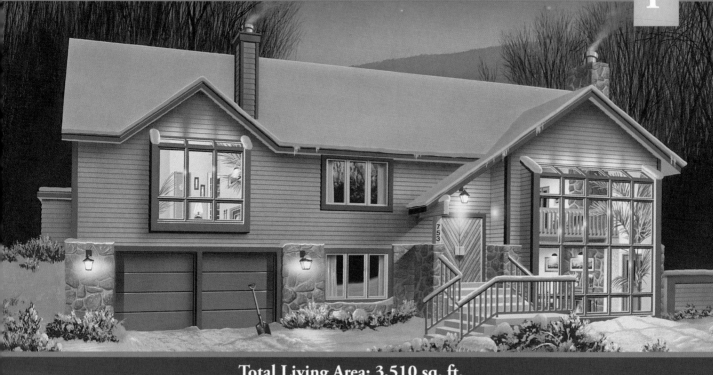

Total Living Area: 3,510 sq. ft.

Lower Level
1,270 sq. ft.

Shop

Mech.

D W

Bar

Pool Rm
18-6x10-8

Garage
23-6x32-2

Br 3
12-0x13-0

Lounge
19-0x14-10

Up

Solarium
19-0x12-3

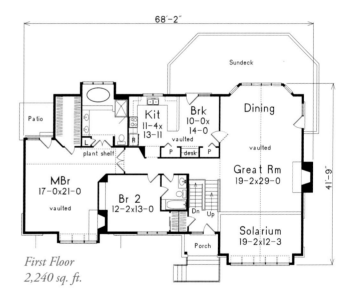

First Floor
2,240 sq. ft.

68'-2"

Sundeck

Patio

Kit
11-4x
13-11
vaulted

Brk
10-0x
14-0
vaulted

Dining

vaulted

plant shelf

P desk P

MBr
17-0x21-0
vaulted

Br 2
12-2x13-0

Great Rm
19-2x29-0

Dn Up

Solarium
19-2x12-3

Porch

41'-9"

Plan Features

- Great room has open solarium with balcony, greenhouse window, bay window, stone fireplace and vaulted ceiling creating a magical ambiance
- Master bedroom boasts a sitting area with fireplace and luxury bath with private courtyard, both featuring greenhouse windows
- 3 bedrooms, 3 baths, 2-car drive under garage
- Walk-out basement foundation

Total Living Area: 3,168 sq. ft.

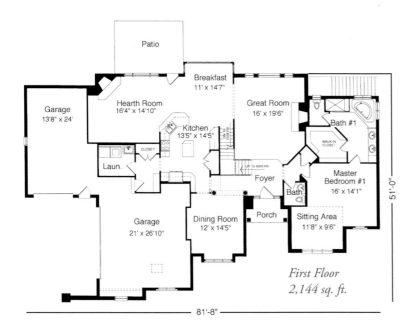

First Floor
2,144 sq. ft.

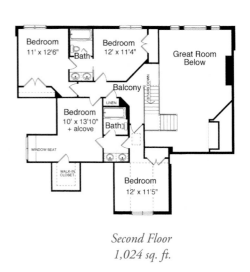

Second Floor
1,024 sq. ft.

Plan Features

- The great room with an 18' ceiling is decorated with a gas fireplace and high windows
- The hearth room, breakfast area and kitchen provide comfortable family living areas
- The master bedroom with sitting area and luxurious bath pamper the homeowner
- The second floor offers a balcony that overlooks the great room
- 5 bedrooms, 3 1/2 baths, 3-car side entry garage
- Basement foundation

Total Living Area: 2,126 sq. ft.

First Floor
1,583 sq. ft.

Second Floor
543 sq. ft.

Plan Features

- Kitchen overlooks vaulted family room with a handy serving bar
- Two-story foyer creates an airy feeling
- Second floor includes an optional bonus room with an additional 251 square feet of living area
- 4 bedrooms, 3 baths, 2-car side entry garage
- Walk-out basement, crawl space or slab foundation, please specify when ordering

Total Living Area: 1,808 sq. ft.

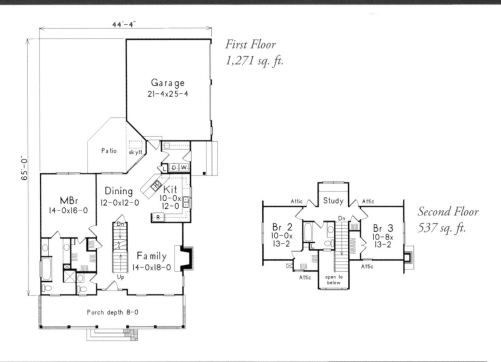

First Floor
1,271 sq. ft.

Second Floor
537 sq. ft.

Plan Features

- Master bedroom has a walk-in closet, double vanities and a separate tub and shower
- Two second floor bedrooms share a study area and full bath
- Partially covered patio is complete with a skylight
- Side entrance opens to utility room with convenient counterspace and laundry sink
- 3 bedrooms, 2 1/2 baths, 2-car side entry garage
- Basement foundation

Total Living Area: 1,855 sq. ft.

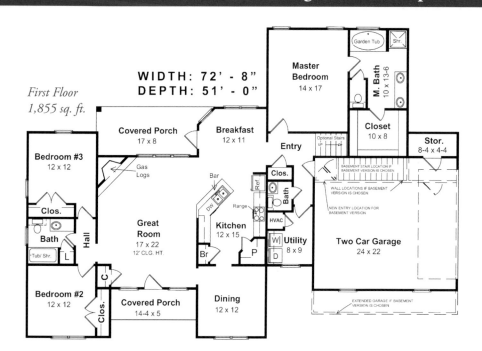

First Floor
1,855 sq. ft.

WIDTH: 72' - 8"
DEPTH: 51' - 0"

Master Bedroom 14 x 17

Garden Tub · Shr.

M. Bath 10 x 13-6

Covered Porch 17 x 8

Breakfast 12 x 11

Entry

Closet 10 x 8

Optional Stairs UP

Stor. 8-4 x 4-4

Bedroom #3 12 x 12

Clos.

Bath

Tub/Shr.

Gas Logs

Bar

Ref.

Clos.

Bath

BASEMENT STAIR LOCATION IF BASEMENT VERSION IS CHOSEN

WALL LOCATIONS IF BASEMENT VERSION IS CHOSEN

Great Room 17 x 22 12' CLG. HT.

DW

Range

Kitchen 12 x 15

HVAC

NEW ENTRY LOCATION FOR BASEMENT VERSION

Br

P

W D

Utility 8 x 9

Two Car Garage 24 x 22

Bedroom #2 12 x 12

Clos.

C

Covered Porch 14-4 x 5

Dining 12 x 12

EXTENDED GARAGE IF BASEMENT VERSION IS CHOSEN

Optional
Second Floor

Down

Clos.

Opt. Bath

Sloped Ceiling

Bonus Room 14 x 22 8' Flat Ceiling

Sloped Ceiling

EXTENDED BONUS ROOM IF BASEMENT VERSION IS CHOSEN

Plan Features

- The great room boasts a 12' ceiling and corner fireplace
- Bayed breakfast area adjoins the kitchen that features a walk-in pantry
- The relaxing master bedroom includes a private bath with walk-in closet and garden tub
- Optional second floor has an additional 352 square feet of living area
- 3 bedrooms, 2 1/2 baths, 2-car side entry garage
- Basement, crawl space or slab foundation, please specify when ordering

Total Living Area: 1,851 sq. ft.

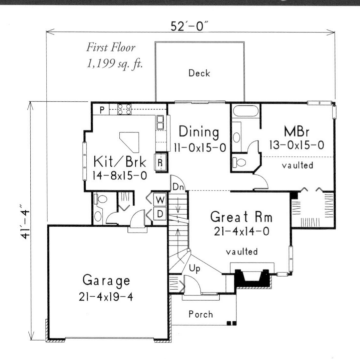

52'-0"

First Floor
1,199 sq. ft.

Deck

P

Kit/Brk
14-8x15-0

Dining
11-0x15-0

MBr
13-0x15-0

vaulted

R

Dn

W
D

41'-4"

Great Rm
21-4x14-0

vaulted

Up

Garage
21-4x19-4

Porch

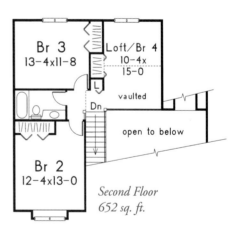

Br 3
13-4x11-8

Loft/Br 4
10-4x
15-0

vaulted

Dn

open to below

Br 2
12-4x13-0

Second Floor
652 sq. ft.

Plan Features

- High-impact entrance to great room also leads directly to the second floor
- First floor master bedroom suite with corner window and walk-in closet
- Kitchen/breakfast room has center work island and pass-through to the dining room
- Second floor bedrooms share a bath
- 4 bedrooms, 2 1/2 baths, 2-car garage
- Basement foundation

Total Living Area: 1,818 sq. ft.

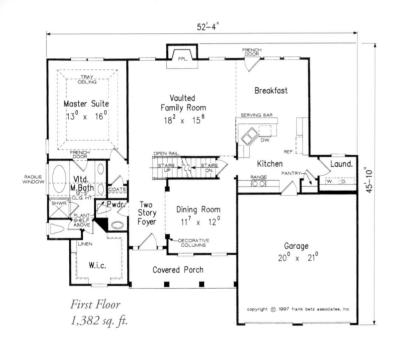

First Floor
1,382 sq. ft.

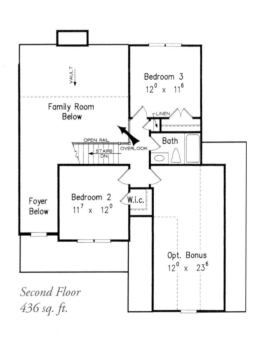

Second Floor
436 sq. ft.

Plan Features

- Spacious breakfast area extends into the family room and kitchen
- Master suite has a tray ceiling and vaulted bath with walk-in closet
- Optional bonus room above the garage has an additional 298 square feet of living area
- 3 bedrooms, 2 1/2 baths, 2-car garage
- Walk-out basement, slab or crawl space foundation, please specify when ordering

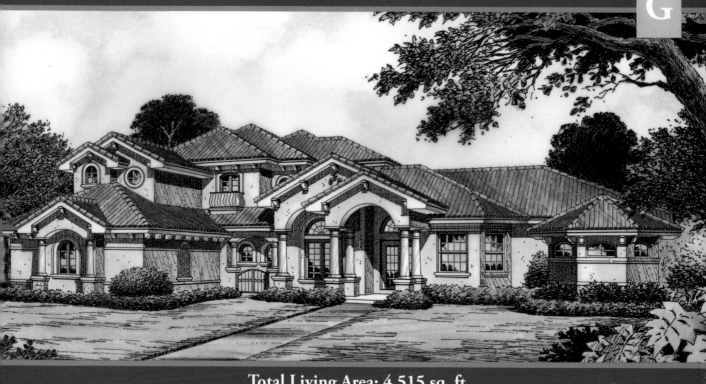

Total Living Area: 4,515 sq. ft.

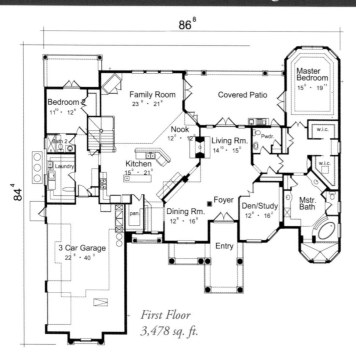

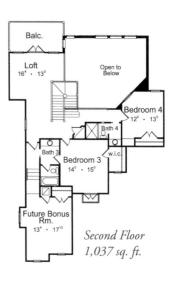

First Floor
3,478 sq. ft.

Second Floor
1,037 sq. ft.

Plan Features

- Covered patio includes an outdoor kitchen
- Spacious kitchen overlooks breakfast nook which features a see-through fireplace
- Framing - only concrete block available
- Bonus room on the second floor has an additional 314 square feet of living area
- 4 bedrooms, 4 1/2 baths, 3-car side entry garage
- Slab foundation

Total Living Area: 1,149 sq. ft.

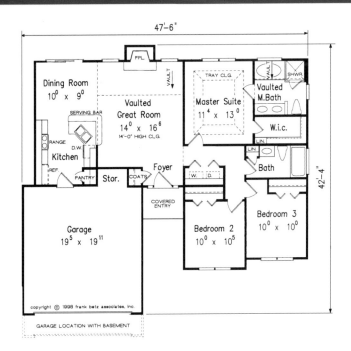

DID YOU KNOW?

Trees are a huge influence on a landscape so take time to locate them properly. Be careful when planting near a house - a tree that could spread 40 feet wide should be at least 20 feet from the house. Avoid planting where the tree will overhang your house, block a door, or obstruct a desirable view from inside. Plant where roots have ample room to grow. Don't plant a tree beneath power lines if it will grow to be 25 feet tall or more. Don't plant above underground utility lines. For help locating electric, cable, phone and water lines on your property, contact each of your utility companies directly.

Plan Features

- Vaulted great room creates an open, airy feel
- Oversized serving bar in kitchen allows for extra seating in dining area
- 9' ceilings throughout home
- 3 bedrooms, 2 baths, 2-car garage
- Crawl space or walk-out basement foundation, please specify when ordering

Total Living Area: 2,726 sq. ft.

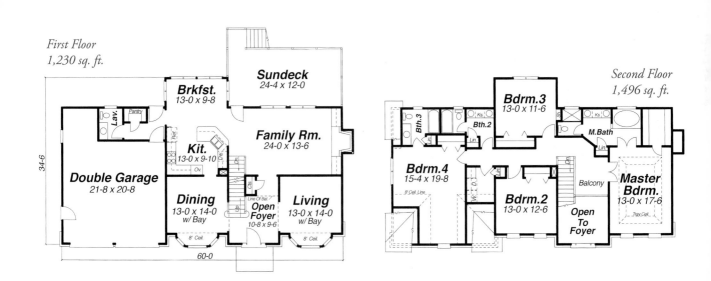

First Floor
1,230 sq. ft.

Sundeck
24-4 x 12-0

Brkfst.
13-0 x 9-8

Lav.

Pantry

Family Rm.
24-0 x 13-6

Kit.
13-0 x 9-10

Double Garage
21-8 x 20-8

Dining
13-0 x 14-0
w/ Bay

Open Foyer
10-8 x 9-6

Living
13-0 x 14-0
w/ Bay

8' Ceil.

8' Ceil.

34-6

60-0

Second Floor
1,496 sq. ft.

Bdrm.3
13-0 x 11-6

Bth.3

Bth.2

M.Bath

Bdrm.4
15-4 x 19-8

Master Bdrm.
13-0 x 17-6

Balcony

Bdrm.2
13-0 x 12-6

Open To Foyer

Tray Ceil.

Plan Features

- French doors access the master bedroom and bath
- Large family room has a fireplace, built-in bookshelves and access to the sundeck
- Large bedroom #4 has a private bath perfect for an in-law suite
- Convenient laundry room is located on the second floor
- 4 bedrooms, 3 1/2 baths, 2-car garage
- Walk-out basement, crawl space or slab foundation, please specify when ordering

Total Living Area: 2,508 sq. ft.

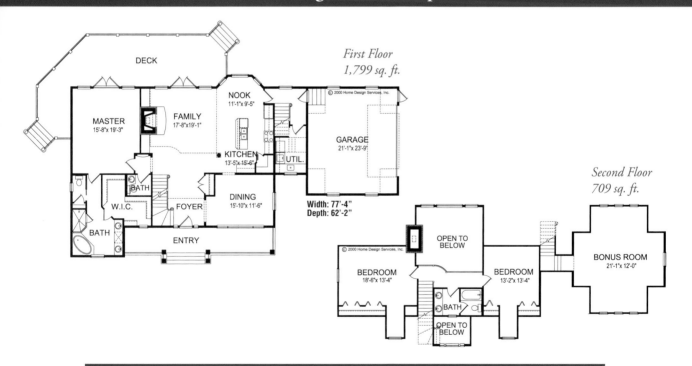

First Floor
1,799 sq. ft.

DECK

MASTER
15'-8"x 19'-3"

FAMILY
17'-8"x19'-1"

NOOK
11'-1"x 9'-5"

© 2000 Home Design Services, Inc.

GARAGE
21'-1"x 23'-9"

KITCHEN
13'-5"x 15'-6"

UTIL.

BATH

W.I.C.

FOYER

DINING
15'-10"x 11'-6"

BATH

ENTRY

Width: 77'-4"
Depth: 62'-2"

Second Floor
709 sq. ft.

© 2000 Home Design Services, Inc.

OPEN TO
BELOW

BONUS ROOM
21'-1"x 12'-0"

BEDROOM
18'-6"x 13'-4"

BEDROOM
13'-2"x 13'-4"

BATH

OPEN TO
BELOW

Plan Features

- Family room, bayed nook and kitchen combine for a spacious living area
- The formal dining room provides an elegant entertaining space
- The master bedroom and family room feature double-door access onto the rear deck
- The bonus room above the garage has an additional 384 square feet of living area
- 3 bedrooms, 2 1/2 baths, 2-car side entry garage
- Basement or walk-out basement foundation, please specify when ordering

Total Living Area: 3,085 sq. ft.

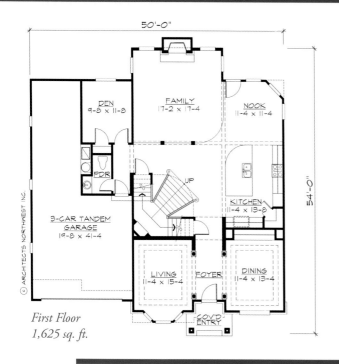

First Floor
1,625 sq. ft.

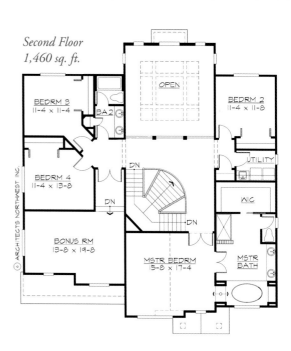

Second Floor
1,460 sq. ft.

Plan Features

- The foyer boasts symmetrical formal living and dining rooms with decorative columns
- Central two-story family room is spectacular with fireplace and beamed ceiling
- Unique see-through area from master bedroom into bath
- Bonus room on the second floor has an additional 315 square feet of living area
- 4 bedrooms, 2 1/2 baths, 3-car tandem garage
- Crawl space foundation

Total Living Area: 1,482 sq. ft.

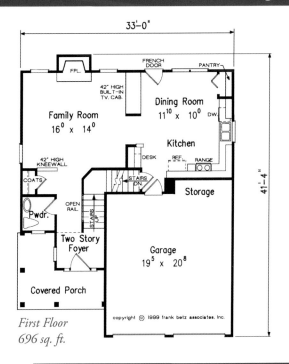

First Floor
696 sq. ft.

copyright © 1999 frank betz associates, inc.

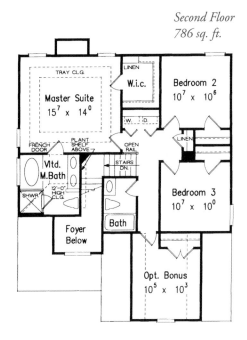

Second Floor
786 sq. ft.

Plan Features

- Family room includes 42" high built-in TV cabinet
- Spacious kitchen and dining room includes a built-in desk and a French door leading to the outdoors
- Optional bonus room on the second floor has an additional 141 square feet of living area
- 3 bedrooms, 2 1/2 baths, 2-car garage
- Walk-out basement, crawl space or slab foundation, please specify when ordering

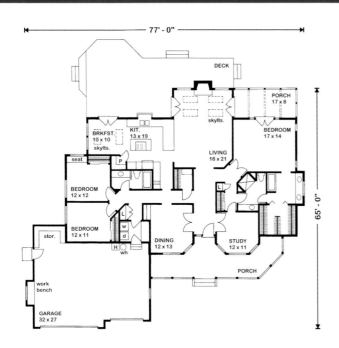

Total Living Area: 2,300 sq. ft.

77' - 0"

65' - 0"

DECK

PORCH
17 x 8

skylts.

BEDROOM
17 x 14

BRKFST.
10 x 10
skylts.

KIT.
13 x 19

LIVING
16 x 21

seat

P

BEDROOM
12 x 12

BEDROOM
12 x 11

stor.

L

w
d

H

wh

DINING
12 x 13

STUDY
12 x 11

work
bench

PORCH

GARAGE
32 x 27

DID YOU KNOW?

On open decks, water drains through gaps in the deck boards, but flooring on a covered porch fits tightly and therefore needs a pitch of at least $1/4$ inch per foot to shed water. Choose quality materials. Rot-resistant woods (redwood, cedar or cypress), stainless-steel fasteners, and protective coats of high-quality paint all help ensure that a porch will be able to withstand the elements for years to come.

Plan Features

- The living room boasts a vaulted ceiling, skylights, fireplace and French doors to the deck and solarium
- The open kitchen includes a cooking island, breakfast bar and large pantry
- The bedroom on the right of the home features a vaulted ceiling, private entrance to the solarium and a luxury bath making it an ideal master suite
- 3 bedrooms, 2 baths, 3-car garage
- Basement or crawl space foundation, please specify when ordering

Total Living Area: 2,286 sq. ft.

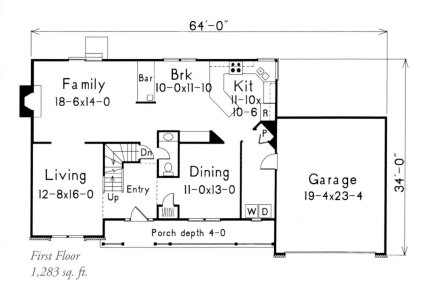

First Floor
1,283 sq. ft.

Second Floor
1,003 sq. ft.

Plan Features

- Fine architectural detail makes this home a showplace with its large windows, intricate brickwork and fine woodwork and trim
- Stunning two-story entry with attractive wood railing and balustrades in the foyer
- Convenient wrap-around kitchen enjoys a window view, planning center and pantry
- 4 bedrooms, 2 1/2 baths, 2-car garage
- Basement foundation, drawings also include crawl space and slab foundations

Total Living Area: 2,968 sq. ft.

*First Floor
2,968 sq. ft.*

Wood Deck

Covered Porch

Breakfast
14'x12'1"

Living
24'8"x19'3"

Master Bedroom
16'9"x21'5"

Master Bath

WIC

Bedroom
12'4"x12'1"

Kitchen
18'4"x14'10"

Dining
13'1"x14'7"

Foyer

Bedroom
13'x12'

Bedroom
12'1"x13'

Utility

Porch

Width: 72'-5"
Depth: 83'-5"

Garage
21'2"x27'2"

*Optional
Second Floor*

Gameroom
13'5"x17'

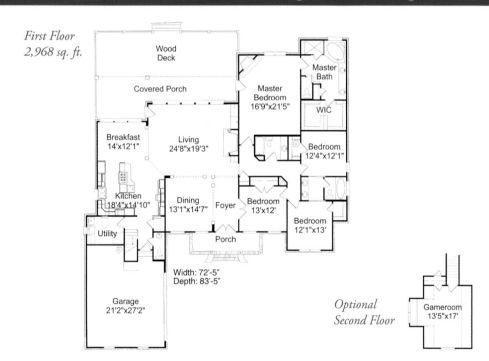

Plan Features

- Decorative columns accent the entrance and define the formal dining room
- A full wall of windows brightens the living room which also enjoys a cozy fireplace
- The spacious kitchen is designed for efficiency and opens to the breakfast room
- The optional second floor has an additional 304 square feet of living area
- 4 bedrooms, 3 1/2 baths, 2-car side entry garage
- Slab foundation

Total Living Area: 3,882 sq. ft.

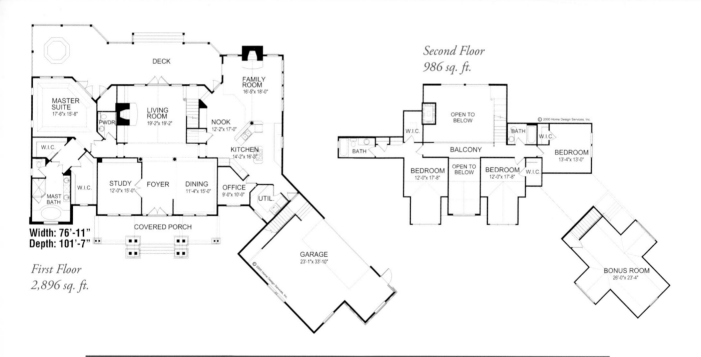

First Floor
2,896 sq. ft.

Width: 76'-11"
Depth: 101'-7"

DECK

MASTER SUITE 17'-6"x 15'-8"

LIVING ROOM 19'-2"x 19'-2"

FAMILY ROOM 16'-5"x 18'-0"

PWDR

W.I.C.

NOOK 12'-2"x 17'-0"

KITCHEN 14'-2"x 16'-3"

MAST BATH

W.I.C.

STUDY 12'-0"x 15'-0"

FOYER

DINING 11'-4"x 15'-0"

OFFICE 9'-0"x 10'-0"

UTIL.

COVERED PORCH

GARAGE 23'-1"x 33'-10"

Second Floor
986 sq. ft.

OPEN TO BELOW

W.I.C.

BATH

BALCONY

BATH

W.I.C.

BEDROOM 13'-4"x 13'-0"

BEDROOM 12'-0"x 17'-8"

OPEN TO BELOW

BEDROOM 12'-0"x 17'-8"

W.I.C.

BONUS ROOM 26'-0"x 23'-4"

Plan Features

- Covered porch creates a relaxing atmosphere and welcomes guests
- The master suite boasts two walk-in closets, a deluxe bath and access onto the rear deck
- The kitchen opens to the charming nook and cozy family room
- The bonus room above the garage has an additional 480 square feet of living area
- 4 bedrooms, 3 1/2 baths, 2-car rear entry garage
- Crawl space foundation

Total Living Area: 2,247 sq. ft.

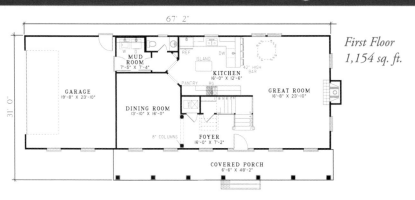

First Floor
1,154 sq. ft.

Second Floor
1,093 sq. ft.

Plan Features

- Enormous great room with fireplace extends into the kitchen with a center island
- Formal dining area is quiet, yet convenient to kitchen
- All bedrooms are located on the second floor to maintain privacy
- 3 bedrooms, 2 1/2 baths, 2-car side entry garage
- Basement, crawl space or slab foundation, please specify when ordering

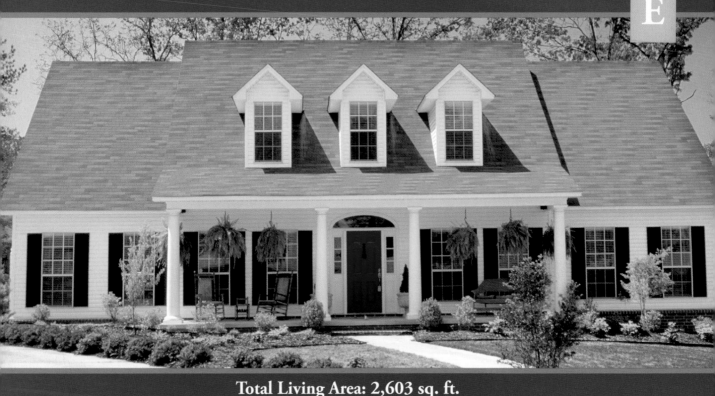

Total Living Area: 2,603 sq. ft.

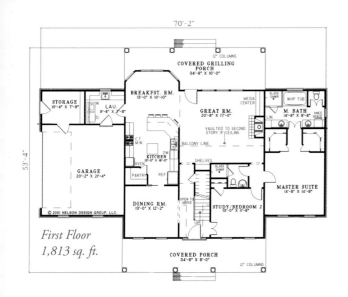

First Floor
1,813 sq. ft.

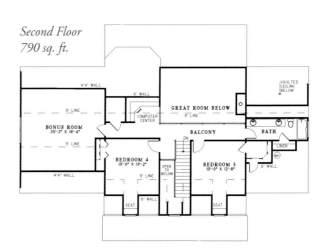

Second Floor
790 sq. ft.

Plan Features

- The vaulted great room includes a media center, fireplace and access to the covered grilling porch
- The second floor bedrooms share a unique computer center
- The bonus room on the second floor has an additional 410 square feet of living space
- 4 bedrooms, 2 1/2 baths, 2-car side entry garage
- Slab or crawl space foundation, please specify when ordering

Total Living Area: 2,585 sq. ft.

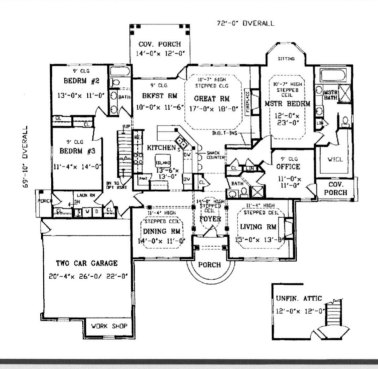

Plan Features

- Kitchen includes walk-in pantry and an angled serving counter
- Master bedroom enjoys a bayed sitting area, huge walk-in closet and private bath
- Flanking the foyer, the formal living and dining rooms have pillar framed entrances and stepped ceilings
- 3 bedrooms, 2 1/2 baths, 2-car side entry garage
- Basement, slab or crawl space foundation, please specify when ordering

Total Living Area: 2,695 sq. ft.

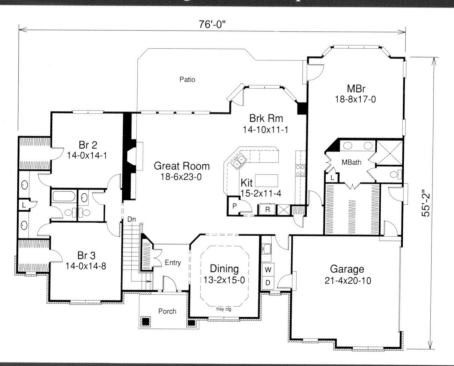

Plan Features

- A grand-scale great room features a fireplace with flanking shelves, handsome entry foyer with staircase and opens to a large kitchen and breakfast room
- Roomy master bedroom has a bay window, walk-in closet and a shower built for two
- Bedrooms #2 and #3 are generously oversized with walk-in closets and a Jack and Jill style bath
- 3 bedrooms, 2 1/2 baths, 2-car side entry garage
- Basement foundation

Total Living Area: 2,135 sq. ft.

First Floor
1,109 sq. ft.

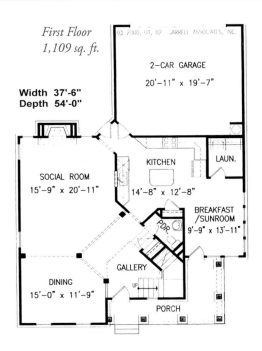

Width 37'-6"
Depth 54'-0"

2-CAR GARAGE
20'-11" x 19'-7"

KITCHEN
14'-8" x 12'-8"

LAUN.

SOCIAL ROOM
15'-9" x 20'-11"

BREAKFAST /SUNROOM
9'-9" x 13'-11"

PDR.

GALLERY

DINING
15'-0" x 11'-9"

UP

PORCH

Second Floor
1,026 sq. ft.

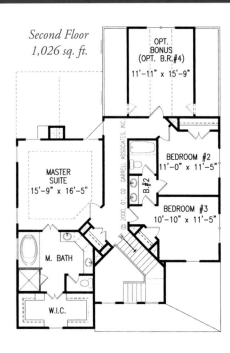

OPT. BONUS
(OPT. B.R. #4)
11'-11" x 15'-9"

MASTER SUITE
15'-9" x 16'-5"

B. #2

BEDROOM #2
11'-0" x 11'-5"

BEDROOM #3
10'-10" x 11'-5"

M. BATH

W.I.C.

Plan Features

- 10' ceilings throughout the first floor and 9' ceilings on the second floor
- Wonderful angled entry leads through columns into a cozy social room
- Spacious kitchen has center island with a place for dining as well as food preparation
- Bonus room on the second floor has an additional 247 square feet of living area
- 3 bedrooms, 2 1/2 baths, 2-car rear entry garage
- Slab foundation

Total Living Area: 2,052 sq. ft.

First Floor
1,135 sq. ft.

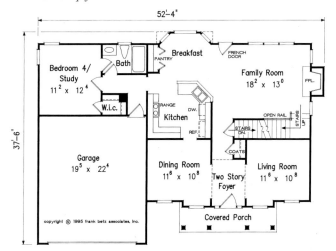

Second Floor
917 sq. ft.

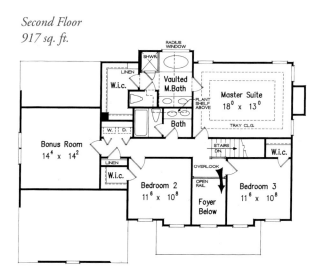

Plan Features

- Terrific family room has a fireplace and several windows adding sunlight
- Bedroom #4/study has a private bath making it an ideal in-law suite
- Bonus room on the second floor has an additional 216 square feet of living area
- 4 bedrooms, 3 baths, 2-car garage
- Walk-out basement, crawl space or slab foundation, please specify when ordering

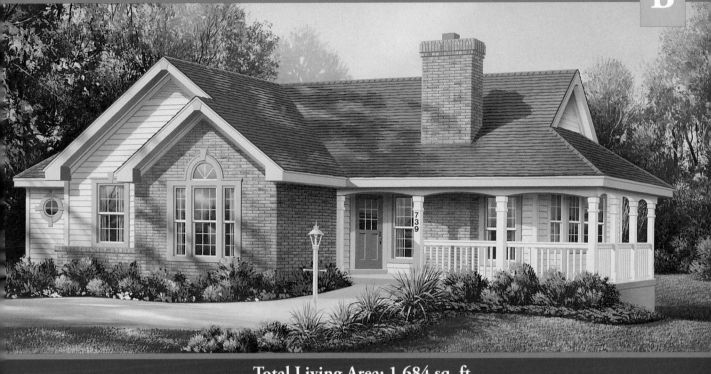

Total Living Area: 1,684 sq. ft.

Optional Lower Level

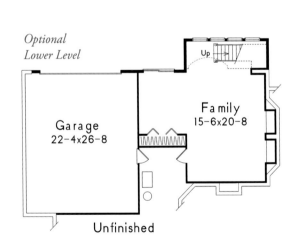

Garage
22-4x26-8

Family
15-6x20-8

Up

Unfinished

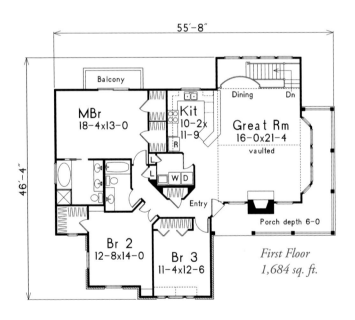

55'-8"

46'-4"

Balcony

MBr
18-4x13-0

Kit
10-2x
11-9

Dining

Dn

Great Rm
16-0x21-4
vaulted

L

W D

Entry

Porch depth 6-0

Br 2
12-8x14-0

Br 3
11-4x12-6

*First Floor
1,684 sq. ft.*

Plan Features

Rear View

- The great room has a bay window, fireplace, dining balcony and atrium window wall
- The master bedroom features double walk-in closets, large luxury bath and sliding doors to exterior balcony
- Atrium opens to 611 square feet of optional living area on the lower level
- 3 bedrooms, 2 baths, 2-car drive under garage
- Walk-out basement foundation

Total Living Area: 3,138 sq. ft.

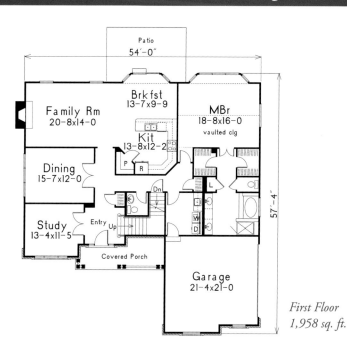

Patio

54'-0"

Brkfst
13-7x9-9

Family Rm
20-8x14-0

MBr
18-8x16-0
vaulted clg

Kit
13-8x12-2

Dining
15-7x12-0

57'-4"

Study
13-4x11-5

Entry Up

Dn

Covered Porch

Garage
21-4x21-0

First Floor
1,958 sq. ft.

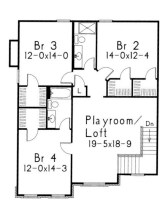

Second Floor
1,180 sq. ft.

Br 3
12-0x14-0

Br 2
14-0x12-4

Playroom/
Loft
19-5x18-9

Dn

Br 4
12-0x14-3

Plan Features

- Impressive stair descends into the large entry and through double-doors to the study
- Private dining is spacious and secluded
- Master bedroom, family and laundry rooms are among the many generously sized rooms
- Three large bedrooms, two baths and four walk-in closets compose the second floor
- 4 bedrooms, 3 1/2 baths, 2-car side entry garage
- Basement foundation

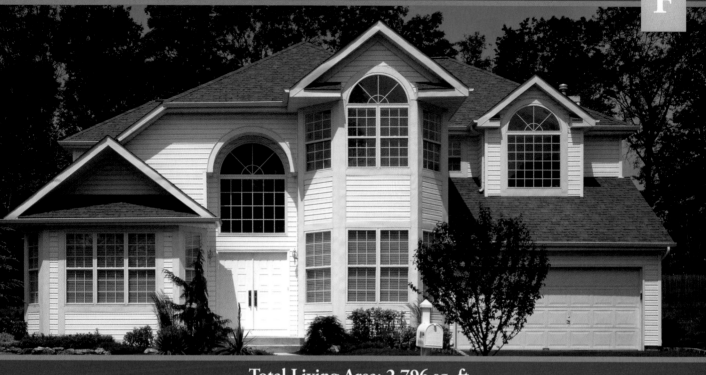

Total Living Area: 2,796 sq. ft.

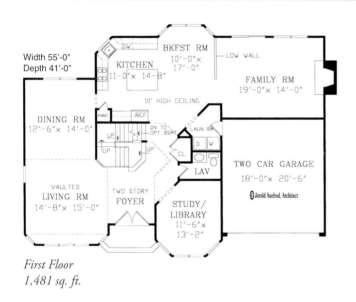

Width 55'-0"
Depth 41'-0"

BKFST RM
10'-0" x 17'-0"

LOW WALL

KITCHEN
11'-0" x 14'-8"

DW

FAMILY RM
19'-0" x 14'-0"

10' HIGH CEILING

DINING RM
12'-6" x 14'-0"

PANT

REF

DN TO OPT BSMT

LAUN RM

UP

D W

CL

LAV

TWO CAR GARAGE
18'-0" x 20'-6"

© Jerold Axelrod, Architect

VAULTED
LIVING RM
14'-8" x 15'-0"

TWO STORY
FOYER

STUDY/
LIBRARY
11'-6" x 13'-2"

First Floor
1,481 sq. ft.

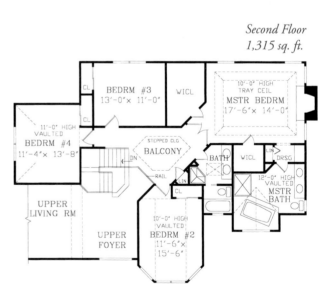

Second Floor
1,315 sq. ft.

BEDRM #3
13'-0" x 11'-0"

WICL

CL

CL

10'-0" HIGH
TRAY CEIL
MSTR BEDRM
17'-6" x 14'-0"

11'-0" HIGH
VAULTED
BEDRM #4
11'-4" x 13'-8"

STEPPED CLG
BALCONY

RAIL

BATH

LIN

WICL

DRSG

12'-0" HIGH
VAULTED
MSTR
BATH

UPPER
LIVING RM

CL

UPPER
FOYER

10'-0" HIGH
VAULTED
BEDRM #2
11'-6" x 15'-6"

Plan Features

- Open stairway leads to a railed balcony and four second floor bedrooms
- Family room has fireplace and glass doors to the backyard
- Master bedroom has a 10' tray ceiling, a cozy fireplace and two walk-in closets
- 4 bedrooms, 2 1/2 baths, 2-car garage
- Basement foundation

Total Living Area: 1,769 sq. ft.

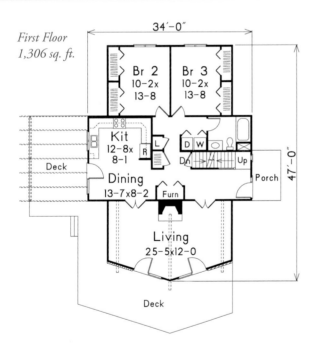

First Floor
1,306 sq. ft.

34'-0"

Br 2
10-2x
13-8

Br 3
10-2x
13-8

Kit
12-8x
8-1

L
R

D W

Dn

Up

Porch

47'-0"

Deck

Dining
13-7x8-2

Furn

Living
25-5x12-0

Deck

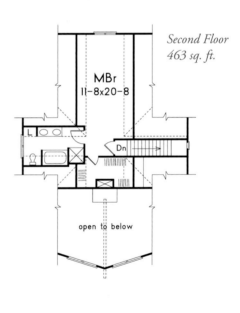

Second Floor
463 sq. ft.

MBr
11-8x20-8

L

Dn

open to below

Plan Features

- Living room boasts an elegant cathedral ceiling and fireplace
- U-shaped kitchen and dining area combine for easy living
- Secondary bedrooms include double closets
- Secluded master bedroom features a sloped ceiling, large walk-in closet and private bath
- 3 bedrooms, 2 baths
- Basement foundation, drawings also include crawl space and slab foundations

Plan #583-055D-0137

Total Living Area: 2,444 sq. ft.

Plan Features

- The patio is surrounded by a low wall making it a private outdoor retreat
- The kitchen has open counterspace facing the family and breakfast rooms for quick snacks or meals
- The great room has French doors opening onto the patio
- 3 bedrooms, 2 1/2 baths, 2-car side entry garage
- Slab, crawl space, basement or walk-out basement foundation, please specify when ordering

---

Plan #583-025D-0019

C

Total Living Area: 2,074 sq. ft.

Plan Features

- Unique sewing room is ideal for hobby enthusiasts and has counterspace for convenience
- Double walk-in closets are located in the luxurious master bath
- A built-in bookcase in the great room adds charm
- 3 bedrooms, 2 baths, 2-car side entry garage
- Slab foundation

Total Living Area: 1,700 sq. ft.

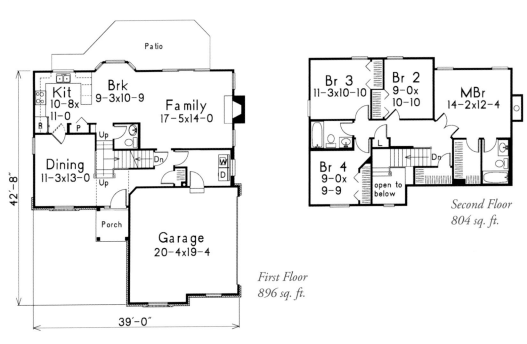

First Floor
896 sq. ft.

Second Floor
804 sq. ft.

Plan Features

- Two-story entry with T-stair is illuminated with a decorative oval window
- Skillfully designed U-shaped kitchen has a built-in pantry
- All bedrooms have generous closet storage and are common to spacious hall with walk-in cedar closet
- 4 bedrooms, 2 1/2 baths, 2-car side entry garage
- Basement foundation

Plan #583-001D-0045

DID YOU KNOW?

To preserve and protect exterior doors and trim without hiding the wood's beauty, do what boaters do: use marine varnish. Also known as spar varnish, the high oil content of this finish coating makes it more flexible than other clear finishes. And marine varnish contains ultraviolet inhibitors, which act as a sunscreen to preserve the finish.

Total Living Area: 1,197 sq. ft.

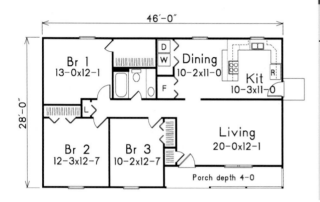

Plan Features

- U-shaped kitchen includes ample workspace, breakfast bar, laundry area and direct access to the outdoors
- Large living room has a convenient coat closet
- Bedroom #1 features a large walk-in closet
- 3 bedrooms, 1 bath
- Crawl space foundation, drawings also include basement and slab foundations

---

Plan #583-048D-0008

Total Living Area: 2,089 sq. ft.

Plan Features

- Family room features a fireplace, built-in bookshelves and triple sliders opening to the covered patio
- Kitchen features a pantry and desk
- The secluded master bedroom is a quiet retreat with patio access
- Master bedroom features an oversized bath with walk-in closet and corner tub
- 4 bedrooms, 3 baths, 2-car garage
- Slab foundation

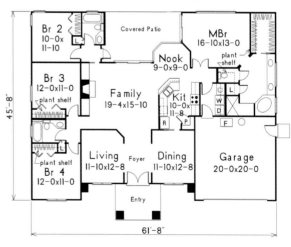

Total Living Area: 1,978 sq. ft.

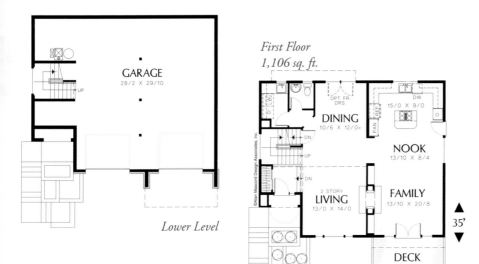

GARAGE
28/2 X 29/10

UP

Lower Level

First Floor
1,106 sq. ft.

OPT. FR. DRS.

DW
15/0 X 9/0

DINING
10/6 X 12/0+

PAN
REF

DN

UP

DN

NOOK
13/10 X 8/4

2 STORY
LIVING
13/0 X 14/0

FAMILY
13/10 X 20/8

35'

DECK

◀ 38' ▶

BR. 3
11/0 X 10/8

©Alan Mascord Design Associates, Inc.

BR. 2
11/0 X 10/0

DN

LOFT

FOYER
BELOW

©Alan Mascord Design Associates, Inc.

LIN

LIVING
BELOW

VAULTED
MASTER
15/2 X 12/0

Second Floor
872 sq. ft.

Plan Features

- Designed for a sloping lot, this multi-level home intrigues the eye
- Sunlight filters into the grand two-story foyer and living room from tall windows
- Master suite has elegant front-facing windows and a private bath
- 3 bedrooms, 2 1/2 baths, 2-car drive under garage
- Basement foundation

Plan #583-056D-0027

Optional Second Floor

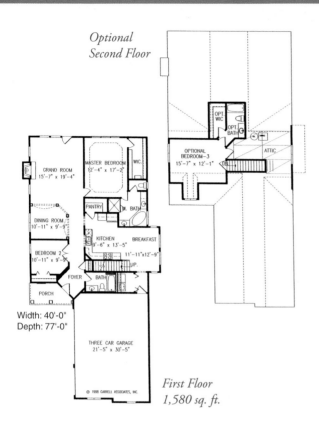

Width: 40'-0"
Depth: 77'-0"

First Floor 1,580 sq. ft.

Total Living Area: 1,580 sq. ft.

Plan Features

- Dining room has columns which maintain an open feeling
- Sunny breakfast room is located off the kitchen
- 9' ceilings throughout the first floor
- Optional second floor has an additional 336 square feet of living area
- 2 bedrooms, 2 baths, 3-car side entry garage
- Slab foundation

Plan #583-007D-0030

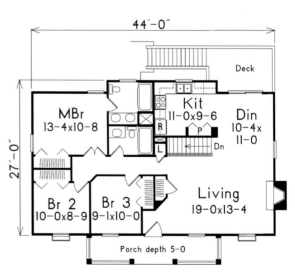

Total Living Area: 1,140 sq. ft.

Plan Features

- Open and spacious living and dining areas for family gatherings
- Well-organized kitchen with an abundance of cabinetry and a built-in pantry
- Roomy master bath features a double-bowl vanity
- 3 bedrooms, 2 baths, 2-car drive under garage
- Basement foundation

Total Living Area: 1,380 sq. ft.

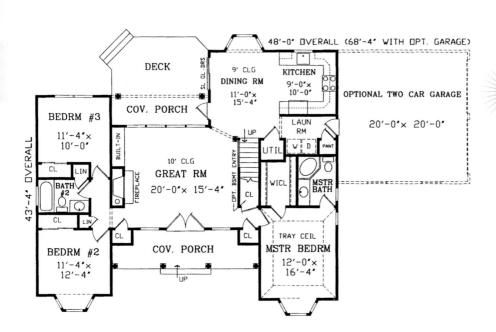

DID YOU KNOW?

Engineered wood siding is a lot easier and less costly to install than real wood siding. It's lighter in weight and includes advancements making it easier to install. Engineered wood can be bought pre-primed, ready to paint or pre-finished in a number of options which reduces field and labor costs.

Plan Features

- Built-in bookshelves complement the fireplace in the great room
- An abundance of storage space is near the laundry room and kitchen
- Covered porch has a view of the backyard
- 3 bedrooms, 2 baths, optional 2-car side entry garage
- Basement, crawl space or slab foundation, please specify when ordering

Width 75'-0"
Depth 45'-0"

Total Living Area: 1,902 sq. ft.

Plan Features

- Great room with fireplace is easily viewable from the kitchen and breakfast area
- Luxury master bedroom has a bay window and two walk-in closets
- Formal living and dining rooms create a wonderful entertaining space
- 3 bedrooms, 2 baths, 2-car side entry garage
- Basement, crawl space or slab foundation, please specify when ordering

Total Living Area: 1,375 sq. ft.

Plan Features

- Den can easily convert to a second bedroom
- A center island in the kitchen allows extra space for organizing and food preparation
- Centrally located laundry room
- 1 bedroom, 2 baths, 2-car rear entry garage
- Basement foundation

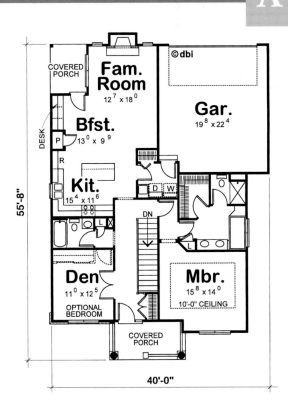

Total Living Area: 2,954 sq. ft.

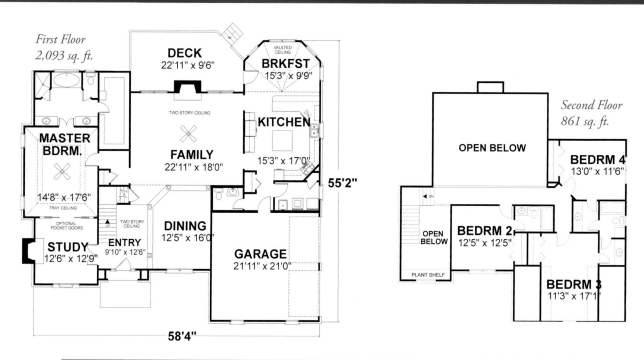

First Floor
2,093 sq. ft.

DECK
22'11" x 9'6"

BRKFST
15'3" x 9'9"

VAULTED CEILING

TWO STORY CEILING

KITCHEN
15'3" x 17'0"

MASTER BDRM.
14'8" x 17'6"
TRAY CEILING

FAMILY
22'11" x 18'0"

OPTIONAL POCKET DOORS

TWO STORY CEILING

STUDY
12'6" x 12'9"

ENTRY
9'10" x 12'6"

UP

DINING
12'5" x 16'0"

GARAGE
21'11" x 21'0"

55'2"

58'4"

Second Floor
861 sq. ft.

OPEN BELOW

BEDRM 4
13'0" x 11'6"

DN

OPEN BELOW

BEDRM 2
12'5" x 12'5"

PLANT SHELF

BEDRM 3
11'3" x 17'1"

Plan Features

- Master bedroom has a double-door entry into the luxurious bath
- Private study has direct access into the master bedroom
- Vaulted ceiling and bay window add light and dimension to the breakfast room
- 4 bedrooms, 3 1/2 baths, 2-car side entry garage
- Basement foundation

Plan #583-024D-0044

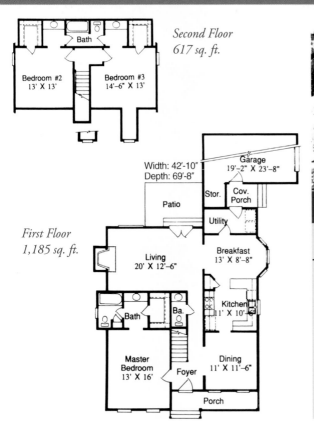

Second Floor 617 sq. ft.

First Floor 1,185 sq. ft.

Width: 42'-10"
Depth: 69'-8"

Total Living Area: 1,802 sq. ft.

Plan Features

- The secluded master bedroom includes a private master bath and large walk-in closet
- The efficient kitchen easily serves the dining room and bayed breakfast area
- The spacious secondary bedrooms enjoy walk-in closets and share the bath
- 3 bedrooms, 2 1/2 baths, 2-car side entry garage
- Slab or crawl space foundation, please specify when ordering

Plan #583-055D-0055

Total Living Area: 1,739 sq. ft.

Plan Features

- 10' ceiling in foyer makes an impressive entrance
- 9' ceiling in great room
- Handy computer center located in hallway off main living areas for privacy
- 3 bedrooms, 2 baths, 2-car garage
- Basement, slab or crawl space foundation, please specify when ordering

Total Living Area: 2,365 sq. ft.

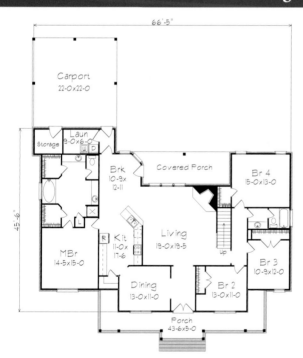

DID YOU KNOW?

Ebony is an extremely hard, close-grained wood used as an early inlay and for turned woods. Today, although expensive, it is used to make handsome staircases and furniture.

Plan Features

- 9' ceilings throughout the home
- Expansive central living room is complemented by a corner fireplace
- Master bedroom features a bath with two walk-in closets and vanities, separate tub and shower and handy linen closet
- 4 bedrooms, 2 baths, 2-car carport
- Slab foundation

Plan #583-011D-0001

VAULTED
MASTER
13/8 X 11/8

PATIO

BR. 2
10/4 X 10/0
(9' CLG.)

DINING
10/0 X 13/6
(9' CLG.)

BR. 3
10/0 X 10/0
(9' CLG.)

VAULTED
LIVING
14/0 X 14/6

58'

PAN. REF.

D. W. L

GARAGE
19/4 X 21/8

PORCH

©Alan Mascord Design Associates, Inc.

◀ 40' ▶

Total Living Area: 1,275 sq. ft.

Plan Features

- The kitchen expands into the dining area with the help of a center island
- Decorative columns keep the living area open to other areas
- Covered front porch adds charm to the entry
- 3 bedrooms, 2 baths, 2-car garage
- Crawl space foundation

Plan #583-062D-0036

Total Living Area: 1,018 sq. ft.

Plan Features

- Living room enjoys a grand fireplace and a large picture window
- U-shaped compact kitchen offers efficiency
- The master bedroom has a convenient half bath
- Lower level has an additional 1,018 square feet of living area
- 3 bedrooms, 1 1/2 baths, 1-car carport
- Basement foundation

mbr
10'4 x 12'

br2
8'1 x 12'

k
9'2 x 7'6

din

9'x 8'6
br3

Width: 27'-0"
Depth: 42'-0"

*First Floor
1,018 sq. ft.*

20'2 x 16'9

liv

12 x 22
CARPORT

UNFINISHED

UNFINISHED

D

W

F

UNFINISHED

*Optional
Lower Level*

Total Living Area: 1,945 sq. ft.

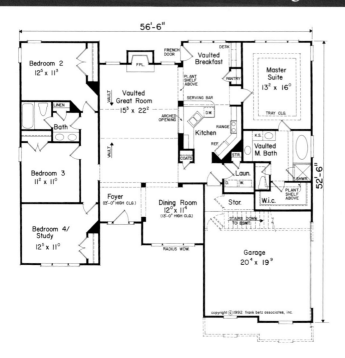

DID YOU KNOW?

Pictures and ornaments give traditional bathrooms an inviting feel, but make sure any treasured items will tolerate a steamy atmosphere. You can protect paintings or photos by framing them behind glass or Lucite.

Plan Features

- Master suite is separate from other bedrooms for privacy
- Vaulted breakfast room is directly off great room
- Kitchen includes a built-in desk area
- Elegant dining room has an arched window
- 4 bedrooms, 2 baths, 2-car side entry garage
- Walk-out basement, crawl space or slab foundation, please specify when ordering

Plan #583-058D-0014

Price Code:

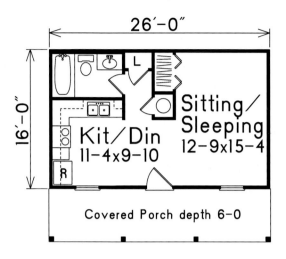

26'-0"

16'-0"

Kit/Din
11-4x9-10

Sitting/
Sleeping
12-9x15-4

L

R

Covered Porch depth 6-0

Total Living Area: 416 sq. ft.

Plan Features

- Open floor plan creates a spacious feeling
- Covered porch has rustic appeal
- Plenty of cabinetry and workspace in the kitchen
- Large linen closet is centrally located and close to the bath
- Sleeping area, 1 bath
- Slab foundation

Plan #583-070D-0011

Price Code:

C

Total Living Area: 2,198 sq. ft.

Plan Features

- Double walk-in closets in the master bedroom, as well as direct access to the laundry room, creates the perfect opportunity for organization
- Varied ceiling heights throughout this home
- Large study includes a walk-in closet and cathedral ceiling
- 2 bedrooms, 2 baths, 2-car garage
- Basement foundation

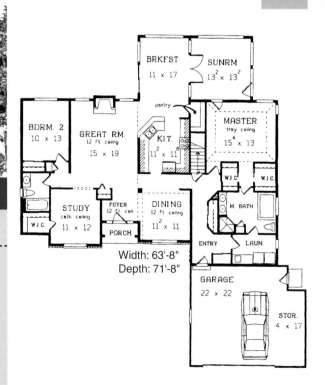

BRKFST
11 x 17

SUNRM
$13^2 \times 13^2$

BDRM. 2
10 x 13

GREAT RM.
12 ft. ceiling
15 x 19

pantry

KIT.
$11^2 \times 11^8$

MASTER
tray ceiling
$15^4 \times 13$

STUDY
cath. ceiling
11 x 12

FOYER
12 ft. ceil.

DINING
12 ft. ceiling
$11^2 \times 11$

W.I.C.

W.I.C.

W.I.C.

M. BATH

PORCH

ENTRY

LAUN

Width: 63'-8"
Depth: 71'-8"

GARAGE
22 x 22

STOR.
4 x 17

Total Living Area: 3,059 sq. ft.

First Floor
1,925 sq. ft.

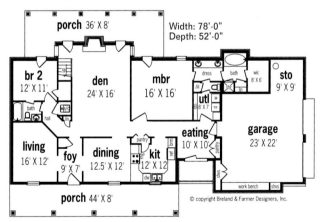

Width: 78'-0"
Depth: 52'-0"

porch 36' X 8'

br 2 12' X 11'
den 24' X 16'
mbr 16' X 16'
dress
bath
wic 8' X 6'
sto 9' X 9'
utl 8' X 7'
bath
living 16' X 12'
foy 9' X 7'
dining 12.5' X 12'
kit 12' X 12'
pantry
eating 10' X 10'
garage 23' X 22'
work bench

porch 44' X 8'

© copyright Breland & Farmer Designers, Inc.

Second Floor
1,134 sq. ft.

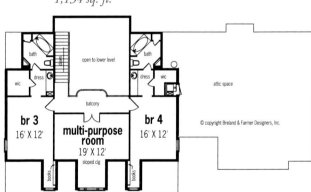

open to lower level
bath
wic
dress
bath
dress
wic
attic space
balcony
br 3 16' X 12'
multi-purpose room 19' X 12'
sloped clg
br 4 16' X 12'
books
books

© copyright Breland & Farmer Designers, Inc.

Plan Features

- The den, master bedroom and bedroom #2 all access the relaxing rear porch
- Formal living and dining rooms are great for entertaining
- Bedrooms #3 and #4 each enjoy built-in bookshelves, a walk-in closet and a private bath
- The garage includes plenty of storage space and a work bench
- 4 bedrooms, 4 baths, 2-car side entry garage
- Crawl space foundation, drawings also include slab foundation

Plan #583-022D-0003

A

Second Floor
677 sq. ft.

48'-0"

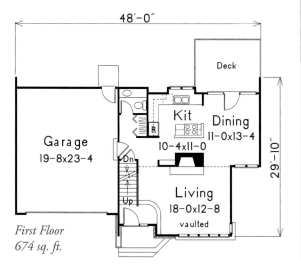

First Floor
674 sq. ft.

29'-10"

Total Living Area: 1,351 sq. ft.

Plan Features

- Roof lines and vaulted ceilings make home appear larger
- Central fireplace provides a focal point for dining and living areas
- Master bedroom features a roomy window seat and a walk-in closet
- Loft can easily be converted to a third bedroom
- 2 bedrooms, 2 1/2 baths, 2-car garage
- Basement foundation

Plan #583-007D-0105

AA

Total Living Area: 1,084 sq. ft.

Plan Features

- Delightful country porch for quiet evenings
- The living room offers a front feature window which invites the sun and includes a fireplace and dining area with private patio
- Both bedrooms have walk-in closets and access to their own bath
- 2 bedrooms, 2 baths
- Basement foundation

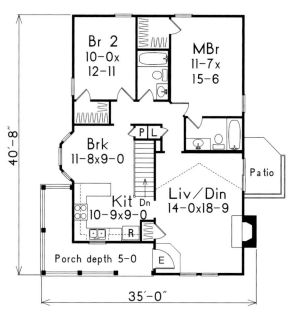

40'-8"

35'-0"

Total Living Area: 717 sq. ft.

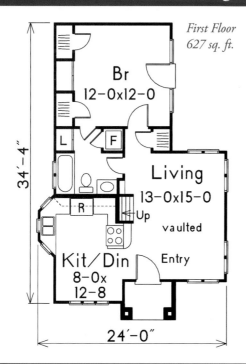

First Floor
627 sq. ft.

Br
12-0x12-0

L   F

34'-4"

Living
13-0x15-0
vaulted

Up

R

Entry

Kit/Din
8-0x
12-8

24'-0"

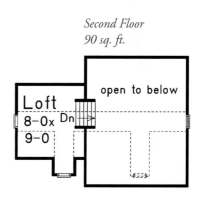

Second Floor
90 sq. ft.

open to below

Loft
8-0x
9-0

Dn

Plan Features

- Incline ladder leads up to cozy loft area
- Living room features plenty of windows and a vaulted ceiling
- U-shaped kitchen includes a small bay window at the sink
- 1 bedroom, 1 bath
- Slab foundation

Plan #583-062D-0048

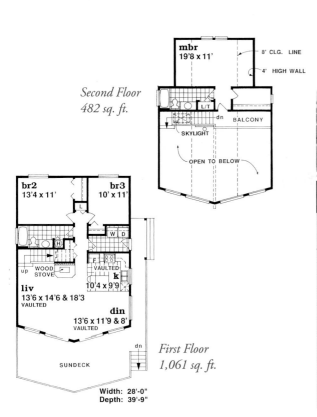

Second Floor
482 sq. ft.

mbr
19'8 x 11'

8' CLG. LINE
4' HIGH WALL

SKYLIGHT
dn BALCONY
OPEN TO BELOW

br2
13'4 x 11'

br3
10' x 11'

W D

up
WOOD
STOVE

VAULTED
k
10'4 x 9'9

liv
13'6 x 14'6 & 18'3
VAULTED

din
13'6 x 11'9 & 8'
VAULTED

dn

First Floor
1,061 sq. ft.

SUNDECK

dn

Width: 28'-0"
Depth: 39'-9"

Total Living Area: 1,543 sq. ft.

Plan Features

- Enormous sundeck makes this a popular vacation style
- A woodstove warms the vaulted living and dining rooms
- A vaulted kitchen has a prep island and breakfast bar
- Second floor vaulted master bedroom has a private bath and walk-in closet
- 3 bedrooms, 2 baths
- Crawl space foundation

Plan #583-055D-0195

Total Living Area: 1,746 sq. ft.

Plan Features

- The centrally located kitchen serves the breakfast room and formal dining room with ease
- The screened porch expands the living area to the outdoors
- The secondary bedrooms enjoy walk-in closets and a central bath
- 3 bedrooms, 2 baths, 2-car garage
- Slab or crawl space foundation, please specify when ordering

67'-0"

MASTER
SUITE
12'-8" x 18'-0"

M. BATH
9'-4" x 11'-8"

GLASS
BLOCKS

BEDROOM 2
13'-10" x 11'-0"

SCREENED
PORCH
17'-0" x 10'-0"

BREAKFAST
ROOM
13'-0" x 8'-8"

LAU.
6'-0" x 5'-6"

STORAGE
9'-4" x 5'-6"

54'-10"

KITCHEN
13'-0" x 10'-0"

GREAT ROOM
17'-0" x 16'-4"

GARAGE
22'-4" x 22'-0"

OPTIONAL
SIDE LOAD
GARAGE

BEDROOM 3
13'-0" x 11'-0"

DINING
ROOM
13'-10" x 11'-6"

FOYER
17'-0" x 4'-0"

COVERED PORCH
44'-10" x 8'-0"

Total Living Area: 3,335 sq. ft.

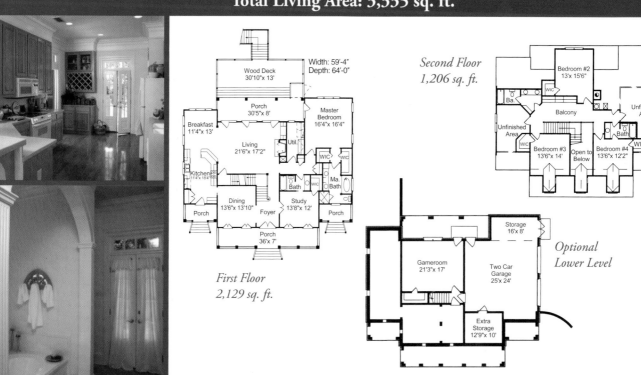

Width: 59'-4"
Depth: 64'-0"

Wood Deck
30'10"x 13'

Porch
30'5"x 8'

Master
Bedroom
16'4"x 16'4"

Breakfast
11'4"x 13'

Living
21'6"x 17'2"

Util.

WIC   WIC

Kitchen
11'4" 18'4"

Bath

WIC

Ma.
Bath

Dining
13'6"x 13'10"

Study
13'8"x 12'

Porch   Foyer

Porch

Porch
36'x 7'

*First Floor
2,129 sq. ft.*

*Second Floor
1,206 sq. ft.*

Bedroom #2
13'x 15'6"

WIC

Ba.

Balcony

Unfinished
Area

Unfinished
Area

WIC

Bedroom #3
13'6"x 14'

Open to
Below

Bath

Bedroom #4
13'6"x 12'2"

WIC

Storage
16'x 8'

Gameroom
21'3"x 17'

Two Car
Garage
25'x 24'

*Optional
Lower Level*

Extra
Storage
12'9"x 10'

Plan Features

- Provides the comfort of a country cottage with modern amenities and luxury
- The dining room and study have two sets of French doors brightening the area
- Unfinished areas on the second floor have an additional 422 square feet of living space
- The lower level gameroom has an additional 435 square feet of living space
- 4 bedrooms, 4 baths, 2-car drive under garage
- Basement foundation

Plan #583-016D-0053

Price Code: B

Total Living Area: 1,466 sq. ft.

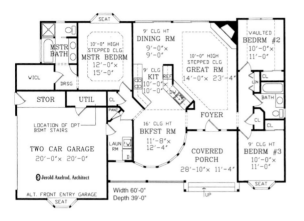

Plan Features

- Sliding French doors open to the backyard from both the great room and adjoining formal dining room
- A turreted breakfast room overlooks the front porch
- The master bedroom is separated for privacy and includes its own bath
- 3 bedrooms, 2 baths, 2-car side entry garage
- Basement, crawl space or slab foundation, please specify when ordering

---

Plan #583-065D-0012

Price Code: E

Total Living Area: 2,738 sq. ft.

Plan Features

- An open entrance offers a spectacular view of the windowed rear wall, fireplace and open staircase in the great room
- The kitchen, breakfast and hearth rooms combine to offer an open and comfortable gathering place
- The master bedroom is topped with an 11' ceiling and features a sitting alcove and deluxe bath
- 4 bedrooms, 3 1/2 baths, 2-car side entry garage
- Basement foundation

Second Floor
823 sq. ft.

First Floor
1,915 sq. ft.

Total Living Area: 2,044 sq. ft.

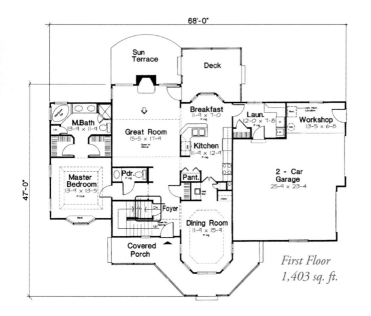

First Floor
1,403 sq. ft.

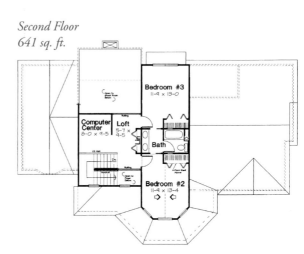

Second Floor
641 sq. ft.

Plan Features

- Elegant French doors lead from the kitchen to the formal dining room
- Two-car garage features a workshop area for projects or extra storage
- Second floor includes loft space ideal for an office area and a handy computer center
- Master bedroom boasts double walk-in closets, a private bath and bay window seat
- 3 bedrooms, 2 1/2 baths, 2-car side entry garage
- Basement, crawl space or slab foundation, please specify when ordering

Plan #583-007D-0114

B

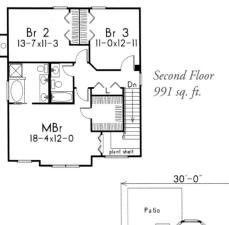

Second Floor 991 sq. ft.

Br 2
13-7x11-3

Br 3
11-0x12-11

MBr
18-4x12-0

plant shelf

First Floor 680 sq. ft.

30'-0"

Patio

Din

Family
19-4x15-8

Kit
10-0
11-0

37'-0"

Dn

Garage
18-4x20-4

Entry

Up

Porch

Total Living Area: 1,671 sq. ft.

Plan Features

- Triple gables and stone facade create great curb appeal
- Two-story entry with hallway leads to a spacious family room, dining area with bay window and U-shaped kitchen
- Second floor features a large master bedroom with luxury bath, huge walk-in closet, overlook to entry and two secondary bedrooms with hall bath
- 3 bedrooms, 2 1/2 baths, 2-car garage
- Basement foundation

Plan #583-065D-0074

B

Total Living Area: 1,640 sq. ft.

Plan Features

- An open great room and dining area is topped by a stepped ceiling treatment that reaches a 9' height
- The functional kitchen enjoys a walk-in pantry, angles and a delightful snack bar
- Warmth and charm radiates through the combined living areas from the corner fireplace; while a covered porch offers outdoor enjoyment
- 3 bedrooms, 2 baths, 2-car garage
- Basement foundation

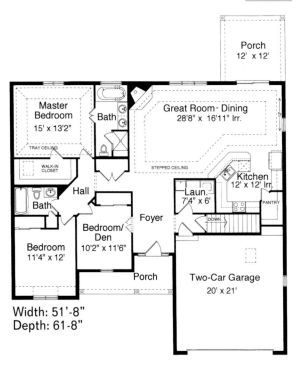

Porch
12' x 12'

Master
Bedroom
15' x 13'2"

Bath

Great Room- Dining
28'8" x 16'11" Irr.

TRAY CEILING

WALK-IN
CLOSET

STEPPED CEILING

Kitchen
12' x 12' Irr.

Laun.
7'4" x 6'

PANTRY

Hall

Bath

Foyer

DOWN

Bedroom
11'4" x 12'

Bedroom/
Den
10'2" x 11'6"

Porch

Two-Car Garage
20' x 21'

Width: 51'-8"
Depth: 61-8"

D

Total Living Area: 2,384 sq. ft.

First Floor
2,384 sq. ft.

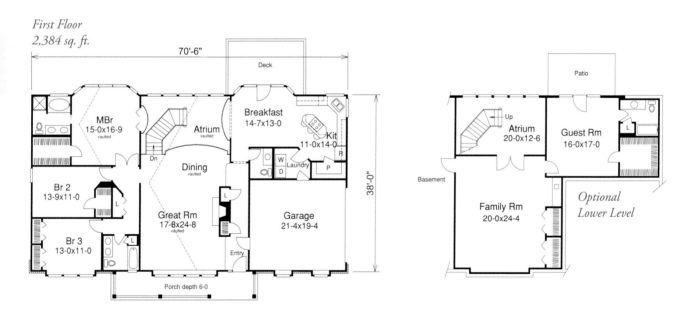

70'-6"

Deck

MBr
15-0x16-9
vaulted

Atrium
vaulted

Breakfast
14-7x13-0

Kit
11-0x14-0

Dn

Dining
vaulted

W
D

Laundry

P

38'-0"

Br 2
13-9x11-0

L

Great Rm
17-8x24-8
vaulted

Garage
21-4x19-4

Br 3
13-0x11-0

L

Entry

Porch depth 6-0

Patio

Up

Atrium
20-0x12-6

Guest Rm
16-0x17-0

L

Basement

Family Rm
20-0x24-4

Optional
Lower Level

Plan Features

- Bracketed box windows create an exterior with country charm
- Great room features an atrium, fireplace, box window wall and vaulted ceilings
- An atrium balcony with large bay window is enjoyed by the spacious breakfast room
- Optional lower level has an additional 1,038 square feet of living area
- 3 bedrooms, 2 1/2 baths, 2-car side entry garage
- Walk-out basement foundation

Second Floor 1,125 sq. ft.

First Floor 1,255 sq. ft.

47' · 48'

Total Living Area: 2,383 sq. ft.

Plan Features

- Loft/bedroom #4 can remain open or finished as your family grows
- All bedrooms located on the second floor for privacy
- Built-in shelves in the family room make an ideal entertainment center
- 4 bedrooms, 2 1/2 baths, 2-car garage
- Crawl space foundation

Total Living Area: 950 sq. ft.

Plan Features

- The combined living and dining areas are warmed by a hearth fireplace and brightened by palladian windows
- Wrap-around kitchen offers a pantry, laundry area and plant window beyond the sink
- A spectacular loft overlooking the living and dining areas provides an additional 270 square feet of living area
- 2 bedrooms, 1 bath
- Crawl space foundation

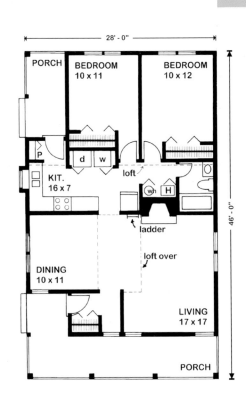

Price Code:

E

Total Living Area: 3,057 sq. ft.

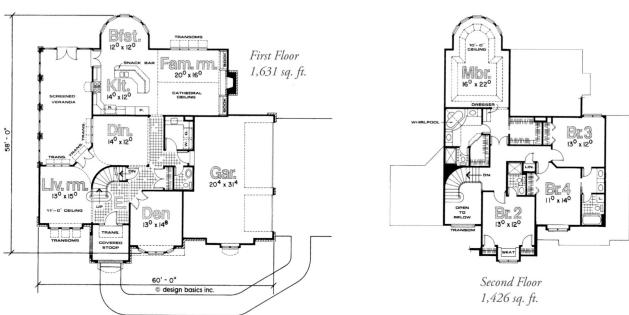

First Floor
1,631 sq. ft.

Second Floor
1,426 sq. ft.

Plan Features

- Oversized rooms throughout
- Peaceful second floor master bedroom enjoys a dramatic bay window
- Living and dining rooms lead to the screened veranda through a beautiful double-door entry
- 4 bedrooms, 3 1/2 baths, 3-car side entry garage
- Basement foundation

Plan #583-062D-0062

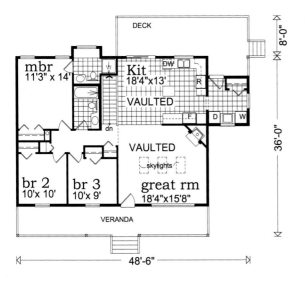

Total Living Area: 1,298 sq. ft.

Plan Features

- Energy efficient home with 2"x 6" exterior walls
- A cozy veranda offers an enchanting spot to unwind
- The spacious vaulted kitchen offers space for dining and has access to a large rear deck
- The laundry area is located next to the kitchen
- 3 bedrooms, 2 baths
- Basement or crawl space foundation, please specify when ordering

---

Plan #583-007D-0032

Total Living Area: 1,294 sq. ft.

Plan Features

- Great room features a fireplace and large bay with windows and patio doors
- Vaulted master bedroom features a bay window and two walk-in closets
- Bedroom #2 boasts a vaulted ceiling, plant shelf and half bath, perfect for a studio
- 2 bedrooms, 1 full bath, 2 half baths, 1-car rear entry garage
- Basement foundation

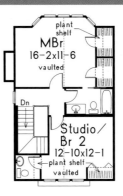

Second Floor
576 sq. ft.

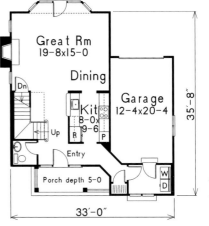

First Floor
718 sq. ft.

Total Living Area: 2,073 sq. ft.

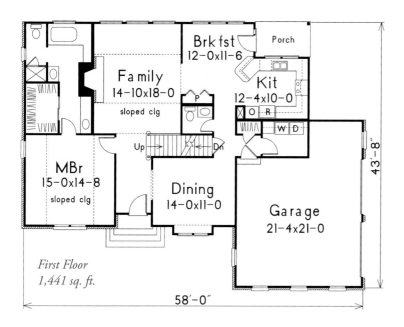

First Floor
1,441 sq. ft.

58'-0"

43'-8"

Brk fst
12-0x11-6

Porch

Family
14-10x18-0
sloped clg

Kit
12-4x10-0

MBr
15-0x14-8
sloped clg

Up   Dn

Dining
14-0x11-0

Garage
21-4x21-0

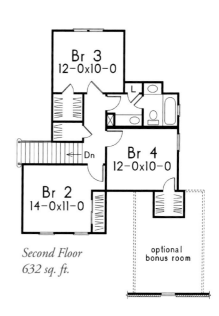

Second Floor
632 sq. ft.

Br 3
12-0x10-0

Br 4
12-0x10-0

Br 2
14-0x11-0

Dn

optional
bonus room

Plan Features

- Family room provides an ideal gathering area with a fireplace, large windows and vaulted ceiling
- Private first floor master bedroom enjoys a vaulted ceiling and luxury bath
- Kitchen features an angled bar connecting the kitchen and breakfast area
- 4 bedrooms, 2 1/2 baths, 2-car side entry garage
- Basement foundation

Plan #583-039D-0013

Price Code: C

Width: 56'-4"
Depth: 68'-6"

Porch
11 x 6/10

Family Room
14 x 17/1

12' Vaulted Clg.

Bookcase

Breakfast
10/9 x 11/6

9' Ceiling

Master
14 x 16

9' Ceiling

Skylight

Kitchen
17/5 x 9

Br. #2
11 x 12/10

9' Ceiling

Skylight

Foyer
6 x 8

Dining
11 x12

10' Ceiling

Utility
W D

Br. #3
11 x12

9' Ceiling

Porch

Garage
22 x 22

Total Living Area: 1,842 sq. ft.

Plan Features

- Vaulted family room features a fireplace and an elegant bookcase
- Island countertop in kitchen makes cooking convenient
- Rear facade has an intimate porch area ideal for relaxing
- 3 bedrooms, 2 baths, 2-car garage
- Slab or crawl space foundation, please specify when ordering

---

Plan #583-038D-0018

Price Code: B

Total Living Area: 1,792 sq. ft.

Plan Features

- Master bedroom has a private bath and large walk-in closet
- A central stone fireplace and windows on two walls are focal points in the living room
- Decorative beams and sloped ceilings add interest to the kitchen, living and dining rooms
- 3 bedrooms, 2 baths, 2-car drive under garage
- Basement foundation

56'-0"

Deck

Kitchen
12 x 11-4

Dining Rm
9 x 11-4

Ldry

pantry

MBr 1
14-2 x 14-4

32'-0"

Living Rm
21-6 x 19-4

decor. beams

slope

Br 3
12 x 12-6

Br 2
12 x 12-6

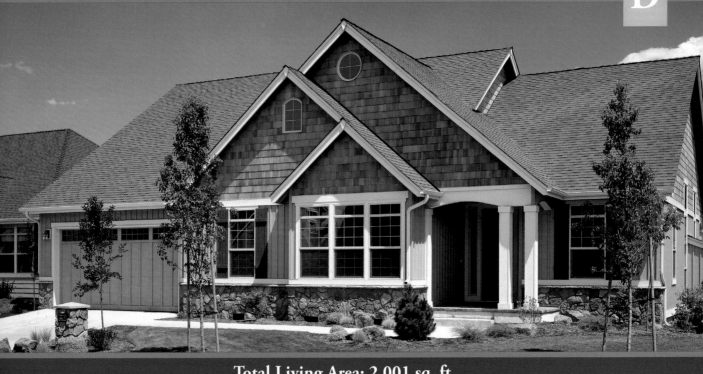

Total Living Area: 2,001 sq. ft.

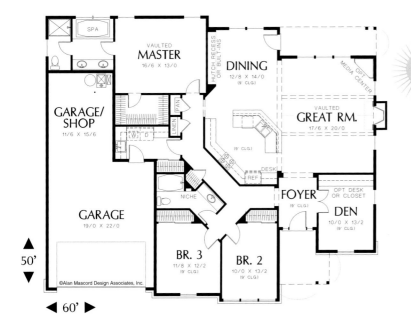

©Alan Mascord Design Associates, Inc.

50'

60'

DID YOU KNOW?

Relaxing in a warm, bubbling spa or hot tub can relieve sore muscles, invigorate the skin, and contribute to a sense of calm. Once only available at great expense, many manufacturers now offer kits for home use that are affordable, easy to install, and can be adapted to just about any home. Most spa and hot tub dealers will assist you with delivery and installation of the unit. In most cases, you just place the hot tub, fill it with a water hose, set the controls and you're ready to go.

Plan Features

- Large wrap-around counter in kitchen is accessible from the dining area
- A double-door entry keeps the den secluded from other living areas making it an ideal home office
- Decorative columns adorn the entry leading into the great room
- 3 bedrooms, 2 baths, 3-car garage
- Crawl space foundation

Plan #583-028D-0005

Price Code: C

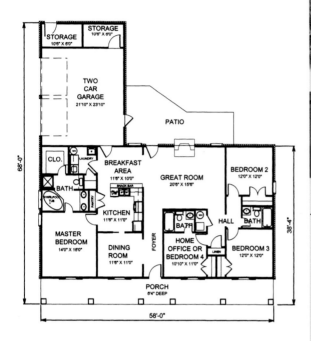

Total Living Area: 1,856 sq. ft.

Plan Features

- Kitchen is well positioned between the formal dining room and the casual breakfast area
- Master bedroom has a luxurious bath with all the amenities
- Home office or bedroom #4 has its own private bath
- 4 bedrooms, 3 baths, 2-car side entry garage
- Crawl space or slab foundation, please specify when ordering

---

Plan #583-072D-0007

Price Code: C

Total Living Area: 2,143 sq. ft.

Plan Features

- The kitchen handles every task because of its efficiency
- A cozy casual family room has a fireplace for warmth and a convenient log bin accessible from the garage as well
- Dining and living rooms combine, perfect for entertaining
- 4 bedrooms, 3 baths, 2-car garage
- Basement foundation

Second Floor
943 sq. ft.

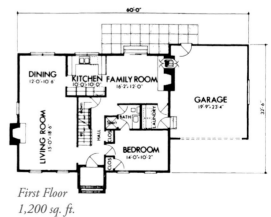

First Floor
1,200 sq. ft.

Total Living Area: 1,699 sq. ft.

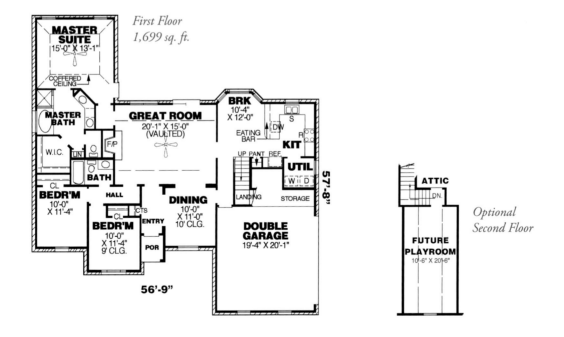

First Floor 1,699 sq. ft.

Optional Second Floor

Plan Features

- Master suite is filled with luxury including a private bath with glass shower, oversized tub, large walk-in closet and double vanity
- Wonderful kitchen and breakfast room arrangement makes great use of space
- Bonus room on the second floor has an additional 260 square feet of living area
- 3 bedrooms, 2 baths, 2-car side entry garage
- Slab foundation

Plan #583-021D-0018

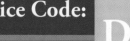

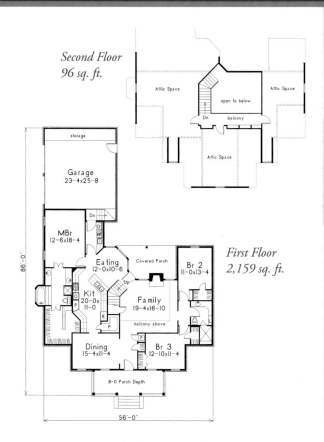

Second Floor
96 sq. ft.

First Floor
2,159 sq. ft.

Total Living Area: 2,255 sq. ft.

Plan Features

- Master bedroom with adjoining bath has an enormous walk-in closet
- Energy efficient home with 2"x 6" exterior walls
- Kitchen has a planning desk and convenient eating area
- Balcony library overlooks living area
- 3 bedrooms, 2 baths, 2-car side entry garage
- Crawl space foundation, drawings also include slab and basement foundations

---

Plan #583-055D-0064

Price Code: **B**

Total Living Area: 1,544 sq. ft.

Plan Features

- Great room has a vaulted ceiling and fireplace
- 32' x 8' grilling porch in rear
- Kitchen features a center island
- 3 bedrooms, 2 baths
- Crawl space or slab foundation, please specify when ordering

Second Floor
513 sq. ft.

First Floor
1,031 sq. ft.

Total Living Area: 3,144 sq. ft.

Second Floor
1,420 sq. ft.

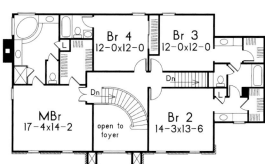

Br 4
12-0x12-0

Br 3
12-0x12-0

Dn

Dn

MBr
17-4x14-2

open to foyer

Br 2
14-3x13-6

First Floor
1,724 sq. ft.

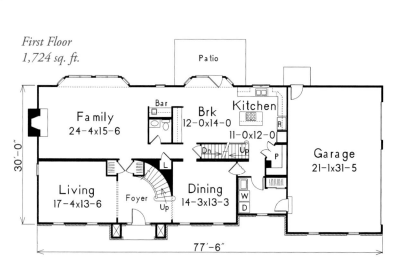

Patio

Family
24-4x15-6

Bar

Brk
12-0x14-0

Kitchen
11-0x12-0

R

Garage
21-1x31-5

Dn   Up

P

30'-0"

Living
17-4x13-6

Foyer

L

Up

Dining
14-3x13-3

W
D

77'-6"

Plan Features

- 9' ceilings on the first floor
- Kitchen offers large pantry, island cooktop and close proximity to laundry and dining rooms
- Expansive family room includes wet bar, fireplace and an attractive bay window
- 4 bedrooms, 4 1/2 baths, 3-car side entry garage
- Basement foundation

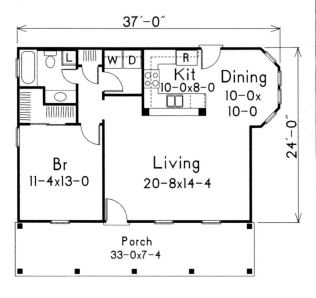

37'-0"

24'-0"

L W D R

Kit
10-0x8-0

Dining
10-0x
10-0

Br
11-4x13-0

Living
20-8x14-4

Porch
33-0x7-4

Total Living Area: 829 sq. ft.

Plan Features

- U-shaped kitchen opens into living area by a 42" high counter
- Oversized bay window and French door accent dining room
- Gathering space is created by the large living room
- Convenient utility room and linen closet
- 1 bedroom, 1 bath
- Slab foundation

Total Living Area: 2,288 sq. ft.

Plan Features

- Truly sumptuous master bedroom includes a 12' ceiling, two walk-in closets, sitting area and full bath
- Family room features a 14' ceiling and a rear window wall with French doors leading to an enormous deck
- Cozy hearth room includes a TV niche
- 3 bedrooms, 2 1/2 baths, 2-car side entry garage
- Basement or crawl space foundation, please specify when ordering

DECK
19'-8" x 15'-0"

DINING
15'10" x 11'-0"

HEARTH ROOM
16'-7" x 13'-0"

MASTER BDRM
16'-0" x 15'-0"

FAMILY ROOM
16'-0" x 19'-0"

KITCHEN
16'-0" x 13'-0"

BRKFST
10'-0" x 10'-6"

BEDROOM 2
11'-0" x 14'-0"

BEDROOM 3
11'-0" x 14'-0"

ENTRY

PORCH

GARAGE
21'-0" x 23'-0"

62'-9"

69'-4"

Total Living Area: 1,643 sq. ft.

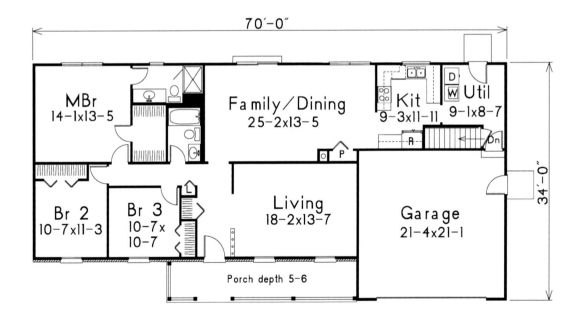

70'-0"

MBr
14-1x13-5

Family/Dining
25-2x13-5

Kit
9-3x11-11

Util
9-1x8-7

P

R

Dn

Br 2
10-7x11-3

Br 3
10-7x
10-7

Living
18-2x13-7

Garage
21-4x21-1

34'-0"

Porch depth 5-6

Plan Features

- An attractive front entry porch gives this ranch a country accent
- Kitchen and utility room are conveniently located near gathering areas
- Formal living room in the front of the home provides area for quiet and privacy
- Master bedroom has view to the rear of the home and a generous walk-in closet
- 3 bedrooms, 2 baths, 2-car garage
- Basement foundation, drawings also include crawl space and slab foundations

Plan #583-007D-0103

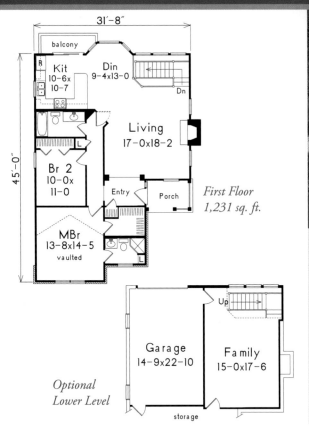

First Floor
1,231 sq. ft.

Optional
Lower Level

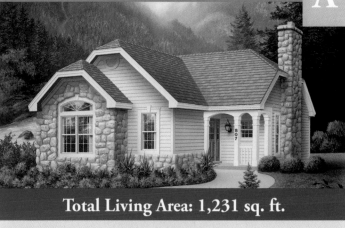

Total Living Area: 1,231 sq. ft.

Plan Features

- The spacious living room offers a masonry fireplace, atrium with window wall and is open to a dining area with bay window
- Kitchen has a breakfast counter, lots of cabinet space and glass sliding doors to a balcony
- 380 square feet of optional living area on the lower level
- 2 bedrooms, 2 baths, 1-car drive under garage
- Walk-out basement foundation

Plan #583-013D-0026

Total Living Area: 2,187 sq. ft.

Plan Features

- Lots of windows create a sunny atmosphere in the breakfast room
- Exceptional master bedroom enjoys an enormous bath and unique morning porch
- The roomy deck may be accessed from the family room and master bedroom
- 4 bedrooms, 2 1/2 baths, 2-car side entry garage
- Basement, crawl space or slab foundation, please specify when ordering

D

Total Living Area: 1,945 sq. ft.

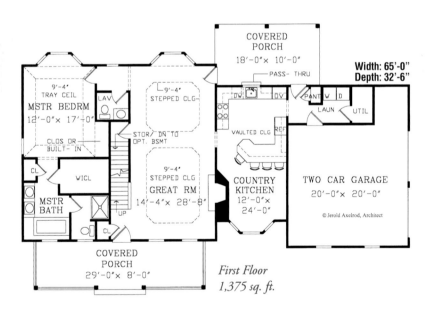

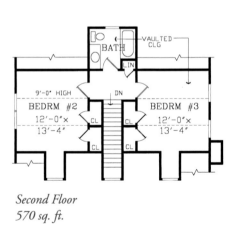

COVERED PORCH
18'-0" x 10'-0"

—PASS-THRU—

Width: 65'-0"
Depth: 32'-6"

9'-4"
TRAY CEIL
MSTR BEDRM
12'-0" x 17'-0"

LAV

9'-4"
STEPPED CLG

DW

DV

PANT W D

LAUN UTIL

CLOS OR
BUILT-IN

STOR/ DN TO
OPT. BSMT

VAULTED CLG

REF

CL

WICL

9'-4"
STEPPED CLG
GREAT RM
14'-4" x 28'-8"

UP

MSTR BATH

CL

COUNTRY KITCHEN
12'-0" x 24'-0"

TWO CAR GARAGE
20'-0" x 20'-0"

© Jerold Axelrod, Architect

COVERED PORCH
29'-0" x 8'-0"

First Floor
1,375 sq. ft.

BATH

VAULTED CLG

LIN

9'-0" HIGH

BEDRM #2
12'-0" x
13'-4"

DN

CL

CL

BEDRM #3
12'-0" x
13'-4"

CL

CL

Second Floor
570 sq. ft.

Plan Features

- Great room has a stepped ceiling and a fireplace
- Bayed dining area enjoys a stepped ceiling and French door leading to a covered porch
- Master bedroom has a tray ceiling, bay window and large walk-in closet
- 3 bedrooms, 2 1/2 baths, 2-car side entry garage
- Basement, crawl space or slab foundation, please specify when ordering

Second Floor
784 sq. ft.

First Floor
716 sq. ft.

Total Living Area: 1,500 sq. ft.

Plan Features

- Kitchen and dining area are perfectly organized with a center island, large pantry and work desk
- Vaulted master bedroom has its own bath
- A plant shelf graces the foyer
- 3 bedrooms, 2 1/2 baths, 2-car garage
- Crawl space foundation

Total Living Area: 1,609 sq. ft.

Plan Features

- Laundry area is adjacent to kitchen for convenience
- Two storage areas; one can be accessed from the outdoors and the other from the garage
- Eating bar overlooks from kitchen into dining area
- 3 bedrooms, 2 baths, 2-car side entry garage
- Slab foundation

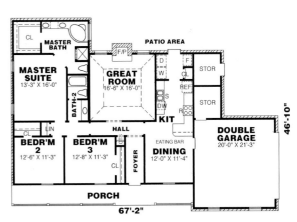

Total Living Area: 2,597 sq. ft.

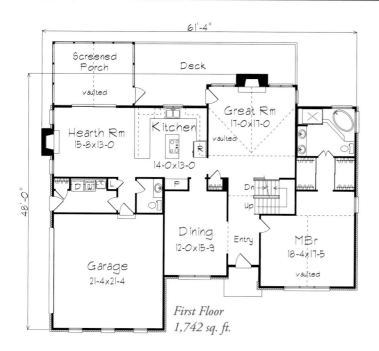

First Floor
1,742 sq. ft.

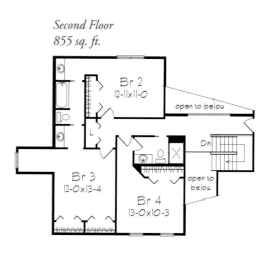

Second Floor
855 sq. ft.

Plan Features

- Large U-shaped kitchen features an island cooktop and breakfast bar
- Entry and great room are enhanced by sweeping balcony
- Bedrooms #2 and #3 share a bath, while the fourth bedroom has a private bath
- Vaulted great room includes transomed arch windows
- 4 bedrooms, 3 1/2 baths, 2-car side entry garage
- Walk-out basement foundation, drawings also include crawl space and slab foundations

Plan #583-024D-0010

Price Code: **B**

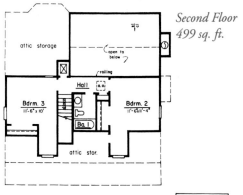

Second Floor 499 sq. ft.

attic storage

open to below

ceiling

railing

Hall

Bdrm. 3
11'-6" x 10'

Ba.

Bdrm. 2
11'-6" x 11'-4"

attic stor.

Total Living Area: 1,737 sq. ft.

Width: 36'-0"
Depth: 49'-0"

Patio

First Floor 1,238 sq. ft.

Util.

Brkfst.
9' x 11'

Living
20'-6" x 14'

Kit.
11'-6" x 10'-8"

1/2 Ba.

Dr.

Ba.

Dining
11'-6" x 13'

Bdrm. 1
16'-6" x 13'-6"

Foyer

Porch
36' x 5'

Plan Features

- U-shaped kitchen, sunny bayed breakfast room and living area become one large gathering area
- Living area has a sloped ceiling and a balcony overlook from the second floor
- Second floor includes lots of storage area
- 3 bedrooms, 2 1/2 baths
- Slab or crawl space foundation, please specify when ordering

---

Plan #583-011D-0026

Price Code: **E**

Total Living Area: 2,320 sq. ft.

Plan Features

- Family room is flooded with sunlight from wall of windows
- Decorative columns help separate dining area from living area
- Breakfast nook has sliding glass doors leading to the outdoors
- 4 bedrooms, 2 1/2 baths, 2-car garage
- Crawl space foundation

Second Floor 1,100 sq. ft.

MASTER
12/0 X 14/8

BR. 2
11/4 X 10/0

LOFT
10/10 X 9/8

3 CAR VER.
20/4 X 10/0

BR. 4
11/4 X 10/0

LIVING RM.
BELOW

BR. 3
10/8 X 10/8

©Alan Mascord Design Associates, Inc.

NOOK
11/0 X 8/0
(9' CLG.)

FAMILY
16/4 X 14/8
(9' CLG.)

First Floor 1,220 sq. ft.

DINING
11/2 X 10/0
(9' CLG.)

GARAGE
19/2 X 22/8
3 CAR - 29/2 X 22/8

VAULTED
LIVING
14/10 X 12/6

50'

DEN
11/0 X 11/2

◀ 40' ▶
3 CAR VER. 49' WIDE

Plan #583-024D-0062

Price Code: H

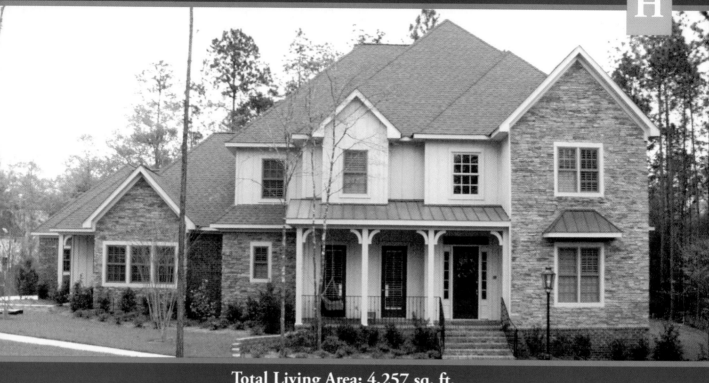

Total Living Area: 4,257 sq. ft.

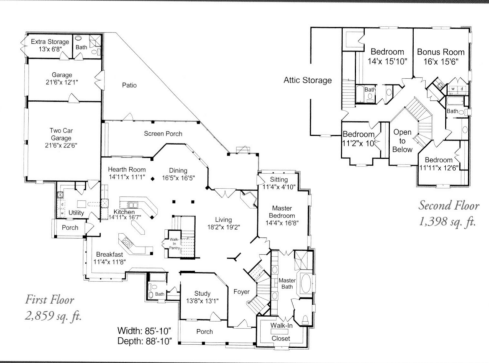

First Floor
2,859 sq. ft.

Width: 85'-10"
Depth: 88'-10"

Second Floor
1,398 sq. ft.

Plan Features

- Unique angles throughout the house add style
- The dining area is defined by decorative columns
- The utility room doubles as a hobby room and includes a TV cabinet
- The master bedroom enjoys a sitting area, exquisite bath and a large walk-in closet
- 4 bedrooms, 4 1/2 baths, 3-car side entry garage
- Crawl space foundation

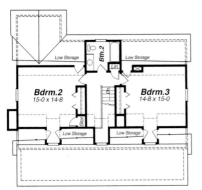

Second Floor
711 sq. ft.

Low Storage   Bth.2   Lin.   Low Storage

Bdrm.2
15-0 x 14-8

Bdrm.3
14-8 x 15-0

Low Storage   Low Storage

First Floor
1,159 sq. ft.

6-0

Sundeck
16-0 x 12-0

Brkfst.
10-6 x 7-6

Kit.
10-6 x 10-0

Dining
10-10 x 8-10

Lav.   W. D.   M.Bath

38-0

Living Area
20-6 x 13-6

Master Bedroom
17-6 x 14-6

Entry

44-4

Total Living Area: 1,870 sq. ft.

Plan Features

- Kitchen is open to the living and dining areas
- Breakfast area has a cathedral ceiling creating a sunroom effect
- Master bedroom is spacious with all the amenities
- Second floor bedrooms share hall bath
- 3 bedrooms, 2 1/2 baths, 2-car drive under garage
- Basement foundation

Total Living Area: 2,547 sq. ft.

Plan Features

- Grand-sized great room features a 12' volume ceiling, fireplace with built-in wrap-around shelving and patio doors with sidelights and transom windows
- The kitchen features a walk-in pantry, computer desk, breakfast island for seven and bayed breakfast area
- The master bedroom suite enjoys a luxurious bath, large walk-in closets and patio access
- 4 bedrooms, 2 1/2 baths, 3-car side entry garage
- Basement foundation

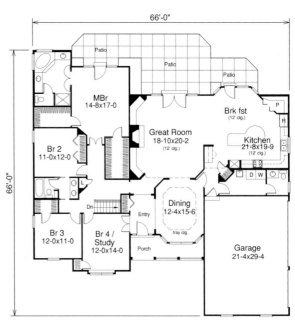

66'-0"

66'-0"

Patio   Patio   Patio

MBr
14-8x17-0

Brk fst
(12' clg.)

Great Room
18-10x20-2
(12' clg.)

Kitchen
21-8x19-9
(12' clg.)

Br 2
11-0x12-0

D   W

Dn

Dining
12-4x15-6
tray clg.

Entry

Br 3
12-0x11-0

Br 4 /
Study
12-0x14-0

Porch

Garage
21-4x29-4

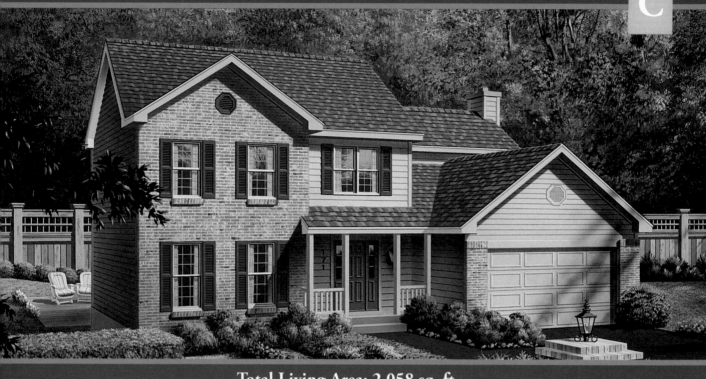

Total Living Area: 2,058 sq. ft.

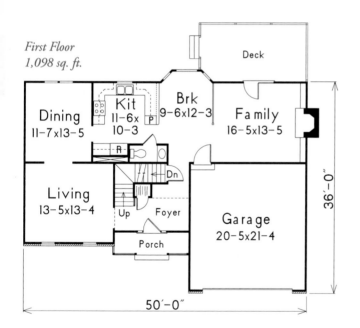

First Floor 1,098 sq. ft.

Deck

Dining
11-7x13-5

Kit
11-6x
10-3

Brk
9-6x12-3

Family
16-5x13-5

Living
13-5x13-4

Up   Foyer   Dn

Garage
20-5x21-4

Porch

36'-0"

50'-0"

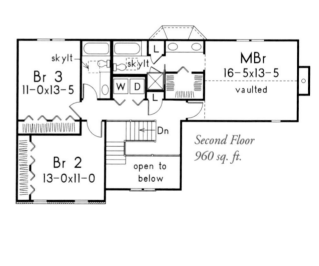

Br 3
11-0x13-5

skylt   skylt

W D

MBr
16-5x13-5
vaulted

L

L

Dn

Br 2
13-0x11-0

open to below

Second Floor 960 sq. ft.

Plan Features

- Handsome two-story foyer with balcony creates a spacious entrance area
- Vaulted ceiling in the master bedroom with private dressing area and large walk-in closet
- Skylights furnish natural lighting in the hall and master bath
- Laundry closet is conveniently located on the second floor near the bedrooms
- 3 bedrooms, 2 1/2 baths, 2-car garage
- Basement foundation, drawings also include slab and crawl space foundations

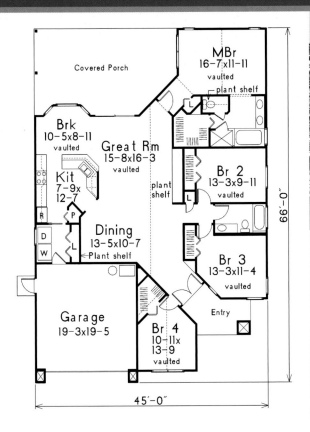

Total Living Area: 1,865 sq. ft.

Plan Features

- The large foyer opens into an expansive dining area and great room
- Home features vaulted ceilings throughout
- Master bedroom features an angled entry, vaulted ceiling, plant shelf and bath with double vanity, tub and shower
- 4 bedrooms, 2 baths, 2-car garage
- Slab foundation, drawings also include crawl space foundation

Total Living Area: 2,156 sq. ft.

Plan Features

- Secluded master bedroom has spa-style bath with corner whirlpool tub, large shower, double sinks and a walk-in closet
- Kitchen overlooks rear patio
- Plenty of windows add an open, airy feel to the great room
- 4 bedrooms, 3 baths, 2-car side entry garage
- Basement, crawl space or slab foundation, please specify when ordering

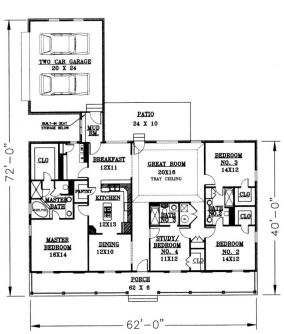

Total Living Area: 3,246 sq. ft.

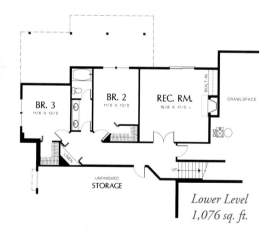

BR. 3
11/6 X 13/0

BR. 2
11/0 X 13/0

REC. RM.
16/8 X 17/0 +

BUILT-IN

CRAWLSPACE

LINEN

UNFINISHED
STORAGE

UP

Lower Level
1,076 sq. ft.

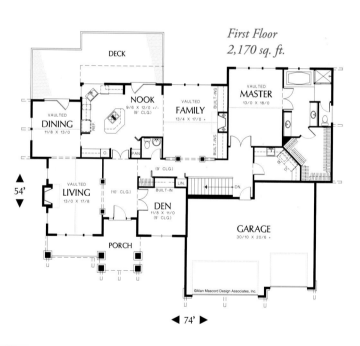

DECK

First Floor
2,170 sq. ft.

NOOK
9/6 X 12/0
(9' CLG.)

VAULTED
FAMILY
13/4 X 17/0

VAULTED
MASTER
13/0 X 18/0

BUILT-INS

VAULTED
DINING
11/8 X 13/0

REF.

PAN.

(9' CLG.)

W.I.C.

54'

VAULTED
LIVING
13/0 X 17/8

(10' CLG.)

BUILT-IN

LIN

DN.

DEN
11/8 X 11/0
(9' CLG.)

GARAGE
30/10 X 20/6 +

PORCH

©Alan Mascord Design Associates, Inc.

◄ 74' ►

Plan Features

- Private master bedroom has a sumptuous bath and large walk-in closet
- Lower level recreation room is a great casual family area
- L-shaped kitchen has a large center island with stove top and dining space
- 3 bedrooms, 2 1/2 baths, 3-car garage
- Walk-out basement foundation

Plan #583-058D-0010

Price Code:

26'-0"

26'-0"

Br 1
11-6x11-0

Kit
7-10x8-0

R

P

F

Din
11-2x8-5

Living
14-2x14-0

Covered Porch depth 6-0

Total Living Area: 676 sq. ft.

Plan Features

- See-through fireplace between bedroom and living area adds character
- Combined dining and living areas create an open feeling
- Full-length front covered porch is perfect for enjoying the outdoors
- Additional storage is available in the utility room
- 1 bedroom, 1 bath
- Crawl space foundation

Plan #583-032D-0036

Price Code:

Total Living Area: 1,285 sq. ft.

Plan Features

- Energy efficient home with 2"x 6" exterior walls
- Dining and living areas both access a large wrap-around porch
- First floor bath has convenient laundry closet as well as a shower
- 2 bedrooms, 2 baths
- Basement foundation

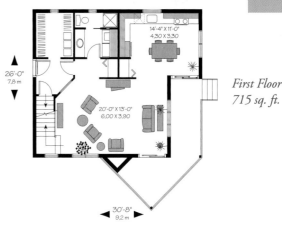

26'-0"
7,8 m

*First Floor
715 sq. ft.*

14'-4" X 11'-0"
4,30 X 3,30

20'-0" X 13'-0"
6,00 X 3,90

30'-8"
9,2 m

*Second Floor
570 sq. ft.*

11'-0" X 11'-4"
3,30 X 3,40

11'-8" X 19'-4"
3,50 X 5,80

Total Living Area: 1,597 sq. ft.

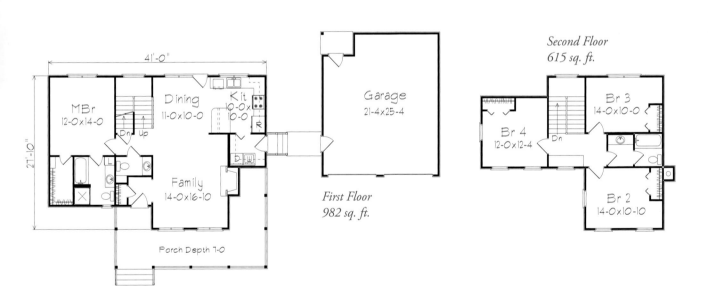

First Floor
982 sq. ft.

Second Floor
615 sq. ft.

Plan Features

- Spacious family room includes a fireplace and coat closet
- Open kitchen and dining room provide a breakfast bar and access to the outdoors
- Convenient laundry area is located near the kitchen
- Secluded master bedroom enjoys a walk-in closet and private bath
- 4 bedrooms, 2 1/2 baths, 2-car detached garage
- Basement foundation

Plan #583-032D-0041

Second Floor
587 sq. ft.

First Floor
895 sq. ft.

Total Living Area: 1,482 sq. ft.

Plan Features

- Energy efficient home with 2"x 6" exterior walls
- Corner fireplace warms living area
- Screened porch is spacious and connects to main living area in the home
- Two bedrooms on second floor share a spacious bath
- 2 bedrooms, 1 1/2 baths
- Basement foundation

Plan #583-025D-0013

Total Living Area: 1,686 sq. ft.

Plan Features

- Secondary bedrooms are separate from the master suite maintaining privacy
- Island in kitchen is ideal for food preparation
- Dramatic foyer leads to the great room
- Covered side porch has direct access into the great room
- 3 bedrooms, 2 baths, 2-car side entry garage
- Slab foundation

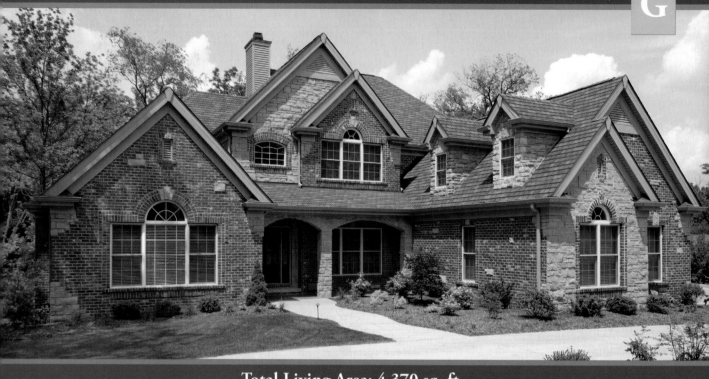

Total Living Area: 4,370 sq. ft.

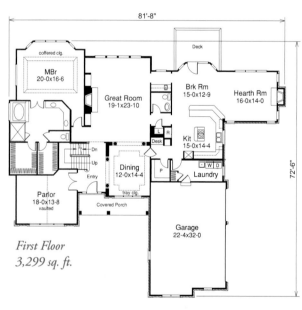

First Floor
3,299 sq. ft.

Second Floor
1,071 sq. ft.

Plan Features

- Two-story great room has a large fireplace, flanking bookshelves, massive window wall and balcony overlook
- The state-of-the-art kitchen has an island cooktop, built-in oven/microwave oven, large pantry, menu desk and opens to the breakfast and hearth rooms
- A coffered ceiling, bay window, and two walk-in closets adorn the master bedroom
- 4 bedrooms, 3 1/2 baths, 3-car side entry garage
- Walk-out basement foundation

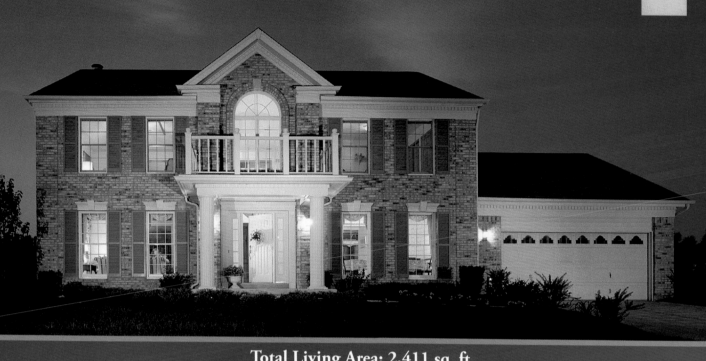

Total Living Area: 2,411 sq. ft.

First Floor
1,293 sq. ft.

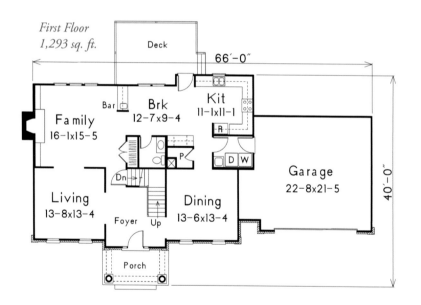

Deck

66'-0"

40'-0"

Bar
Brk
12-7x9-4
Kit
11-1x11-1

Family
16-1x15-5

R

Garage
22-8x21-5

Dn

P

D W

Living
13-8x13-4

Dining
13-6x13-4

Foyer
Up

Porch

Second Floor
1,118 sq. ft.

Study
11-5x11-8
Br 3
11-11x10-0

MBr
13-8x15-4

Dn

open to
below

vaulted

Br 2
13-8x11-0

L

Plan Features

- Elegant entrance features a two-story vaulted foyer
- Large family room is enhanced by a masonry fireplace and wet bar
- Master bath includes a walk-in closet, oversized tub and separate shower
- Second floor study could easily convert to a fourth bedroom
- 3 bedrooms, 2 1/2 baths, 2-car garage
- Basement foundation, drawings also include slab and crawl space foundations

Total Living Area: 1,840 sq. ft.

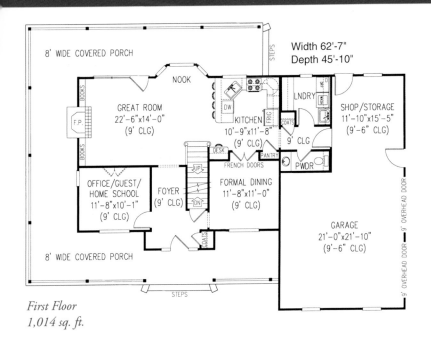

8' WIDE COVERED PORCH

NOOK

Width 62'-7"
Depth 45'-10"

GREAT ROOM
22'-6"x14'-0"
(9' CLG)

F.P.

BOOKS

BOOKS

KITCHEN
10'-9"x11'-8"
(9' CLG)

DW

FRIG

LNDRY

COATS

9' CLG

SHOP/STORAGE
11'-10"x15'-5"
(9'-6" CLG)

DESK

FRENCH DOORS

PANTRY

PWDR

OFFICE/GUEST/
HOME SCHOOL
11'-8"x10'-1"
(9' CLG)

FOYER
(9' CLG)

UP

DN

FORMAL DINING
11'-8"x11'-0"
(9' CLG)

COATS

GARAGE
21'-0"x21'-10"
(9'-6" CLG)

9' OVERHEAD DOOR

9' OVERHEAD DOOR

9' OVERHEAD DOOR

8' WIDE COVERED PORCH

STEPS

STEPS

First Floor
1,014 sq. ft.

BEDROOM #3
11'-8"x11'-9"

HALL
BATH

LIN

TUB/SHWR

TUB/SHWR

MSTR
BATH

LIN

W.I.C.

LIN

BEDROOM #2
10'-8"x10'-0"

6'-7"

DN

MASTER
BEDROOM
11'-8"x16'-0"
(10' TRAY CLG)

SITTING AREA
(VAULTED)

BOOKS

Second Floor
826 sq. ft.

Plan Features

- All bedrooms are located on the second floor for privacy
- Counter dining space is provided in the kitchen
- Formal dining room connects to the kitchen through French doors
- 4 bedrooms, 2 1/2 baths, 2-car side entry garage with shop/storage
- Basement, crawl space or slab foundation, please specify when ordering

Total Living Area: 1,680 sq. ft.

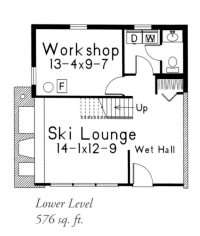

Workshop
13-4x9-7

D W

F

Ski Lounge
14-1x12-9   Wet Hall

Up

Lower Level
576 sq. ft.

26'-8"

Br 1
9-4x10-3

Kit
8-1x
9-1

R

24'-0"

Dn   Up

Living/Dining
23-4x12-9

Deck

First Floor
576 sq. ft.

Dorm
8-8x13-7

Dorm
8-8x13-7

sloped
clg

sloped
clg

Dn

Br 2
11-6x9-5

Br 3
11-6x9-5

Balcony

Second Floor
528 sq. ft.

Plan Features

- Highly functional lower level includes a wet hall with storage, laundry area, workshop and cozy ski lounge with an enormous fireplace
- First floor is warmed by a large fireplace in living/dining area which features a spacious wrap-around deck
- Lots of sleeping space for guests or a large family
- 5 bedrooms, 2 1/2 baths
- Basement foundation

To order call toll-free 1-800-DREAM HOME or visit www.houseplansandmore.com

Total Living Area: 1,991 sq. ft.

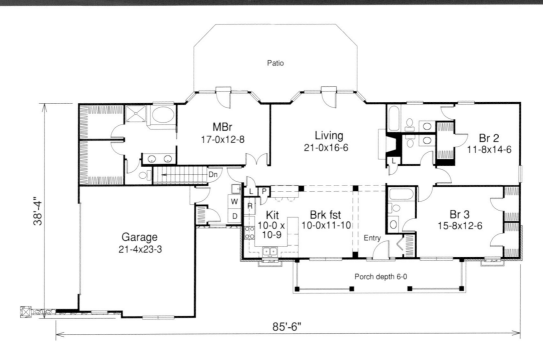

Plan Features

- A large porch with roof dormers and flanking stonework creates a distinctive country appeal
- The highly functional U-shaped kitchen is open to the dining and living rooms defined by a colonnade
- Large bay windows are enjoyed by both the living room and master bedroom
- 3 bedrooms, 3 1/2 baths, 2-car side entry garage
- Basement foundation

To order call toll-free 1-800-DREAM HOME or visit www.houseplansandmore.com

Total Living Area: 2,018 sq. ft.

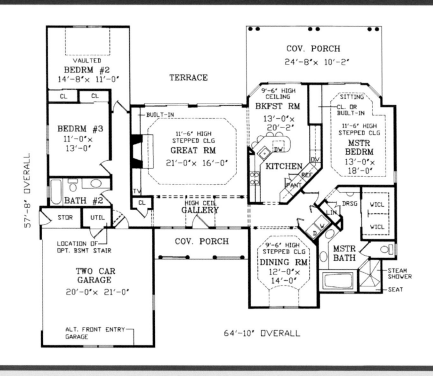

Plan Features

- Large expanses of elegant curved transomed windows flank the beautiful entrance
- Great room includes French doors leading to a large terrace
- Luxurious master bedroom has fabulous master bath, double closets and accesses rear porch
- 3 bedrooms, 2 baths, 2-car side entry garage
- Basement, slab or crawl space foundation, please specify when ordering

Total Living Area: 1,841 sq. ft.

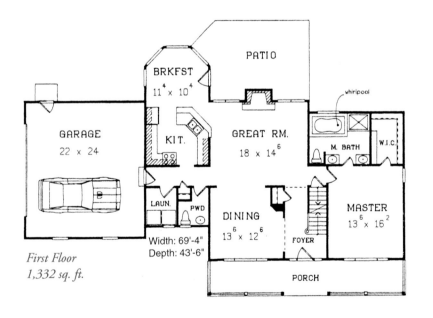

PATIO

BRKFST
11⁴ x 10⁴

GARAGE
22 x 24

KIT.

GREAT RM.
18 x 14⁶

whirlpool

M. BATH

W.I.C.

LAUN.

PWD

DINING
13⁶ x 12⁶

FOYER

MASTER
13⁶ x 16²

Width: 69'-4"
Depth: 43'-6"

First Floor
1,332 sq. ft.

PORCH

Second Floor
509 sq. ft.

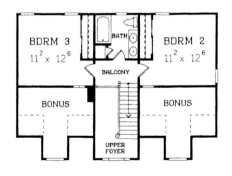

BDRM 3
11² x 12⁶

BATH

BDRM 2
11² x 12⁶

BALCONY

BONUS

BONUS

UPPER
FOYER

Plan Features

- Sunny bayed breakfast room is cheerful for meals
- The master suite remains separate from the other bedrooms for privacy
- Second floor bonus rooms have a total of 295 square feet of additional living area
- 3 bedrooms, 2 1/2 baths, 2-car side entry garage
- Basement foundation

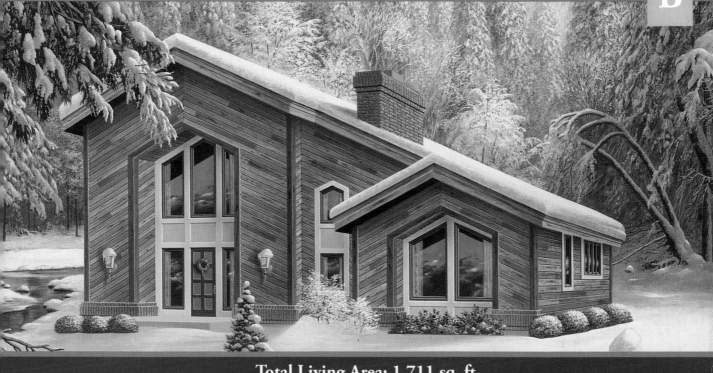

Total Living Area: 1,711 sq. ft.

40'-0"

Deck

First Floor
1,314 sq. ft.

34'-0"

Great Rm
19-3x18-6
vaulted

Kit/Brk
17-3x
14-0

P R

Up

Entry

L

MBr
13-7x14-7
vaulted

Dn

Porch

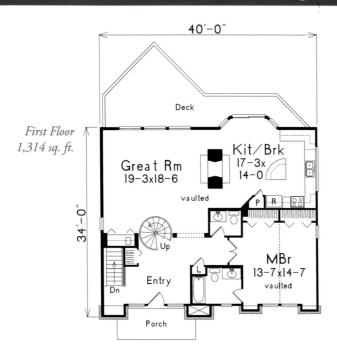

Second Floor
397 sq. ft.

open to below

plant shelf

Dn

Loft/Br 2
19-3x12-0
vaulted

MBr
below

Plan Features

- Vaulted great room has exposed beams, two-story window wall, fireplace, wet bar and balcony
- Bayed breakfast room shares the fireplace and joins a sun-drenched kitchen and deck
- Spiral stairs and a balcony dramatize the loft that doubles as a second bedroom
- 2 bedrooms, 2 1/2 baths
- Basement foundation

Rear View

Total Living Area: 1,425 sq. ft.

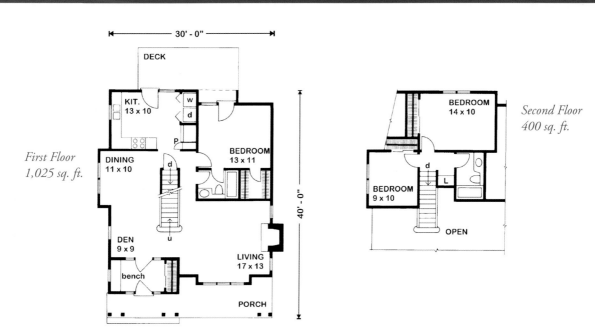

First Floor 1,025 sq. ft.

Second Floor 400 sq. ft.

Plan Features

- Double-door vestibule entrance features a large closet and window seat
- The living and dining rooms boast vaulted ceilings for added volume and drama
- The kitchen is equipped with a pantry, laundry alcove and French doors opening to a deck
- 3 bedrooms, 2 baths
- Basement or crawl space foundation, please specify when ordering

Total Living Area: 2,689 sq. ft.

First Floor
1,703 sq. ft.

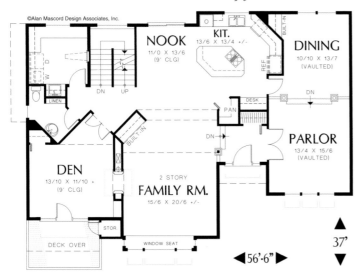

©Alan Mascord Design Associates, Inc.

NOOK
11/0 X 13/6
(9' CLG)

KIT.
13/6 X 13/4

DINING
10/10 X 13/7
(VAULTED)

REF.

BUILT-IN

DESK

PAN

DN

PARLOR
13/4 X 15/6
(VAULTED)

DN

DN

UP

LINEN

BUILT-IN

DEN
13/10 X 11/10 +
(9' CLG)

2 STORY
FAMILY RM.
15/6 X 20/6 +/-

STOR

DECK OVER

WINDOW SEAT

▲
37'
▼

◄ 56'-6" ►

Second Floor
986 sq. ft.

BR. 2
10/0 X 12/8

BR. 3
11/0 X 12/8

SH.

DN

LINEN

VAULTED
MASTER
15/2 X 15/8 +/-

OPEN TO
FAMILY ROOM
BELOW

DECK

STOR

Plan Features

- A private parlor and dining area off the kitchen are perfect for entertaining
- All bedrooms are located on the second floor for privacy
- A see-through fireplace warms both the family room and the den
- 3 bedrooms, 2 1/2 baths, 3-car drive under garage
- Crawl space foundation

D

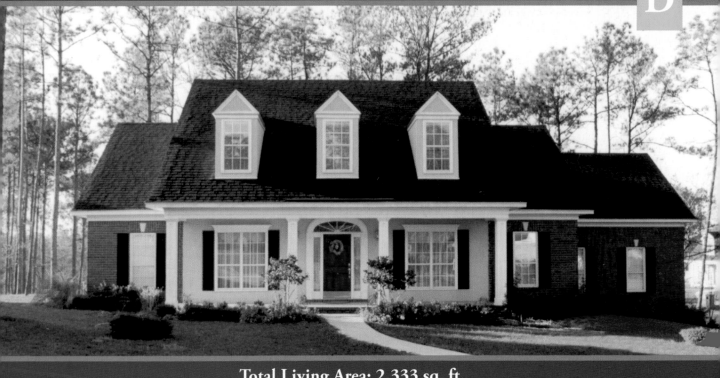

Total Living Area: 2,333 sq. ft.

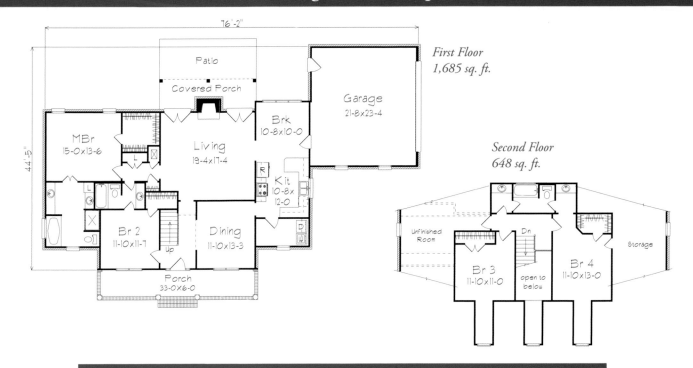

First Floor
1,685 sq. ft.

Second Floor
648 sq. ft.

Plan Features

- 9' ceilings on the first floor
- Master bedroom features a large walk-in closet and an inviting double-door entry into a spacious bath
- Convenient laundry room is located near the kitchen
- 4 bedrooms, 3 baths, 2-car side entry garage
- Slab foundation, drawings also include crawl space and partial crawl space/basement foundations

Total Living Area: 1,595 sq. ft.

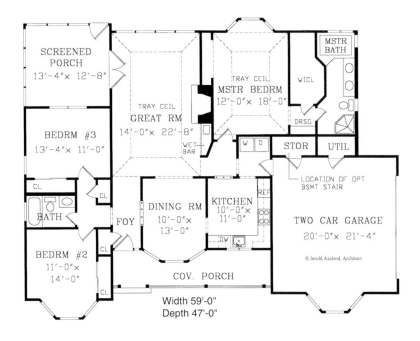

SCREENED PORCH
13'-4" x 12'-8"

TRAY CEIL
GREAT RM
14'-0" x 22'-8"

MSTR BATH

TRAY CEIL
MSTR BEDRM
12'-0" x 18'-0"

WICL

DRSG

BEDRM #3
13'-4" x 11'-0"

WET BAR

W D

STOR

UTIL

CL

CL

BATH

FOY

DINING RM
10'-0" x 13'-0"

KITCHEN
10'-0" x 11'-0"

REF

LOCATION OF OPT BSMT STAIR

TWO CAR GARAGE
20'-0" x 21'-4"

© Jerold Axelrod, Architect

BEDRM #2
11'-0" x 14'-0"

CL

DW

CL

COV. PORCH

Width 59'-0"
Depth 47'-0"

Plan Features

- Large great room features a tray ceiling and French doors to a screened porch
- Dining room and bedroom #2 have bay windows
- Master bedroom has a tray ceiling and a bay window
- 3 bedrooms, 2 baths, 2-car side entry garage
- Basement, crawl space, slab or walk-out basement foundation, please specify when ordering

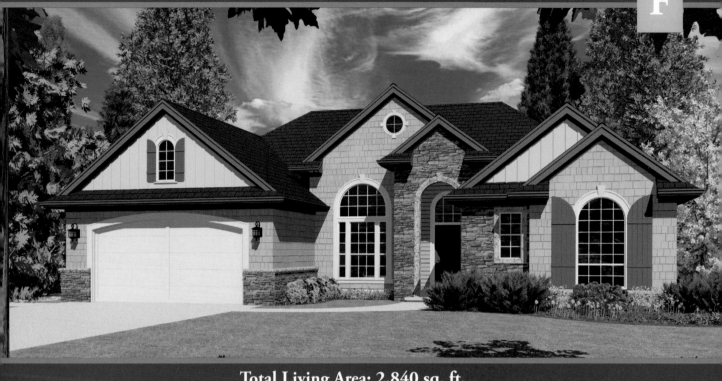

Total Living Area: 2,840 sq. ft.

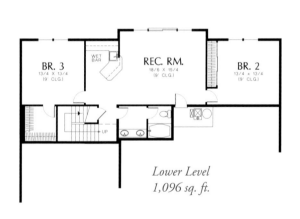

Lower Level
1,096 sq. ft.

First Floor
1,744 sq. ft.

Plan Features

- Secluded den has a half bath perfect for a home office
- Corner columns separate the formal dining room while maintaining openness
- Built-in bookshelves flank each side of the fireplace in the great room
- 3 bedrooms, 2 1/2 baths, 2-car garage
- Crawl space foundation

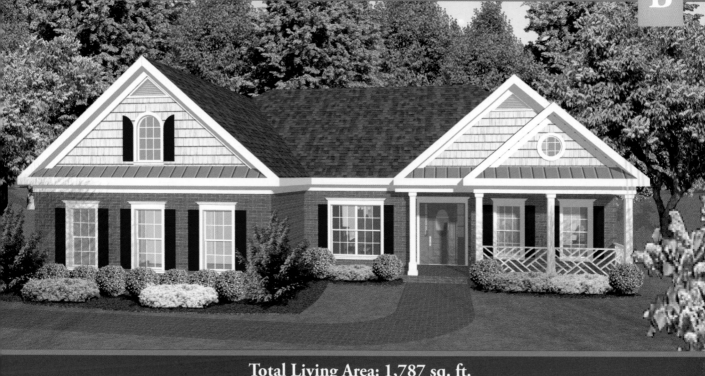

Total Living Area: 1,787 sq. ft.

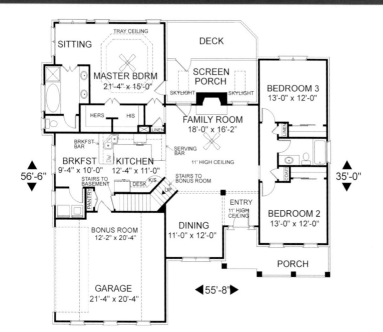

DID YOU KNOW?

Block sunlight from reaching weeds to stop growth in your vegetable garden. This can be done by spreading plastic or newspaper over the soil, but these materials can make it difficult for water to reach plant roots.

A better choice is to use landscaping fabric. Cover the entire area before planting, anchoring with brick or wire clips. Then cover the area with mulch. Cut small holes in the fabric to plant your seeds.

Plan Features

- Skylights brighten the screen porch connecting to the family room and deck outdoors
- Master bedroom features a comfortable sitting area, large private bath and direct access to the screen porch
- Kitchen has a serving bar which extends dining into the family room
- 3 bedrooms, 2 baths, 2-car side entry garage
- Basement, crawl space or slab foundation, please specify when ordering

Total Living Area: 2,176 sq. ft.

Second Floor
505 sq. ft.

First Floor
1,671 sq. ft.

Plan Features

- Outdoor living is created by the screened porch located off the great room
- Corner whirlpool tub in master bath is eye-catching
- Bedroom #3 has an enormous closet and additional cedar closet storage
- 3 bedrooms, 2 1/2 baths, 2-car garage
- Basement, crawl space or slab foundation, please specify when ordering

Total Living Area: 1,865 sq. ft.

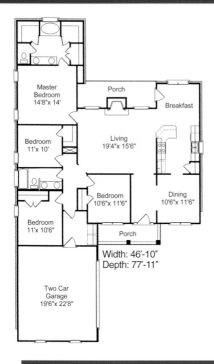

DID YOU KNOW?

For a stylish flower arrangement, pick flowers from your garden in the early morning or late evening. Place them in water immediately, or the stems will form an air-lock that prevents them from drinking.

Plan Features

- The foyer leads to the grand living room which displays a fireplace flanked by windows
- The master bedroom retreat features a private bath including three closets, a whirlpool tub and double-bowl vanity
- The garage entrance passes through the large utility area
- 4 bedrooms, 2 baths, 2-car side entry garage
- Slab foundation

Total Living Area: 2,061 sq. ft.

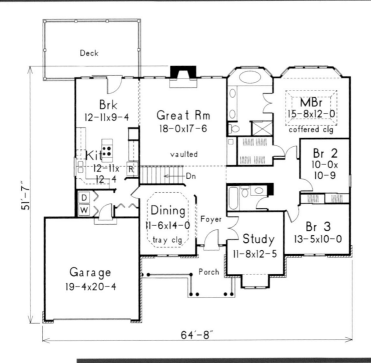

DID YOU KNOW?

Watering your lawn can be a tricky task as watering too much can be as harmful as too little. Too much water drains nutrients, including fertilizer, out of the soil and drives it down beyond the root system. Apply only enough water to soak the soil slightly below the roots. To determine root depth, excavate a small area of the lawn. On average roots are 6 to 8 inches deep.

Plan Features

- Master bedroom features a walk-in closet and double-door entrance into master bath with an oversized tub
- Formal dining room enjoys a tray ceiling
- Kitchen features island cooktop and breakfast room
- 3 bedrooms, 2 baths, 2-car garage
- Basement foundation

Total Living Area: 2,245 sq. ft.

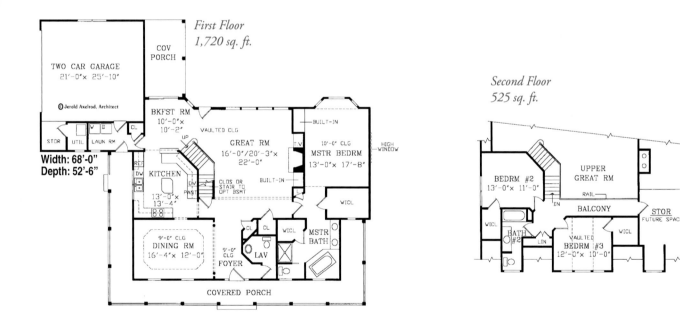

First Floor
1,720 sq. ft.

TWO CAR GARAGE
21'-0" x 25'-10"

COV
PORCH

© Jerold Axelrod, Architect

BKFST RM
10'-0" x
10'-2"

VAULTED CLG

STOR | UTIL | LAUN RM | CL

Width: 68'-0"
Depth: 52'-6"

GREAT RM
16'-0"/20'-3" x
22'-0"

BUILT-IN

10'-0" CLG
MSTR BEDRM
13'-0" x 17'-8"

HIGH
WINDOW

KITCHEN
13'-0" x
13'-4"

CLOS. OR
STAIR TO
OPT BSMT

BUILT-IN

PANT

WICL

DINING RM
16'-4" x 12'-0"
9'-0" CLG

9'-0"
CLG
LAV

FOYER

CL | CL | WICL

MSTR
BATH

COVERED PORCH

Second Floor
525 sq. ft.

BEDRM #2
13'-0" x 11'-0"

UPPER
GREAT RM

DN

RAIL

BALCONY

STOR
FUTURE SPACE

WICL

BATH
#2

LIN

VAULTED
BEDRM #3
12'-0" x 10'-0"

WICL

Plan Features

- Covered wrap-around porch and arched windows create wonderful curb appeal
- Great room with an 18' vaulted ceiling has a fireplace set into a media wall
- Master bedroom has a 10' ceiling and bay window
- 3 bedrooms, 2 1/2 baths, 2-car side entry garage
- Basement, crawl space or slab foundation, please specify when ordering

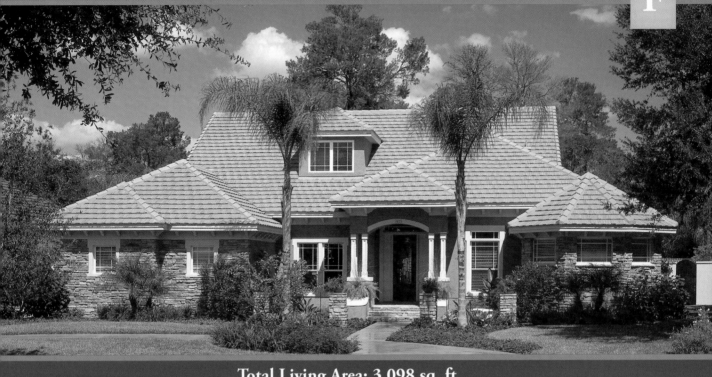

Total Living Area: 3,098 sq. ft.

First Floor
3,098 sq. ft.

Optional Second Floor

Plan Features

- Master bedroom has a private bath, enormous walk-in closet and sitting area
- Secluded study has double closets and built-ins
- Optional second floor has an additional 849 square feet of living area
- Framing - only concrete block available
- 4 bedrooms, 4 baths, 3-car side entry garage
- Slab foundation

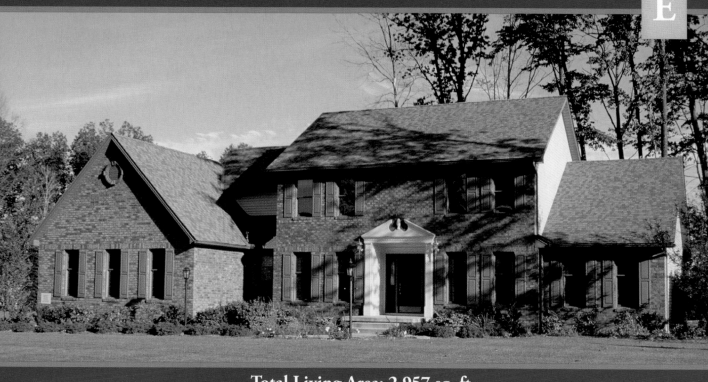

Total Living Area: 2,957 sq. ft.

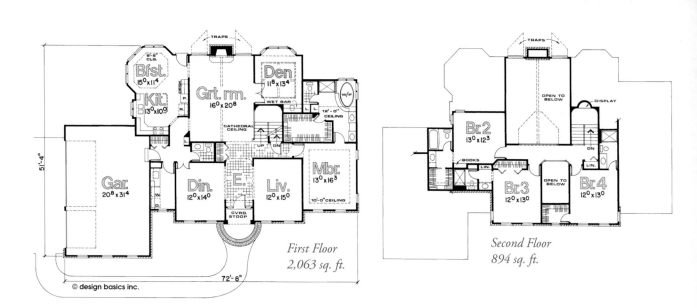

First Floor
2,063 sq. ft.

Second Floor
894 sq. ft.

© design basics inc.

Plan Features

- Expansive great room features a cathedral ceiling, a fireplace and opens into the den which includes a wet bar
- Charming bayed breakfast area connects with kitchen and has access to the outdoors
- All bedrooms boast their own private bath
- 4 bedrooms, 4 1/2 baths, 3-car garage
- Basement, crawl space or slab foundation, please specify when ordering

Total Living Area: 2,357 sq. ft.

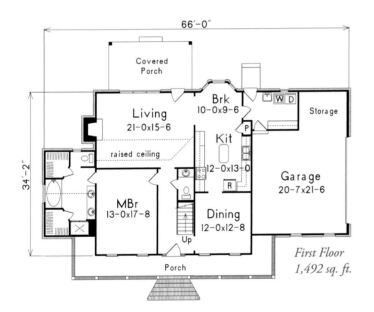

66'-0"

Covered Porch

Living
21-0x15-6

Brk
10-0x9-6

W D

Storage

raised ceiling

Kit
12-0x13-0

P

34'-2"

MBr
13-0x17-8

R

Garage
20-7x21-6

Dining
12-0x12-8

Up

Porch

First Floor
1,492 sq. ft.

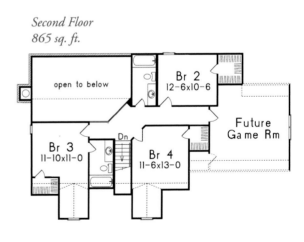

Second Floor
865 sq. ft.

open to below

Br 2
12-6x10-6

Future Game Rm

Br 3
11-10x11-0

Dn

Br 4
11-6x13-0

Plan Features

- 9' ceilings on the first floor
- Secluded master bedroom includes a private bath with double walk-in closets and vanity
- Balcony overlooks living room with large fireplace
- Future game room on the second floor has an additional 303 square feet of living area
- 4 bedrooms, 3 1/2 baths, 2-car side entry garage
- Slab foundation, drawings also include crawl space foundation

To order call toll-free 1-800-DREAM HOME or visit www.houseplansandmore.com

Total Living Area: 2,576 sq. ft.

First Floor
1,385 sq. ft.

Second Floor
1,191 sq. ft.

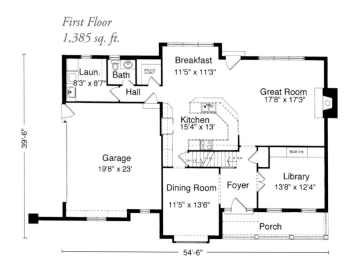

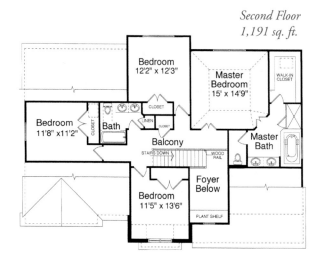

Plan Features

- The combined kitchen, breakfast and great rooms provide a centralized gathering place for family time
- The formal dining room creates an elegant entertaining space
- All bedrooms are located on the second floor for privacy
- 4 bedrooms, 2 1/2 baths, 2-car side entry garage
- Basement foundation

Total Living Area: 1,657 sq. ft.

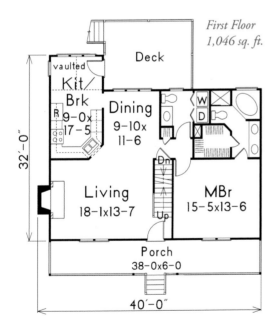

First Floor
1,046 sq. ft.

Deck

vaulted

Kit/
Brk
9-0x
17-5

Dining
9-10x
11-6

W
D

Living
18-1x13-7

Dn

Up

MBr
15-5x13-6

32'-0"

Porch
38-0x6-0

40'-0"

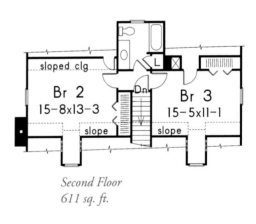

sloped clg

Br 2
15-8x13-3

Dn

Br 3
15-5x11-1

slope   slope

Second Floor
611 sq. ft.

Plan Features

- Stylish pass-through between living and dining areas
- Master bedroom is secluded from living area for privacy
- Large windows in breakfast and dining areas
- 3 bedrooms, 2 1/2 baths, 2-car drive under garage
- Basement foundation

Total Living Area: 3,160 sq. ft.

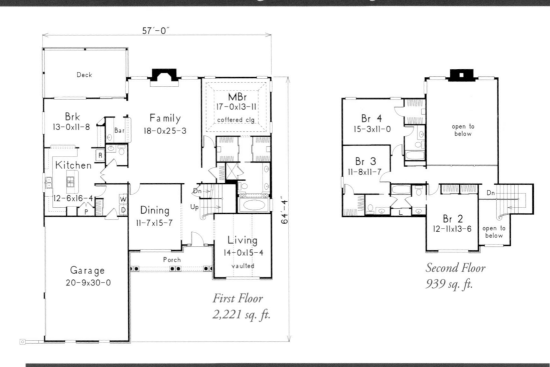

57'-0"

Deck

Brk
13-0x11-8

Family
18-0x25-3

MBr
17-0x13-11
coffered clg.

Bar

R

Kitchen

12-6x16-4

W
D

P

Dining
11-7x15-7

Dn

Up

64'-4"

Living
14-0x15-4
vaulted

Garage
20-9x30-0

Porch

First Floor
2,221 sq. ft.

Br 4
15-3x11-0

open to
below

Br 3
11-8x11-7

L

Dn

Br 2
12-11x13-6

open to
below

Second Floor
939 sq. ft.

Plan Features

- Covered entry porch leads into a magnificent two-story foyer which accesses formal rooms on either side
- First floor master bedroom features two walk-in closets and a large master bath
- Kitchen includes island cooktop and pass-through to breakfast room
- 4 bedrooms, 3 1/2 baths, 3-car side entry garage
- Basement foundation

Total Living Area: 2,874 sq. ft.

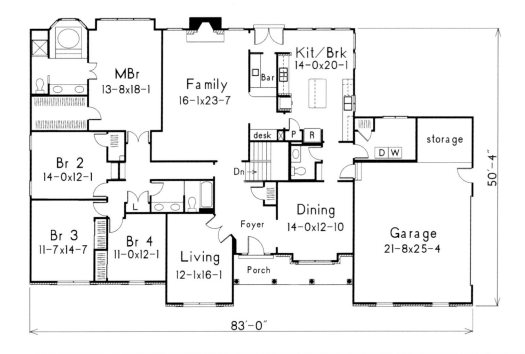

Plan Features

- Family room with sloped ceiling and wood beams adjoins the kitchen and breakfast area
- Large foyer opens to family room with massive stone fireplace and open stairs to the basement
- Private master bedroom includes a raised tub under the bay window, dramatic dressing area and a walk-in closet
- 4 bedrooms, 2 1/2 baths, 2-car side entry garage
- Basement foundation

Total Living Area: 3,199 sq. ft.

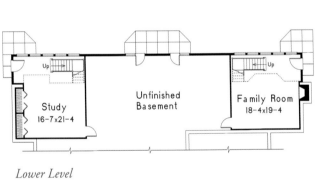

Lower Level
850 sq. ft.

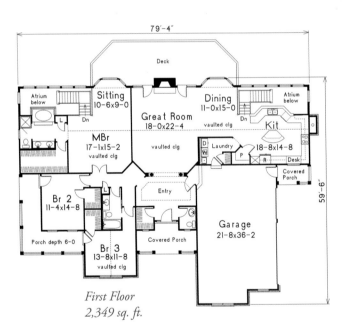

First Floor
2,349 sq. ft.

Plan Features

- Grand-scale kitchen features bay-shaped cabinetry built over an atrium that overlooks a two-story window wall
- A second atrium dominates the master bedroom that boasts a sitting area with bay window as well as a luxurious bath that has a whirlpool tub open to the garden atrium and lower level study
- 3 bedrooms, 2 1/2 baths, 3-car side entry garage
- Walk-out basement foundation

Rear View

Price Code:

B

Total Living Area: 1,559 sq. ft.

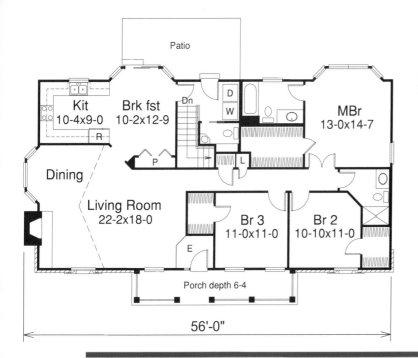

Patio

Kit
10-4x9-0

Brk fst
10-2x12-9

Dn

D

W

MBr
13-0x14-7

Dining

P

L

Living Room
22-2x18-0

Br 3
11-0x11-0

Br 2
10-10x11-0

E

Porch depth 6-4

56'-0"

DID YOU KNOW?

When you're done painting for the day, and know you need to continue on the next day, scrape off the excess paint, stick your brush in a resealable plastic bag, press the air out and seal. This keeps the brush from drying out even if you don't get back to the job for a couple of days. The same trick works for rollers too, sealing the bag with a twist-tie around the handle. As soon as you're finished with your project, give your brushes a thorough cleaning to ensure they will last a long time.

Plan Features

- A cozy country appeal is provided by a spacious porch, masonry fireplace, roof dormers and a perfect balance of stonework and siding
- Large living room enjoys a fireplace, bayed dining area and separate entry
- A U-shaped kitchen is adjoined by a breakfast room with bay window and large pantry
- 3 bedrooms, 2 1/2 baths, 2-car drive under side entry garage
- Basement foundation

Total Living Area: 1,516 sq. ft.

First Floor
817 sq. ft.

40'-0"

41'-4"

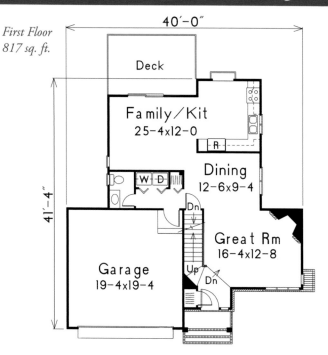

Deck

Family/Kit
25-4x12-0

Dining
12-6x9-4

W D

Great Rm
16-4x12-8

Dn

Up

Dn

Garage
19-4x19-4

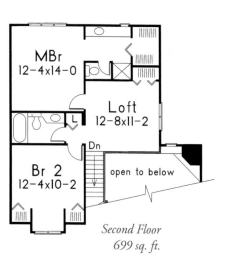

MBr
12-4x14-0

Loft
12-8x11-2

L

Br 2
12-4x10-2

Dn

open to below

Second Floor
699 sq. ft.

Plan Features

- All living and dining areas are interconnected for a spacious look and easy movement
- Covered entrance leads into sunken great room with a rugged corner fireplace
- Second floor loft opens to rooms below and can convert to a third bedroom
- The dormer in bedroom #2 adds interest
- 2 bedrooms, 2 1/2 baths, 2-car garage
- Basement foundation

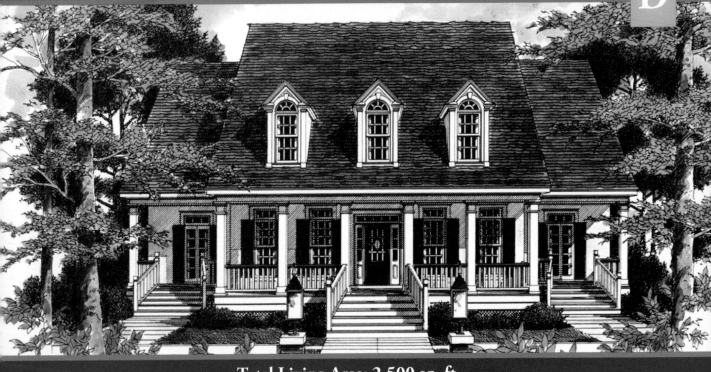

Total Living Area: 2,500 sq. ft.

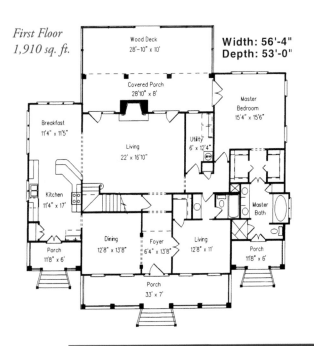

First Floor
1,910 sq. ft.

Wood Deck
28'-10" x 10'

Width: 56'-4"
Depth: 53'-0"

Covered Porch
28'10" x 8'

Breakfast
11'4" x 11'5"

Master
Bedroom
15'4" x 15'6"

Living
22' x 16'10"

Utility
6' x 12'4"

Kitchen
11'4" x 17'

Master
Bath

Dining
12'8" x 13'8"

Foyer
6'4" x 13'8"

Living
12'8" x 11'

Porch
11'8" x 6'

Porch
11'8" x 6'

Porch
33' x 7'

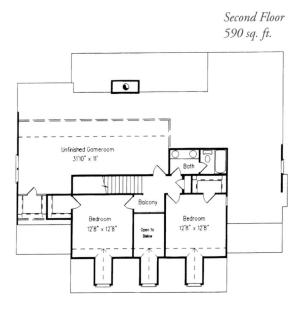

Second Floor
590 sq. ft.

Unfinished Gameroom
31'10" x 11'

Bath

Bedroom
12'8" x 12'8"

Balcony

Open to
Below

Bedroom
12'8" x 12'8"

Plan Features

- Master bedroom has its own separate wing with front porch, double walk-in closets, private bath and access to back porch and patio
- Large unfinished gameroom on the second floor has an additional 359 square feet of living area
- Living area is oversized and has a fireplace
- 3 bedrooms, 3 baths
- Basement, slab or crawl space foundation, please specify when ordering

Total Living Area: 3,231 sq. ft.

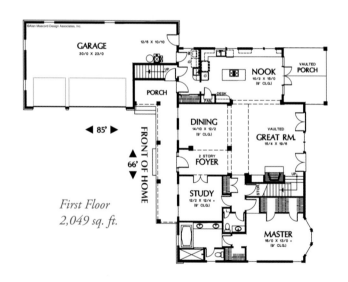

First Floor
2,049 sq. ft.

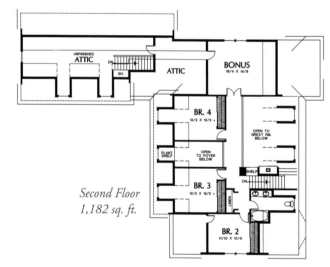

Second Floor
1,182 sq. ft.

Plan Features

- Breakfast nook and kitchen combine creating a large open dining space
- A cozy and private study is convenient to the master bedroom perfect for an office
- Decorative columns enhance the formal dining room
- Bonus room on the second floor is included in the square footage
- 4 bedrooms, 2 1/2 baths, 3-car garage
- Crawl space foundation

Total Living Area: 1,754 sq. ft.

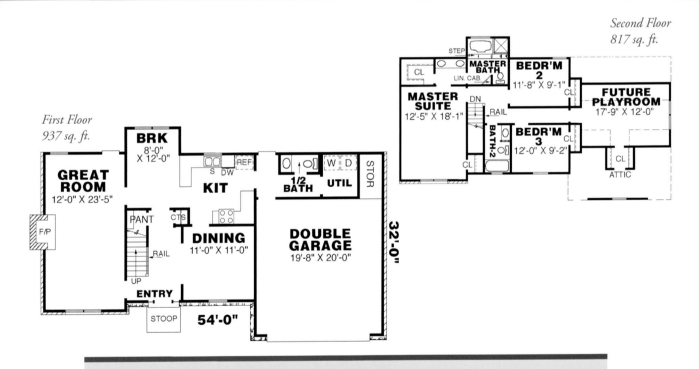

Second Floor
817 sq. ft.

MASTER BATH
CL
LIN. CAB.
STEP
BEDR'M 2
11'-8" X 9'-1"
CL
FUTURE PLAYROOM
17'-9" X 12'-0"
MASTER SUITE
12'-5" X 18'-1"
DN
RAIL
BATH-2
BEDR'M 3
12'-0" X 9'-2"
CL
CL
CL
ATTIC

First Floor
937 sq. ft.

BRK
8'-0" X 12'-0"
REF
S DW
GREAT ROOM
12'-0" X 23'-5"
KIT
1/2 BATH
W D
UTIL
STOR
F/P
PANT
CTS
DINING
11'-0" X 11'-0"
DOUBLE GARAGE
19'-8" X 20'-0"
32'-0"
RAIL
UP
ENTRY
STOOP
54'-0"

Plan Features

- All bedrooms are located on the second floor for privacy
- Master bath features a step-up tub as well as many other luxuries
- Expansive great room offers plenty of space for entertaining
- Future playroom on the second floor has an additional 258 square feet of living area
- 3 bedrooms, 2 1/2 baths, 2-car garage
- Slab foundation

Total Living Area: 2,000 sq. ft.

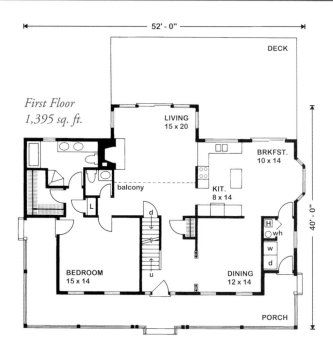

First Floor
1,395 sq. ft.

52' - 0"

DECK

LIVING
15 x 20

BRKFST.
10 x 14

balcony

KIT.
8 x 14

40' - 0"

BEDROOM
15 x 14

DINING
12 x 14

PORCH

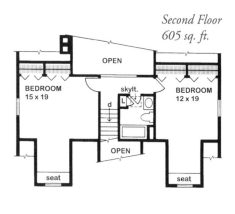

Second Floor
605 sq. ft.

OPEN

BEDROOM
15 x 19

skylt.

BEDROOM
12 x 19

OPEN

seat

seat

Plan Features

- The impressive living room features a dazzling wall of glass and a cozy fireplace
- First floor bedroom boasts a private porch entrance, walk-in closet and luxury bath making an ideal master suite
- Secondary bedrooms each include two closets and a charming window seat
- 3 bedrooms, 2 1/2 baths
- Basement or crawl space foundation, please specify when ordering

Total Living Area: 2,356 sq. ft.

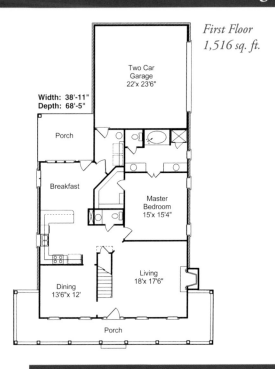

First Floor
1,516 sq. ft.

Two Car Garage
22'x 23'6"

Width: 38'-11"
Depth: 68'-5"

Porch

Breakfast

Master Bedroom
15'x 15'4"

Dining
13'6"x 12'

Living
18'x 17'6"

Porch

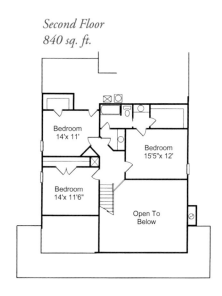

Second Floor
840 sq. ft.

Bedroom
14'x 11'

Bedroom
15'5"x 12'

Bedroom
14'x 11'6"

Open To Below

Plan Features

- Transoms above front windows create a custom feel to this design
- Spacious master bath has double vanities, toilet closet, and an oversized whirlpool tub
- Covered rear porch off the sunny breakfast area is ideal for grilling or relaxing
- 4 bedrooms, 2 1/2 baths, 2-car side entry garage
- Slab foundation

Total Living Area: 2,665 sq. ft.

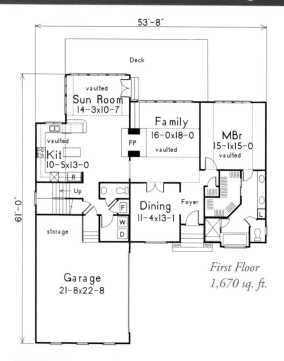

53'-8"

Deck

vaulted
Sun Room
14-3x10-7

vaulted
Kit
10-5x13-0

R

Up

F
W
D

storage

Garage
21-8x22-8

61'-0"

Family
16-0x18-0
vaulted

FP

Dining
11-4x13-1

Foyer

MBr
15-1x15-0
vaulted

L

First Floor
1,670 sq. ft.

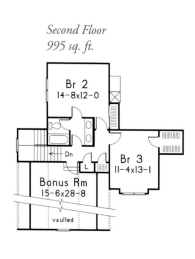

Second Floor
995 sq. ft.

Br 2
14-8x12-0

Dn

L

Bonus Rm
15-6x28-8

vaulted

Br 3
11-4x13-1

Plan Features

- The fireplace provides a focus for family living by connecting the central living quarters
- An abundance of windows and vaulted ceilings give this plan a spacious feel
- Master suite features a huge walk-in closet, vaulted ceiling and luxurious bath facilities
- Bonus room on the second floor is included in the total square footage
- 3 bedrooms, 2 1/2 baths, 2-car side entry garage
- Crawl space foundation

Total Living Area: 1,856 sq. ft.

DID YOU KNOW?

Don't crowd out a small spare room with a double bed, especially if you have to place one of its sides against a wall. A single bed and futon combination frees up floor space and also provides more flexibility for sleeping arrangements.

Plan Features

- The kitchen easily serves the formal dining room and informal breakfast area
- The grand master bedroom is the perfect place to relax with a corner whirlpool tub and large walk-in closet
- Home office/bedroom #4 enjoys a private bath
- 4 bedrooms, 3 baths, 2-car side entry garage
- Slab or crawl space foundation, please specify when ordering

Total Living Area: 3,746 sq. ft.

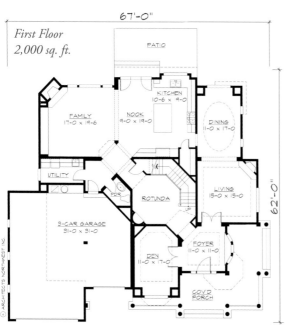

First Floor
2,000 sq. ft.

Second Floor
1,746 sq. ft.

Plan Features

- The foyer enters into a beautiful central two-story rotunda with circular staircase
- An oval tray ceiling in the formal dining room creates a Victorian feel
- Two-story family room is sunny and bright with windows on two floors
- Bonus room on the second floor has an additional 314 square feet of living area
- 4 bedrooms, 3 1/2 baths, 3-car garage
- Crawl space foundation

Total Living Area: 1,284 sq. ft.

First Floor
1,284 sq. ft.

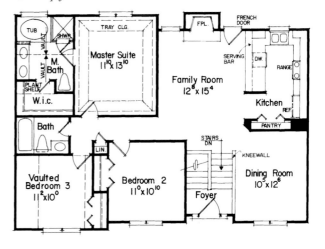

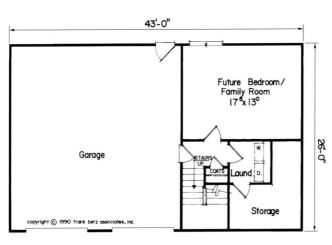

Optional
Lower Level

Plan Features

- Vaulted master bath has extras like a double-vanity and separate shower
- Future bedroom/family room on the lower level has an additional 226 square feet of living area
- Kitchen has convenient serving bar that overlooks family room
- 3 bedrooms, 2 baths, 2-car drive under garage
- Walk-out basement foundation

Total Living Area: 2,252 sq. ft.

First Floor
1,358 sq. ft.

Second Floor
894 sq. ft.

Plan Features

- Cathedral ceiling in the family room adds spaciousness
- 9' ceilings on the first floor
- Energy efficient home with 2"x 6" exterior walls
- 4 bedrooms, 3 1/2 baths, 2-car side entry garage
- Basement foundation

Total Living Area: 3,650 sq. ft.

Second Floor
1,075 sq. ft.

First Floor
2,575 sq. ft.

Plan Features

- Expansive kitchen/nook area features a cooktop island with seating and walk-in pantry
- A two-story vaulted ceiling enhances the spacious great room with grand fireplace
- Entertain with ease in the formal dining room with step ceiling and butler's pantry
- Bedroom #4 is a wonderful suite with a study area, walk-in closet and private bath
- 4 bedrooms, 3 1/2 baths, 4-car side entry garage
- Basement foundation

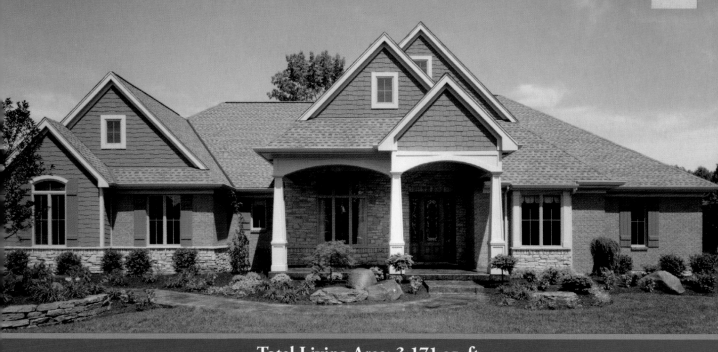

Total Living Area: 3,171 sq. ft.

First Floor
3,171 sq. ft.

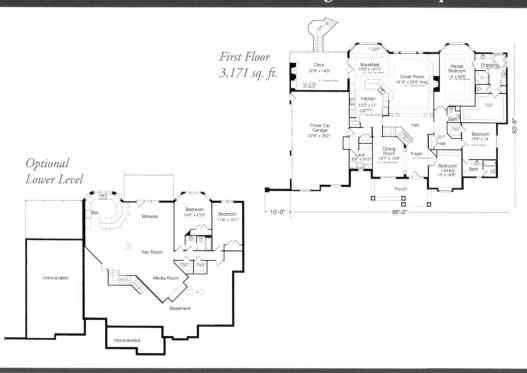

Optional
Lower Level

Plan Features

- The great room, breakfast area and kitchen combine with 12' ceilings to create an open feel
- The optional lower level has an additional 1,897 square feet of living area and is designed for entertaining featuring a wet bar with seating, a billiards room, large media room, two bedrooms and a full bath
- 3 bedrooms, 2 1/2 baths, 3-car side entry garage
- Walk-out basement foundation

Total Living Area: 1,550 sq. ft.

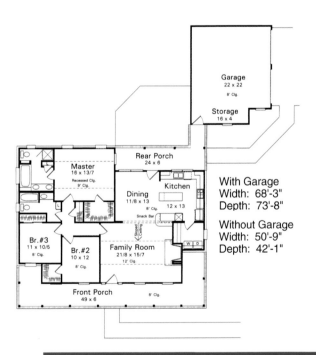

Garage
22 x 22
8' Clg.

Storage
16 x 4

Rear Porch
24 x 6

Master
16 x 13/7
Recessed Clg.
9' Clg.

Dining
11/8 x 13
8' Clg.

Kitchen
12 x 13

Snack Bar

Br.#3
11 x 10/5
8' Clg.

Br.#2
10 x 12
8' Clg.

Family Room
21/8 x 15/7
12' Clg.

W | D

Front Porch
49 x 6   8' Clg.

With Garage
Width: 68'-3"
Depth: 73'-8"

Without Garage
Width: 50'-9"
Depth: 42'-1"

DID YOU KNOW?
Make sure that any fabrics you use for upholstery and curtains are flame retardant. All new sofas have to meet strict fire regulations but second-hand ones may have been made before they came into force.

Plan Features

- Wrap-around front porch is an ideal gathering place
- Handy snack bar is positioned so the kitchen flows into the family room
- Master bedroom has many amenities
- 3 bedrooms, 2 baths, 2-car detached side entry garage
- Slab or crawl space foundation, please specify when ordering

Total Living Area: 1,553 sq. ft.

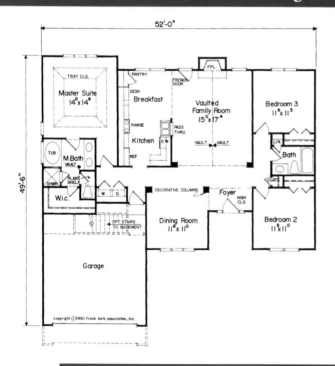

DID YOU KNOW?

Sealing a driveway is just as necessary in warmer climates as in cold ones. Asphalt sealers protect the pavement from oxidizing and becoming brittle in the harsh sun. This also provides prevention from water seeping through hairline cracks and reaching the base, which can cause deterioration almost as bad as the damage caused by freeze/thaw cycles.

Plan Features

- Master suite has tray ceiling and trio of windows adding a bright, spacious feel
- Decorative columns grace the entrance to the dining room
- Breakfast room includes a large pantry and built-in desk
- 3 bedrooms, 2 baths, 2-car garage
- Slab, crawl space or walk-out basement foundation, please specify when ordering

Total Living Area: 2,272 sq. ft.

Width 38'-0"
Depth 55'-0"

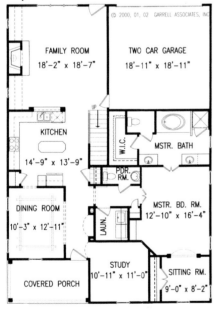

First Floor
1,587 sq. ft.

FAMILY ROOM
18'-2" x 18'-7"

TWO CAR GARAGE
18'-11" x 18'-11"

KITCHEN
14'-9" x 13'-9"

W.I.C.

MSTR. BATH

PDR. RM.

DINING ROOM
10'-3" x 12'-11"

MSTR. BD. RM.
12'-10" x 16'-4"

LAUN.

STUDY
10'-11" x 11'-0"

SITTING RM.
9'-0" x 8'-2"

COVERED PORCH

© 2000, 01, 02 GARRELL ASSOCIATES, INC.

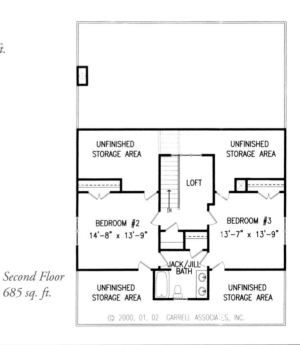

Second Floor
685 sq. ft.

UNFINISHED STORAGE AREA

UNFINISHED STORAGE AREA

LOFT

BEDROOM #2
14'-8" x 13'-9"

BEDROOM #3
13'-7" x 13'-9"

JACK/JILL BATH

UNFINISHED STORAGE AREA

UNFINISHED STORAGE AREA

© 2000, 01, 02 GARRELL ASSOCIATES, INC.

Plan Features

- 10' ceilings throughout the first floor and 9' ceilings on the second floor
- Lots of storage area on the second floor
- First floor master bedroom has a lovely sitting area with an arched entry
- Second floor bedrooms share a Jack and Jill bath
- 3 bedrooms, 2 1/2 baths, 2-car rear entry garage
- Slab foundation

Total Living Area: 1,544 sq. ft.

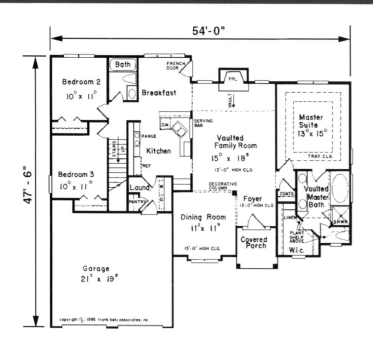

DID YOU KNOW?

Get rid of pests while beautifying your yard. Avoid using insecticides by planting marigolds, basil, mint, chives, onions and chrysanthemums near or in your garden. Secretions from these and many other plants act as a natural insect repellent.

Plan Features

- Well-designed floor plan has a vaulted family room with fireplace
- Decorative columns separate the dining area from the foyer
- A vaulted ceiling adds spaciousness to the master bath with walk-in closet
- Bonus room above garage has an additional 284 square feet of living area
- 3 bedrooms, 2 baths, 2-car garage
- Walk-out basement or crawl space foundation, please specify when ordering

Total Living Area: 2,813 sq. ft.

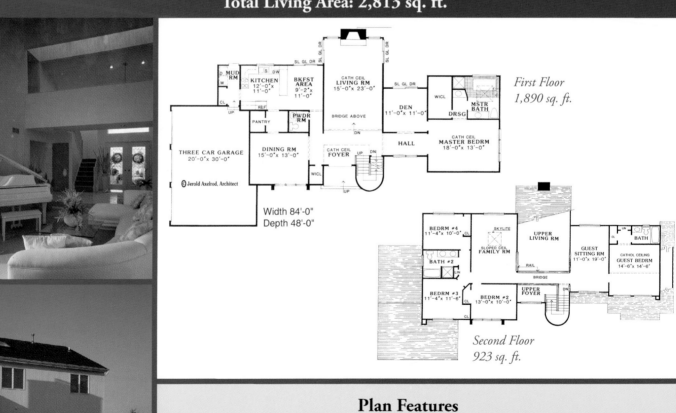

First Floor
1,890 sq. ft.

Width 84'-0"
Depth 48'-0"

Second Floor
923 sq. ft.

Plan Features

- Lovely guest bedroom on the second floor has lots of privacy with its own sitting room
- Cathedral ceiling in foyer adds spaciousness upon entering this home
- Bonus room on the second floor has an additional 500 square feet of living area
- 4 bedrooms, 2 1/2 baths, 3-car side entry garage
- Basement, crawl space or slab foundation, please specify when ordering

Total Living Area: 1,978 sq. ft.

Lower Level
742 sq. ft.

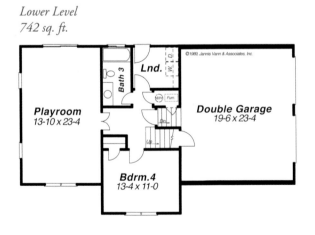

First Floor
1,236 sq. ft.

Plan Features

- Sloped ceiling in living area adds spaciousness
- Bedroom #4 on the lower level is ideal for college student, elderly parent or as a home office
- Playroom on the lower level makes a great children's play area
- 4 bedrooms, 3 baths, 2-car drive under garage
- Basement foundation

D

Total Living Area: 2,236 sq. ft.

DID YOU KNOW?

Wood flooring is no longer used solely in living and family rooms. Increasingly it is being used in high-traffic areas such as hallways and kitchens. If you choose to go this route, be sure to pick the right wood as some types are less likely to hold up in these locations. Avoid softwoods such as pine and spruce. Instead, look for species such as oak, maple, ash or even bamboo.

Plan Features

- Luxurious master suite has an enormous sitting room with a fireplace and vaulted private bath
- Cozy family room is off the kitchen and breakfast area
- Two secondary bedrooms share a bath
- 3 bedrooms, 2 1/2 baths, 2-car side entry garage
- Walk-out basement or crawl space foundation, please specify when ordering

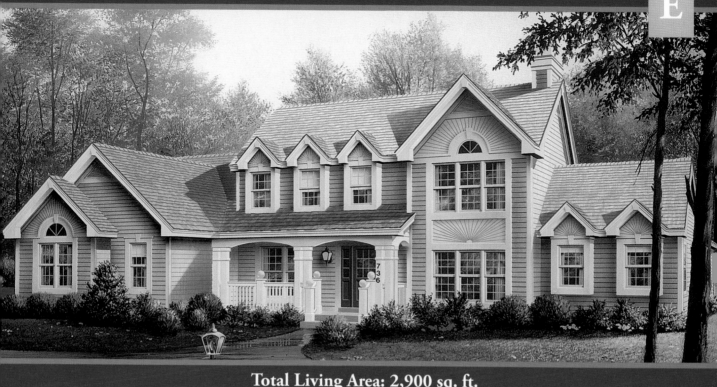

Total Living Area: 2,900 sq. ft.

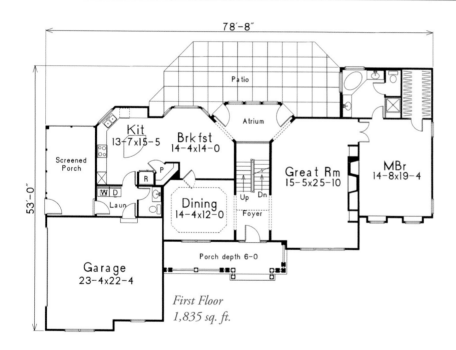

78'-8"

53'-0"

Patio

Atrium

Kit
13-7x15-5

Brk fst
14-4x14-0

Screened
Porch

W D

Laun

P

R

Dining
14-4x12-0

Up Dn

Foyer

Great Rm
15-5x25-10

MBr
14-8x19-4

Garage
23-4x22-4

Porch depth 6-0

First Floor
1,835 sq. ft.

Second Floor
1,065 sq. ft.

Atrium
below

Br 2
14-4x12-4

Br 3
15-2x12-4

L

Dn

Foyer
below

Br 4
13-10x13-2

Plan Features

- Entry foyer leads to the second floor balcony overlook of the vaulted two-story atrium
- Spacious kitchen features an island breakfast bar, walk-in pantry, bayed breakfast room and adjoining screened porch
- Two large second floor bedrooms and stair balconies overlook a sun-drenched two-story vaulted atrium
- 4 bedrooms, 3 1/2 baths, 2-car side entry garage
- Basement foundation

Total Living Area: 2,193 sq. ft.

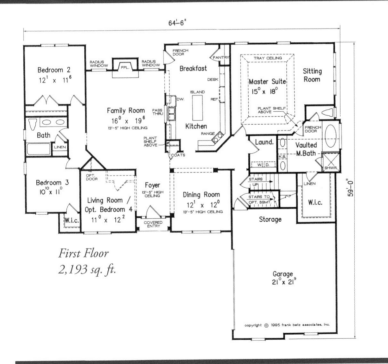

First Floor
2,193 sq. ft.

Optional
Second Floor

Plan Features

- Master suite includes a sitting room
- Dining room has decorative columns and overlooks the family room
- Optional bonus room with bath on the second floor has an additional 400 square feet of living area
- 3 bedrooms, 3 baths, 2-car side entry garage
- Walk-out basement, crawl space or slab foundation, please specify when ordering

Total Living Area: 1,668 sq. ft.

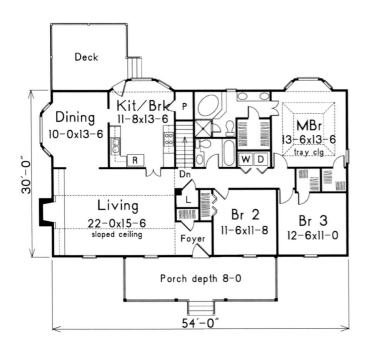

DID YOU KNOW?

Emphasize favorite accessories or pictures by giving them their own special lighting. Spotlights fitted into the top of display boxes or niches, or wall lamps that shine directly down onto prints or paintings, will increase their decorative value and impact.

Plan Features

- Large bay windows grace the breakfast area, master bedroom and dining room
- Extensive walk-in closets and storage spaces are located throughout the home
- Handy covered entry porch
- Large living room has a fireplace, built-in bookshelves and sloped ceiling
- 3 bedrooms, 2 baths, 2-car drive under garage
- Basement foundation

Total Living Area: 2,729 sq. ft.

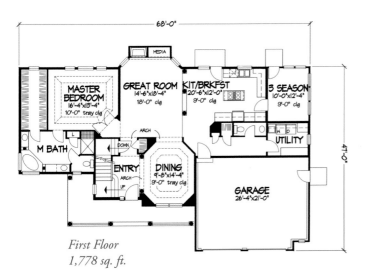

First Floor
1,778 sq. ft.

MASTER BEDROOM 16'-4"x15'-4" 10'-0" tray clg

GREAT ROOM 14'-6"x18'-4" 18'-0" clg

KIT/BRKFST 20'-6"x12'-0" 9'-0" clg

3 SEASON 10'-0"x12'-4" 9'-0" clg

M BATH

MEDIA

ARCH

UTILITY

ENTRY

DINING 9'-8"x14'-4" 9'-0" tray clg

GARAGE 26'-4"x21'-0"

68'-0"

47'-0"

Second Floor
951 sq. ft.

UPPER GREAT ROOM

DESK

BEDRM 2 12'-8"x12'-0"

SHELVES

LOFT

NICHE

SKYLIGHT

DOWN

OPEN TO BELOW

BEDRM 3 12'-8"x13'-4"

SKYLIGHTS

BONUS 16'-2"x21'-2"

DESK

Rear View

Plan Features

- Formal dining room has lovely views into the beautiful two-story great room
- Second floor loft area makes a perfect home office or children's computer area
- Bonus room on the second floor has an additional 300 square feet of living area
- 3 bedrooms, 2 1/2 baths, 2-car garage
- Basement foundation

Total Living Area: 1,869 sq. ft.

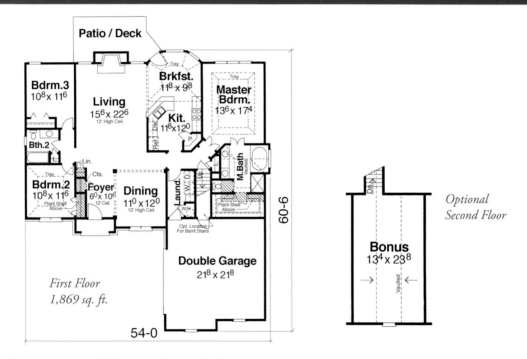

Plan Features

- Bayed breakfast area walks out to a sunny patio/deck
- Master bath has an intricate ceiling, double vanity, spa tub and a large walk-in closet
- Elegant columns frame the formal dining area
- Bonus room on the second floor has an additional 336 square feet of living area
- 3 bedrooms, 2 baths, 2-car side entry garage
- Basement, crawl space or slab foundation, please specify when ordering

Total Living Area: 1,491 sq. ft.

First Floor
1,061 sq. ft.

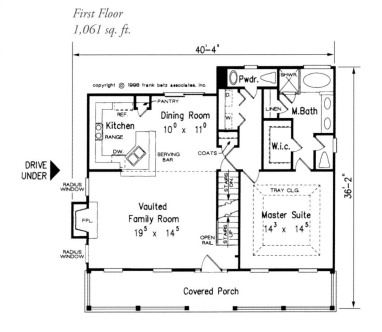

Second Floor
430 sq. ft.

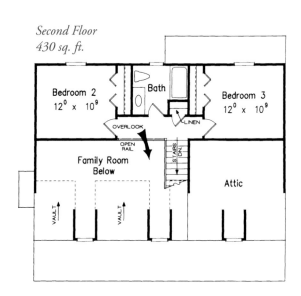

Plan Features

- Two-story family room has a vaulted ceiling
- Well-organized kitchen has serving bar which overlooks family and dining rooms
- First floor master suite has a tray ceiling, walk-in closet and master bath
- 3 bedrooms, 2 1/2 baths, 2-car drive under garage
- Walk-out basement foundation

Total Living Area: 1,821 sq. ft.

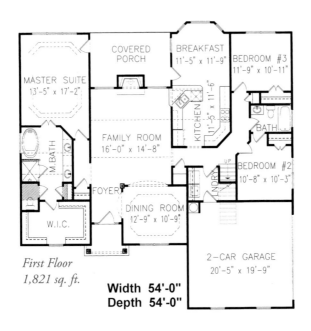

COVERED PORCH

BREAKFAST
11'-5" x 11'-9"

BEDROOM #3
11'-9" x 10'-11"

MASTER SUITE
13'-5" x 17'-2"

KITCHEN
11'-5" x 11'-6"

FAMILY ROOM
16'-0" x 14'-8"

BATH

M.BATH

FOYER

BEDROOM #2
10'-8" x 10'-3"

LNDRY

W.I.C.

DINING ROOM
12'-9" x 10'-9"

2-CAR GARAGE
20'-5" x 19'-9"

First Floor
1,821 sq. ft.

Width 54'-0"
Depth 54'-0"

Optional Second Floor

BONUS ROOM
11'-5" x 15'-3"

Plan Features

- 9' ceilings throughout the first floor
- Master suite is secluded for privacy and has a spacious bath
- Sunny breakfast room features a bay window
- Bonus room on the second floor has an additional 191 square feet of living area
- 3 bedrooms, 2 baths, 2-car side entry garage
- Basement or slab foundation, please specify when ordering

A

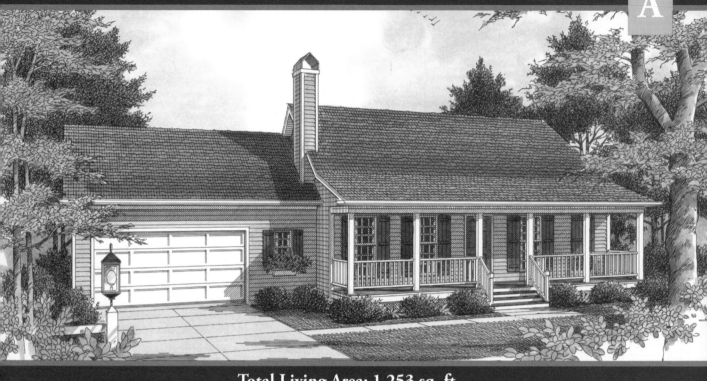

Total Living Area: 1,253 sq. ft.

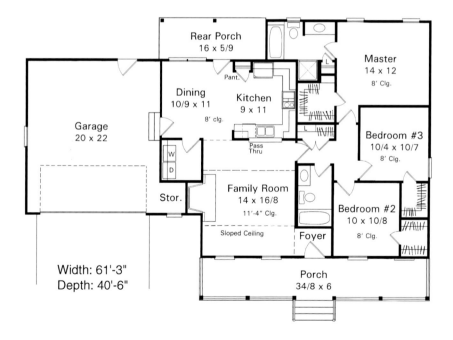

Rear Porch
16 x 5/9

Master
14 x 12
8' Clg.

Pant.

Dining
10/9 x 11
8' clg.

Kitchen
9 x 11

Garage
20 x 22

Bedroom #3
10/4 x 10/7
8' Clg.

Pass
Thru

W
D

Stor.

Family Room
14 x 16/8
11'-4" Clg.

Bedroom #2
10 x 10/8
8' Clg.

Sloped Ceiling

Foyer

Width: 61'-3"
Depth: 40'-6"

Porch
34/8 x 6

Plan Features

- Sloped ceiling and fireplace in family room add drama
- U-shaped kitchen is efficiently designed
- Large walk-in closets are found in all the bedrooms
- 3 bedrooms, 2 baths, 2-car garage
- Crawl space or slab foundation, please specify when ordering

Total Living Area: 1,650 sq. ft.

First Floor
1,562 sq. ft.

Lower Level
88 sq. ft.

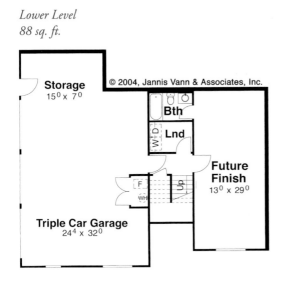

Width: 46'-0"
Depth: 40'-0"

© 2004, Jannis Vann & Associates, Inc.

Plan Features

- The master bath features all the amenities including a separate tub and shower and double-bowl vanity
- The oversized linen closet can convert to a washer/dryer closet if the ground level location is not used
- Future finish on the lower level has an additional 377 square feet of living area
- 3 bedrooms, 2 baths, 3-car side entry garage
- Basement foundation

Total Living Area: 2,336 sq. ft.

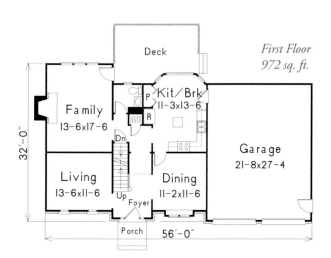

First Floor
972 sq. ft.

Deck

Family
13-6x17-6

Kit/Brk
11-3x13-6
P
R

Garage
21-8x27-4

Living
13-6x11-6

Dining
11-2x11-6

Foyer
Up
Dn

32'-0"

Porch

56'-0"

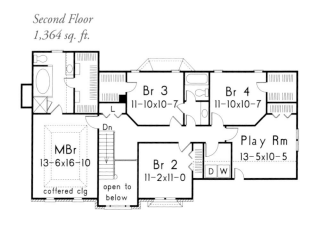

Second Floor
1,364 sq. ft.

Br 3
11-10x10-7

Br 4
11-10x10-7

L

MBr
13-6x16-10

coffered clg

Dn

Br 2
11-2x11-0

open to
below

D W

Play Rm
13-5x10-5

Plan Features

- Two-story foyer with large second floor window creates a sunny, spacious entrance area
- Second floor play room is conveniently located near bedrooms and laundry room
- Master bath has a vaulted ceiling and luxurious appointments
- Coffered ceiling in master bedroom
- 4 bedrooms, 2 1/2 baths, 2-car garage
- Basement foundation

Total Living Area: 2,205 sq. ft.

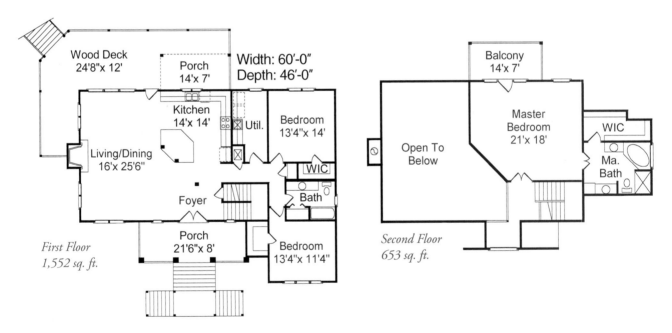

Wood Deck
24'8"x 12'

Porch
14'x 7'

Width: 60'-0"
Depth: 46'-0"

Kitchen
14'x 14'

Util.

Bedroom
13'4"x 14'

Living/Dining
16'x 25'6"

WIC

Foyer

Bath

First Floor
1,552 sq. ft.

Porch
21'6"x 8'

Bedroom
13'4"x 11'4"

Balcony
14'x 7'

Master
Bedroom
21'x 18'

WIC

Open To
Below

Ma.
Bath

Second Floor
653 sq. ft.

Plan Features

- The double-door entry opens to the spacious two-story living/dining area and kitchen with unique center island
- Two secondary bedrooms enjoy walk-in closets and a shared bath
- The master bedroom enjoys a deluxe bath and private balcony
- 3 bedrooms, 2 baths, 2-car drive under carport
- Pier foundation

Rear View

Total Living Area: 2,155 sq. ft.

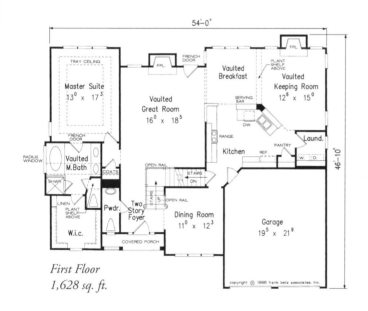

First Floor
1,628 sq. ft.

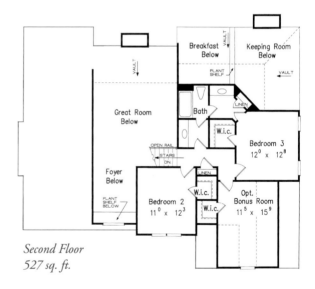

Second Floor
527 sq. ft.

Plan Features

- Vaulted breakfast and keeping rooms create an informal area off the kitchen
- All bedrooms have walk-in closets
- Optional bonus room on the second floor has an additional 207 square feet of living area
- 3 bedrooms, 2 1/2 baths, 2-car garage
- Walk-out basement, slab or crawl space foundation, please specify when ordering

Total Living Area: 1,829 sq. ft.

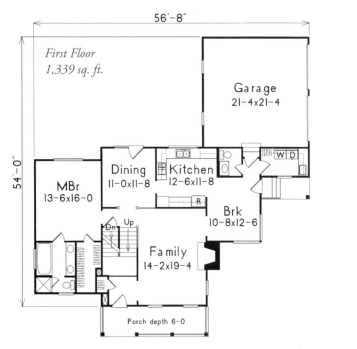

First Floor 1,339 sq. ft.

56'-8"

54'-0"

Garage
21-4x21-4

MBr
13-6x16-0

Dining
11-0x11-8

Kitchen
12-6x11-8

W D
R

Brk
10-8x12-6

Dn Up

Family
14-2x19-4

Porch depth 6-0

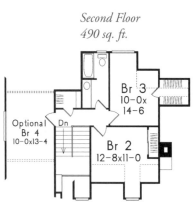

Second Floor 490 sq. ft.

Br 3
10-0x14-6

Optional Br 4
10-0x13-4

Dn

Br 2
12-8x11-0

Plan Features

- Entry foyer with coat closet opens to a large family room with fireplace
- Two second floor bedrooms share a full bath
- Optional bedroom #4 on the second floor adds 145 square feet of living area
- Cozy porch provides a convenient side entrance into the home
- 3 bedrooms, 2 1/2 baths, 2-car side entry garage
- Partial basement/crawl space foundation

Total Living Area: 4,868 sq. ft.

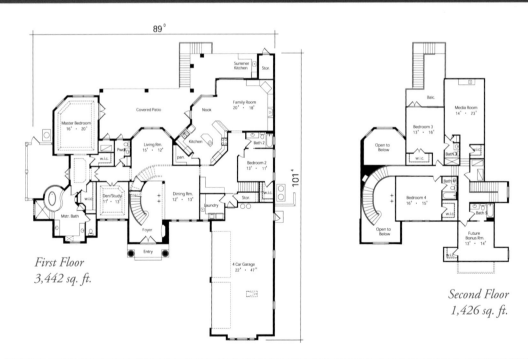

First Floor
3,442 sq. ft.

Second Floor
1,426 sq. ft.

Plan Features

- Unforgettable foyer has an enormous curved staircase and built-in niche
- Master bath includes a step-up whirlpool tub with window wall looking out to patio
- Framing - only concrete block available
- Optional bonus room on the second floor has an additional 251 square feet of living area
- 4 bedrooms, 5 1/2 baths, 4-car side entry garage
- Slab foundation

Total Living Area: 1,342 sq. ft.

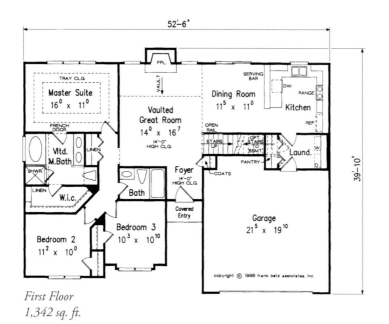

First Floor
1,342 sq. ft.

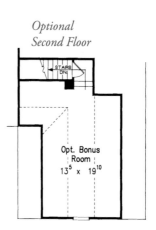

*Optional
Second Floor*

Plan Features

- 9' ceilings throughout the home
- Master suite has a tray ceiling and wall of windows that overlook the backyard
- Dining room includes a serving bar and sliding glass doors that lead outdoors
- Optional second floor has an additional 350 square feet of living area
- 3 bedrooms, 2 baths, 2-car garage
- Slab, walk-out basement or crawl space foundation, please specify when ordering

Total Living Area: 1,782 sq. ft.

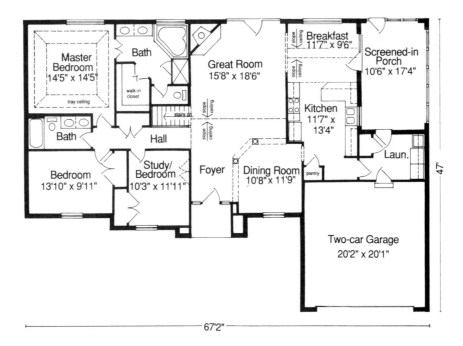

Plan Features

- Outstanding breakfast area accesses the outdoors through French doors
- Generous counterspace and cabinets combine to create an ideal kitchen
- The master bedroom is enhanced with a beautiful bath featuring a whirlpool tub and double-bowl vanity
- 3 bedrooms, 2 baths, 2-car garage
- Basement foundation

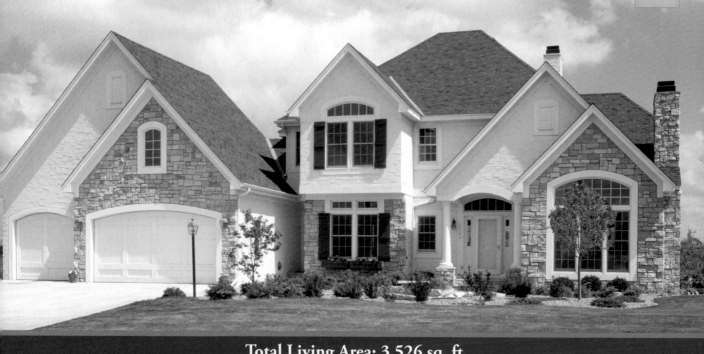

Total Living Area: 3,526 sq. ft.

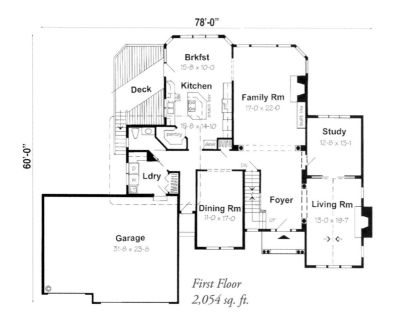

78'-0"

60'-0"

Deck

Brkfst
15-8 x 10-0

Kitchen
15-8 x 14-10

pantry

DW

snack bar

desk

Family Rm
17-0 x 22-0

built-ins

Study
12-8 x 13-1

Ldry
D W

DN

Dining Rm
11-0 x 17-0

Foyer
UP

Living Rm
13-0 x 19-7

Garage
31-8 x 23-8

First Floor
2,054 sq. ft.

Master Suite
15-8 x 18-6
pan vaults

whirlpool

chimney

Lin

Br 2
12-0 x 11-4

niche

Lin

Lin

DN

railing

open to foyer

Br 4
12-8 x 13-0

Br 3
11-0 x 13-0

Second Floor
1,472 sq. ft.

Plan Features

Interior View

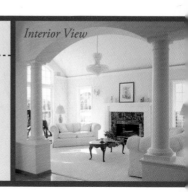

- The breakfast and family rooms have enormous windows overlooking the backyard
- The living room has an elegant sloped ceiling and broad hearth fireplace
- The study is a secluded room providing peace and quiet
- 4 bedrooms, 3 1/2 baths, 3-car garage
- Walk-out basement foundation

Total Living Area: 3,420 sq. ft.

First Floor
1,894 sq. ft.

Second Floor
1,526 sq. ft.

Plan Features

- Elliptical windows and brick facade with quoins emphasize stylish sophisticated living
- Kitchen features a cooktop island, walk-in pantry, breakfast bar and computer desk
- Splendid gallery connects family room and wet bar with vaulted hearth room
- Master bedroom has a coffered ceiling, double walk-in closets and a lavish bath
- 4 bedrooms, 3 1/2 baths, 3-car rear entry garage
- Walk-out basement foundation

Total Living Area: 1,583 sq. ft.

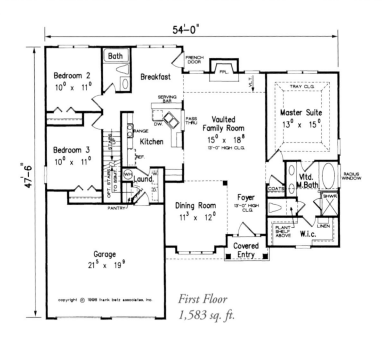

First Floor
1,583 sq. ft.

copyright © 1998 frank betz associates, inc.

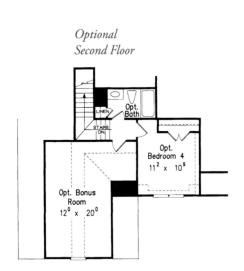

Optional Second Floor

Plan Features

- 9' ceilings throughout this home
- Additional bedrooms are located away from the master suite for privacy
- Optional second floor has an additional 544 square feet of living area
- 3 bedrooms, 2 baths, 2-car garage
- Walk-out basement, slab or crawl space foundation, please specify when ordering

Total Living Area: 3,094 sq. ft.

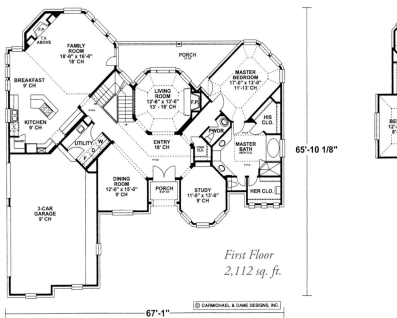

First Floor
2,112 sq. ft.

65'-10 1/8"

67'-1"

© CARMICHAEL & DAME DESIGNS, INC.

Second Floor
982 sq. ft.

Plan Features

- Unique angles throughout home add character and style
- Entry opens to spacious gazebo-style living room
- Bayed family room is flooded with natural light and opens to kitchen and breakfast area
- Vaulted ceilings bring elegance to all bedrooms
- 4 bedrooms, 3 1/2 baths, 3-car side entry garage
- Slab foundation

Plan #583-071D-0003

Price Code:

E

Total Living Area: 2,890 sq. ft.

First Floor
1,630 sq. ft.

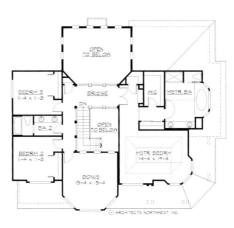

Second Floor
1,260 sq. ft.

Plan Features

- Formal dining and living rooms create a private place for entertaining
- Kitchen features a large island with cooktop and lots of extra counterspace
- A stunning oversized whirlpool tub is showcased in the private master bath
- Bonus room on the second floor has an additional 240 square feet of living area
- 3 bedrooms, 2 1/2 baths, 3-car side entry garage
- Crawl space foundation

To order call toll-free 1-800-DREAM HOME or visit www.houseplansandmore.com

Total Living Area: 2,508 sq. ft.

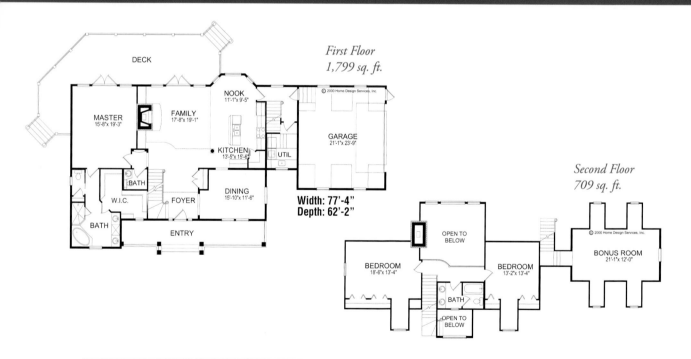

First Floor
1,799 sq. ft.

Second Floor
709 sq. ft.

Width: 77'-4"
Depth: 62'-2"

Plan Features

- The kitchen opens to the bayed nook and expansive family room
- The master bedroom features private access onto the rear deck and a deluxe bath with a whirlpool tub and walk-in closet
- The bonus room above the garage has an additional 384 square feet of living area
- 3 bedrooms, 2 1/2 baths, 2-car side entry garage
- Basement or walk-out basement foundation, please specify when ordering

Total Living Area: 2,632 sq. ft.

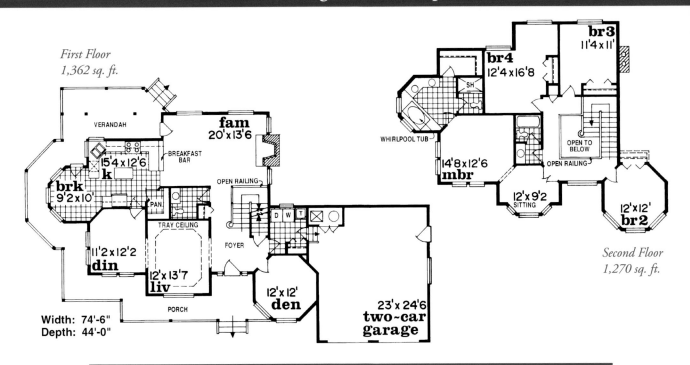

First Floor
1,362 sq. ft.

VERANDAH

fam
20'x13'6

BREAKFAST BAR

15'4 x 12'6
k

OPEN RAILING

brk
9'2 x 10'

PAN.

TRAY CEILING

DW T

FOYER

11'2 x 12'2
din

12'x 13'7
liv

PORCH

12'x 12'
den

23'x 24'6
two-car garage

Width: 74'-6"
Depth: 44'-0"

Second Floor
1,270 sq. ft.

br4
12'4 x 16'8

br3
11'4 x 11'

SH

WHIRLPOOL TUB

OPEN TO BELOW

14'8 x 12'6
mbr

OPEN RAILING

12'x 9'2
SITTING

12'x 12'
br2

Plan Features

- Energy efficient home with 2"x 6" exterior walls
- Master bedroom has a cheerful octagon-shaped sitting area
- Arched entrances create a distinctive living room with a lovely tray ceiling and help define the dining room
- 4 bedrooms, 2 1/2 baths, 2-car garage
- Basement or crawl space foundation, please specify when ordering

Total Living Area: 2,483 sq. ft.

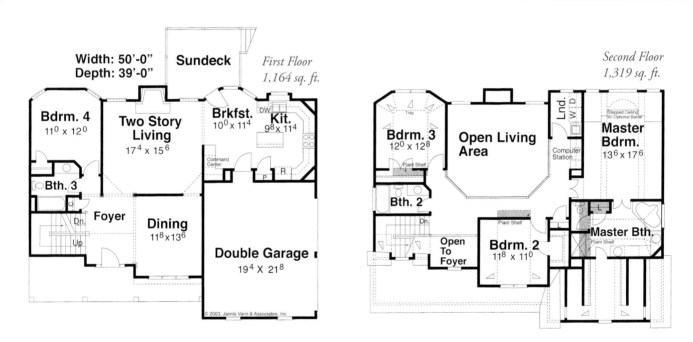

Width: 50'-0"
Depth: 39'-0"

Sundeck

First Floor
1,164 sq. ft.

Second Floor
1,319 sq. ft.

Bdrm. 4
11⁰ x 12⁰

Two Story Living
17⁴ x 15⁶

Brkfst.
10⁰ x 11⁴

Kit.
9⁸ x 11⁴

DW

Command Center

Bth. 3

Foyer

Dining
11⁸ x 13⁶

P

R

Dn.

Up

Double Garage
19⁴ X 21⁸

© 2003, Jannis Vann & Associates, Inc.

Bdrm. 3
12⁰ x 12⁸

Tray

Plant Shelf

Open Living Area

Lnd.

W. D.

Computer Station

Stepped Ceiling W/ Optional Barrel

Master Bdrm.
13⁶ x 17⁶

Bth. 2

Dn.

Open To Foyer

Plant Shelf

Bdrm. 2
11⁸ x 11⁰

Plant Shelf

Master Bth.

Plan Features

- The efficient kitchen and breakfast area includes space for the family computer
- The first floor bedroom provides space for guests or can double as a home office
- The master bedroom offers the option of a dramatic ceiling treatment with windows overlooking the rear of the house
- 4 bedrooms, 3 baths, 2-car side entry garage
- Walk-out basement foundation

Total Living Area: 1,375 sq. ft.

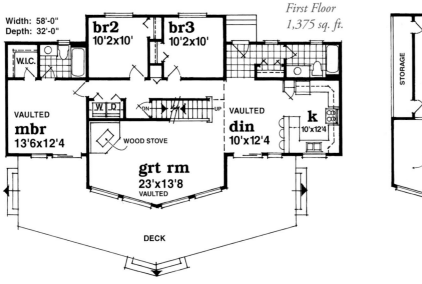

Width: 58'-0"
Depth: 32'-0"

First Floor
1,375 sq. ft.

br2
10'2x10'

br3
10'2x10'

W.I.C.

VAULTED
mbr
13'6x12'4

W D

DN   UP

VAULTED
din
10'x12'4

k
10'x12'4

WOOD STOVE

grt rm
23'x13'8
VAULTED

DECK

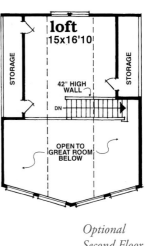

loft
15x16'10

STORAGE

STORAGE

42" HIGH
WALL

DN

OPEN TO
GREAT ROOM
BELOW

Optional
Second Floor

Plan Features

- Open U-shaped kitchen shares an eating bar with the dining room
- Two secondary bedrooms share a full bath
- Master bedroom provides a walk-in closet and private bath
- Loft on the second floor has an additional 284 square feet of living area
- 3 bedrooms, 2 baths
- Basement or crawl space foundation, please specify when ordering

Total Living Area: 3,116 sq. ft.

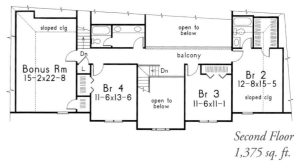

Second Floor
1,375 sq. ft.

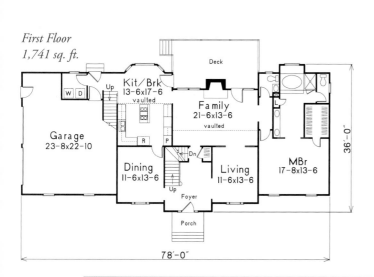

First Floor
1,741 sq. ft.

Plan Features

- Arched mullioned windows provide balance across the impressive facade
- Master bedroom and bedroom #2 have private baths and walk-in closets
- Bonus room above the garage, which is included in the square footage, is available for future use
- 4 bedrooms, 3 1/2 baths, 2-car side entry garage
- Basement foundation

Total Living Area: 1,765 sq. ft.

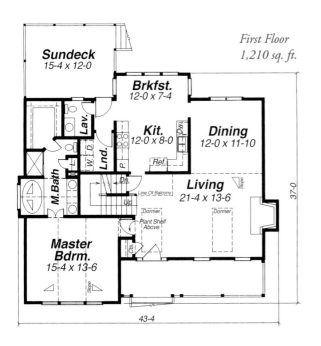

First Floor
1,210 sq. ft.

Sundeck
15-4 x 12-0

Brkfst.
12-0 x 7-4

Lav.

Kit.
12-0 x 8-0

Dw.

Dining
12-0 x 11-10

W.I.D.

Lnd.

P.

Ref.

Slope

M.Bath

Dn.

Line Of Balcony

Living
21-4 x 13-6

Up

Dormer

Dormer

Plant Shelf Above

Cts.

Master Bdrm.
15-4 x 13-6

Slope

37-0

43-4

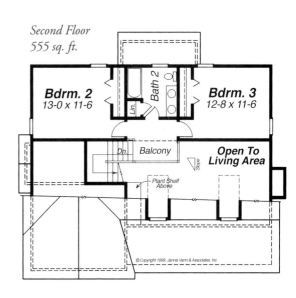

Second Floor
555 sq. ft.

Bdrm. 2
13-0 x 11-6

Bath 2

Lin.

Bdrm. 3
12-8 x 11-6

Dn.

Balcony

Slope

Open To Living Area

Plant Shelf Above

© Copyright 1998 Jannis Vann & Associates, Inc.

Plan Features

- A palladian window accenting the stone gable adds a new look to a popular cottage design
- Dormers above open the vaulted living room
- Kitchen extends to breakfast room with access to sundeck
- 3 bedrooms, 2 1/2 baths, 2-car drive under garage
- Basement foundation

Total Living Area: 3,882 sq. ft.

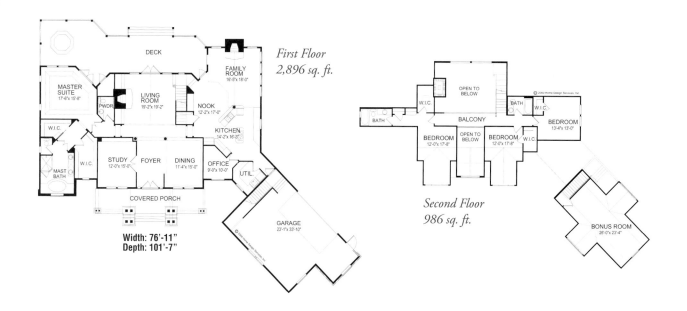

First Floor
2,896 sq. ft.

DECK

FAMILY ROOM 16'-5"x 18'-0"

MASTER SUITE 17'-6"x 15'-8"

LIVING ROOM 19'-2"x 19'-2"

NOOK 12'-2"x 17'-0"

PWDR

W.I.C.

KITCHEN 14'-2"x 16'-3"

MAST BATH

W.I.C.

STUDY 12'-0"x 15'-0"

FOYER

DINING 11'-4"x 15'-0"

OFFICE 9'-0"x 10'-0"

UTIL

COVERED PORCH

GARAGE 23'-1"x 33'-10"

Width: 76'-11"
Depth: 101'-7"

Second Floor
986 sq. ft.

OPEN TO BELOW

W.I.C.

BATH

W.I.C.

BATH

BALCONY

BEDROOM 12'-0"x 17'-8"

OPEN TO BELOW

BEDROOM 12'-0"x 17'-8"

W.I.C.

BEDROOM 13'-4"x 13'-0"

BONUS ROOM 26'-0"x 23'-4"

Plan Features

- The living room includes a fireplace flanked by built-in shelves
- The entrance from the garage leads to a large utility room and private office
- Secondary bedrooms enjoy walk-in closets
- The bonus room above the garage has an additional 480 square feet of living area
- 4 bedrooms, 3 1/2 baths, 2-car rear entry garage
- Crawl space foundation

Total Living Area: 2,546 sq. ft.

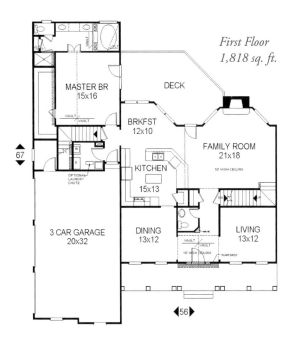

First Floor
1,818 sq. ft.

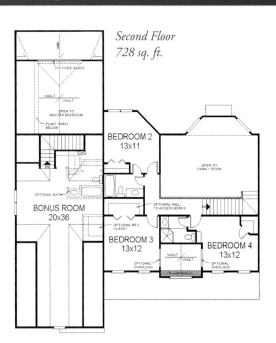

Second Floor
728 sq. ft.

Plan Features

- Bay windows create a warm and sunny feel in the family and breakfast rooms
- Center island in kitchen creates more space for food preparation
- Bonus room on the second floor has an additional 579 square feet of living area
- 4 bedrooms, 3 1/2 baths, 3-car side entry garage
- Basement or crawl space foundation, please specify when ordering

Total Living Area: 1,978 sq. ft.

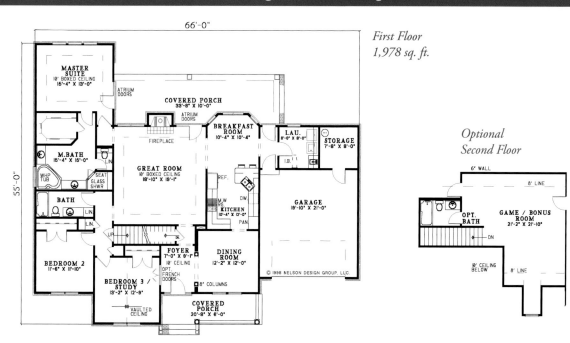

First Floor
1,978 sq. ft.

Optional
Second Floor

Plan Features

- 9' ceilings throughout this home
- Master suite has 10' boxed ceiling and atrium doors to rear porch
- Optional second floor has an additional 479 square feet of living area
- 3 bedrooms, 2 baths, 2-car garage
- Basement, walk-out basement, slab or crawl space foundation, please specify when ordering

Total Living Area: 2,920 sq. ft.

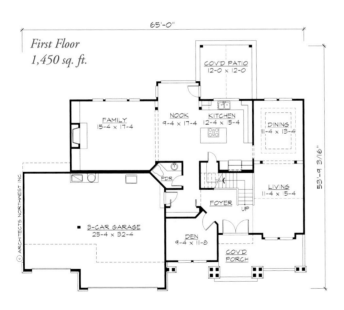

First Floor
1,450 sq. ft.

65'-0"

53'-9 3/16"

COV'D PATIO
12-0 x 12-0

FAMILY
15-4 x 17-4

NOOK
9-4 x 17-4

KITCHEN
12-4 x 15-4

DINING
11-4 x 13-4

LIVING
11-4 x 15-4

PDR

FOYER

UP

3-CAR GARAGE
25-4 x 32-4

DEN
9-4 x 11-8

COV'D PORCH

© ARCHITECTS NORTHWEST INC.

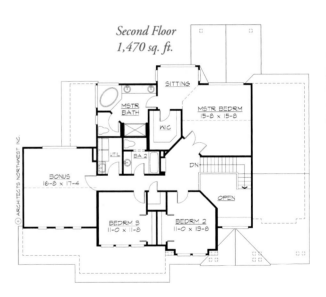

Second Floor
1,470 sq. ft.

SITTING

MSTR BATH

MSTR BEDRM
15-8 x 15-8

WIC

UTIL

BA 2

BONUS
16-8 x 17-4

DN

OPEN

BEDRM 3
11-0 x 11-8

BEDRM 2
11-0 x 13-8

© ARCHITECTS NORTHWEST INC.

Plan Features

- A large, cheerful sitting room connects the master bedroom to the private bath
- A cozy den features a unique angled entrance for interest
- The open kitchen flows into the breakfast nook for maximum convenience
- Second floor bonus room is included in the square footage
- 3 bedrooms, 2 1/2 baths, 3-car garage
- Crawl space foundation

Total Living Area: 1,575 sq. ft.

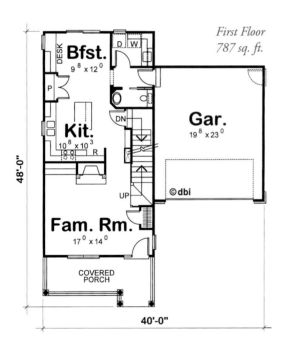

First Floor
787 sq. ft.

Bfst.
9⁸ x 12⁰

Kit.
10⁸ x 10³

Fam. Rm.
17⁰ x 14⁰

Gar.
19⁸ x 23⁰

COVERED PORCH

48'-0"

40'-0"

© dbi

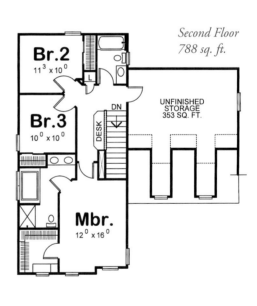

Second Floor
788 sq. ft.

Br.2
11³ x 10⁰

Br.3
10⁰ x 10⁰

Mbr.
12⁰ x 16⁰

UNFINISHED STORAGE
353 SQ. FT.

Plan Features

- A half bath is tucked away in the laundry area for convenience
- Second floor hall has a handy desk
- Bonus area on the second floor has an additional 353 square feet of living area
- 3 bedrooms, 2 1/2 baths, 2-car garage
- Basement foundation

Total Living Area: 3,422 sq. ft.

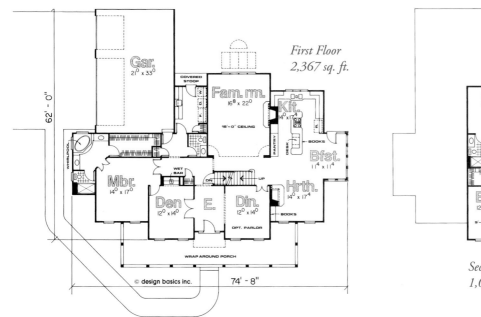

First Floor
2,367 sq. ft.

© design basics inc.

74' - 8"

62' - 0"

Second Floor
1,055 sq. ft.

Plan Features

- Kitchen island includes space for the stove as well as a desk and bookshelves underneath
- Corner whirlpool tub is the focal point in the master bath
- A corner fireplace is enjoyed by both the hearth room and the breakfast room nearby
- Bonus room on the second floor has an additional 228 square feet of living area
- 4 bedrooms, 3 1/2 baths, 3-car side entry garage
- Basement foundation

Total Living Area: 2,241 sq. ft.

First Floor
1,722 sq. ft.

Dining Room
12'10" x 14'6"

Breakfast
15'2" x 8'10"

Great Room
16' x 23'2"

Kitchen

Dressing

Bath

BUILT-IN ENT. CENTER

PLANT LEDGE ABOVE

Laun.

Hall

Foyer

Master Bedroom
13'3" x 16'6"

Two-Car Garage
22' x 23'10"

Landing

Porch

First Floor Plan

55'-6"

56'-8"

Bedroom
13'2" x 11'

Bedroom
11' x 12'2"

Bath

Great Room Below

Balcony

WALK-IN CLOSET

Bonus Room
11'2" x 16'

Second Floor
519 sq. ft.

Plan Features

- The dining and great rooms combine for a beautiful gathering place
- An island with extended counter seating defines the kitchen and breakfast area
- Bonus room on the second floor has an additional 283 square feet of living area
- 4 bedrooms, 2 1/2 baths, 2-car side entry garage
- Basement foundation

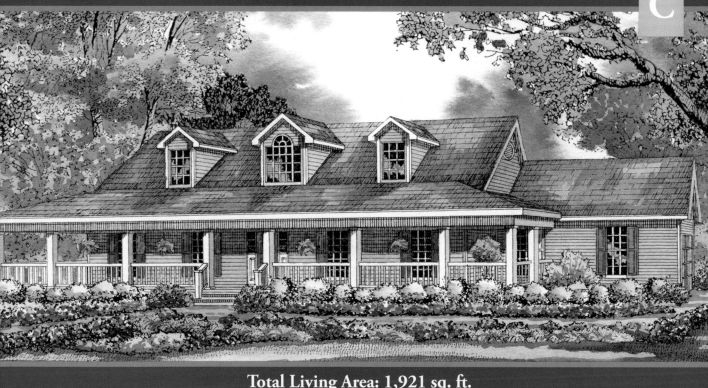

Total Living Area: 1,921 sq. ft.

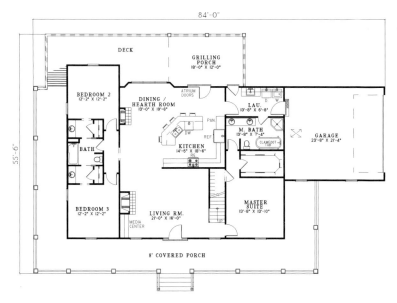

First Floor
1,921 sq. ft.

Optional
Second Floor

Plan Features

- The charming front porch wraps around the house providing a relaxing outdoor retreat
- Fireplaces in the living and dining rooms warm the house
- The optional second floor has an additional 812 square feet of living space
- 3 bedrooms, 3 baths, 2-car side entry garage
- Slab, crawl space, basement or walk-out basement foundation, please specify when ordering

---

Total Living Area: 2,797 sq. ft.

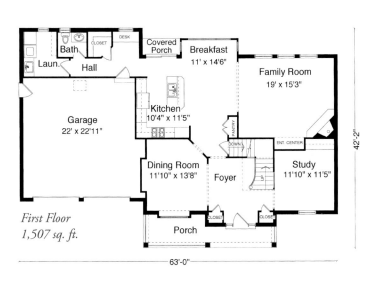

First Floor
1,507 sq. ft.

Second Floor
1,290 sq. ft.

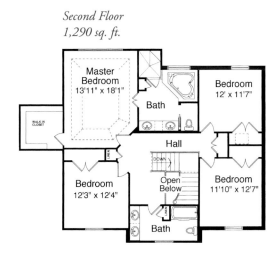

Plan Features

- Brick and siding with a covered porch and wood trim add dimension to the exterior
- A gas fireplace, furniture alcoves, a study with built-ins, angled stairs and large work areas enhance this family home
- A second floor master bedroom enjoys a sloped ceiling, walk-in closet and a bath with a whirlpool tub and double-bowl vanity
- 4 bedrooms, 2 1/2 baths, 2-car garage
- Basement foundation

Total Living Area: 2,096 sq. ft.

DID YOU KNOW?

Masking tape is one of the least expensive but most useful painting tools you'll find. But buy only the good stuff. Standard masking tape is often too sticky, and leaves behind a residue that can interfere with a painted finish. It's also thicker than genuine painter's masking tape, making it more likely to cause drips.

Plan Features

- The foyer opens to the great room which features a fireplace and built-in bookshelves
- The secondary bedrooms are secluded with a central bath and laundry room
- The grand kitchen has an eating counter, pantry, optional island and connects to the bayed breakfast room
- 3 bedrooms, 2 1/2 baths, 3-car side entry garage
- Slab, crawl space, basement or walk-out basement foundation, please specify when ordering

Total Living Area: 2,160 sq. ft.

First Floor
1,541 sq. ft.

Porch

Laun.

Bath

Hall

Breakfast
12'1" x 12'2"

Kitchen
12' x 12'10"

Great Room
23' x 15'4"

WOOD RAIL

Garage
21' x 20'

Dining Room
11'10" x 11'4"

STAIRS UP

Foyer

WOOD RAIL

Bath

Width: 58'-0"
Depth: 44'-4"

Porch

Master
Bedroom
12' x 15'

SLOPE
CEIL.

SLOPE
CEIL.

Second Floor
619 sq. ft.

Bedroom
12'2" x 12'

Great Room
Below

PLANT
SHELF

CLOSET

WOOD RAIL

Bath

LIN

CLOSET

STAIRS DOWN

Bedroom
12'2" x 11'10"

Loft

Plan Features

- Arched windows, a brick facade, covered porch and wood trim add color and dimension
- The great room with gas fireplace and 17' ceiling, the kitchen with breakfast bar and the bayed breakfast area form a wonderful family center
- The formal dining room provides additional space for special occasions
- 3 bedrooms, 2 1/2 baths, 2-car garage
- Basement foundation

Total Living Area: 2,951 sq. ft.

DID YOU KNOW?

Not crazy about draperies to decorate your windows? Then shutters may be your treatment of choice. Uncluttered and classically stylish, shutters offer a range of choices in color, depth and style. They also look fabulous in any home style, from traditional to contemporary.

Plan Features

- The master suite is luxurious with a see-through fireplace, two walk-in closets, deluxe bath and sitting room with access to the lanai
- The great room features a 12' ceiling, wet bar, built-in cabinets and a fireplace that also warms the adjoining kitchen and breakfast area
- 4 bedrooms, 3 baths, 3-car side entry garage
- Slab, crawl space, basement or walk-out basement foundation, please specify when ordering

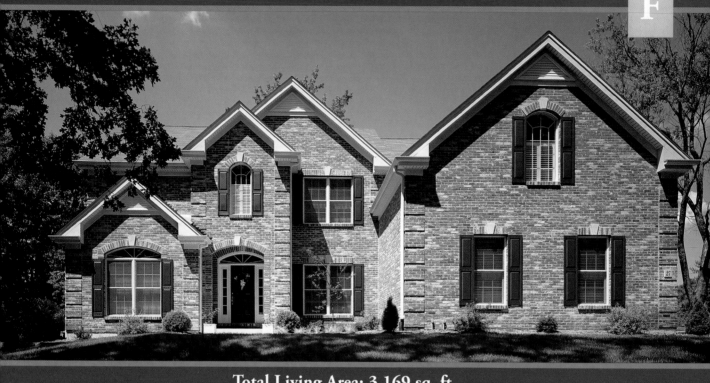

Total Living Area: 3,169 sq. ft.

Patio

Family
18-9x17-4

Wet Bar

Brkfst
12-0x14-8

Kitchen

13-8x12-8

Menu Desk

Pantry

Laundry

W D

Dn

Up

Dining
12-9x14-0
tray clg

Entry

Living
12-4x15-8

vaulted clg

Porch

Garage
20-4x29-4

49'-4"

First Floor
1,679 sq. ft.

55'-0"

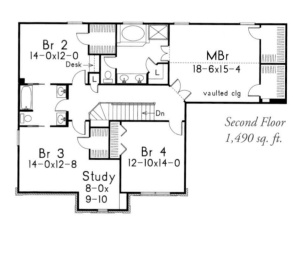

Br 2
14-0x12-0
Desk

L

L

MBr
18-6x15-4

vaulted clg

Dn

Br 3
14-0x12-8

Br 4
12-10x14-0

Study
8-0x
9-10

Second Floor
1,490 sq. ft.

Plan Features

- Formal areas include an enormous entry with handcrafted stairway and powder room, French doors to living room and an open dining area with tray ceiling
- Informal areas consist of a large family room with bay window, fireplace, walk-in wet bar and kitchen open to breakfast room
- Bedroom #3 includes a private study
- 4 bedrooms, 2 1/2 baths, 3-car side entry garage
- Basement foundation

Plan #583-052D-0077

Price Code:

D

Total Living Area: 2,476 sq. ft.

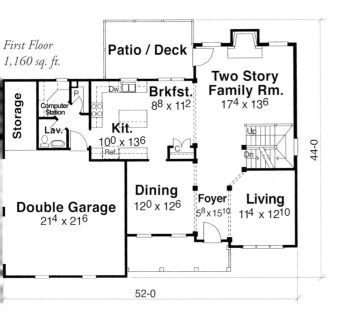

First Floor
1,160 sq. ft.

- Patio / Deck
- Two Story Family Rm. 17⁴ x 13⁶
- Brkfst. 8⁸ x 11²
- Storage
- Computer Station
- P
- Dw.
- Lav.
- Kit. 10⁰ x 13⁶
- Ref.
- C
- Up
- Dn
- Dining 12⁰ x 12⁶
- Foyer 5⁸ x 15¹⁰
- Living 11⁴ x 12¹⁰
- Double Garage 21⁴ x 21⁶
- 44-0
- 52-0

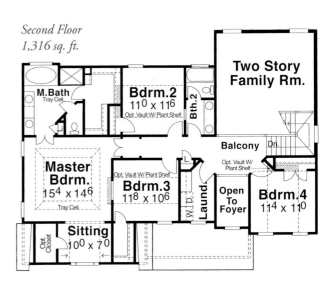

Second Floor
1,316 sq. ft.

- M. Bath Tray Ceil.
- Bdrm. 2 11⁰ x 11⁶ Opt. Vault W/ Plant Shelf
- Bth.2
- Two Story Family Rm.
- Balcony
- Master Bdrm. 15⁴ x 14⁶ Tray Ceil.
- Opt. Vault W/ Plant Shelf
- Bdrm. 3 11⁸ x 10⁶
- W.I.C.
- Laund.
- Opt. Vault W/ Plant Shelf
- Open To Foyer
- Bdrm. 4 11⁴ x 11⁰
- Dn.
- Opt. Closet
- Sitting 10⁰ x 7⁰

Plan Features

- Two-story family room with fireplace and access to patio/deck
- Laundry room on second floor
- First floor has 9' ceilings with open floor plan
- 4 bedrooms, 2 1/2 baths, 2-car side entry garage
- Walk-out basement foundation

To order call toll-free 1-800-DREAM HOME or visit www.houseplansandmore.com

503

Total Living Area: 2,534 sq. ft.

Plan Features

- The private master suite enjoys a 10' box ceiling and a deluxe bath with two vanities and walk-in closets
- A large laundry room is conveniently located adjacent to the garage entrance and the kitchen
- Elegant French doors lead into the study
- 3 bedrooms, 2 baths, 3-car side entry garage
- Slab or crawl space foundation, please specify when ordering

Total Living Area: 2,431 sq. ft.

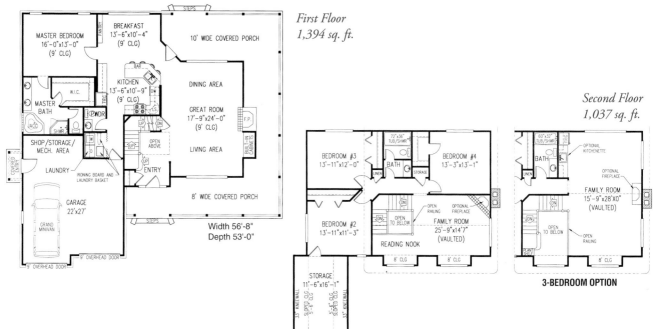

First Floor
1,394 sq. ft.

Second Floor
1,037 sq. ft.

Width 56'-8"
Depth 53'-0"

3-BEDROOM OPTION

Plan Features

- Second floor includes a wonderful casual family room with corner fireplace and reading nook
- The great room, living and dining areas all combine to create one large space ideal for entertaining or family gatherings
- Built-in pantry in breakfast area
- 4 bedrooms, 2 1/2 baths, 2-car garage with shop/storage area
- Basement, crawl space or slab foundation, please specify when ordering

Total Living Area: 1,591 sq. ft.

Plan Features

- Large entry foyer leads to a cheery kitchen and breakfast room which welcomes the sun through a wide array of windows
- Great room features a vaulted ceiling, corner fireplace, wet bar and access to the patio
- Double walk-in closets, private porch and a luxury bath are special highlights of the vaulted master bedroom suite
- 3 bedrooms, 2 baths, 2-car side entry garage
- Basement foundation

Total Living Area: 2,248 sq. ft.

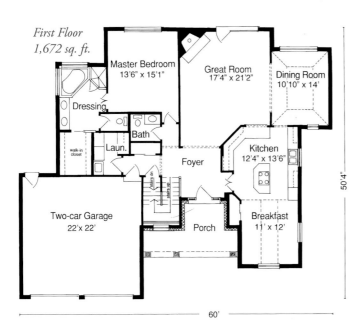

First Floor
1,672 sq. ft.

Master Bedroom
13'6" x 15'1"

Great Room
17'4" x 21'2"

Dining Room
10'10" x 14'

Dressing

Bath

walk-in closet

Laun.

Foyer

Kitchen
12'4" x 13'6"

Two-car Garage
22' x 22'

Porch

Breakfast
11' x 12'

50'4"

60'

Bedroom
11'1" x 13'3"

Bedroom
11'5" x 12'0"

linen

Bath

bookshelves

computer desk

Balcony

wood rail

Foyer Below

Bonus Room
11'0" x 22'0"

wood rail

Second Floor
576 sq. ft.

Plan Features

- Raised ceilings grace the great room, formal dining room and breakfast area
- The large kitchen features an island, pantry and pass-through to the great room
- The master bedroom includes a deluxe bath with a whirlpool tub and walk-in closet
- The second floor bonus room has an additional 242 square feet of living area
- 3 bedrooms, 2 1/2 baths, 2-car garage
- Basement foundation

Total Living Area: 2,391 sq. ft.

Width: 61'-10"
Depth: 59'-11"

DID YOU KNOW?

Garden furniture can be found in a variety of materials. Consider the pros and cons of each before selecting. Wicker has a traditional look and moderate cost but needs protection from weather. Metal is highly durable, usually needs cushions and can be cold to the touch. Resin is an inexpensive and light material and is easily cleaned with soap and water. Weather-resistant hardwood can be left natural for low maintenance and is durable but costly. Regular hardwood or treated softwood is inexpensive but will need regular painting or staining.

Plan Features

- Stucco, brick and quoins combine to create a beautiful facade
- The spacious foyer and formal dining room are topped with 12' ceilings
- The grand fireplace flanked by built-in shelves warms the living room and adjoining breakfast area and kitchen
- 4 bedrooms, 3 baths, 2-car side entry garage
- Slab foundation

Total Living Area: 2,207 sq. ft.

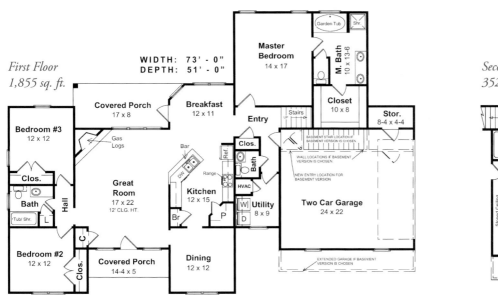

First Floor
1,855 sq. ft.

WIDTH: 73' - 0"
DEPTH: 51' - 0"

Master Bedroom 14 x 17

M. Bath 10 x 13-6

Garden Tub   Shr.

Closet 10 x 8

Covered Porch 17 x 8

Breakfast 12 x 11

Entry

Stairs

Stor. 8-4 x 4-4

Bedroom #3 12 x 12

Gas Logs

Clos.

Bath

Tub/ Shr.

Hall

Great Room 17 x 22 12' CLG. HT.

Bar

Clos.

Ref.

Bath

BASEMENT STAIR LOCATION IF BASEMENT VERSION IS CHOSEN.

WALL LOCATIONS IF BASEMENT VERSION IS CHOSEN.

NEW ENTRY LOCATION FOR BASEMENT VERSION

DW

Range

Kitchen 12 x 15

HVAC

Two Car Garage 24 x 22

Br

P

W   Utility 8 x 9

D

Bedroom #2 12 x 12

Clos.

Covered Porch 14-4 x 5

Dining 12 x 12

EXTENDED GARAGE IF BASEMENT VERSION IS CHOSEN.

Second Floor
352 sq. ft.

Down

Clos.

Opt. Bath

Sloped Ceiling

BEDROOM #4/ LIVING 14 x 22 8' Flat Ceiling

Sloped Ceiling

EXTENDED BONUS ROOM IF BASEMENT VERSION IS CHOSEN.

Plan Features

- The spacious great room boasts a 12' ceiling and corner fireplace
- The kitchen connects to the breakfast area and great room with an eating bar
- Extra storage is located in the garage
- 3 bedrooms, 2 1/2 baths, 2-car side entry garage
- Basement, crawl space or slab foundation, please specify when ordering

Total Living Area: 1,300 sq. ft.

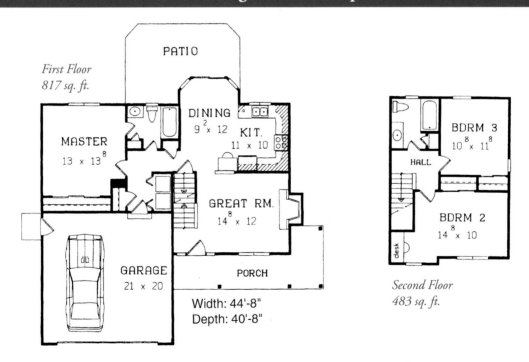

*First Floor
817 sq. ft.*

PATIO

DINING
9² x 12

KIT.
11 x 10

MASTER
13 x 13⁸

GREAT RM.
14⁸ x 12

GARAGE
21 x 20

PORCH

Width: 44'-8"
Depth: 40'-8"

BDRM 3
10⁸ x 11⁸

HALL

BDRM 2
14⁸ x 10

desk

*Second Floor
483 sq. ft.*

Plan Features

- Bayed dining room has sliding glass doors that open onto an outdoor patio
- Large bedroom #2 has a built-in desk
- Charming wrap-around front porch adds curb appeal
- 3 bedrooms, 2 baths, 2-car garage
- Basement foundation

Total Living Area: 2,405 sq. ft.

First Floor
2,405 sq. ft.

Optional
Second Floor

Plan Features

- Grilling porch and covered porch combine for a relaxing outdoor living area
- The master suite enjoys a bayed sitting area and luxurious bath with large walk-in closet
- Kitchen, breakfast and hearth rooms combine for a cozy family living area
- The optional second floor has an additional 358 square feet of living area
- 4 bedrooms, 3 baths, 3-car side entry garage
- Slab or crawl space foundation, please specify when ordering

Total Living Area: 2,493 sq. ft.

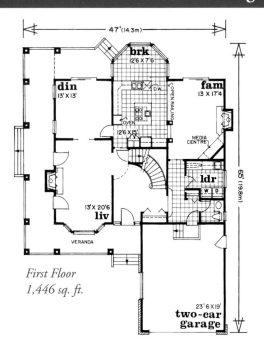

First Floor
1,446 sq. ft.

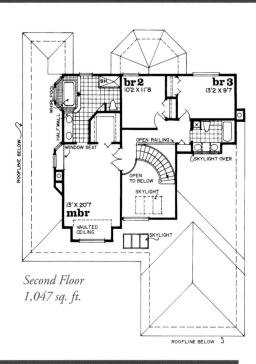

Second Floor
1,047 sq. ft.

Plan Features

- Energy efficient home with 2"x 6" exterior walls
- Breakfast room is nestled in a bay window
- Master bedroom boasts a vaulted ceiling alcove, window seat and walk-in closet
- Sunken family room features a state-of-the-art built-in media center
- 3 bedrooms, 2 1/2 baths, 2-car garage
- Basement foundation

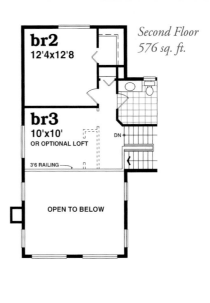

Total Living Area: 1,588 sq. ft.

First Floor
1,012 sq. ft.

PORCH

mbr
12'4"x12'8"

W D

CABINETS

din
12'x10'

k
8'4"x10'

DN

UP

BREAKFAST BAR

great rm
17'x13'6"

PORCH

Width: 34'-0"
Depth: 38'-0"

Second Floor
576 sq. ft.

br2
12'4"x12'8"

br3
10'x10'
OR OPTIONAL LOFT

DN

3'6" RAILING

OPEN TO BELOW

Plan Features

- Master bedroom is located on the first floor for convenience
- Cozy great room has a fireplace
- Dining room has access to both the front and rear porches
- Two secondary bedrooms and a bath complete the second floor
- 3 bedrooms, 2 1/2 baths
- Basement or crawl space foundation, please specify when ordering

Total Living Area: 3,688 sq. ft.

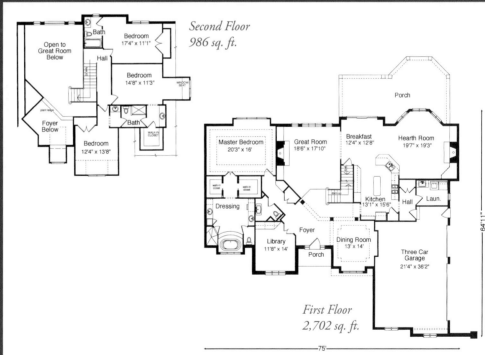

Second Floor
986 sq. ft.

Open to Great Room Below

Bath

Bedroom
17'4" x 11'1"

Hall

Bedroom
14'8" x 11'3"

WINDOW SEAT

Foyer Below

Bath

WALK-IN CLOSET

Bedroom
12'4" x 13'8"

Porch

Master Bedroom
20'3" x 16'

Great Room
18'6" x 17'10"

Breakfast
12'4" x 12'8"

Hearth Room
19'7" x 19'3"

Kitchen
13'1" x 15'6"

Hall

Laun.

Dressing

Foyer

Dining Room
13' x 14'

Library
11'8" x 14'

Porch

Three Car Garage
21'4" x 36'2"

64'11"

75'

First Floor
2,702 sq. ft.

Plan Features

- A gourmet kitchen with open bar and island serves the dining room and breakfast area with equal ease
- A secluded hall creates an orderly transition from the kitchen to the laundry and garage
- A wonderful master bedroom is decorated by a stepped ceiling, crown molding, boxed window and lavish bath with a platform whirlpool tub
- 4 bedrooms, 3 1/2 baths, 3-car side entry garage
- Basement foundation

Plan #583-026D-0167

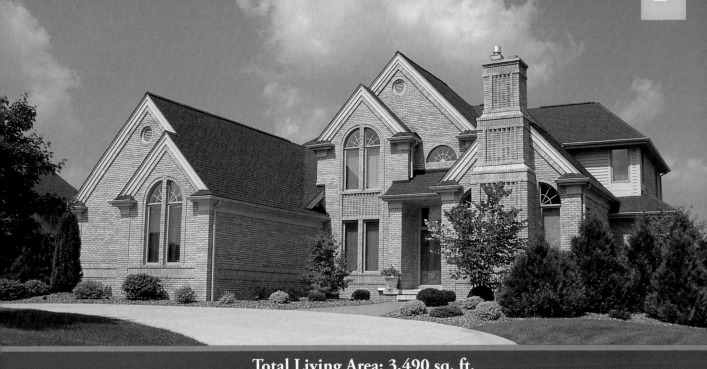

Total Living Area: 3,490 sq. ft.

First Floor
2,355 sq. ft.

© design basics inc.

64'-8"

65'-4"

Second Floor
1,135 sq. ft.

Plan Features

- Master bedroom boasts a walk-in closet, whirlpool tub and a double vanity
- Gourmet kitchen offers a pantry, planning desk and snack bar
- The spacious great room features an elegant fireplace viewed through columned entry
- Each secondary bedroom enjoys bath access and a walk-in closet
- 4 bedrooms, 3 1/2 baths, 3-car side entry garage
- Basement foundation

Rear View

Total Living Area: 2,153 sq. ft.

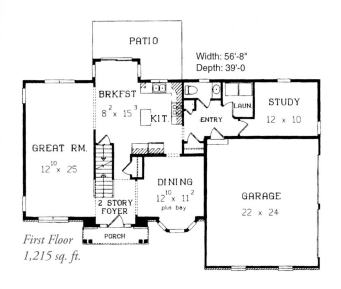

Width: 56'-8"
Depth: 39'-0"

PATIO

BRKFST
8² x 15³

KIT.

STUDY
12 x 10

LAUN.

ENTRY

GREAT RM.
12¹⁰ x 25

2 STORY FOYER

DINING
12¹⁰ x 11²
plus bay

GARAGE
22 x 24

PORCH

First Floor
1,215 sq. ft.

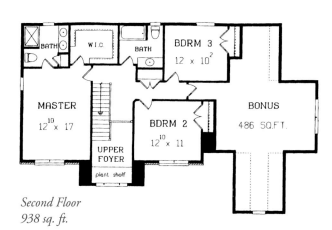

BATH

W.I.C.

BATH

BDRM 3
12 x 10²

MASTER
12¹⁰ x 17

BDRM 2
12¹⁰ x 11

BONUS
486 SQ.FT.

UPPER FOYER

plant shelf

Second Floor
938 sq. ft.

Plan Features

- Secluded first floor study would make an ideal home office
- Breakfast room flows into the great room creating an open feel
- Bonus room on the second floor has an additional 486 square feet of living area
- 3 bedrooms, 2 1/2 baths, 2-car side entry garage
- Basement foundation

Plan #583-062D-0052

Total Living Area: 1,795 sq. ft.

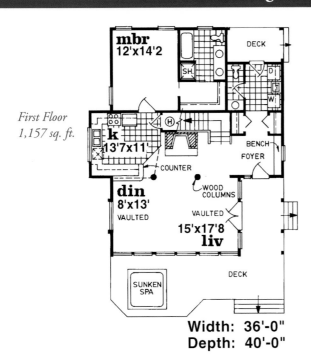

First Floor
1,157 sq. ft.

mbr
12'x14'2

SH

DECK

D
W

k
13'7"x11'

H

COUNTER

BENCH

FOYER

WOOD COLUMNS

VAULTED

din
8'x13'
VAULTED

15'x17'8
liv
VAULTED

SUNKEN SPA

DECK

Width: 36'-0"
Depth: 40'-0"

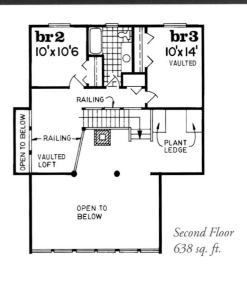

br2
10'x10'6

br3
10'x14'
VAULTED

RAILING

OPEN TO BELOW

RAILING

PLANT LEDGE

VAULTED LOFT

OPEN TO BELOW

Second Floor
638 sq. ft.

Plan Features

- Window wall in living and dining areas brings the outdoors in
- Master bedroom has a full bath and walk-in closet
- Vaulted loft on the second floor is a unique feature
- 3 bedrooms, 2 1/2 baths
- Basement or crawl space foundation, please specify when ordering

Plan #583-024D-0056

Price Code:

G

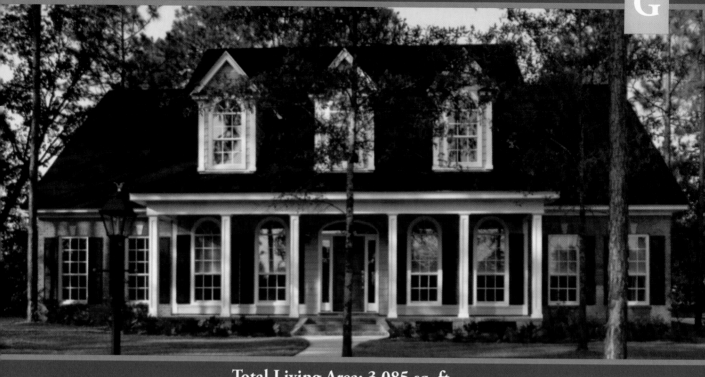

Total Living Area: 3,085 sq. ft.

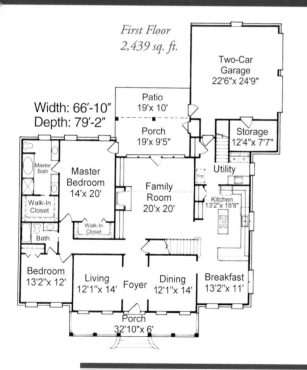

First Floor
2,439 sq. ft.

Two-Car Garage
22'6"x 24'9"

Patio
19'x 10'

Porch
19'x 9'5"

Storage
12'4"x 7'7"

Utility

Width: 66'-10"
Depth: 79'-2"

Master Bath

Master Bedroom
14'x 20'

Walk-In Closet

Family Room
20'x 20'

Kitchen
13'2"x 18'8"

Walk-In Closet

Bath

Bedroom
13'2"x 12'

Living
12'1"x 14'

Foyer

Dining
12'1"x 14'

Breakfast
13'2"x 11'

Porch
32'10"x 6'

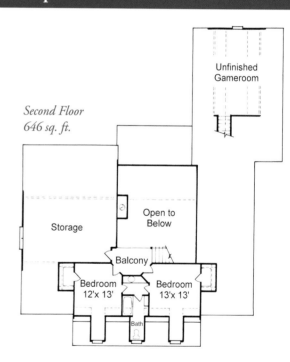

Second Floor
646 sq. ft.

Unfinished Gameroom

Storage

Open to Below

Balcony

Bedroom
12'x 13'

Bedroom
13'x 13'

Bath

Plan Features

- The wonderful family room features a two-story ceiling, full wall of windows and a raised hearth fireplace flanked by built-in bookshelves
- The family chef is sure to enjoy the kitchen with a cooktop island and snack bar that opens to the breakfast area
- The unfinished gameroom has an additional 180 square feet of living area
- 4 bedrooms, 3 baths, 2-car side entry garage
- Slab, crawl space or basement foundation, please specify when ordering

To order call toll-free 1-800-DREAM HOME or visit www.houseplansandmore.com

Total Living Area: 3,422 sq. ft.

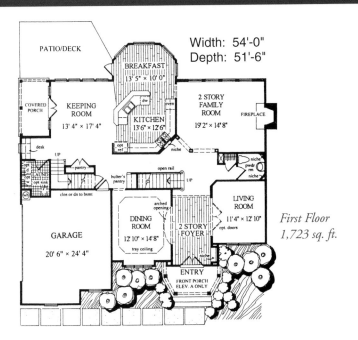

PATIO/DECK

BREAKFAST
13' 5" × 10' 0"

Width: 54'-0"
Depth: 51'-6"

COVERED PORCH

KEEPING ROOM
13' 4" × 17' 4"

KITCHEN
13' 6" × 12' 6"

2 STORY FAMILY ROOM
19' 2" × 14' 8"

FIREPLACE

desk

UP

pantry

LAUND
opt sink

hutler's pantry

open rail

UP

pwdr rm

niche
niche
niche

closs or dn to bsmt

DINING ROOM
12' 10" × 14' 8"
tray ceiling

arched opening

2 STORY FOYER

LIVING ROOM
11' 4" × 12' 10"
opt. doors

*First Floor
1,723 sq. ft.*

GARAGE
20' 6" × 24' 4"

ENTRY

FRONT PORCH ELEV. A ONLY

*Second Floor
1,699 sq. ft.*

MASTER BEDROOM
13' 4" × 22' 8"

ks

12' 6" × 13' 4"

SITTING
9' 0"
× 11' 4"

MASTER BATH

shwr

lin

lin

w.i.c.

trey ceiling

OPEN TO BELOW

plant ledge

open rail

w.i.c.

BATH
vinyl

opt laundry chute

open rail

DN

DN

open rail

BEDROOM 4
13' 10" × 13' 6"

lin

arched opening

BEDROOM 3
12' 11" × 12' 5"

BATH
vinyl

arched opening

OPEN TO BELOW

trey ceiling

BEDROOM 2
11' 6" × 13' 6"

attic access

w.i.c.

attic access

Plan Features

- Tudor influenced brick and stucco exterior
- Arched openings in dining and living rooms create a dramatic feel
- The kitchen is open to the keeping room
- Two-story family room has fireplace and balcony on second floor
- 4 bedrooms, 3 1/2 baths, 2-car side entry garage
- Basement foundation

Total Living Area: 1,000 sq. ft.

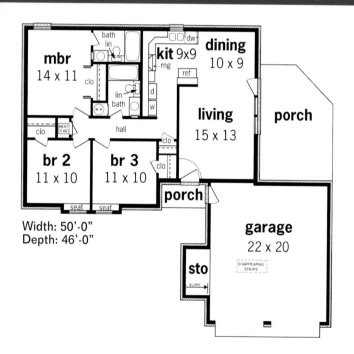

Width: 50'-0"
Depth: 46'-0"

DID YOU KNOW?

Organic gardeners like to quote an old Chinese proverb: "The best fertilizer in the garden may be the gardener's own shadow." It is their belief that the daily attendance of a living presence, as opposed to a chemical or artificial one, may be the best tonic growing plants can have.

Plan Features

- Energy efficient home with 2"x 6" exterior walls
- This three bedroom home has abundant closet space and exterior storage
- A simple design and all brick exterior make this home easy to build and easy to maintain
- 3 bedrooms, 2 baths, 2-car garage
- Slab foundation, drawings also include crawl space foundation

Total Living Area: 1,921 sq. ft.

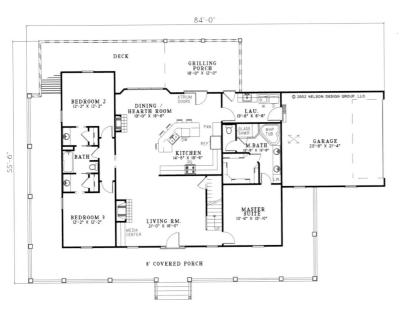

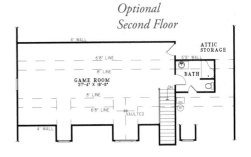

First Floor
1,921 sq. ft.

Optional
Second Floor

Plan Features

- A massive living room is warmed by a fireplace and includes a built-in media center
- Wrap-around kitchen counter with seating opens to the dining/hearth room
- The optional second floor has an additional 812 square feet of living space
- 3 bedrooms, 3 baths, 2-car side entry garage
- Slab, crawl space, basement or walk-out basement foundation, please specify when ordering

Total Living Area: 1,368 sq. ft.

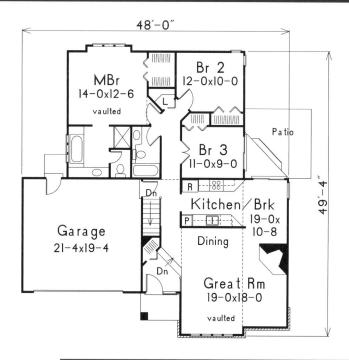

DID YOU KNOW?

To keep rodents out of your house tidy up your garage. Store pet food and birdseed in hard plastic containers. Remove shoes, blankets and other cozy home sites. A mouse can squeeze through holes as small as a dime, so plug gaps around pipes with coarse steel wool and then caulk over it.

Plan Features

- Entry foyer steps down to an open living area which combines the great room and formal dining area
- Vaulted master bedroom includes a box-bay window and a bath with a large vanity, separate tub and shower
- Cozy breakfast area features direct access to the patio and pass-through kitchen
- 3 bedrooms, 2 baths, 2-car garage
- Basement foundation

Total Living Area: 1,793 sq. ft.

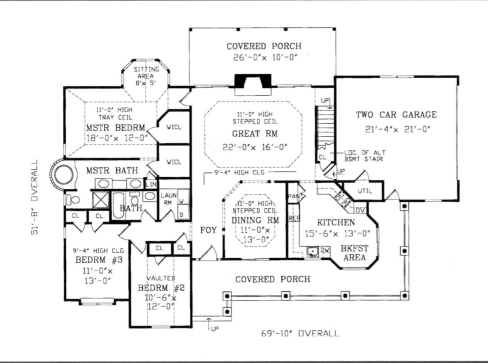

COVERED PORCH
26'-0" x 10'-0"

SITTING AREA
8' x 5'

11'-0" HIGH TRAY CEIL
MSTR BEDRM
18'-0" x 12'-0"

WICL

WICL

11'-0" HIGH STEPPED CEIL
GREAT RM
22'-0" x 16'-0"

TWO CAR GARAGE
21'-4" x 21'-0"

UP

51'-8" OVERALL

MSTR BATH

LIN

LOC. OF ALT BSMT STAIR

9'-4" HIGH CLG

UP

CL

BATH

LAUN RM

W

D

UTIL

DV

9'-4" HIGH CLG
BEDRM #3
11'-0" x 13'-0"

CL

CL

CL

11'-0" HIGH STEPPED CEIL
DINING RM
11'-0" x 13'-0"

FOY

PANT

KITCHEN
15'-6" x 13'-0"

REF

DV

VAULTED
BEDRM #2
10'-6" x 12'-0"

COVERED PORCH

BKFST AREA

UP

DV

69'-10" OVERALL

Plan Features

- Beautiful foyer leads into the great room that has a fireplace flanked by two sets of beautifully transomed doors both leading to a large covered porch
- Dramatic eat-in kitchen includes an abundance of cabinets and workspace
- Optional bonus room above garage has an additional 779 square feet of living area
- 3 bedrooms, 2 baths, 2-car side entry garage
- Basement, crawl space or slab foundation, please specify when ordering

Total Living Area: 1,989 sq. ft.

Plan Features

- The kitchen includes a counter with seating that opens to the charming breakfast room
- The guest bedroom is privately located and includes a bath and walk-in closet
- A tray ceiling, deluxe bath and massive walk-in closet enhance the master suite
- 4 bedrooms, 3 baths, 2-car side entry garage
- Slab, crawl space, basement or walk-out basement foundation, please specify when ordering

Total Living Area: 1,404 sq. ft.

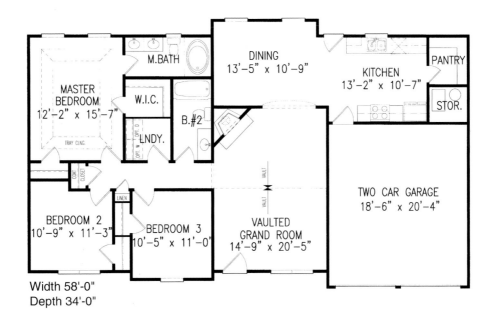

Width 58'-0"
Depth 34'-0"

Plan Features

- Dining area and kitchen connect allowing for convenience and ease
- Well-located laundry area is within steps of bedrooms and baths
- Vaulted grand room creates a feeling of spaciousness for this gathering area
- 3 bedrooms, 2 1/2 baths, 2-car garage
- Slab foundation

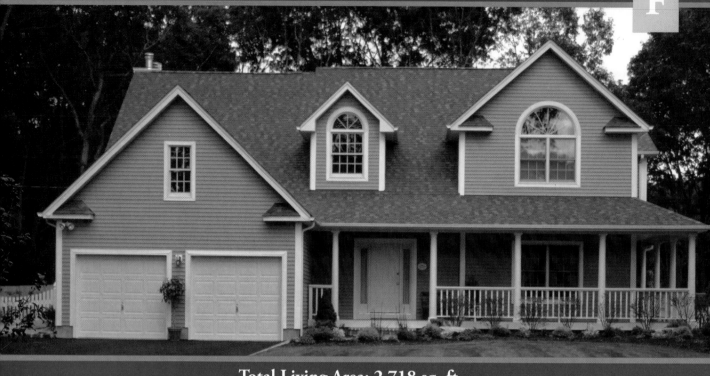

Total Living Area: 2,718 sq. ft.

Second Floor
1,203 sq. ft.

First Floor
1,515 sq. ft.

BEDRM #2 10'-6" x 13'-6"

BEDRM #3 11'-0" x 12'-0"

MSTR BATH

WICL

UPPER FAMILY RM

RAIL

BATH

WICL

OPT LOFT/ BEDRM #4 20'-4" x 11'-0"

BALCONY

RAIL

DN

UPPER FOYER

VAULTED CLG

MSTR BEDRM 16'-0" x 15'-4"

WOOD DECK

9' SL GL DR

FIREPLACE

VAULTED CLG
FAMILY RM 20'-4" x 15'-4"

9'-0" HIGH CEIL
BKFST RM 11'-0" x 17'-0"

KITCHEN 10'-0" x 15'-4"

FRENCH DR

9'-0" HIGH CEIL
DINING RM 14'-0" x 15'-4"

REF.

UTIL

LAUN RM

D W

CL

LAV

CL

9'-0" HIGH CEIL
LIVING RM 16'-0" x 15'-4"

DN TO OPT BSMT

TWO STORY FOYER

UP

UP

TWO CAR GARAGE 20'-4" x 22'-0"

COVERED PORCH

FRENCH DR

© Jerold Axelrod, Architect

ALT FRONT ENTRY GARAGE

Width 56'-0"
Depth 45'-0"

Plan Features

- The two-story foyer opens into the central kitchen which enjoys an island work station
- The master bedroom offers two walk-in closets and a private bath with garden tub
- An optional loft easily converts into a fourth bedroom and has an additional 223 square feet of living area
- 4 bedrooms, 2 1/2 baths, 2-car side entry garage
- Basement, crawl space or slab foundation, please specify when ordering

Total Living Area: 2,828 sq. ft.

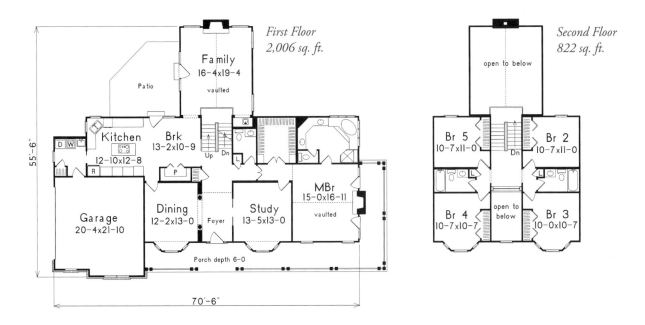

First Floor
2,006 sq. ft.

Family
16-4x19-4
vaulted

Patio

Kitchen
12-10x12-8

Brk
13-2x10-9

Up   Dn

Garage
20-4x21-10

Dining
12-2x13-0

Foyer

Study
13-5x13-0

MBr
15-0x16-11
vaulted

Porch depth 6-0

55'-6"

70'-6"

Second Floor
822 sq. ft.

open to below

Br 5
10-7x11-0

Dn

Br 2
10-7x11-0

Br 4
10-7x10-7

open to below

Br 3
10-0x10-7

Plan Features

- Popular wrap-around porch gives home country charm
- Secluded family room with vaulted ceiling and wet bar features many windows
- Any chef would be delighted to cook in this smartly designed kitchen with island and corner windows
- 5 bedrooms, 3 1/2 baths, 2-car side entry garage
- Basement foundation, drawings also include crawl space and slab foundations

D

Total Living Area: 2,449 sq. ft.

First Floor
1,925 sq. ft.

Width: 56'-4"
Depth: 53'-4"

Master Bedroom
14'4" x 14'8"

Breakfast
11'2" x 11'8"

Porch

Great Room
18'1" x 18'11"

Kitchen
15'5" x 11'2"

Laun.

WALK-IN CLOSET

STAIRS UP

DOWN

Dining Room
11' x 13'

Foyer

Library
11'4" x 12'2"

Porch

Two-car Garage
22' x 21'

Second Floor
524 sq. ft.

Bedroom
11' x 12'2"

Bath

Loft

STAIRS DOWN

Computer desk

Bedroom
11' x 12'6"

Plan Features

- Separated by columns and varied ceiling treatments the great room and formal dining room create a functional gathering area
- A delightfully spacious breakfast area with sloped ceiling and multiple windows offers a bright and cheery place to start the day
- The first floor master bedroom features a raised ceiling treatment and deluxe bath
- 3 bedrooms, 2 1/2 baths, 2-car garage
- Basement foundation

Plan #583-047D-0050

Optional Second Floor

Balc. Bonus Rm. 21⁴ • 16⁴

First Floor 2,293 sq. ft.

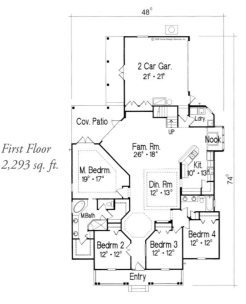

48⁰

2 Car Gar. 21⁰ • 21⁰

Cov. Patio

Ldry

UP

Fam. Rm. 26⁰ • 18⁰

Nook

M. Bedrm. 19⁰ • 17⁴

Kit. 10⁰ • 13⁰

Din. Rm 12⁰ • 13⁰

74⁰

M.Bath

Bedrm 2 12⁰ • 12⁰

Bedrm 3 12⁰ • 12⁰

Bedrm 4 12⁰ • 12⁰

Entry

Total Living Area: 2,293 sq. ft.

Plan Features

- Formal dining area flows into large family room making great use of space
- Cozy nook off kitchen makes an ideal breakfast area
- Optional second floor has an additional 509 square feet of living area
- Framing - only concrete block available
- 4 bedrooms, 2 baths, 2-car side entry garage
- Slab foundation

Plan #583-053D-0037

Total Living Area: 1,388 sq. ft.

Plan Features

- Handsome see-through fireplace offers a gathering point for the kitchen, family and breakfast rooms
- A dramatic angular wall and large windows add brightness to the kitchen and breakfast room
- Kitchen, breakfast and family rooms have vaulted ceilings, adding to this central living area
- 3 bedrooms, 2 baths, 2-car garage
- Crawl space foundation, drawings also include slab foundation

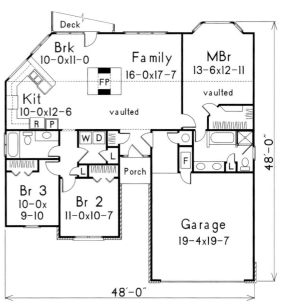

Deck

Brk 10-0x11-0

Family 16-0x17-7

MBr 13-6x12-11

FP

vaulted

Kit 10-0x12-6

vaulted

R P

W D

L

F

Porch

48'-0"

Br 3 10-0x 9-10

Br 2 11-0x10-7

Garage 19-4x19-7

48'-0"

Total Living Area: 2,806 sq. ft.

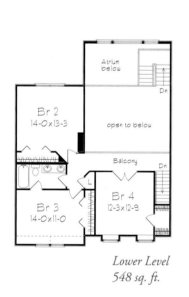

Lower Level
548 sq. ft.

Br 2
14-0x13-3

Atrium below

open to below

Balcony

Br 3
14-0x11-0

Br 4
12-3x12-9

Dn

Dn

54'-8"

51'-0"

Atrium below

Deck

Great Rm
18-0x19-10

Dining
10-2x13-3

Kit
11-0x13-3

vaulted

MBr
14-0x16-9

vaulted

Bar

W
D

P

Foyer

Up

Dn

Garage
21-4x21-4

Porch

First Floor
1,473 sq. ft.

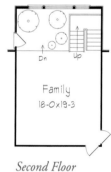

Family
18-0x19-3

Dn   Up

Second Floor
785 sq. ft.

Rear View

Plan Features

- Harmonious charm throughout
- A sweeping balcony and vaulted ceiling soar above the spacious great room and walk-in bar
- Atrium with lower level family room is a unique touch, creating an open and airy feeling
- 4 bedrooms, 2 1/2 baths, 2-car garage
- Walk-out basement foundation

Plan #583-001D-0028

Price Code: D

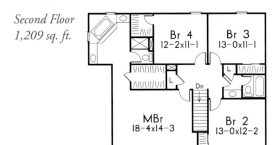

Second Floor
1,209 sq. ft.

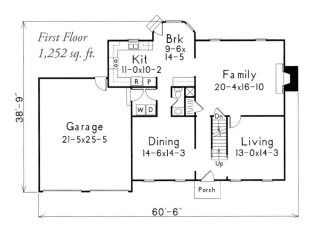

Br 4
12-2x11-1

Br 3
13-0x11-1

MBr
18-4x14-3

Br 2
13-0x12-2

Dn

First Floor
1,252 sq. ft.

Brk
9-6x 14-5

Kit
11-0x10-2

Family
20-4x16-10

38'-9"

Garage
21-5x25-5

Dining
14-6x14-3

Living
13-0x14-3

Up

Dn

Porch

60'-6"

Total Living Area: 2,461 sq. ft.

Plan Features

- Unique corner tub, double vanities and walk-in closet enhance the large master bedroom
- Fireplace provides focus in the spacious family room
- Centrally located half bath for guests
- 4 bedrooms, 2 1/2 baths, 2-car garage
- Basement foundation, drawings also include slab and crawl space foundations

---

Plan #583-008D-0110

Price Code: B

Total Living Area: 1,500 sq. ft.

Plan Features

- Living room features a cathedral ceiling and opens to the breakfast room
- Breakfast room has a spectacular bay window and adjoins a well-appointed kitchen with generous storage
- Laundry room is convenient and includes a large closet
- Walk-in closet gives the master bedroom plenty of storage
- 3 bedrooms, 2 baths, 2-car garage
- Basement foundation

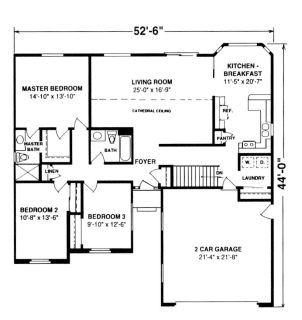

52'-6"

MASTER BEDROOM
14'-10" x 13'-10"

LIVING ROOM
25'-0" x 16'-9"

CATHEDRAL CEILING

KITCHEN - BREAKFAST
11'-5" x 20'-7"

REF.

PANTRY

MASTER BATH

BATH

FOYER

DN

W. D.

LAUNDRY

LINEN

44'-0"

BEDROOM 2
10'-8" x 13'-6"

BEDROOM 3
9'-10" x 12'-6"

2 CAR GARAGE
21'-4" x 21'-8"

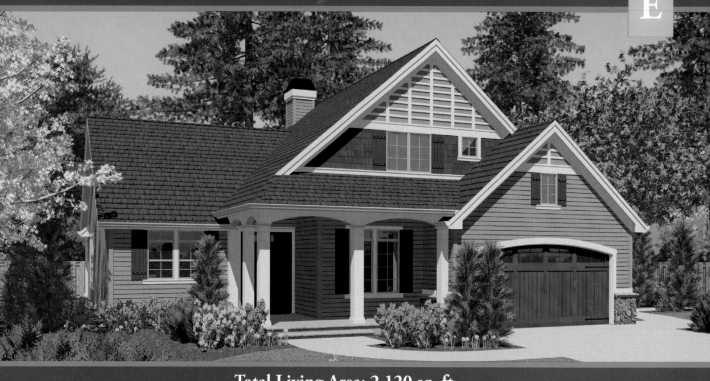

Total Living Area: 2,120 sq. ft.

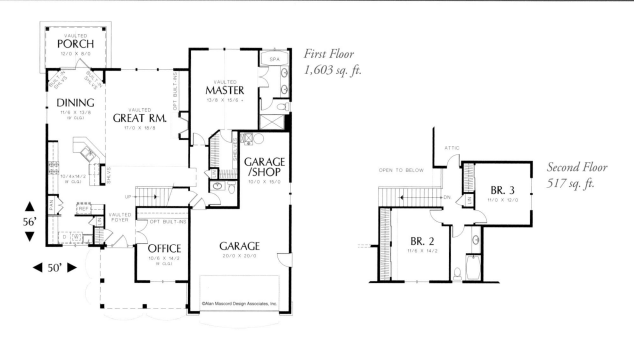

First Floor
1,603 sq. ft.

Second Floor
517 sq. ft.

©Alan Mascord Design Associates, Inc.

Plan Features

- First floor vaulted master bedroom has a spacious and open feel
- Built-in shelves adorn the dining room
- Office has a double-door entry helping to maintain privacy
- 3 bedrooms, 2 1/2 baths, 3-car garage
- Crawl space foundation

Plan #583-013D-0001

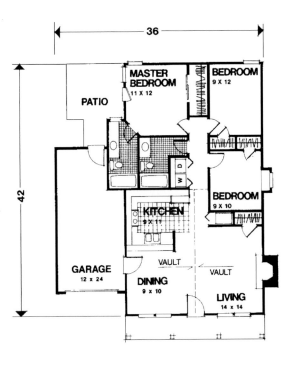

Total Living Area: 1,050 sq. ft.

Plan Features

- Master bedroom has its own private bath and access to the outdoors onto a private patio
- Vaulted ceilings in the living and dining areas create a feeling of spaciousness
- Laundry closet is convenient to all bedrooms
- 3 bedrooms, 2 baths, 1-car garage
- Basement or slab foundation, please specify when ordering

Plan #583-040D-0003

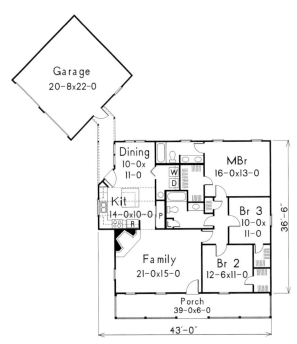

Total Living Area: 1,475 sq. ft.

Plan Features

- Family room features a high ceiling and corner fireplace
- Kitchen with island counter and garden window connects to the family and dining rooms
- Covered breezeway joins main house and garage
- Full-width covered porch entry lends a country touch
- 3 bedrooms, 2 baths, 2-car detached side entry garage
- Slab foundation, drawings also include crawl space foundation

Total Living Area: 2,356 sq. ft.

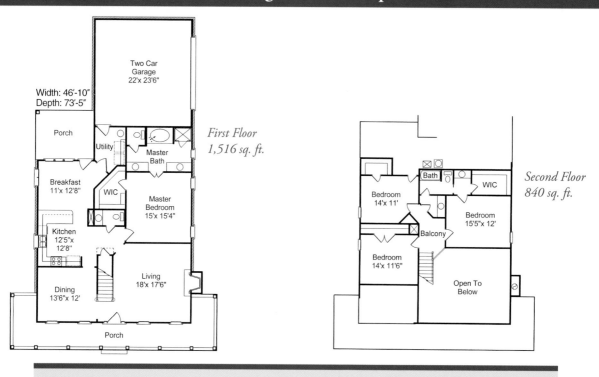

Width: 46'-10"
Depth: 73'-5"

Two Car Garage 22'x 23'6"

First Floor 1,516 sq. ft.

Porch

Utility

Master Bath

Breakfast 11'x 12'8"

WIC

Master Bedroom 15'x 15'4"

Kitchen 12'5"x 12'8"

Dining 13'6"x 12'

Living 18'x 17'6"

Porch

Second Floor 840 sq. ft.

Bath

WIC

Bedroom 14'x 11'

Bedroom 15'5"x 12'

Balcony

Bedroom 14'x 11'6"

Open To Below

Plan Features

- Arched windows add elegance to the facade and shed an abundance of light into the dining and living rooms
- The kitchen includes a snack bar counter that opens to the relaxing breakfast area
- The secondary bedrooms share a Jack and Jill bath
- 4 bedrooms, 2 1/2 baths, 2-car side entry garage
- Slab foundation

Plan #583-052D-0037

Price Code: B

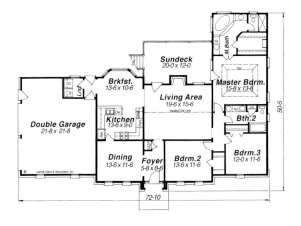

Total Living Area: 1,781 sq. ft.

Plan Features

- Massive arched entry welcomes visitors
- Charming master bath has double vanities split by a corner tub and large walk-in closet
- The sundeck is accessible from the living area and master bedroom
- 3 bedrooms, 2 baths, 2-car side entry garage
- Slab or crawl space foundation, please specify when ordering

---

Plan #583-052D-0020

Price Code: B

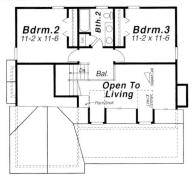

Second Floor 498 sq. ft.

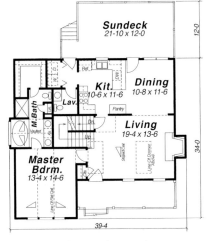

First Floor 1,055 sq. ft.

Total Living Area: 1,553 sq. ft.

Plan Features

- Two-story living area creates an open and airy feel to the interior especially with two dormers above
- First floor master bedroom is private and includes its own bath and walk-in closet
- Two secondary bedrooms share a full bath with double vanity
- 3 bedrooms, 2 1/2 baths, 2-car drive under garage
- Walk-out basement foundation

Total Living Area: 1,609 sq. ft.

First Floor
1,072 sq. ft.

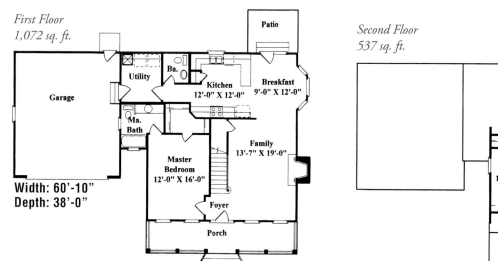

Width: 60'-10"
Depth: 38'-0"

Second Floor
537 sq. ft.

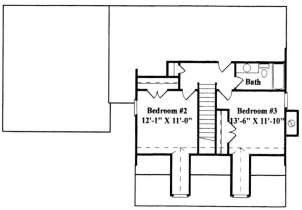

Plan Features

- U-shaped kitchen has a conveniently located pantry
- Spacious utility room creates easy access from the garage to the rest of the home
- Both bedrooms on the second floor feature dormers
- Family room includes plenty of space for entertaining
- 3 bedrooms, 2 1/2 baths, 2-car garage
- Slab foundation

Plan #583-062D-0058

Width: 38'-0"
Depth: 32'-0"

First Floor
1,108 sq. ft.

DECK

mbr 13'8x11'4

VAULTED **K** 8'6x11'4

din 9'x11'4 VAULTED

OPTIONAL BUFFET

VAULTED **liv** 15'2x13'4

SKYLIGHT

br2 9'4x11'

br3 9'4x12'8

PORCH

DN

Optional Lower Level

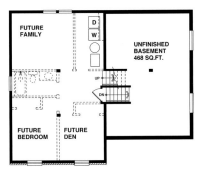

FUTURE FAMILY

D W

UNFINISHED BASEMENT 468 SQ.FT.

UP

DN

FUTURE BEDROOM

FUTURE DEN

Total Living Area: 1,108 sq. ft.

Plan Features

- Master bedroom offers a walk-in closet, a full bath and a box-bay window
- Vaulted ceilings in the kitchen, living and dining rooms make this home appear larger than its actual size
- Optional lower level has an additional 1,108 square feet of living area
- 3 bedrooms, 2 baths
- Partial basement/crawl space or basement foundation, please specify when ordering

---

Plan #583-055D-0024

Total Living Area: 1,680 sq. ft.

Plan Features

- Enormous and luxurious master suite
- Kitchen and dining room have vaulted ceilings creating an open feeling
- Double sinks grace the secondary bath
- 3 bedrooms, 2 baths, 2-car garage
- Walk-out basement, basement, crawl space or slab foundation, please specify when ordering

51' 6"

COVERED GRILLING PORCH 17'-4" X 9'-4"

MASTER SUITE 20'-10" X 13'-0" 9' PAN CEILING

BEDROOM 2 12'-4" X 10'-0"

GREAT ROOM 17'-0" X 20'-0" 9' PAN CEILING

GLASS SHWR

LIN

LAU. 5'-6" X 6'-2"

D W

WHP TUB

GLASS BLOCKS

BATH

LIN

DN

OPTIONAL BASEMENT PLAN

GARAGE 20'-10" X 20'-0"

BEDROOM 3 12'-4" X 11'-8"

REF PAN

RC

KITCHEN 12'-4" X 12'-0"

DW

FOYER

PRCH

DINING 12'-0" X 10'-0"

VAULTED CEILING

52' 4"

© 2006 NELSON DESIGN GROUP, LLC

Total Living Area: 2,336 sq. ft.

First Floor
1,291 sq. ft.

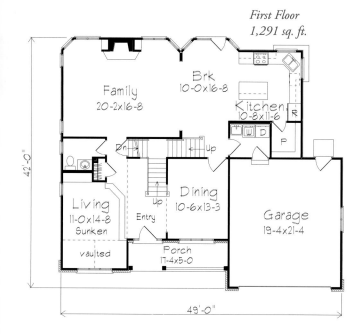

Family
20-2x16-8

Brk
10-0x16-8

Kitchen
10-8x11-6

Dn

Up

Up

Living
11-0x14-8
Sunken

vaulted

Entry

Dining
10-6x13-3

Garage
19-4x21-4

Porch
17-4x5-0

42'-0"

49'-0"

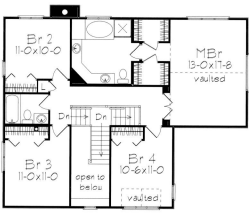

Br 2
11-0x10-0

MBr
13-0x17-8
vaulted

Dn

Dn

Br 3
11-0x11-0

open to
below

Br 4
10-6x11-0

vaulted

Second Floor
1,045 sq. ft.

Plan Features

- Stately sunken living room with partially vaulted ceiling and classic arched transom windows create a pleasant, inviting atmosphere
- Family room features plenty of windows and a fireplace with flanking bookshelves
- 4 bedrooms, 2 1/2 baths, 2-car garage
- Basement foundation

Plan #583-077D-0006

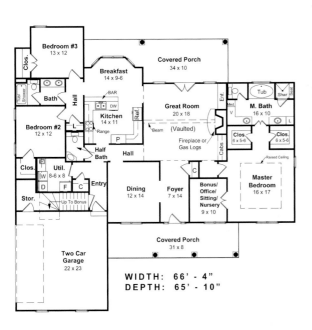

WIDTH: 66'-4"
DEPTH: 65'-10"

Total Living Area: 2,307 sq. ft.

Plan Features

- The bayed breakfast area warms the home
- The spacious master bedroom boasts two walk-in closets, private bath and a bonus area
- The vaulted great room includes a grand fireplace, built-in shelves and a double-door entry onto the covered porch
- 3 bedrooms, 2 1/2 baths, 2-car side entry garage
- Basement, crawl space or slab foundation, please specify when ordering

---

Plan #583-025D-0010

Total Living Area: 1,677 sq. ft.

Plan Features

- Master suite has a secluded feel with a private and remote location from other bedrooms
- Great room is complete with fireplace and beautiful windows
- Optional second floor has an additional 350 square feet of living area
- 3 bedrooms, 2 baths, 2-car side entry garage
- Slab foundation

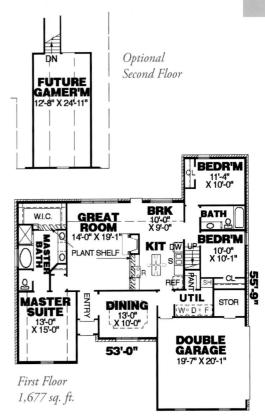

Optional Second Floor

First Floor
1,677 sq. ft.

A

Total Living Area: 1,281 sq. ft.

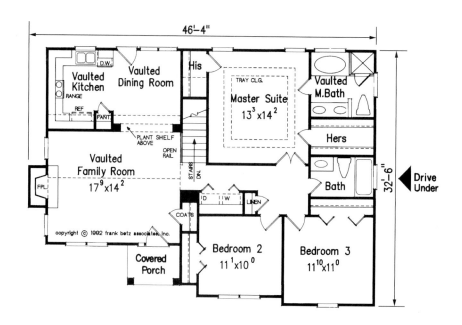

46'-4"

Vaulted Kitchen

D.W.

RANGE

REF

PANT

Vaulted Dining Room

His

TRAY CLG.

Master Suite
13³x14²

Vaulted M.Bath

Hers

PLANT SHELF ABOVE

OPEN RAIL

STAIRS DN

Vaulted Family Room
17⁹x14²

FPL

Bath

32'-6"

Drive Under

D   W

LINEN

COATS

copyright © 1992 frank betz associates, inc.

Covered Porch

Bedroom 2
11¹x10⁰

Bedroom 3
11¹⁰x11⁰

Plan Features

- Spacious master suite has a tray ceiling, double closets and a private bath
- Vaulted family room has lots of sunlight from multiple windows and a fireplace
- Plant shelf above kitchen and dining room is a nice decorative touch
- 3 bedrooms, 2 baths, 2-car drive under garage
- Walk-out basement foundation

Plan #583-013D-0033

Second Floor 651 sq. ft.

First Floor 1,689 sq. ft.

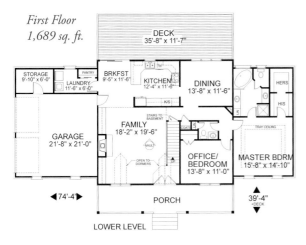

Total Living Area: 2,340 sq. ft.

Plan Features

- Large family room has a vaulted ceiling, bookcases and an entertainment center which surrounds a brick fireplace
- Highly functional kitchen is easily accessible
- The second floor consists of two secondary bedrooms each having direct access to the bath
- The loft can serve as a recreation area or fifth bedroom
- 3 bedrooms, 2 1/2 baths, 2-car side entry garage
- Walk-out basement foundation

Plan #583-028D-0012

Price Code: **D**

Total Living Area: 2,293 sq. ft.

Plan Features

- The arched opening between the kitchen and breakfast area leads to two of the secondary bedrooms, the laundry area and a full bath
- Bedroom #2/study could easily convert to an office area
- The corner fireplace in the great room demands attention
- 4 bedrooms, 3 baths, 3-car side entry garage
- Crawl space or slab foundation, please specify when ordering

Total Living Area: 1,820 sq. ft.

Plan Features

- Living room has a stunning cathedral ceiling
- Spacious laundry room with easy access to kitchen, garage and the outdoors
- Plenty of closet space throughout
- Covered front porch enhances outdoor living
- 3 bedrooms, 2 baths, 2-car garage
- Basement foundation

Plan #583-038D-0043

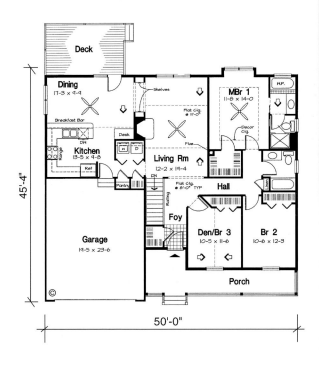

Total Living Area: 1,539 sq. ft.

Plan Features

- A tray ceiling tops the master bedroom
- The peninsula counter in the kitchen doubles as a breakfast bar
- A walk-in closet in the foyer has space for additional storage
- 3 bedrooms, 2 baths, 2-car garage
- Basement, crawl space or slab foundation, please specify when ordering

Plan #583-007D-0014

Total Living Area: 1,985 sq. ft.

Plan Features

- Charming design for a narrow lot
- Dramatic sunken great room features a vaulted ceiling, large double-hung windows and transomed patio doors
- Grand master bedroom includes a double-door entry, large closet, elegant bath and patio access
- 4 bedrooms, 3 1/2 baths, 2-car garage
- Basement foundation

Second Floor
871 sq. ft.

First Floor
1,114 sq. ft.

Total Living Area: 1,621 sq. ft.

Lower Level with Optional Laundry Area

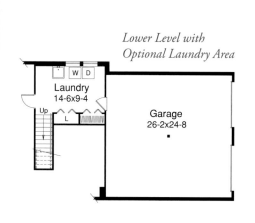

Laundry
14-6x9-4

Garage
26-2x24-8

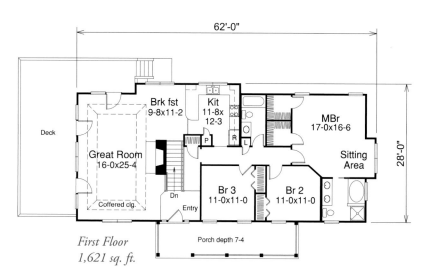

62'-0"

28'-0"

Deck

Brk fst
9-8x11-2

Kit
11-8x12-3

MBr
17-0x16-6

Great Room
16-0x25-4

Sitting
Area

Coffered clg.

Dn

Entry

Br 3
11-0x11-0

Br 2
11-0x11-0

Porch depth 7-4

*First Floor
1,621 sq. ft.*

Plan Features

- The front exterior includes an attractive gable-end arched window and extra-deep porch
- A grand-scale great room enjoys a coffered ceiling, fireplace, access to the wrap-around deck and is brightly lit with numerous French doors and windows
- 223 square feet of optional finished space on the lower level
- 3 bedrooms, 2 baths, 2-car drive under side entry garage
- Basement foundation

Plan #583-008D-0162

Second Floor
370 sq. ft.

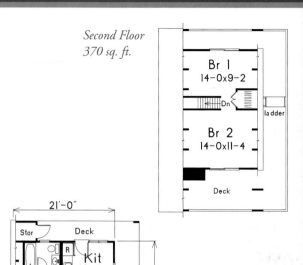

Br 1
14-0x9-2

Dn   ladder

Br 2
14-0x11-4

Deck

21'-0"

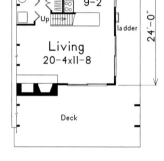

Stor   Deck

Kit
10-4x
9-2

R

Up   ladder

Living
20-4x11-8

24'-0"

First Floor
495 sq. ft.

Deck

Total Living Area: 865 sq. ft.

Plan Features

- Central living area provides an enormous amount of space for gathering around the fireplace
- The outdoor ladder on the wrap-around deck connects the top deck with the main deck
- Kitchen is bright and cheerful with lots of windows and access to the deck
- 2 bedrooms, 1 bath
- Pier foundation

Plan #583-003D-0004

Total Living Area: 3,357 sq. ft.

Plan Features

- Attractive balcony overlooks entry foyer and living area
- Spacious kitchen also opens into a sunken family room with a fireplace
- Master bedroom boasts walk-in closet and dressing area
- Laundry room has laundry chute from second floor
- 4 bedrooms, 2 full baths, 2 half, 2-car side entry garage
- Basement foundation, drawings also include crawl space and slab foundations

Second Floor
983 sq. ft.

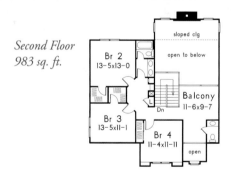

sloped clg

open to below

Br 2
13-5x13-0

Balcony
11-6x9-7

Dn

Br 3
13-5x11-1

Br 4
11-4x11-11

open

69'-0"

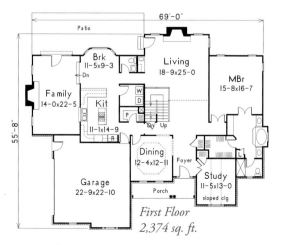

Patio

Brk
11-5x9-3

Living
18-9x25-0

Dn

MBr
15-8x16-7

Family
14-0x22-5

Kit
11-1x14-9

W D

P

Dn Up

R

Dining
12-4x12-11

Foyer

55'-8"

Garage
22-9x22-10

Porch

Study
11-5x13-0
sloped clg

First Floor
2,374 sq. ft.

Total Living Area: 3,072 sq. ft.

First Floor
2,116 sq. ft.

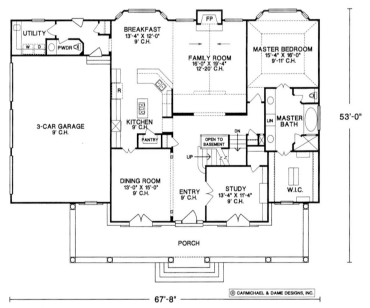

Second Floor
956 sq. ft.

© CARMICHAEL & DAME DESIGNS, INC.

Plan Features

- Charming window seats accent all the secondary bedrooms
- Master bedroom has a luxurious bath and an enormous walk-in closet
- French doors in both the study and the formal dining room lead to the covered front porch
- 4 bedrooms, 3 1/2 baths, 3-car side entry garage
- Slab foundation

To order call toll-free 1-800-DREAM HOME or visit www.houseplansandmore.com

Total Living Area: 1,833 sq. ft.

Plan Features

- Master bedroom suite comes with a garden tub, walk-in closet and bay window
- Walk-through kitchen and breakfast room
- Front bay windows offer a deluxe touch
- Foyer with convenient coat closet opens into large vaulted living room with an attractive fireplace
- 3 bedrooms, 2 baths, 2-car drive under garage
- Basement foundation

Total Living Area: 1,635 sq. ft.

Plan Features

- Large wrap-around front porch
- Open living and dining rooms are separated only by columns for added openness
- Kitchen includes a large work island and snack bar
- Master bedroom with tray ceiling has three closets
- 3 bedrooms, 2 1/2 baths, 2-car garage
- Basement, crawl space or slab foundation, please specify when ordering

Second Floor 755 sq. ft.

First Floor 880 sq. ft.

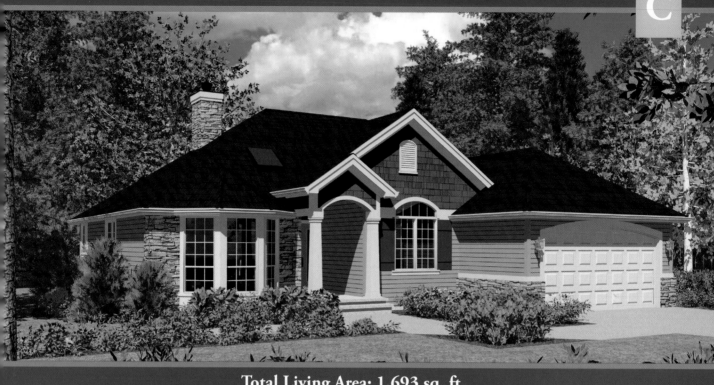

Total Living Area: 1,693 sq. ft.

DID YOU KNOW?

Planning the layout of a living room is as important as choosing the color scheme. To make the task a little easier, draw a floor plan to scale on graph paper and cut out separate pieces for the furniture. Place these on the plan and move them around until you have an arrangement that suits your needs.

Plan Features

- Formal dining and living rooms combine for an open entertaining area
- The kitchen includes a bayed nook for extra dining space and opens to the vaulted family room with a cozy fireplace
- The vaulted master bedroom features a double-door entry and private bath
- 3 bedrooms, 2 baths, 2-car garage
- Crawl space foundation

Plan #583-007D-0042

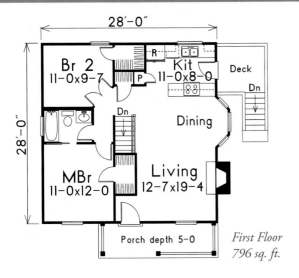

First Floor 796 sq. ft.

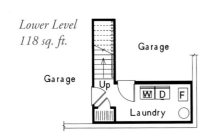

Lower Level 118 sq. ft.

Total Living Area: 914 sq. ft.

Plan Features

- Large porch for leisure evenings
- Dining area with bay window, open stair and pass-through kitchen create openness
- Basement includes generous garage space, storage area, finished laundry and mechanical room
- 2 bedrooms, 1 bath, 2-car drive under garage
- Basement foundation

Plan #583-013D-0024

Total Living Area: 2,088 sq. ft.

Plan Features

- Exceptional master bedroom includes a grand bath, spacious walk-in closet, direct access to the deck and a unique secluded morning porch
- Vaulted and raised ceilings adorn the foyer, kitchen, master bedroom, living, family and dining rooms
- 3 bedrooms, 2 1/2 baths, 2-car garage
- Walk-out basement, crawl space or slab foundation, please specify when ordering

D

Total Living Area: 1,815 sq. ft.

First Floor
1,815 sq. ft.

Width 75'-0"
Depth 43'-0"

Optional
Second Floor

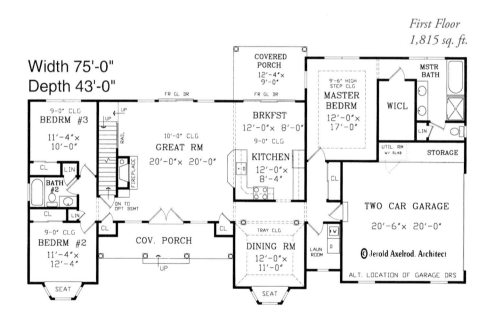

Plan Features

- The great room features a 10' ceiling, built-in fireplace and a bright airy feeling from several windows
- The kitchen and breakfast area are visually connected and the formal dining room is nearby for convenience
- Optional bonus room has an additional 323 square feet of living area
- 3 bedrooms, 2 baths, 2-car side entry garage
- Basement, crawl space or slab foundation, please specify when ordering

Plan #583-039D-0004

Total Living Area: 1,406 sq. ft.

Plan Features

- Master bedroom has a sloped ceiling
- Kitchen and dining area merge becoming a gathering place
- Enter the family room from the charming covered front porch to find a fireplace and lots of windows
- 3 bedrooms, 2 baths, 2-car detached garage
- Slab or crawl space foundation, please specify when ordering

---

Plan #583-026D-0136

Total Living Area: 1,712 sq. ft.

Plan Features

- Cathedral ceiling in family room adds drama and spaciousness
- Roomy utility area
- Master bedroom has a private bath, walk-in closet and whirlpool tub
- Efficient kitchen has a snack bar
- 3 bedrooms, 2 1/2 baths, 2-car garage
- Basement foundation

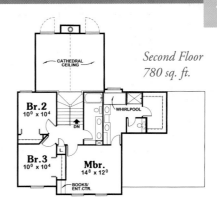

*Second Floor
780 sq. ft.*

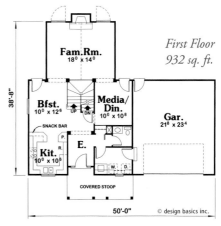

*First Floor
932 sq. ft.*

Total Living Area: 1,798 sq. ft.

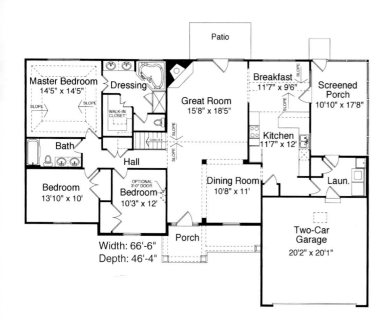

Patio

Master Bedroom
14'5" x 14'5"

Dressing

Great Room
15'8" x 18'5"

Breakfast
11'7" x 9'6"

Screened Porch
10'10" x 17'8"

WALK-IN CLOSET

Kitchen
11'7" x 12'

Bath

Hall

DOWN 13 R.

OPTIONAL 3'-0" DOOR

Bedroom
13'10" x 10'

Bedroom
10'3" x 12'

Dining Room
10'8" x 11'

Laun.

Porch

Two-Car Garage
20'2" x 20'1"

Width: 66'-6"
Depth: 46'-4"

DID YOU KNOW?

Cold weather shouldn't be an issue anymore with exterior painting, Most conventional paints need to be applied during temperatures 55 degrees or warmer. But cold weather paints are designed to resist moisture, frost and blisters in temperatures as low as 35 degrees. They are safe for most surfaces and can easily be applied with a roller or brush.

Plan Features

- The centrally located kitchen is easily accessible to the dining room and breakfast area
- The master bedroom boasts a sloped ceiling and deluxe bath with a corner whirlpool tub and large walk-in closet
- A screened porch offers relaxing outdoor living
- 3 bedrooms, 2 baths, 2-car garage
- Basement foundation

Plan #583-062D-0031

AA

Second Floor 401 sq. ft.

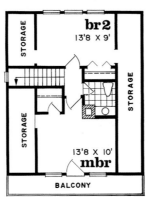

First Floor 672 sq. ft.

Total Living Area: 1,073 sq. ft.

Plan Features

- The front-facing deck and covered balcony add to the outdoor living areas
- The fireplace is the main focus in the living room, while effectively separating the living room from the dining room
- Three large storage areas are found on the second floor
- 3 bedrooms, 1 1/2 baths
- Basement or crawl space foundation, please specify when ordering

---

Plan #583-013D-0037

Price Code:

D

Total Living Area: 2,564 sq. ft.

Plan Features

- Hearth room is surrounded by the kitchen, dining and breakfast rooms making it a focal point of the home
- The master bedroom has a luxurious private bath and a sitting area leading to the deck outdoors
- The secondary bedrooms share a Jack and Jill bath and both have a walk-in closet
- 3 bedrooms, 2 1/2 baths, 2-car side entry garage
- Basement, crawl space or slab foundation, please specify when ordering

Total Living Area: 1,674 sq. ft.

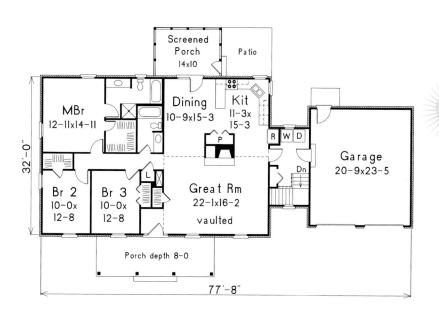

DID YOU KNOW?

Bamboo is an environment-friendly choice of wood that grows fast and energetically. It makes terrific flooring as well as furniture. The planks have a high-gloss finish and are easy to keep clean.

Plan Features

- Convenient laundry/mud room is located between the garage and family area with handy stairs to the basement
- Easily expandable screened porch and adjacent patio access the dining area
- Master bedroom features a full bath with tub, separate shower and walk-in closet
- 3 bedrooms, 2 baths, 2-car garage
- Basement foundation, drawings also include crawl space and slab foundations

Plan #583-055D-0012

Total Living Area: 1,381 sq. ft.

Plan Features

- Plenty of closet space in all bedrooms
- Kitchen has a large eating bar for extra dining
- Great room has a sunny wall of windows creating a cheerful atmosphere
- 3 bedrooms, 2 baths, 2-car garage
- Slab, crawl space, walk-out basement or basement foundation, please specify when ordering

---

Plan #583-065D-0069

Total Living Area: 1,697 sq. ft.

Plan Features

- The large breakfast area and open kitchen with island create a delightful family work and gathering area
- A first floor master bedroom with raised ceiling, super bath and walk-in closet create a luxurious retreat
- The second floor balcony offers a breathtaking view to the open foyer and leads to two additional bedrooms, a bath and storage space
- 3 bedrooms, 2 1/2 baths, 2-car garage
- Basement foundation

Second Floor 434 sq. ft.

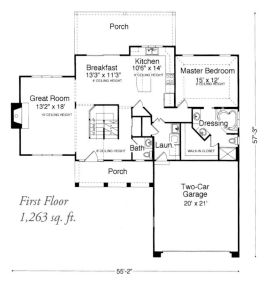

First Floor 1,263 sq. ft.

Total Living Area: 2,464 sq. ft.

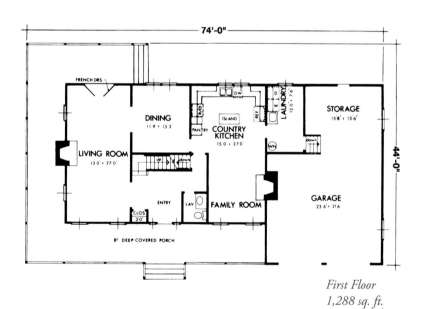

Second Floor
1,176 sq. ft.

First Floor
1,288 sq. ft.

Plan Features

- The dining room is perfect for hosting elegant meals
- Master bedroom is oversized and offers a large shower and a separate dressing area
- The family room features a second fireplace and overlooks the kitchen beyond
- 4 bedrooms, 3 baths, 2-car garage
- Basement foundation

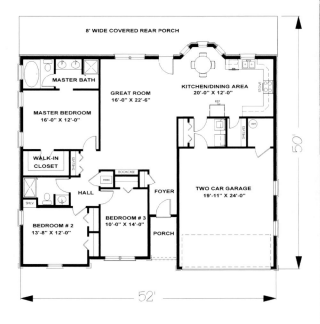

Total Living Area: 1,609 sq. ft.

Plan Features

- The foyer leads into the impressive great room which features access onto the rear porch ideal for relaxing
- Bay windows add charm to the kitchen/dining area
- Master bedroom enjoys a walk-in closet and deluxe bath
- The laundry area is conveniently located between the kitchen and garage
- 3 bedrooms, 2 baths, 2-car garage
- Slab foundation

Total Living Area: 1,444 sq. ft.

Plan Features

- 11' ceilings in the living and dining rooms combine with a central fireplace to create a large open living area
- Both secondary bedrooms have large walk-in closets
- Large storage area in the garage is suitable for a workshop or play area
- Front and rear covered porches add a cozy touch
- 3 bedrooms, 2 baths, 2-car side entry garage
- Slab foundation, drawings also include crawl space foundation

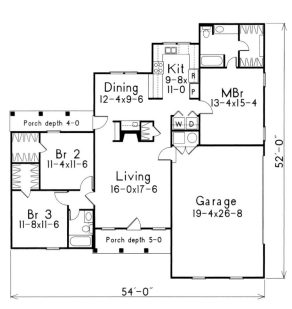

Total Living Area: 2,889 sq. ft.

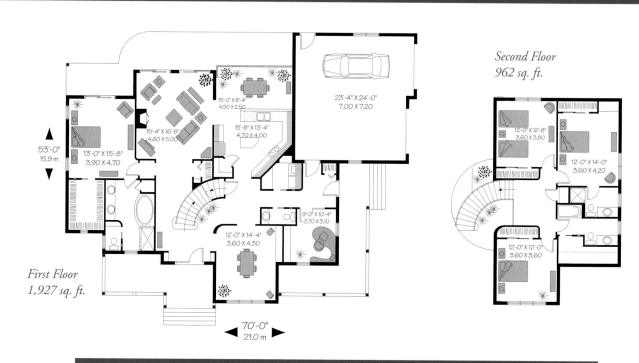

Second Floor
962 sq. ft.

First Floor
1,927 sq. ft.

Plan Features

- Energy efficient home with 2"x 6" exterior walls
- Cathedral ceiling in family room is impressive
- 9' ceilings throughout first floor
- Private home office is located away from traffic flow
- 4 bedrooms, 3 1/2 baths, 2-car side entry garage
- Basement foundation

Plan #583-056D-0023

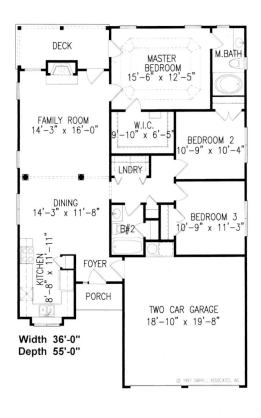

Width 36'-0"
Depth 55'-0"

© 1997 CARRELL ASSOCIATES, INC

Total Living Area: 1,277 sq. ft.

Plan Features

- Both the family room and master bedroom have direct access to an outdoor deck
- The kitchen is compact, yet efficient
- Columns add distinction between the dining and family rooms
- 3 bedrooms, 2 baths, 2-car garage
- Slab foundation

Plan #583-028D-0003

Total Living Area: 1,716 sq. ft.

Plan Features

- Great room boasts a fireplace and access to the kitchen/breakfast area through a large arched opening
- Master bedroom includes a huge walk-in closet and French doors that lead onto an L-shaped porch
- Bedrooms #2 and #3 share a bath and linen closet
- 3 bedrooms, 2 baths, 2-car detached garage
- Crawl space or slab foundation, please specify when ordering

Total Living Area: 1,915 sq. ft.

DID YOU KNOW?

With so many perennials to choose from, it is easy to find one that suits your site, soil and style. Before buying always check the plant for signs of disease and poor growth, and only select healthy specimens. Things to look for: strong, healthy top growth; disease-free vigorous leaves; moist soil mix free of weeds and moss; established thriving roots.

Plan Features

- Large breakfast area overlooks the vaulted great room
- Master suite has a cheerful sitting room and private bath
- Plan features a unique in-law suite with private bath and walk-in closet
- 4 bedrooms, 3 baths, 2-car garage
- Walk-out basement, slab or crawl space foundation, please specify when ordering

Plan #583-007D-0027

Second Floor
528 sq. ft.

Br 1
10-0x
13-8
vaulted

Dn

R

Kit

plant shelf

Living
15-8x10-8
vaulted

Balcony

First Floor
126 sq. ft.

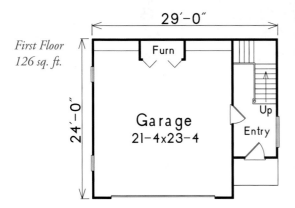

29'-0"

Furn

24'-0"

Garage
21-4x23-4

Up

Entry

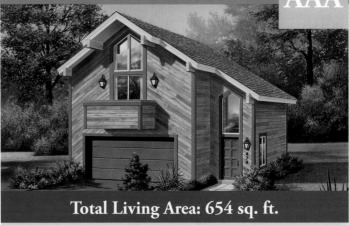

Total Living Area: 654 sq. ft.

Plan Features

- Two-story vaulted entry has a balcony overlook and large windows to welcome the sun
- Vaulted living room is open to a pass-through kitchen and breakfast bar with an overhead plant shelf and features sliding glass doors to an outdoor balcony
- The bedroom with vaulted ceiling offers a private bath and walk-in closet
- 1 bedroom, 1 bath, 2-car garage
- Slab foundation

Plan #583-070D-0004

Total Living Area: 1,791 sq. ft.

Plan Features

- A whirlpool tub adds luxury to the master bath
- Breakfast nook leads to a covered porch
- Double closets create plenty of storage in the foyer
- 3 bedrooms, 2 baths, 2-car side entry garage
- Basement foundation

PATIO

MASTER
cathedral ceiling
15⁴ x 14

BDRM. 2
12⁴ x 11⁴

PORCH

NOOK
9⁴ x 11⁴

W.I.C.

BATH

whirlpool

GREAT
cathedral ceiling
15 x 21

KIT.

GARAGE
22 x 21

BATH

entertainment
center

FOYER

BDRM. 3
12⁴ x 11⁴

PORCH

DINING
12⁴ x 13

Width: 63'-8"
Depth: 51'-0"

Total Living Area: 1,563 sq. ft.

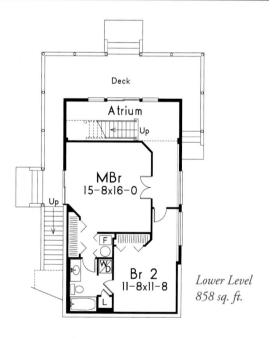

Deck

Atrium

Up

MBr
15-8x16-0

Up

Br 2
11-8x11-8

F

W
D

L

*Lower Level
858 sq. ft.*

22'-0"

Atrium below

Dn

*First Floor
705 sq. ft.*

39'-0"

Great Rm
21-4x16-5

vaulted

Din

Study

Dn

plant
shelves

Kit
7-8x9-0

L

R

Covered Porch
depth 5-0

Rear View

Plan Features

- Enjoyable wrap-around porch and lower sundeck
- Vaulted entry is adorned with a palladian window, plant shelves, stone floor and fireplace
- Vaulted great room has a magnificent view through a two-story atrium window wall
- 2 bedrooms, 1 1/2 baths
- Basement foundation

Second Floor
837 sq. ft.

Total Living Area: 1,805 sq. ft.

First Floor
968 sq. ft.

46'

40'

Plan Features

- Cooktop island, a handy desk and dining area make the kitchen highly functional
- Open floor plan with tall ceilings creates an airy atmosphere
- Family and living rooms are both enhanced with fireplaces
- 3 bedrooms, 2 1/2 baths, 2-car garage
- Crawl space foundation

Total Living Area: 1,408 sq. ft.

Plan Features

- A bright country kitchen boasts an abundance of counterspace and cupboards
- The front entry is sheltered by a broad veranda
- A spa tub is brightened by a box-bay window in the master bath
- 3 bedrooms, 2 baths, 2-car side entry garage
- Basement or crawl space foundation, please specify when ordering

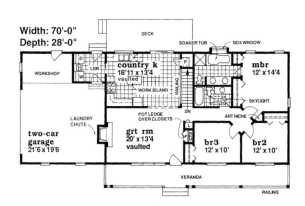

Width: 70'-0"
Depth: 28'-0"

Total Living Area: 632 sq. ft.

First Floor
120 sq. ft.

28'-0"

26'-0"

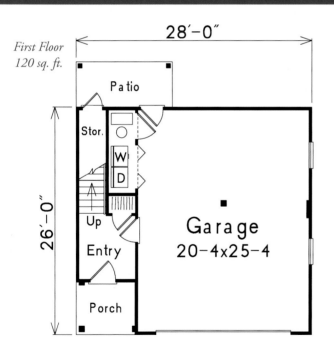

Patio

Stor.

W D

Up

Entry

Porch

Garage
20-4x25-4

Second Floor
512 sq. ft.

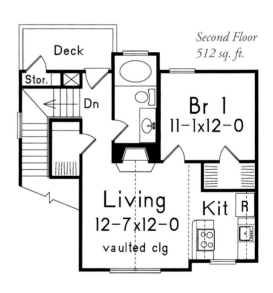

Deck

Stor.

Dn

Br 1
11-1x12-0

Living
12-7x12-0
vaulted clg

Kit

R

Plan Features

- Porch leads to a vaulted entry and stair with feature window, coat closet and access to garage/laundry
- Cozy living room offers a vaulted ceiling, fireplace, large palladian window and pass-through to kitchen
- A garden tub with arched window is part of a very roomy bath
- 1 bedroom, 1 bath, 2-car garage
- Slab foundation

Plan #583-077D-0007

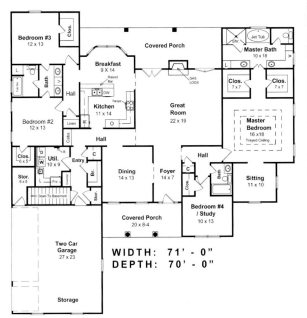

Total Living Area: 2,805 sq. ft.

WIDTH: 71'-0"
DEPTH: 70'-0"

Plan Features

- Wrap-around counter in kitchen opens to breakfast area
- Great room features a grand fireplace flanked by doors that access the rear covered porch
- Secondary bedrooms enjoy walk-in closets
- The large utility room offers an abundance of workspace
- 4 bedrooms, 3 baths, 2-car side entry garage
- Basement, crawl space or slab foundation, please specify when ordering

Plan #583-040D-0015

Total Living Area: 1,655 sq. ft.

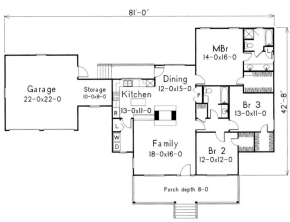

Plan Features

- Master bedroom features a 9' ceiling, walk-in closet and bath with dressing area
- Oversized family room includes a 10' ceiling and masonry see-through fireplace
- Handy covered walkway from the garage leads to the kitchen and dining area
- 3 bedrooms, 2 baths, 2-car garage
- Crawl space foundation

Total Living Area: 2,533 sq. ft.

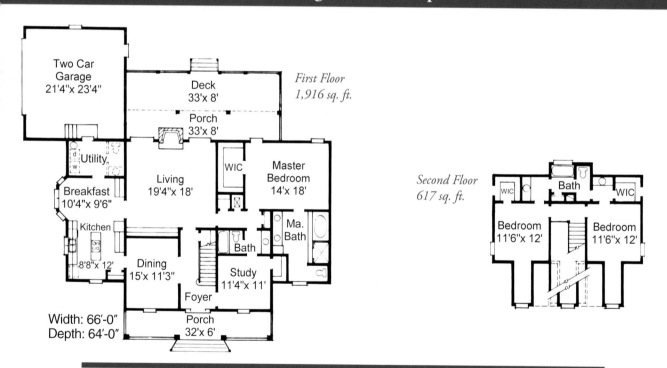

Two Car Garage
21'4"x 23'4"

Deck
33'x 8'

*First Floor
1,916 sq. ft.*

Porch
33'x 8'

Utility

WIC

Master Bedroom
14'x 18'

Living
19'4"x 18'

Breakfast
10'4"x 9'6"

Kitchen

Ma. Bath

8'8"x 12'

Bath

Dining
15'x 11'3"

Study
11'4"x 11'

Foyer

Width: 66'-0"
Depth: 64'-0"

Porch
32'x 6'

*Second Floor
617 sq. ft.*

WIC

Bath

WIC

Bedroom
11'6"x 12'

Bedroom
11'6"x 12'

Plan Features

- The living room includes a fireplace flanked by large windows overlooking the backyard
- The secluded master bedroom accesses the rear porch and features a large walk-in closet and private bath
- The kitchen includes a cooktop island and opens to a sunny bayed breakfast area
- 3 bedrooms, 3 1/2 baths, 2-car side entry garage
- Slab or crawl space foundation, please specify when ordering

Plan #583-020D-0035

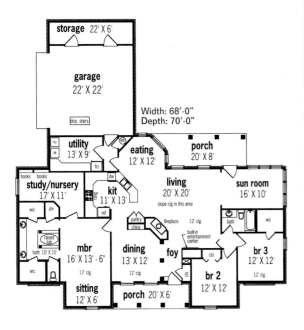

Total Living Area: 2,280 sq. ft.

Plan Features

- The master bedroom boasts a sitting area, private bath and an adjacent room ideal for a study or nursery
- The kitchen, living, dining and eating rooms are open and bright with an adjacent sun room
- The master bedroom, dining room, foyer and bedroom #2 boast 12' ceilings
- 3 bedrooms, 2 baths, 2-car side entry garage
- Slab foundation, drawings also include crawl space foundation

Width: 68'-0"
Depth: 70'-0"

Plan #583-077D-0004

Total Living Area: 2,024 sq. ft.

Plan Features

- Covered porches offer a relaxing atmosphere
- Bedrooms are separated for privacy
- Dining room provides an elegant space for entertaining
- The second floor living area and optional bath are ideal for a guest suite
- 3 bedrooms, 2 baths, 2-car side entry garage
- Basement, crawl space or slab foundation, please specify when ordering

Second Floor
386 sq. ft.

WIDTH: 73'-0"
DEPTH: 41'-0"

First Floor
1,638 sq. ft.

Total Living Area: 2,606 sq. ft.

First Floor
2,606 sq. ft.

Optional
Second Floor

Plan Features

- A corner fireplace in the great room warms the area and the adjoining dining room
- French doors lead into the study/bedroom #4 which features a bay window and has access to a private patio
- The optional second floor has an additional 751 square feet of living space
- 4 bedrooms, 2 1/2 baths, 2-car side entry garage
- Slab, basement, crawl space or walk-out basement foundation, please specify when ordering

Plan #583-021D-0005

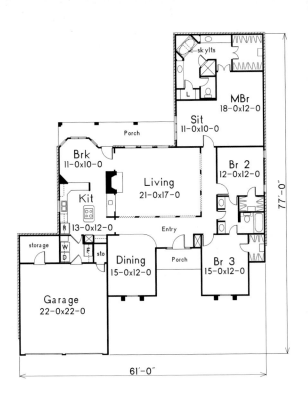

Total Living Area: 2,177 sq. ft.

Plan Features

- Master bedroom features a sitting area and double-door entry to an elegant master bath
- Secondary bedrooms are spacious with walk-in closets and a shared bath
- Kitchen features an island cooktop, eating bar and wet bar that is accessible to the living room
- 3 bedrooms, 2 baths, 2-car garage
- Slab foundation, drawings also include basement and crawl space foundations

Plan #583-026D-0112

Price Code:

C

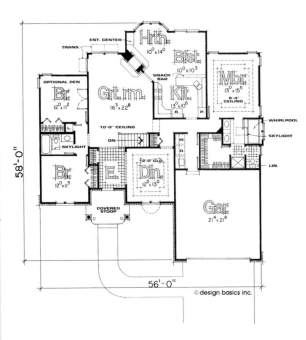

Total Living Area: 1,911 sq. ft.

Plan Features

- Large entry opens into a beautiful great room with an angled see-through fireplace
- Terrific design includes kitchen and breakfast area with adjacent sunny bayed hearth room
- Private master bedroom with bath features skylight and walk-in closet
- 3 bedrooms, 2 baths, 2-car garage
- Basement foundation

Total Living Area: 1,978 sq. ft.

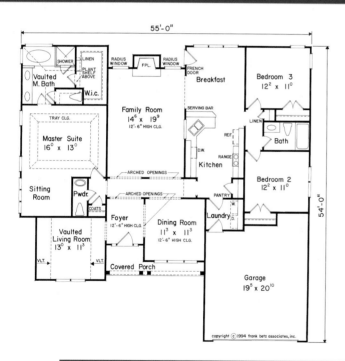

DID YOU KNOW?

Dormers have been featured in American architecture since the late 1600's. Although they come in a variety of shapes and sizes, all dormers are windows with their own roof, which is set vertically into the roof of the house. Being able to recognize different types of dormers will give you a clue to a home's architectural style. For example, gable dormers, as seen here, generally point to these styles: Colonial Revival, Georgian, Tudor and Craftsman to name a few.

Plan Features

- Elegant arched openings throughout interior
- Vaulted living room off foyer is quiet and intimate
- Master suite features a cheerful sitting room and a private bath
- 3 bedrooms, 2 1/2 baths, 2-car garage
- Walk-out basement, slab or crawl space foundation, please specify when ordering

Plan #583-062D-0063

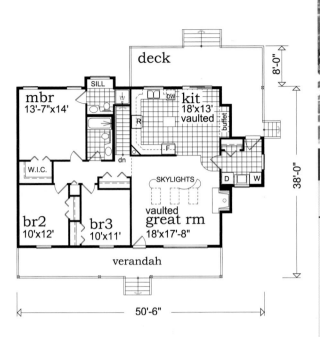

Total Living Area: 1,455 sq. ft.

Plan Features

- Energy efficient home with 2"x 6" exterior walls
- A vaulted ceiling, fireplace and skylights decorate the great room
- The spacious kitchen features a wrap-around counter, buffet alcove and vaulted ceiling
- 3 bedrooms, 2 baths
- Basement or crawl space foundation, please specify when ordering

Plan #583-055D-0043

Total Living Area: 1,654 sq. ft.

Plan Features

- U-shaped kitchen features lots of cabinetry, counter seating and access to the dining room/hearth room
- Great room has a sloped ceiling, media center and fireplace
- Master bath is accented with glass blocks above the whirlpool tub
- 3 bedrooms, 2 baths, 2-car garage
- Walk-out basement, basement, crawl space or slab foundation, please specify when ordering

Total Living Area: 1,780 sq. ft.

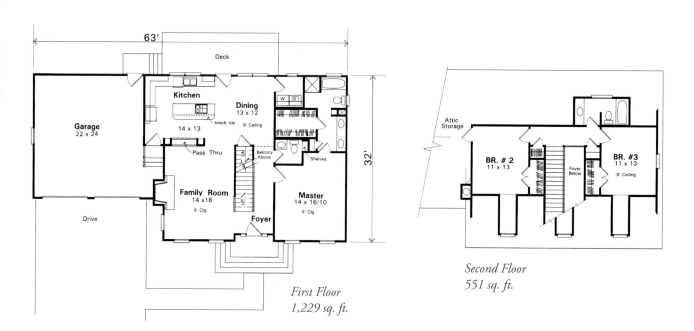

63'

Deck

Kitchen

Dining
13 x 12

14 x 13

snack bar

9' Ceiling

Garage
22 x 24

Pass Thru

Balcony
Above

Shelves

32'

Family Room
14 x18

9' Clg.

Master
14 x 16/10

9' Clg.

Drive

Foyer

First Floor
1,229 sq. ft.

Attic
Storage

BR. # 2
11 x 13

Foyer
Below

BR. #3
11 x 13

8' Ceiling

Second Floor
551 sq. ft.

Plan Features

- Traditional styling with all the comforts of home
- First floor master bedroom has a walk-in closet and bath
- Large kitchen and dining area open to the deck
- 3 bedrooms, 2 1/2 baths, 2-car garage
- Basement, crawl space or slab foundation, please specify when ordering

Plan #583-001D-0067

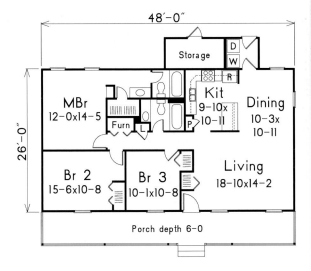

48'-0"

26'-0"

Storage

D W R

MBr
12-0x14-5

Furn L

Kit
9-10x
10-11

Dining
10-3x
10-11

Br 2
15-6x10-8

Br 3
10-1x10-8

Living
18-10x14-2

Porch depth 6-0

Total Living Area: 1,285 sq. ft.

Plan Features

- Accommodating home with ranch-style porch
- Master bedroom includes dressing area, private bath and built-in bookcase
- Kitchen features pantry, breakfast bar and complete view to the dining room
- 3 bedrooms, 2 baths
- Crawl space foundation, drawings also include basement and slab foundations

Plan #583-078D-0013

Total Living Area: 1,175 sq. ft.

Plan Features

- The two-story living room is brightened by rows of double-hung windows creating a dramatic impression
- The compact kitchen is laid out for maximum efficiency
- Both bedrooms enjoy privacy and walk-in closets
- Second floor loft area provides a view of the first floor
- 2 bedrooms, 2 baths
- Basement or crawl space foundation, please specify when ordering

OPEN

BEDROOM
11 x 12

LOFT
7 x 9

OPEN

OPEN

d d w

OPEN

plant shelf

Second Floor
375 sq. ft.

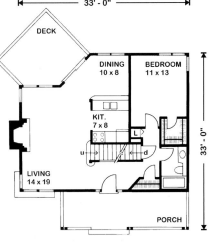

33' - 0"

DECK

DINING
10 x 8

BEDROOM
11 x 13

KIT.
7 x 8

LIVING
14 x 19

PORCH

33' - 0"

First Floor
800 sq. ft.

Total Living Area: 1,246 sq. ft.

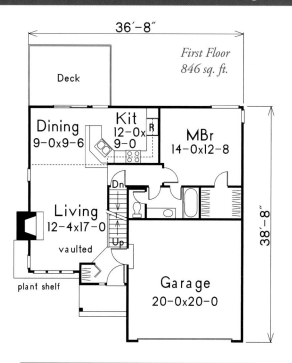

36'-8"

Deck

First Floor 846 sq. ft.

Dining
9-0x9-6

Kit
12-0x
9-0

R

MBr
14-0x12-8

Dn

Living
12-4x17-0

Up

vaulted

plant shelf

Garage
20-0x20-0

38'-8"

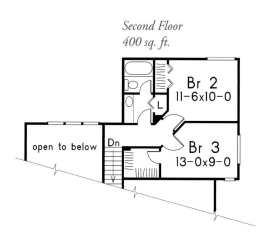

Second Floor 400 sq. ft.

Br 2
11-6x10-0

L

open to below

Dn

Br 3
13-0x9-0

Plan Features

- Corner living room window adds openness and light
- Private first floor master bedroom has a corner window
- Large walk-in closet is located in bedroom #3
- Easily built perimeter allows economical construction
- 3 bedrooms, 2 baths, 2-car garage
- Basement foundation

Plan #583-078D-0002

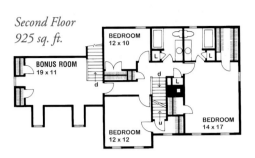

Second Floor
925 sq. ft.

BONUS ROOM
19 x 11

BEDROOM
12 x 10

BEDROOM
12 x 12

BEDROOM
14 x 17

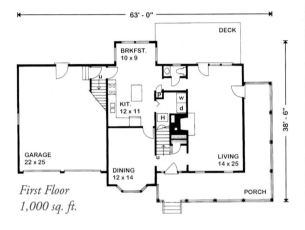

63' - 0"

DECK

BRKFST.
10 x 9

KIT.
12 x 11

GARAGE
22 x 25

DINING
12 x 14

LIVING
14 x 25

PORCH

38' - 6"

First Floor
1,000 sq. ft.

Total Living Area: 1,925 sq. ft.

Plan Features

- The foyer is flanked by formal dining and living rooms
- The centrally located kitchen serves the dining room and breakfast nook with ease
- Master bedroom enjoys a walk-in closet and full bath
- The bonus room above the garage has an additional 209 square feet of living area
- 3 bedrooms, 2 1/2 baths, 2-car garage
- Crawl space foundation

Plan #583-011D-0016

Total Living Area: 1,902 sq. ft.

Plan Features

- A two-story great room is stunning with a fireplace and many windows
- Breakfast nook and kitchen combine creating a warm and inviting place to dine
- Bonus room on the second floor is included in the square footage
- 3 bedrooms, 2 1/2 baths, 2-car garage
- Crawl space foundation

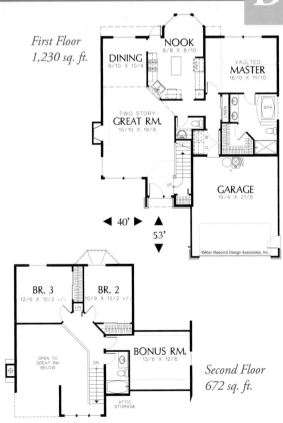

First Floor
1,230 sq. ft.

NOOK
8/8 X 8/10

DINING
9/10 X 10/4

VAULTED
MASTER
16/0 X 11/10

TWO STORY
GREAT RM.
15/10 X 19/8

SPA

GARAGE
19/4 X 21/8

40'

53'

©Alan Mascord Design Associates, Inc.

BR. 3
12/6 X 12/2 +/-

BR. 2
10/9 X 12/2 +/-

OPEN TO
GREAT RM.
BELOW

BONUS RM.
13/6 X 12/6

DN.

ATTIC
STORAGE

Second Floor
672 sq. ft.

F

Total Living Area: 2,600 sq. ft.

Interior View

Plan Features

- The entry opens into the spacious great room which features a wall of windows bringing in an abundance of light
- The master bedroom boasts a double-door entry, sitting area, two walk-in closets and a private bath
- Convenient laundry area includes a closet, sink and stairway to the basement
- 3 bedrooms, 2 1/2 baths, 3-car side entry garage
- Basement foundation

Total Living Area: 2,614 sq. ft.

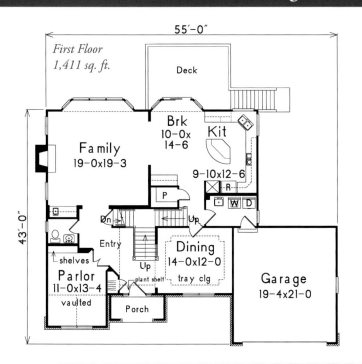

First Floor
1,411 sq. ft.

55'-0"

43'-0"

Deck

Family
19-0x19-3

Brk
10-0x
14-6

Kit

9-10x12-6

P

R

W D

Dn

Up

Up

Entry

shelves

Dining
14-0x12-0
tray clg

plant shelf

Parlor
11-0x13-4
vaulted

Porch

Garage
19-4x21-0

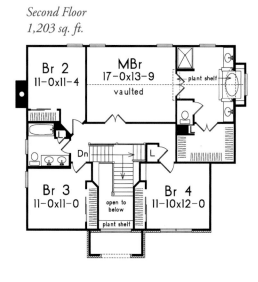

Second Floor
1,203 sq. ft.

Br 2
11-0x11-4

MBr
17-0x13-9
vaulted

plant shelf

Dn

L

L

Br 3
11-0x11-0

open to
below

plant shelf

Br 4
11-10x12-0

Plan Features

- Grand two-story entry features a majestic palladian window, double French doors to the parlor and access to the powder room
- Kitchen has corner sink, island snack bar, menu desk and walk-in pantry
- Master bath is vaulted and offers a luxurious step-up tub, palladian window, built-in shelves and columns with plant shelf
- 4 bedrooms, 2 1/2 baths, 2-car garage
- Basement foundation

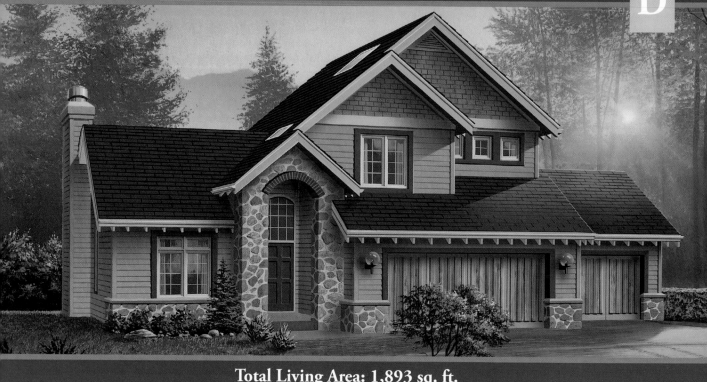

Total Living Area: 1,893 sq. ft.

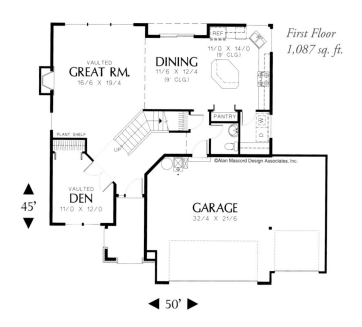

*First Floor
1,087 sq. ft.*

◄ 50' ►

45'

*Second Floor
806 sq. ft.*

Plan Features

- Two-story home delivers comfort and beauty
- Handsome open staircase adds interest
- Master suite includes walk-in closet and a private bath with twin sinks, oversized tub and a shower
- 3 bedrooms, 2 1/2 baths, 3-car garage
- Crawl space foundation

Price Code:

C

Total Living Area: 2,010 sq. ft.

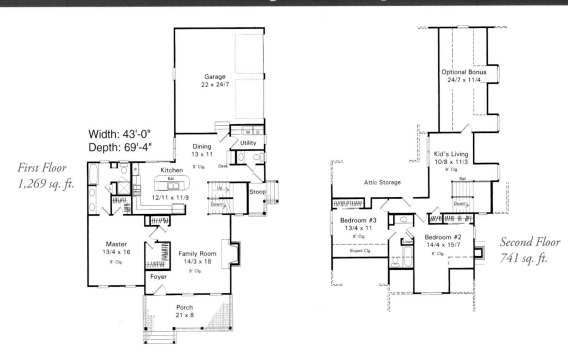

Width: 43'-0"
Depth: 69'-4"

First Floor
1,269 sq. ft.

Second Floor
741 sq. ft.

Plan Features

- Oversized kitchen is a great gathering place with eat-in island bar, dining area nearby and built-in desk
- Unique second floor kid's living area for playroom
- Optional bonus room has an additional 313 square feet of living area
- 3 bedrooms, 2 1/2 baths, 2-car side entry garage
- Basement foundation

Total Living Area: 1,625 sq. ft.

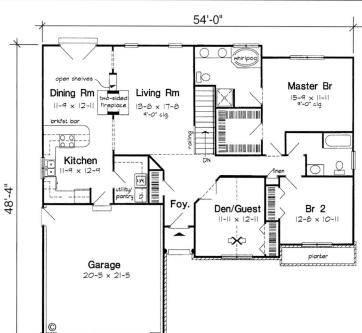

DID YOU KNOW?

Mildew is a nuisance in many parts of the country, and even vinyl siding provides a suitable surface for it to grow. To remove, mix a cup of household bleach into a gallon of water and apply the mix with a pump sprayer. Let the solution sit for about five minutes, taking caution to not let it dry out. Then pull out a hose and rinse the siding thoroughly from top to bottom using fresh water. Bleach can harm plants, so protect them by spraying their leaves with clear water before and after you treat the siding.

Plan Features

- An interesting double-door entry leads to the den/guest room
- Spacious master bath has both a whirlpool tub and a shower
- Welcoming planter boxes in front add curb appeal
- 3 bedrooms, 2 baths, 2-car garage
- Basement or crawl space foundation, please specify when ordering

Total Living Area: 1,667 sq. ft.

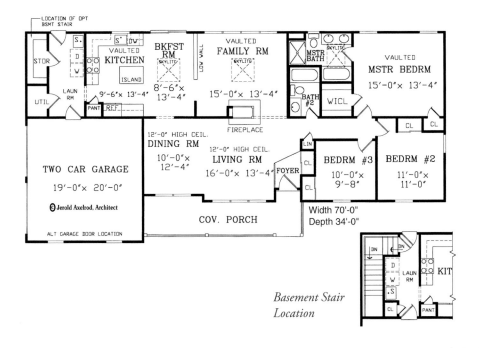

Basement Stair Location

Plan Features

- The centrally located fireplace lends warmth to the surrounding rooms
- The foyer opens into the dining and living rooms with 12' ceilings and a wall of windows for an open and spacious feel
- The large laundry room offers an abundance of storage space
- 3 bedrooms, 2 baths, 2-car side entry garage
- Basement, crawl space or slab foundation, please specify when ordering

Total Living Area: 647 sq. ft.

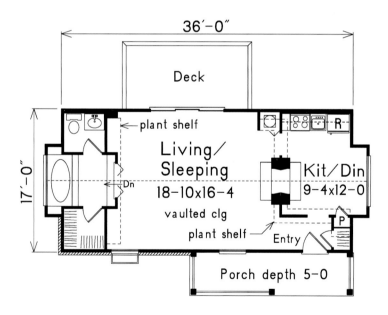

36'-0"

Deck

plant shelf

17'-0"

Living/ Sleeping
18-10x16-4

vaulted clg

plant shelf

Dn

Kit/Din
9-4x12-0

R

P

Entry

Porch depth 5-0

DID YOU KNOW?

Outdoor faucets mounted on the side of a house can freeze in cold weather, causing pipes to burst. Be sure to drain them before the first freeze. To do this, shut off the water supply leading to the faucet, then open the faucet to drain off any remaining water trapped between the faucet and the shut-off valve. An alternative to this seasonal chore is to have a freeze-proof spigot installed.

Plan Features

- Living/sleeping room has plant shelves on each end, stone fireplace and wide glass doors
- Roomy kitchen is vaulted and has a bayed dining area and fireplace
- Step down into a sunken and vaulted bath featuring a 6'-0" whirlpool tub-in-a-bay
- A large palladian window adorns each end of the cottage giving it a cheery atmosphere
- 1 living/sleeping room, 1 bath
- Crawl space foundation

Total Living Area: 1,195 sq. ft.

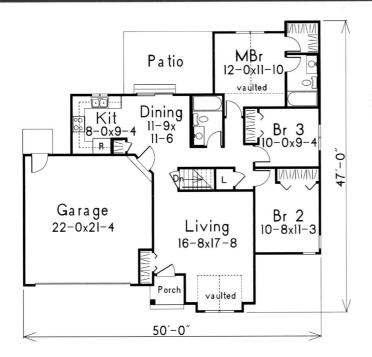

DID YOU KNOW?

Elegant arched windows can be challenging to dress. A rounded track or rod can be installed to follow the line of an arch. Curtains can then be hung from this fixed track though they will have to meet in the middle and gathered on each side. Alternatively, a rod may be fixed across the window below the semicircular part. Then either leave the arched portion bare, or fill it with a fixed, shaped shade or fan-shaped curtain.

Plan Features

- Dining room opens onto the patio
- Master bedroom features a vaulted ceiling, private bath and walk-in closet
- Coat closets are located by both the entrances
- Convenient secondary entrance is located at the back of the garage
- 3 bedrooms, 2 baths, 2-car garage
- Basement foundation

Total Living Area: 2,529 sq. ft.

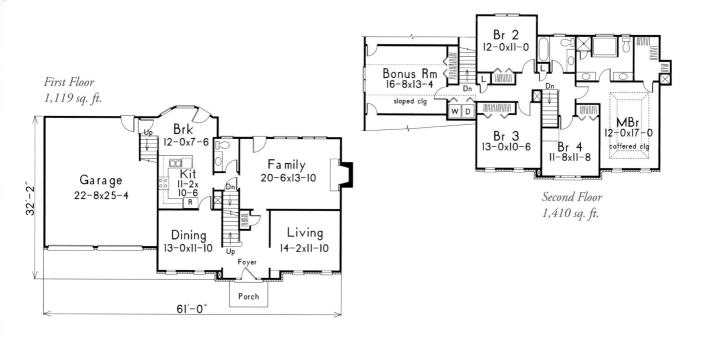

First Floor
1,119 sq. ft.

Second Floor
1,410 sq. ft.

Plan Features

- Distinguished appearance enhances this home's classic interior arrangement
- Bonus room over the garage, which is included in the square footage, has direct access from the attic and the second floor hall
- Garden tub, walk-in closet and coffered ceiling enhance the master bedroom suite
- 4 bedrooms, 2 1/2 baths, 2-car garage
- Basement foundation

Total Living Area: 2,388 sq. ft.

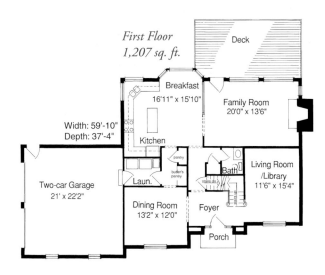

First Floor
1,207 sq. ft.

Deck

Breakfast
16'11" x 15'10"

Family Room
20'0" x 13'6"

Width: 59'-10"
Depth: 37'-4"

Kitchen

pantry
butler's pantry

Laun.

Living Room
/Library
11'6" x 15'4"

Bath

stairs dn.

Two-car Garage
21' x 22'2"

Dining Room
13'2" x 12'0"

Foyer

Porch

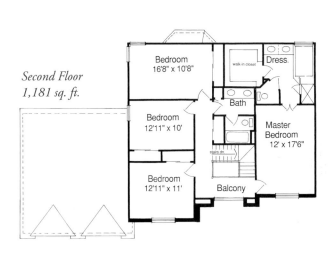

Second Floor
1,181 sq. ft.

Bedroom
16'8" x 10'8"

walk-in closet

Dress.

Bath

Bedroom
12'11" x 10'

Master
Bedroom
12' x 17'6"

stairs dn.

Bedroom
12'11" x 11'

Balcony

Plan Features

- Roomy kitchen, breakfast area and family room with fireplace provide an expansive space for family activities
- The master bedroom pampers with a whirlpool tub, extra large walk-in closet and double vanity
- The formal dining and living rooms offer elegance
- 4 bedrooms, 2 1/2 baths, 2-car side entry garage
- Walk-out basement foundation

Total Living Area: 1,452 sq. ft.

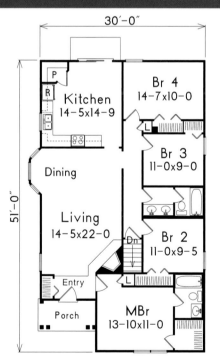

DID YOU KNOW?

Big lawns are the American dream but are extremely labor-intensive. You can reduce yard maintenance by removing a portion of the lawn and replacing it with functional, yet relatively low-maintenance surfaces, such as wood decking, a brick patio or gravel paths. Or put in a range of permanent landscape plants to slice hours off your weekly routine.

Plan Features

- Large living room features a cozy corner fireplace, bayed dining area and access from entry with guest closet
- Forward master bedroom enjoys having its own bath and linen closet
- Three additional bedrooms share a bath with a double-bowl vanity
- 4 bedrooms, 2 baths
- Basement foundation

Total Living Area: 3,565 sq. ft.

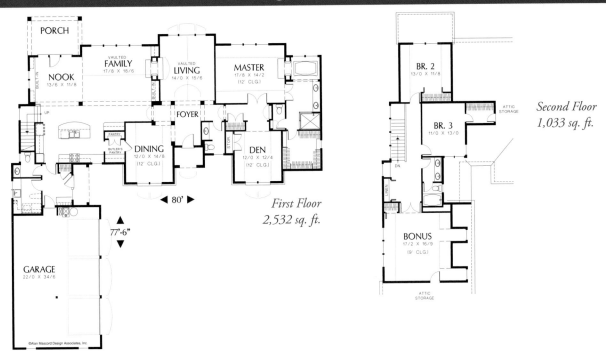

First Floor
2,532 sq. ft.

Second Floor
1,033 sq. ft.

Plan Features

- Spacious master suite has an enormous bath and walk-in closet
- Vaulted living room shares a cozy fireplace with the vaulted family room
- A convenient butler's pantry connects the formal dining room to the kitchen
- Bonus room above the garage is included in the square footage
- 3 bedrooms, 2 full baths, 2 half baths, 3-car side entry garage
- Crawl space foundation

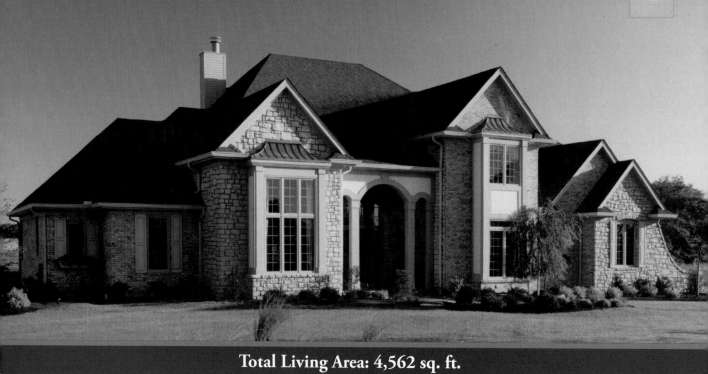

Total Living Area: 4,562 sq. ft.

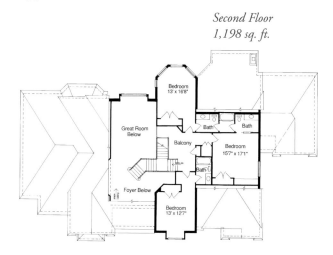

First Floor
3,364 sq. ft.

Second Floor
1,198 sq. ft.

Plan Features

- The cozy hearth room and master bedroom showcase tray ceilings and moldings
- A dressing area, deluxe bath and extra-large walk-in closet crown the master bedroom
- The kitchen with island opens to the breakfast and hearth rooms for an open atmosphere
- 4 bedrooms, 3 1/2 baths, 3-car side entry garage
- Basement foundation

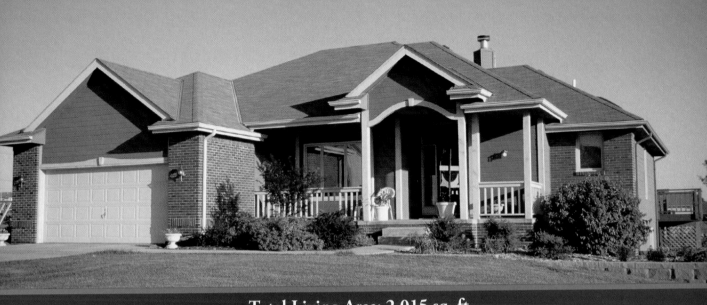

Total Living Area: 2,015 sq. ft.

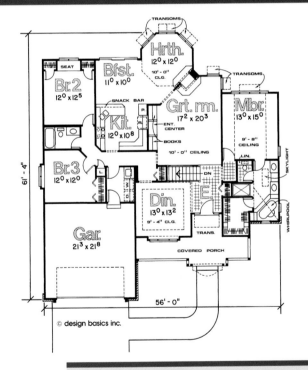

© design basics inc.

DID YOU KNOW?

One of the benefits of aluminum siding is that it generally requires less maintenance than wood siding. The material holds paint very well so you don't have to worry about repainting it often. On the other hand, one of the drawbacks of aluminum is that it dents easily if a rock hits it or you drop your ladder against it. Always use ladder cushions or standoffs.

Plan Features

- Sunny and cheerful hearth room is warmed by the sun as well as the see-through fireplace shared by the great room
- Window seat in bedroom #2 is a nice touch
- Corner whirlpool tub in master bath is a beautiful focal point
- 3 bedrooms, 2 baths, 2-car garage
- Basement foundation

Total Living Area: 2,508 sq. ft.

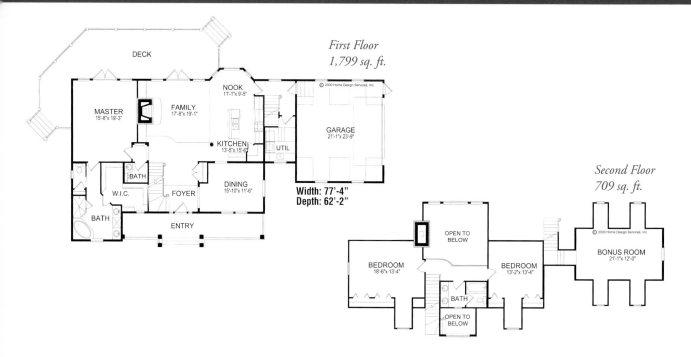

First Floor
1,799 sq. ft.

DECK

NOOK
11'-1"x 9'-5"

MASTER
15'-8"x 19'-3"

FAMILY
17'-8"x 19'-1"

GARAGE
21'-1"x 23'-9"

KITCHEN
13'-5"x 15'-6"

UTIL

BATH

W.I.C.

FOYER

DINING
15'-10"x 11'-6"

Width: 77'-4"
Depth: 62'-2"

BATH

ENTRY

© 2000 Home Design Services, Inc.

Second Floor
709 sq. ft.

OPEN TO BELOW

BONUS ROOM
21'-1"x 12'-0"

BEDROOM
18'-6"x 13'-4"

BEDROOM
13'-2"x 13'-4"

BATH

OPEN TO BELOW

© 2000 Home Design Services, Inc.

Plan Features

- Covered porch creates an inviting entrance to the home
- The bayed nook opens to the kitchen which features an island and walk-in pantry
- The family room enjoys a grand fireplace flanked by built-in shelves
- The bonus room above the garage has an additional 384 square feet of living area
- 3 bedrooms, 2 1/2 baths, 2-car side entry garage
- Basement or walk-out basement foundation, please specify when ordering

Total Living Area: 1,985 sq. ft.

First Floor
1,009 sq. ft.

DECK
30'-6" x 11'-7"

BRKFST

KITCHEN
15'-0" x 17'-0"

DINING
14'-8" x 12'-8"

FAMILY
18'-8" x 16'-0"

ENTRY
7'-11" x 15'-6"

UP

COATS

42'-0"

PORCH
30'-6" x 7'-7"

◀ 31'-2" ▶

Second Floor
976 sq. ft.

TRAY CEILING

MASTER BDRM
16'-4" x 15'-0"

D W

DN

BEDROOM 2
12'-0" x 12'-8"

BEDROOM 3
12'-8" x 12'-0"

WINDOW SEAT

Plan Features

- Cozy family room features a fireplace and double French doors opening onto the porch
- The open kitchen includes a convenient island
- Extraordinary master bedroom has a tray ceiling and a large walk-in closet
- Lovely bayed breakfast area has easy access to the deck
- 3 bedrooms, 2 1/2 baths
- Basement or crawl space foundation, please specify when ordering

Total Living Area: 3,882 sq. ft.

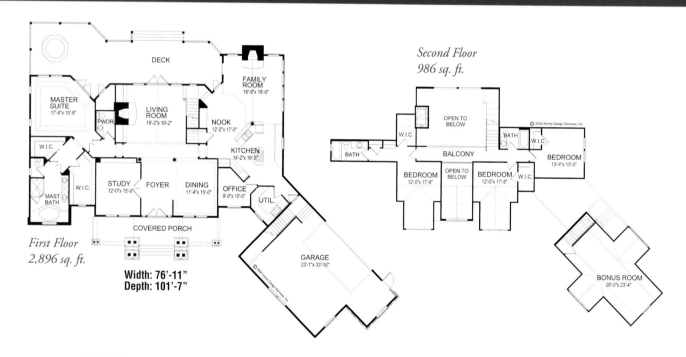

Second Floor
986 sq. ft.

First Floor
2,896 sq. ft.

Width: 76'-11"
Depth: 101'-7"

Plan Features

- The study and dining room flank the foyer which opens into the spacious living room
- A large deck, accessed from the living room and master suite offers a wonderful outdoor entertaining area
- A private stairway leads to the bonus room above the garage which has an additional 480 square feet of living area
- 4 bedrooms, 3 1/2 baths, 2-car rear entry garage
- Crawl space foundation

Total Living Area: 2,636 sq. ft.

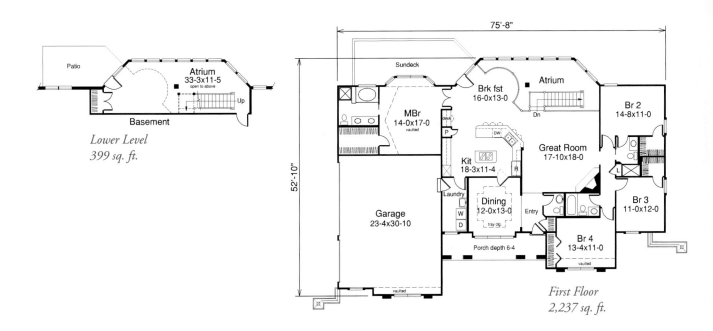

Lower Level
399 sq. ft.

First Floor
2,237 sq. ft.

Plan Features

- The large great room, breakfast room/balcony and spacious kitchen all enjoy dazzling views through the two-story window wall of the atrium bay
- The dining room features a tray ceiling and three patio doors to the front porch
- The secluded master bedroom enjoys a double-door entry, a bay window overlooking the sundeck, a huge walk-in closet and a lavish bath
- 4 bedrooms, 3 1/2 baths, 3-car side entry garage
- Walk-out basement foundation

Total Living Area: 1,551 sq. ft.

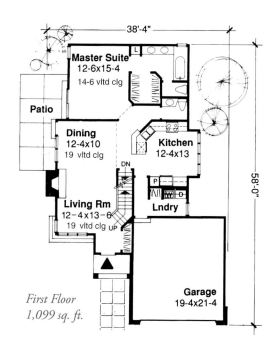

First Floor
1,099 sq. ft.

- 38'-4"
- 58'-0"
- **Master Suite** 12-6x15-4 / 14-6 vltd clg
- **Patio**
- **Dining** 12-4x10 / 19 vltd clg
- **Kitchen** 12-4x13
- **Living Rm** 12-4x13-6 / 19 vltd clg
- **Lndry**
- **Garage** 19-4x21-4
- DN / UP
- P / D

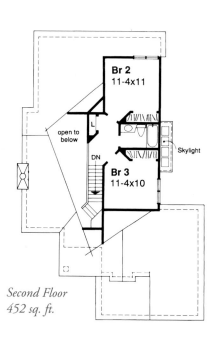

Second Floor
452 sq. ft.

- **Br 2** 11-4x11
- **Br 3** 11-4x10
- open to below
- DN
- Skylight

Plan Features

- Vaulted dining room has a view onto the patio
- Master suite is vaulted with a private bath and walk-in closet
- An arched entry leads to the vaulted living room featuring tall windows and a fireplace
- 3 bedrooms, 3 baths, 2-car garage
- Basement foundation

Plan #583-026D-0067

Price Code:

E

Total Living Area: 3,172 sq. ft.

First Floor
2,252 sq. ft.

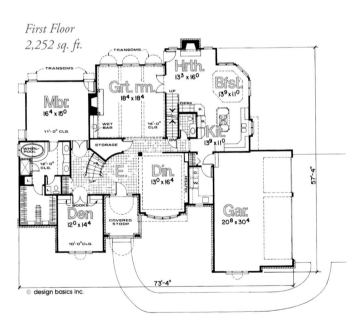

© design basics inc.

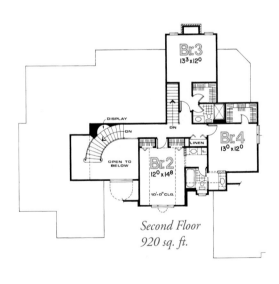

Second Floor
920 sq. ft.

Plan Features

- 9' ceilings on the first floor
- Hearth room shares the warmth of the fireplace with the adjoining bayed breakfast area and kitchen
- The great room is perfect for entertaining with a cozy fireplace, wet bar, 14' ceiling, transom windows and a double-door entry to the hearth room
- 4 bedrooms, 3 1/2 baths, 3-car garage
- Basement foundation

Total Living Area: 2,148 sq. ft.

DID YOU KNOW?

Applying caulk can be messy but, for best results start by practicing on a scrap of paper so you get used to how quick the caulk comes out of the tube. Smoothing the caulk is best done with a damp finger or rag.

Plan Features

- The great room has a double-boxed ceiling providing a subtle point of interest
- The master bath features a whirlpool tub in addition to the shower
- The kitchen has ample counterspace and a bar with seating
- 4 bedrooms, 2 baths, 2-car garage
- Slab or crawl space foundation, please specify when ordering

Total Living Area: 2,194 sq. ft.

Width: 52'-0"
Depth: 74'-0"

First Floor
1,531 sq. ft.

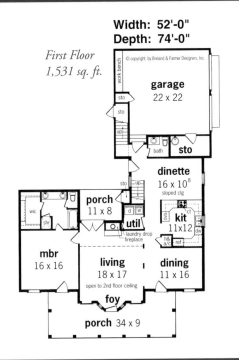

Second Floor
663 sq. ft.

Plan Features

- Energy efficient home with 2"x 6" exterior walls
- Utility room has a laundry drop conveniently located next to the kitchen
- Both second floor bedrooms have large closets and their own bath
- Bonus room on the second floor has an additional 352 square feet of living space
- 3 bedrooms, 3 1/2 baths, 2-car side entry garage
- Crawl space foundation, drawings also include slab and basement foundations

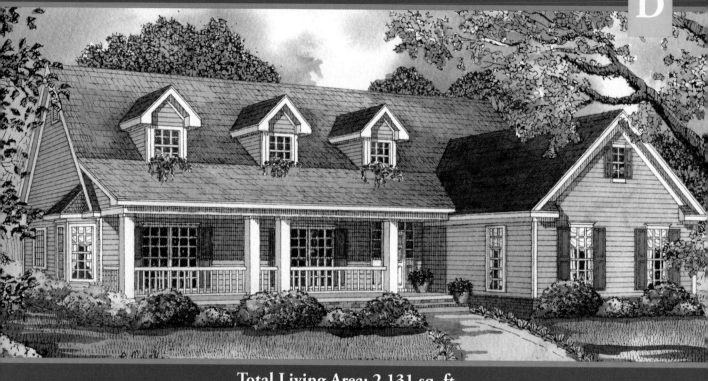

Total Living Area: 2,131 sq. ft.

DID YOU KNOW?

Before dipping a brush in paint, dip it into water (for water based paints) or paint thinner (for oil-based paints) and spin out the excess. This wets the bristles in the ferrule (the metal base) and prevents paint from building up in there, which makes cleanup easier and extends the life of the brush.

Plan Features

- The kitchen, great room and dining room create an expansive living area
- Bedroom #2 features a charming bay window with seat
- The garage includes space for a safe storm shelter
- 3 bedrooms, 2 1/2 baths, 2-car side entry garage
- Slab or crawl space foundation, please specify when ordering

Total Living Area: 2,231 sq. ft.

First Floor
1,586 sq. ft.

Second Floor
645 sq. ft.

Plan Features

- Open and airy L-shaped front porch leads to a spacious entrance foyer
- Great room enjoys vaulted ceiling, fireplace and opens to breakfast room with snack bar
- An abundance of cabinet storage is just one of the many features of this ideal kitchen
- A luxurious first floor master bedroom has been provided along with an oversized bath
- 3 bedrooms, 2 1/2 baths, 2-car garage
- Basement foundation

Total Living Area: 2,935 sq. ft.

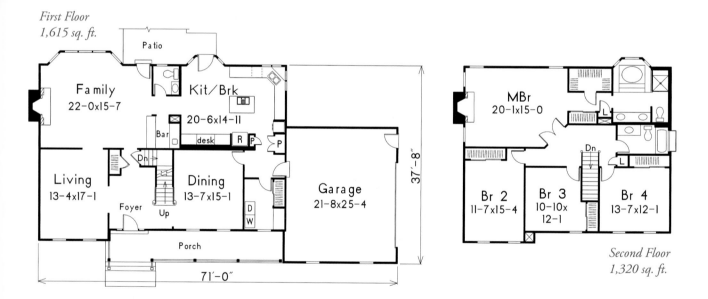

First Floor
1,615 sq. ft.

Patio

Family
22-0x15-7

Kit/Brk
20-6x14-11

Bar

desk   R   P

Living
13-4x17-1

Dn

Dining
13-7x15-1

Garage
21-8x25-4

Foyer   Up

D
W

Porch

37'-8"

71'-0"

Second Floor
1,320 sq. ft.

MBr
20-1x15-0

L

Dn

L

Br 2
11-7x15-4

Br 3
10-10x
12-1

Br 4
13-7x12-1

Plan Features

- Gracious entry foyer with handsome stairway opens to separate living and dining rooms
- Kitchen has a vaulted ceiling and skylight, island worktop, breakfast area with bay window and two separate pantries
- Large second floor master bedroom features a fireplace, raised tub, dressing area with vaulted ceiling and skylight
- 4 bedrooms, 2 1/2 baths, 2-car side entry garage
- Basement foundation

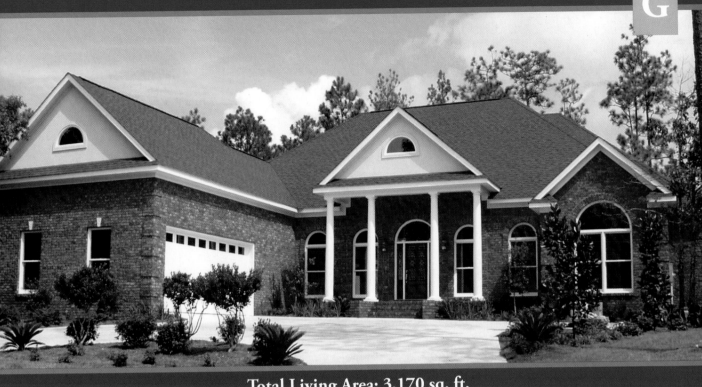

Total Living Area: 3,170 sq. ft.

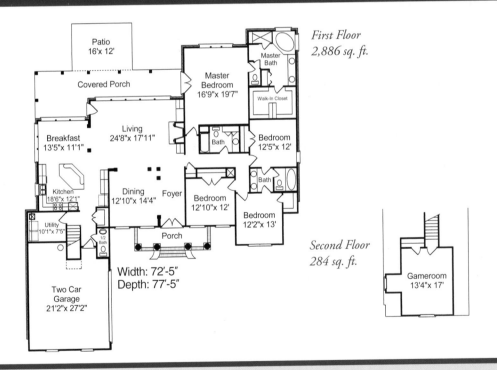

First Floor
2,886 sq. ft.

Second Floor
284 sq. ft.

Width: 72'-5"
Depth: 77'-5"

Plan Features

- The foyer and dining room feature 12' ceilings and are open with three free-standing columns to separate the areas
- The living room offers a stunning view of the backyard
- The flawless master bedroom connects to the covered porch and includes a private bath with an impressive walk-in closet
- 4 bedrooms, 3 1/2 baths, 2-car side entry garage
- Slab foundation

Total Living Area: 2,784 sq. ft.

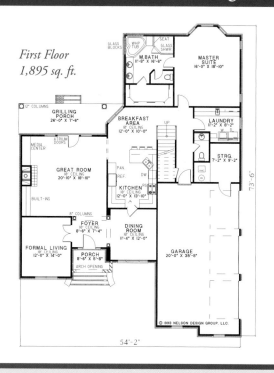

First Floor
1,895 sq. ft.

Second Floor
889 sq. ft.

Plan Features

- Formal living and dining rooms flank the grand foyer
- The great room enjoys a fireplace, a media center and access to the rear grilling porch
- All bedrooms include walk-in closets
- 3 bedrooms, 2 1/2 baths, 3-car side entry garage
- Slab, crawl space, basement or walk-out basement foundation, please specify when ordering

Total Living Area: 2,808 sq. ft.

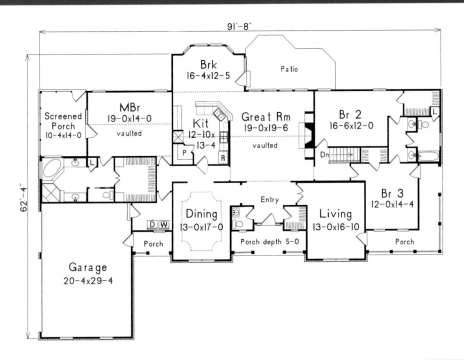

Plan Features

- Bedroom #3 shares a porch with the living room and a spacious bath with bedroom #2
- Vaulted master bedroom enjoys a secluded screened porch and sumptuous bath with corner tub, double vanities and huge walk-in closet
- Living room can easily convert to an optional fourth bedroom
- 3 bedrooms, 2 1/2 baths, 3-car side entry garage
- Basement foundation

Total Living Area: 2,582 sq. ft.

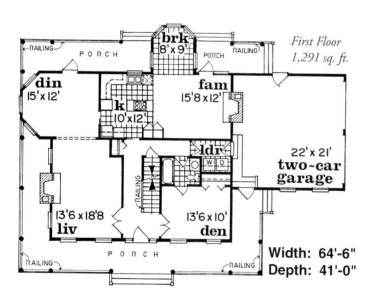

First Floor
1,291 sq. ft.

brk
8' x 9'

PORCH

RAILING

RAILING

PORCH

din
15' x 12'

fam
15'8 x 12'

k
10' x 12'

22' x 21'
two-car garage

ldr

liv
13'6 x 18'8

den
13'6 x 10'

PORCH

RAILING

RAILING

Width: 64'-6"
Depth: 41'-0"

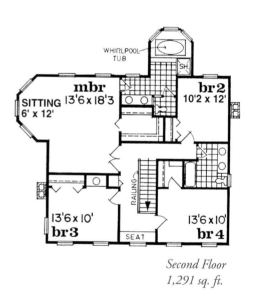

WHIRLPOOL TUB

mbr
13'6 x 18'3

SITTING
6' x 12'

br 2
10'2 x 12'

SH

br 3
13'6 x 10'

SEAT

br 4
13'6 x 10'

Second Floor
1,291 sq. ft.

Plan Features

- Both the family and living rooms are warmed by hearths
- The master bedroom on the second floor has a bayed sitting room and a private bath with whirlpool tub
- Old-fashioned window seat in second floor landing is a charming touch
- 4 bedrooms, 3 baths, 2-car side entry garage
- Basement or crawl space foundation, please specify when ordering

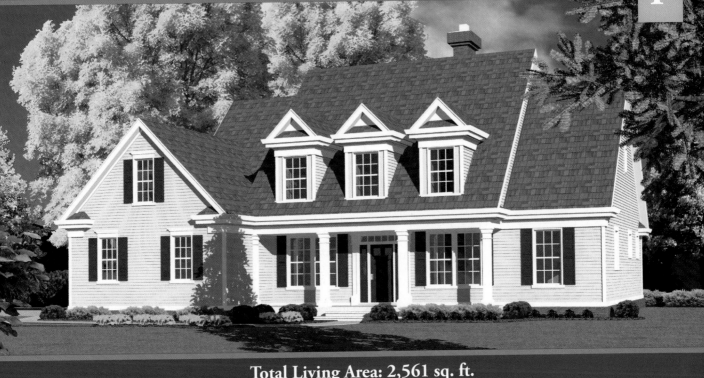

Total Living Area: 2,561 sq. ft.

First Floor
1,784 sq. ft.

Second Floor
777 sq. ft.

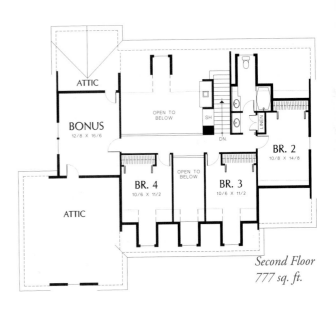

Plan Features

- Sunny vaulted breakfast nook
- Dormers are a charming touch in the second floor bedrooms
- Columns throughout the first floor help separate rooms while creating an open feel
- Bonus room on the second floor has an additional 232 square feet of living area
- 4 bedrooms, 2 1/2 baths, 2-car side entry garage
- Crawl space foundation

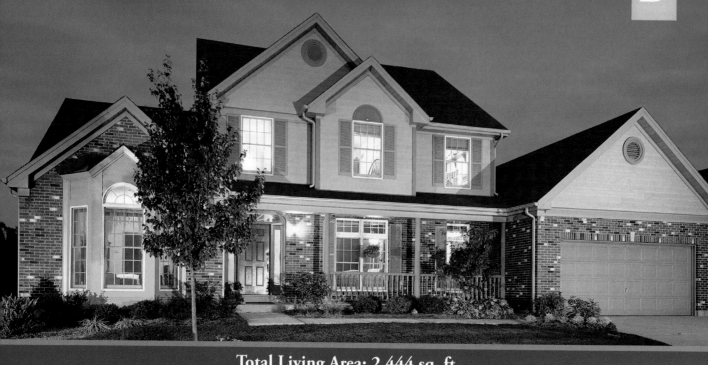

Total Living Area: 2,444 sq. ft.

64'-0"

48'-0"

skylt

Great Rm
17-0x15-9

Brk
11-8x11-6

Patio

Kitchen

First Floor
1,672 sq. ft.

11-8x11-0

Dn

MBr
13-8x
20-0

Up

Dining
14-1x11-11

Garage
19-8x19-5

Porch

open to below

Study
12-0x12-3

Dn

open to
below

Br 2
10-10x14-1

Br 3
10-11x14-1

Second Floor
772 sq. ft.

Plan Features

- Laundry room with workspace, pantry and coat closet is adjacent to the kitchen
- Two bedrooms, a study, full bath and plenty of closets are on the second floor
- Large walk-in closet and private bath make this master bedroom one you're sure to enjoy
- Kitchen enjoys a cooktop island and easy access to living area
- 3 bedrooms, 2 1/2 baths, 2-car side entry garage
- Basement foundation

Plan #583-053D-0028

Price Code:

E

Total Living Area: 2,940 sq. ft.

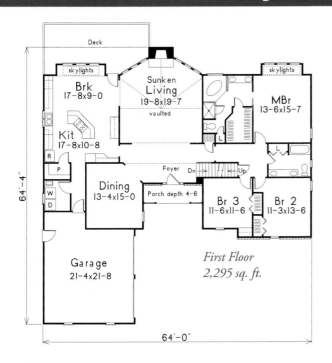

First Floor
2,295 sq. ft.

64'-4"

64'-0"

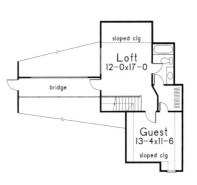

Second Floor
645 sq. ft.

Plan Features

- Two sets of twin dormers add outdoor charm while lighting the indoors
- The foyer leads into the sunken living room below and accesses the second floor attic
- Private master bedroom is complete with a luxurious corner tub and large walk-in closet
- A novel bridge provides view of living room below and access to second floor attic
- 4 bedrooms, 3 baths, 2-car side entry garage
- Basement foundation

Total Living Area: 1,770 sq. ft.

First Floor
924 sq. ft.

Great Room
15'6" x 20'

Dining
12'4" x 11'4"

Kitchen
12'4" x 10'

Two-Car Garage
20' x 22'

Foyer

STAIRS UP

Hall

Bath

Porch

Laun.

Width: 50'-0"
Depth: 36'-8"

Dressing

WALK-IN CLOSET

Master Bedroom
14' x 15'2"

Bedroom
12'4" x 10'

Bath

STAIRS DOWN

Balcony

WALK-IN CLOSET

Bedroom
11'2" x 12'

Second Floor
846 sq. ft.

Plan Features

- The spacious foyer leads to the airy great room which features a corner fireplace that also warms the adjacent dining room and kitchen
- A large laundry room is conveniently located off of the kitchen and garage entrance
- A luxurious whirlpool tub, double-bowl vanity and large walk-in closet enhance the master bedroom suite
- 3 bedrooms, 2 1/2 baths, 2-car garage
- Basement foundation

Plan #583-024D-0017

Price Code:

E

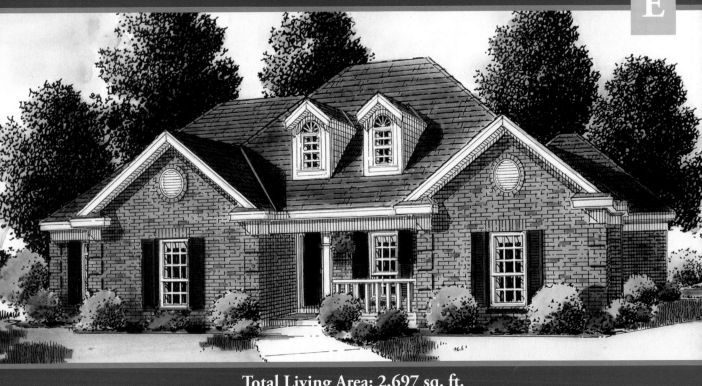

Total Living Area: 2,697 sq. ft.

Width: 59'-10"
Depth: 60'-10"

DID YOU KNOW?

Counters run a close second to floors in the amount of punishment they withstand, so choose your material wisely. Plastic tops run from moderately priced laminate to costly solid acrylic that looks like marble or granite. For slicing, chopping and pounding, hardwood counters or inserts are the gourmet chef's favorite. Small scratches and nicks add character or are easy to smooth out. Hard-surface counters include tile, granite, organic glass, stainless steel and natural and synthetic marble. Any will make a good-looking heat and scratch-proof surface.

Plan Features

- Secluded study with full bath nearby is an ideal guest room or office
- Master bedroom has access to outdoor patio
- 351 square feet of additional unfinished living space available in the attic
- 3 bedrooms, 3 baths, 2-car side entry garage
- Slab foundation

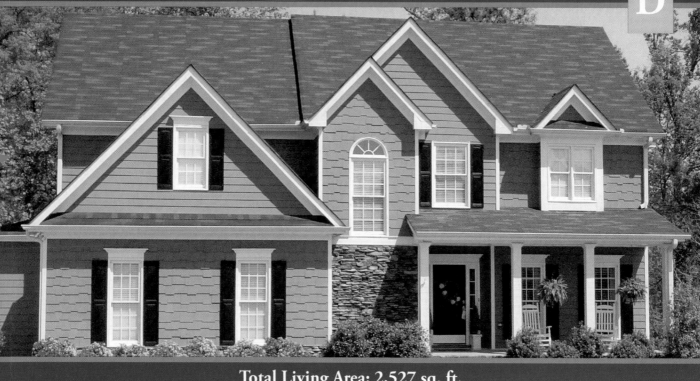

Total Living Area: 2,527 sq. ft.

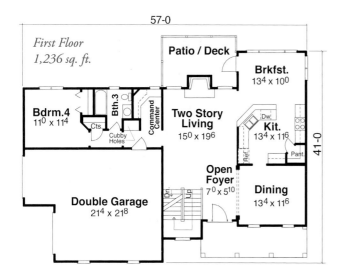

First Floor
1,236 sq. ft.

57-0

Patio / Deck

Brkfst.
13⁴ x 10⁰

Bdrm.4
11⁰ x 11⁴

Bth.3

Command Center

Two Story Living
15⁰ x 19⁶

Kit.
13⁴ x 11⁶

Cubby Holes

Open Foyer
7⁰ x 5¹⁰

Dining
13⁴ x 11⁶

41-0

Double Garage
21⁴ x 21⁸

Second Floor
1,291 sq. ft.

Hinged Window Seat

Opt. Window Seat

Master Bdrm.
13⁶ x 17⁴

Bdrm.2
11⁰ x 13⁴

Linen

Two Story Living

Bth.2

Computer Station

M.Bath Vaulted

Opt. Vaulted Ceil.

Bdrm.3
12⁸ x 11⁸

Laund.

Open To Foyer

Plant Shelf Above

Plant Shelf

Seat

Opt. Club-house

Plan Features

- Open two-story foyer and living area adds charm to this elegant country style home
- Oversized closet and private bath with vaulted ceiling are a few of the many luxuries found in the master bedroom
- Breakfast area has windows on all exterior walls and access to the patio/deck
- 4 bedrooms, 3 baths, 2-car side entry garage
- Walk-out basement foundation

Total Living Area: 2,358 sq. ft.

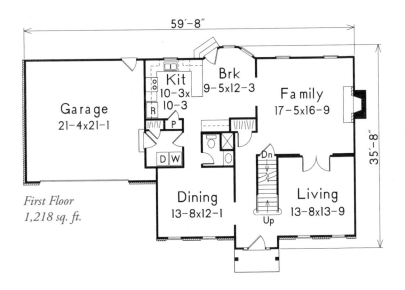

First Floor
1,218 sq. ft.

59'-8"

Garage
21-4x21-1

Kit
10-3x
10-3

Brk
9-5x12-3

Family
17-5x16-9

Dining
13-8x12-1

Living
13-8x13-9

35'-8"

Dn

Up

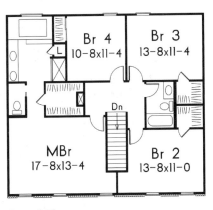

Second Floor
1,140 sq. ft.

Br 4
10-8x11-4

Br 3
13-8x11-4

MBr
17-8x13-4

Br 2
13-8x11-0

L

Dn

Plan Features

- U-shaped kitchen provides an ideal layout; adjoining breakfast room allows for casual dining
- Formal dining and living rooms have attractive floor-to-ceiling windows
- Master bedroom includes deluxe bath
- 4 bedrooms, 2 1/2 baths, 2-car garage
- Basement foundation, drawings also include crawl space and slab foundations

Total Living Area: 1,979 sq. ft.

DID YOU KNOW?

To get your windows to really shine, mix a solution of half vinegar and half water and pour into a spray bottle. This should remove grit and grime from windows with little effort. To minimize lint, wipe windows clean with newspaper, coffee filters or a cloth diaper.

Plan Features

- Striking corner fireplace is a stylish addition to the great room
- Open dining room allows the area to flow into the great room for added spaciousness
- Large pantry in the kitchen
- 3 bedrooms, 2 baths, 2-car side entry garage
- Slab foundation

Total Living Area: 3,192 sq. ft.

First Floor
2,335 sq. ft.

Family Room
17⁰ · 16⁰

Covered Patio

Master Bedroom
14⁴ · 16⁰

Living Rm.
14⁰ · 11⁰

Bath 2

Nook
12³ · 9⁰

w.i.c.

w.i.c.

Kitchen
13⁴ · 12⁰

Dining Rm.
10¹⁰ · 15²

Master Bath

Laundry

Foyer

Study
13⁴ · 10¹⁰

Entry

2 Car Garage
21⁴ · 21⁴

Width: 75'-0"
Depth: 53'-0"

Second Floor
857 sq. ft.

Bedroom 4
14⁴ · 11⁰

Bath 4

w.i.c.

w.i.c.

Bedroom 2
12⁴ · 12⁰

Bedroom 3
12⁴ · 11⁰

w.i.c.

Bath 3

Plan Features

- 12' ceilings throughout first floor and 10' ceilings on second floor
- The kitchen features a walk-in pantry and opens to the bayed nook and family room
- The dining room boasts elegant columns and connects to the formal living room
- Framing - only concrete block available
- 4 bedrooms, 3 1/2 baths, 2-car side entry garage
- Slab foundation

Plan #583-028D-0010

Price Code:

D

Total Living Area: 2,214 sq. ft.

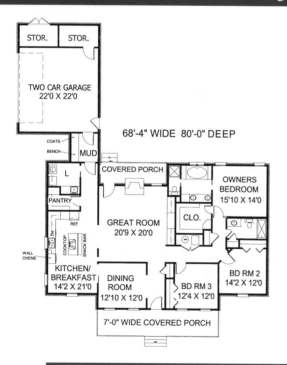

68'-4" WIDE 80'-0" DEEP

DID YOU KNOW?

To get extra life from any outdoor paint job, coat the bare wood with water repellent preservative before priming or painting it. Use only a repellent that is clearly labeled as paintable; some contain substances that will prevent paint from bonding properly.

Plan Features

- Great room has built-in cabinets for an entertainment system, fireplace and French doors leading to a private rear covered porch
- Dining room has an arched opening from the foyer
- Breakfast room has lots of windows for a sunny open feel
- 3 bedrooms, 2 baths, 2-car side entry garage
- Crawl space or slab foundation, please specify when ordering

To order call toll-free 1-800-DREAM HOME or visit www.houseplansandmore.com

Plan #583-053D-0057

Total Living Area: 3,427 sq. ft.

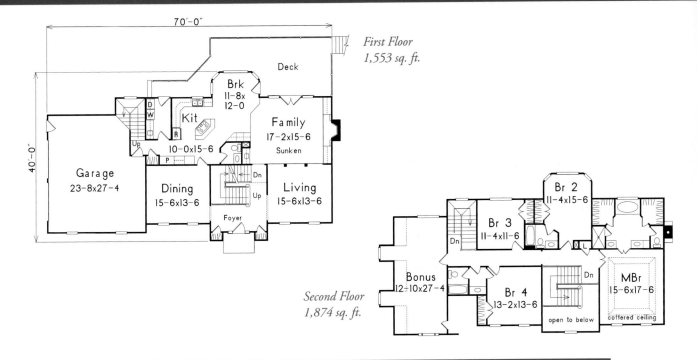

First Floor
1,553 sq. ft.

Second Floor
1,874 sq. ft.

Plan Features

- 10' ceilings on the first floor
- Elaborate master bedroom features a coffered ceiling and luxurious private bath
- Two-story showplace foyer is flanked by the dining and living rooms
- Bonus room above the garage is included in the square footage
- 4 bedrooms, 3 1/2 baths, 2-car side entry garage
- Basement foundation

Total Living Area: 3,216 sq. ft.

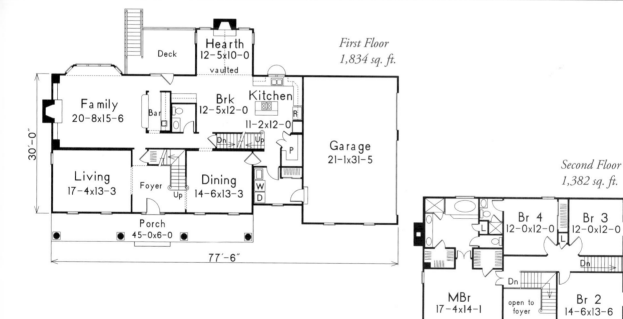

First Floor
1,834 sq. ft.

Second Floor
1,382 sq. ft.

Plan Features

- All bedrooms include private full baths
- Hearth room and kitchen/breakfast area create a large informal gathering area
- Oversized family room boasts a fireplace, wet bar and bay window
- Master bedroom has two walk-in closets and a luxurious bath
- 4 bedrooms, 4 1/2 baths, 3-car side entry garage
- Basement foundation

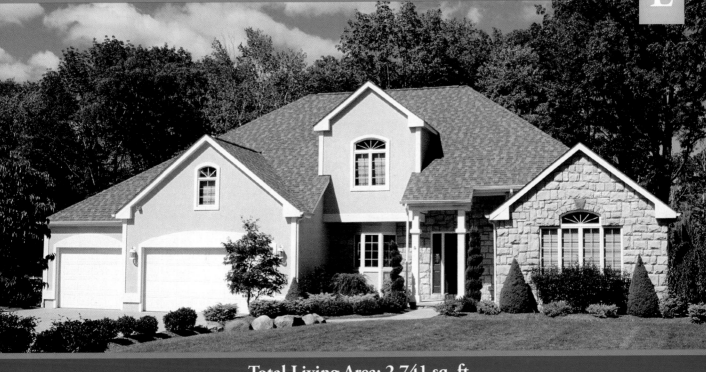

Total Living Area: 2,741 sq. ft.

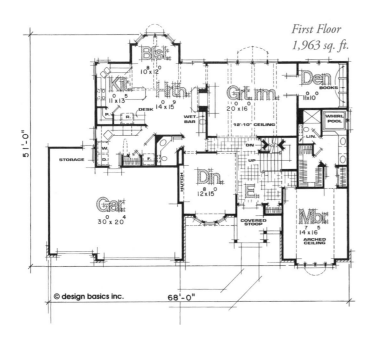

First Floor
1,963 sq. ft.

Second Floor
778 sq. ft.

© design basics inc.

Plan Features

- Formal dining room boasts a bayed window and hutch space
- A see-through fireplace warms the hearth and great rooms
- Kitchen includes an island counter, walk-in pantry, desk, wet bar and bayed dinette
- Convenient laundry area offers a sink, closet, iron-a-way and freezer space
- 4 bedrooms, 2 1/2 baths, 3-car garage
- Basement foundation

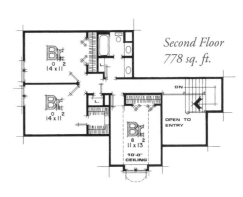

Rear View

Total Living Area: 1,480 sq. ft.

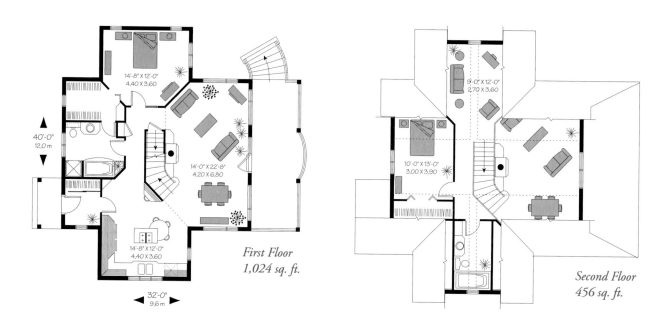

14'-8" X 12'-0"
4,40 X 3,60

40'-0"
12,0 m

14'-0" X 22'-8"
4,20 X 6,80

14'-8" X 12'-0"
4,40 X 3,60

First Floor
1,024 sq. ft.

32'-0"
9,6 m

9'-0" X 12'-0"
2,70 X 3,60

10'-0" X 13'-0"
3,00 X 3,90

Second Floor
456 sq. ft.

Plan Features

- Energy efficient home with 2"x 6" exterior walls
- Cathedral ceilings in the family and dining rooms
- Master bedroom has a walk-in closet and access to bath
- 2 bedrooms, 2 baths
- Basement foundation

Total Living Area: 1,880 sq. ft.

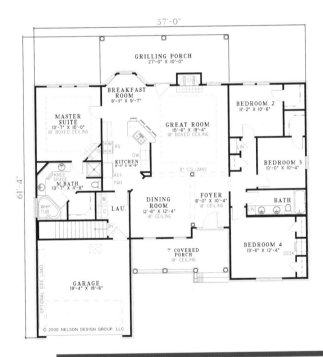

DID YOU KNOW?

As well as serving as decorative features and essential dressing aids, mirrors also play a less obvious role in a room scheme. They are invaluable for reflecting light, and can increase the illusion of space in a small room.

Plan Features

- Dining room conveniently accesses the kitchen
- Sunny breakfast room features a bay window
- Master suite has a cozy fireplace and a luxurious private bath
- 4 bedrooms, 2 baths, 2-car garage
- Slab, crawl space or basement foundation available, please specify when ordering

Total Living Area: 4,220 sq. ft.

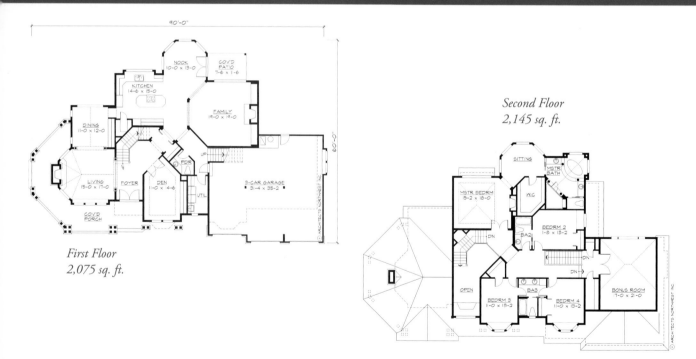

First Floor
2,075 sq. ft.

Second Floor
2,145 sq. ft.

Plan Features

- A large covered porch surrounds and connects to the living room with fireplace
- Octagon-shaped sitting room connects the master bedroom to its own private bath
- Bay windows brighten bedrooms #3 and #4
- Bonus room on the second floor is included in the square footage
- 4 bedrooms, 3 1/2 baths, 3-car garage
- Crawl space foundation

Total Living Area: 1,497 sq. ft.

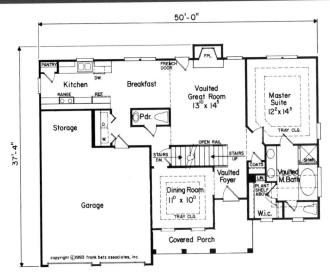

First Floor
1,065 sq. ft.

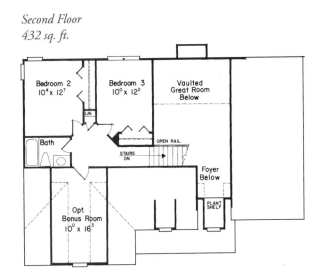

Second Floor
432 sq. ft.

Plan Features

- Master suite has a private luxurious bath with a spacious walk-in closet
- Formal dining room has a tray ceiling and views onto front covered porch
- Bonus room on second floor has an additional 175 square feet of living area
- 3 bedrooms, 2 1/2 baths, 2-car garage
- Crawl space or walk-out basement foundation, please specify when ordering

Plan #583-026D-0170

Total Living Area: 3,827 sq. ft.

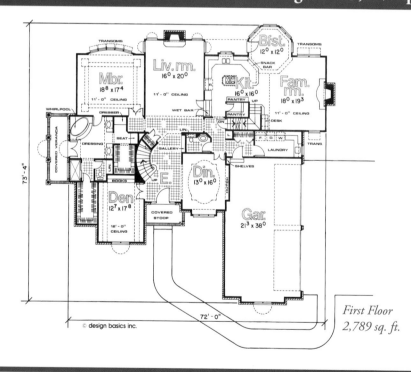

Second Floor 1,038 sq. ft.

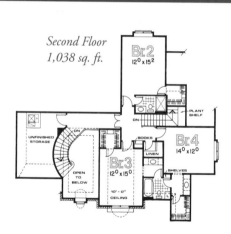

First Floor 2,789 sq. ft.

© design basics inc.

Rear View

Plan Features

- The living room has an 11' ceiling, fireplace flanked by transom windows and a wet bar
- Kitchen features two pantries and opens to a bayed breakfast area and family room
- The master bedroom enjoys a bay window, two walk-in closets, deluxe bath and access onto the covered veranda
- 4 bedrooms, 3 1/2 baths, 4-car side entry garage
- Basement foundation

Total Living Area: 2,208 sq. ft.

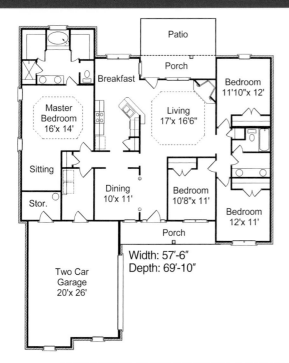

Width: 57'-6"
Depth: 69'-10"

DID YOU KNOW?

Save your back when shoveling with proper technique. Bend at the knees when lifting a shovel full of any material, keeping your back straight, and tighten your stomach muscles as you lift with your legs. Use the momentum generated by the upward thrust of your legs to propel the shovel's contents into a wheelbarrow or onto a tarp. Don't overextend your arms though - the closer the load remains to your body, the lighter it feels. And don't twist your back when shoveling: backbones aren't designed to move that way.

Plan Features

- The kitchen counter with seating opens to the spacious living room which features a corner fireplace and access to the rear porch
- Decorative columns adorn the dining room entry
- The master bedroom sitting area is a quiet place to relax
- 4 bedrooms, 2 baths, 2-car side entry garage
- Slab foundation

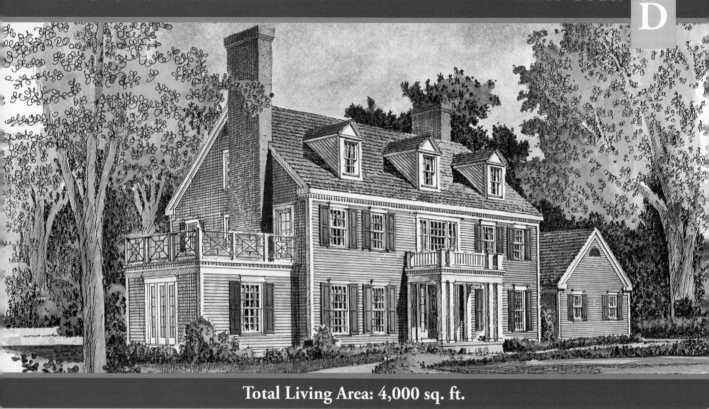

Total Living Area: 4,000 sq. ft.

First Floor
1,875 sq. ft.

Third Floor
775 sq. ft.

Second Floor
1,350 sq. ft.

Plan Features

- The stunning entry foyer showcases the grand spiral staircase
- The family and sun rooms feature bay windows flooding the first floor with warm natural light
- The luxurious second floor master bedroom includes a fireplace, bath with whirlpool tub, walk-in closet and private deck
- 5 bedrooms, 3 1/2 baths, 3-car side entry garage
- Partial basement/crawl space foundation

Total Living Area: 1,977 sq. ft.

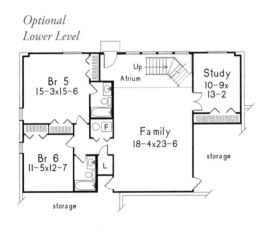

*Optional
Lower Level*

Br 5
15-3x15-6

Study
10-9x
13-2

Up
Atrium

Family
18-4x23-6

storage

Br 6
11-5x12-7

storage

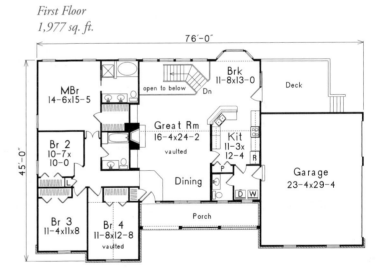

*First Floor
1,977 sq. ft.*

76'-0"

45'-0"

MBr
14-6x15-5

open to below

Brk
11-8x13-0

Deck

Dn

Great Rm
16-4x24-2
vaulted

Kit
11-3x
12-4

Garage
23-4x29-4

Br 2
10-7x
10-0

Dining

Br 3
11-4x11x8

Br 4
11-8x12-8
vaulted

Porch

Plan Features

- Classic traditional exterior is always in style
- Spacious great room boasts a vaulted ceiling, dining area, atrium with elegant staircase and feature windows
- Atrium opens to 1,416 square feet of optional living area below which consists of a family room, two bedrooms, two baths and a study
- 4 bedrooms, 2 1/2 baths, 3-car side entry garage
- Walk-out basement foundation

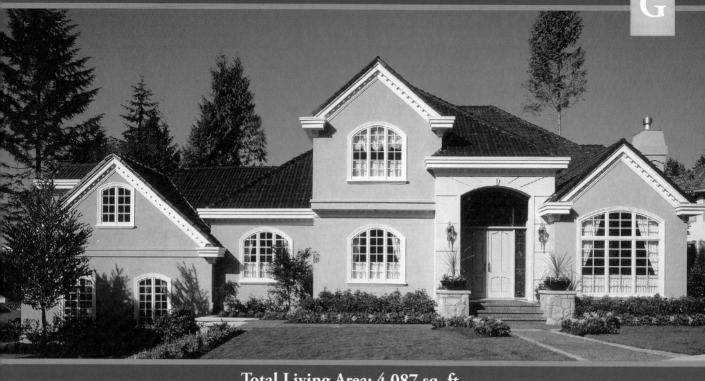

Total Living Area: 4,087 sq. ft.

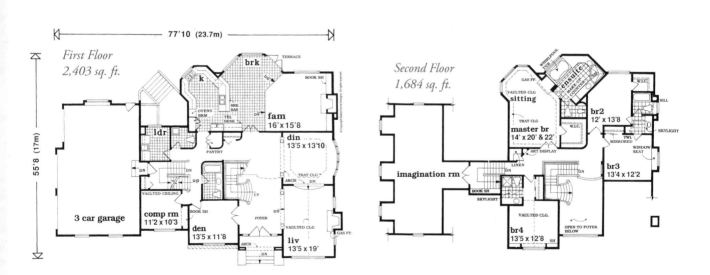

First Floor
2,403 sq. ft.

Second Floor
1,684 sq. ft.

Plan Features

- Second floor offers an imagination room perfect for a children's play area
- Deluxe master bedroom features a vaulted ceiling, fireplace, walk-in closet and bath with whirlpool tub
- 10' ceiling on the first floor
- 4 bedrooms, 4 1/2 baths, 3-car side entry garage
- Basement foundation

To order call toll-free 1-800-DREAM HOME or visit www.houseplansandmore.com

Total Living Area: 1,679 sq. ft.

First Floor
1,134 sq. ft.

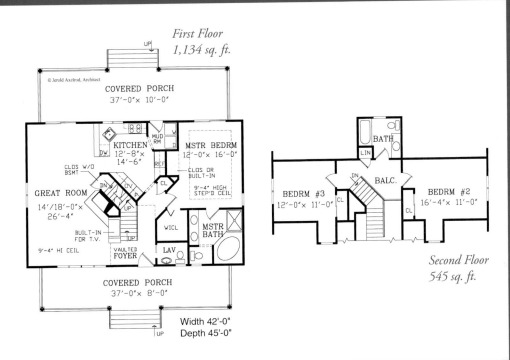

© Jerold Axelrod, Architect

COVERED PORCH
37'-0" x 10'-0"

KITCHEN
12'-8" x 14'-6"

MUD RM

MSTR BEDRM
12'-0" x 16'-0"

DW

REF

CLOS W/D BSMT

CLOS OR BUILT-IN

9'-4" HIGH STEP'D CEIL

CL

GREAT ROOM
14'/18'-0" x 26'-4"

DN

OV

UP

WICL

MSTR BATH

BUILT-IN FOR T.V.

9'-4" HI CEIL

VAULTED FOYER

UP

LAV

COVERED PORCH
37'-0" x 8'-0"

UP

Width 42'-0"
Depth 45'-0"

BATH

LIN

DN

BALC.

BEDRM #3
12'-0" x 11'-0"

CL

BEDRM #2
16'-4" x 11'-0"

CL

Second Floor
545 sq. ft.

Plan Features

- Wide, angled spaces in both the great room and the master bedroom create roomy appeal and year-round comfort
- Master bedroom includes a walk-in closet, whirlpool tub and double bowl vanity
- The nicely appointed kitchen offers nearby laundry facilities and porch access
- 3 bedrooms, 2 1/2 baths, 2-car drive under garage
- Basement, crawl space or slab foundation, please specify when ordering

Total Living Area: 2,245 sq. ft.

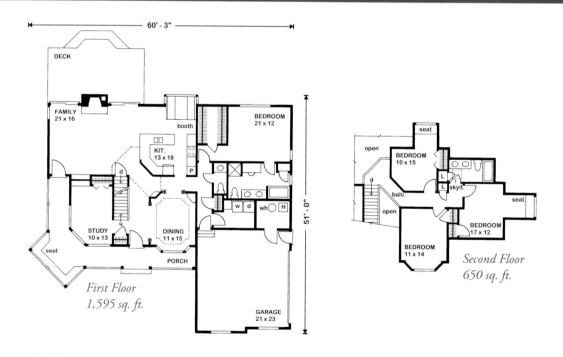

First Floor
1,595 sq. ft.

Second Floor
650 sq. ft.

Plan Features

- A wide entry hallway leads to the vaulted family room, kitchen and breakfast area
- The country kitchen includes a built-in breakfast nook, pantry and fireplace
- The main dining area is defined by elegant columns encircling its perimeter
- Bedroom suite enhanced with a walk-in closet and spacious bath
- 4 bedrooms, 2 1/2 baths, 2-car side entry garage
- Basement or crawl space foundation, please specify when ordering

Total Living Area: 1,779 sq. ft.

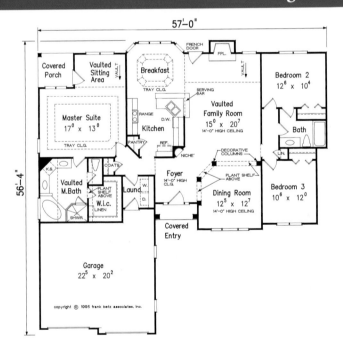

DID YOU KNOW?

Some paint manufacturers offer kitchen and bathroom collections specially formulated for steamy rooms. Designed to resist moisture and inhibit mildew growth, they also give a wipe-clean finish.

Plan Features

- Well-designed floor plan has a vaulted family room with fireplace and access to the outdoors
- Decorative columns separate the dining area from the foyer
- A vaulted ceiling adds spaciousness in the master bath that also features a walk-in closet
- 3 bedrooms, 2 baths, 2-car garage
- Walk-out basement, slab or crawl space foundation, please specify when ordering

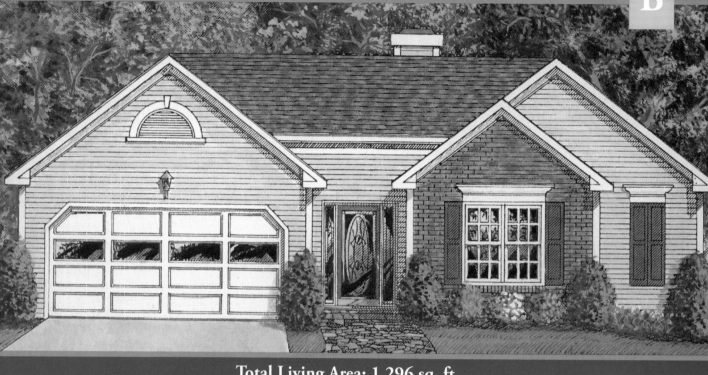

Total Living Area: 1,296 sq. ft.

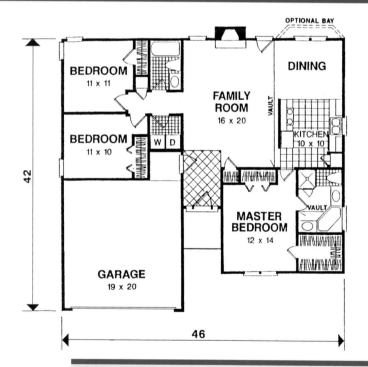

DID YOU KNOW?

Many people water their lawns in the late afternoon, thinking that is the best time in order to minimize evaporation. The best time to water is actually early in the morning. This allows water to soak down to root level before the day warms up. Another reason to get up early, or set your sprinkler timer, is that watering later in the day can leave grass wet all night which can lead to the formation of fungus.

Plan Features

- Two secondary bedrooms share a bath and have convenient access to the laundry room
- Family room has a large fireplace flanked by sunny windows
- Master bedroom includes privacy as well as an amenity-full bath
- 3 bedrooms, 2 baths, 2-car garage
- Basement, crawl space or slab foundation, please specify when ordering

To order call toll-free 1-800-DREAM HOME or visit www.houseplansandmore.com

Total Living Area: 1,862 sq. ft.

First Floor
1,103 sq. ft.

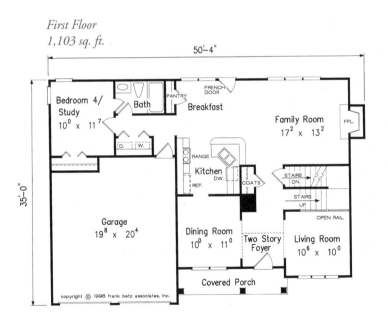

Second Floor
759 sq. ft.

Plan Features

- Dining and living rooms flank the grand two-story foyer
- Open floor plan combines kitchen, breakfast and family rooms
- Bedroom #4/study is tucked away on first floor for privacy
- Second floor bedrooms have walk-in closets
- 4 bedrooms, 3 baths, 2-car garage
- Walk-out basement or crawl space foundation, please specify when ordering

Total Living Area: 2,476 sq. ft.

◄ 60' ►
(50' · 2 CAR)

First Floor
1,786 sq. ft.

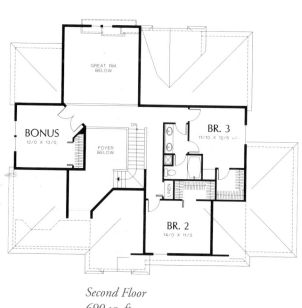

Second Floor
690 sq. ft.

Plan Features

- Luxurious master bath features a dramatic sunlit corner spa tub
- Double-door entry into den creates a private retreat for a home office or study
- Bonus room on the second floor has an additional 204 square feet of living area
- 3 bedrooms, 2 1/2 baths, 3-car garage
- Crawl space foundation

Total Living Area: 2,463 sq. ft.

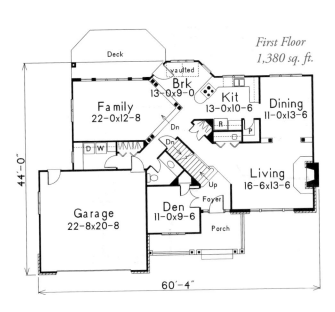

*First Floor
1,380 sq. ft.*

Deck

Brk
13-0x9-0

vaulted

Family
22-0x12-8

Kit
13-0x10-6

Dining
11-0x13-6

Dn

Dn

D W

Living
16-6x13-6

Garage
22-8x20-8

Up

Foyer

Den
11-0x9-6

Porch

44'-0"

60'-4"

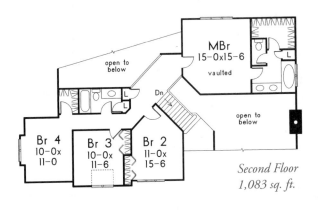

*Second Floor
1,083 sq. ft.*

open to below

MBr
15-0x15-6

vaulted

Dn

open to below

Br 4
10-0x11-0

Br 3
10-0x11-6

Br 2
11-0x15-6

Plan Features

- Exciting angular design with diagonal stairway
- Living room features a vaulted ceiling, fireplace and convenient wet bar
- Generously sized family room features a vaulted ceiling and easy access to the kitchen
- Sunny bay window defines breakfast area which accesses deck
- 4 bedrooms, 2 1/2 baths, 2-car garage
- Basement foundation

Our Blueprint Packages Offer...

Quality plans for building your future, with extras that provide unsurpassed value, ensure good construction and long-term enjoyment.

1 Cover Sheet

Included with many of the plans, the cover sheet is the artist's rendering of the exterior of the home. It will give you an idea of how your home will look when completed and landscaped.

2 Foundation

The foundation plan shows the layout of the basement, walk-out basement, crawl space, slab or pier foundation. All necessary notations and dimensions are included. See plan page for the foundation types included. If the home plan you choose does not have your desired foundation type, our Customer Service Representatives can advise you on how to customize your foundation to suit your specific needs or site conditions.

3 Floor Plans

The floor plans show the placement of walls, doors, closets, plumbing fixtures, electrical outlets, columns, and beams for each level of the home.

4 Interior Elevations

Interior elevations provide views of special interior elements such as fireplaces, kitchen cabinets, built-in units and other features of the home.

5 Exterior Elevations

Exterior elevations illustrate the front, rear and both sides of the house, with all details of exterior materials and the required dimensions.

6 Sections

Show detail views of the home or portions of the home as if it were sliced from the roof to the foundation. This sheet shows important areas such as load-bearing walls, stairs, joists, trusses and other structural elements, which are critical for proper construction.

7 Details

Show how to construct certain components of your home, such as the roof system, stairs, deck, etc.

Plan Number	Square Feet	Price Code	Page	Material List	Right Read. Reverse	Can. Shipping
583-001D-0003	2,286	E	356	•		
583-001D-0007	2,874	E	440	•		
583-001D-0008	2,935	E	600	•		
583-001D-0012	3,368	F	8	•		
583-001D-0013	1,882	D	231	•		
583-001D-0014	2,401	D	113	•		
583-001D-0015	2,618	E	222	•		
583-001D-0016	2,847	E	272	•		
583-001D-0017	2,411	D	417	•		
583-001D-0024	1,360	A	6	•		
583-001D-0026	2,358	D	611	•		
583-001D-0028	2,461	D	531	•		
583-001D-0031	1,501	B	227	•		
583-001D-0034	1,642	B	267	•		
583-001D-0037	3,216	F	616	•		
583-001D-0038	3,144	E	400	•		
583-001D-0045	1,197	AA	371	•		
583-001D-0059	2,050	C	228	•		
583-001D-0067	1,285	B	573	•		
583-001D-0077	1,769	B	368	•		
583-003D-0001	2,058	C	410	•		
583-003D-0002	1,676	B	225	•		
583-003D-0004	3,357	F	545	•		
583-003D-0005	1,708	B	115	•		
583-004D-0001	2,505	D	49	•		
583-004D-0002	1,823	C	72	•		
583-005D-0001	1,400	B	14	•		
583-006D-0002	3,222	F	149	•		
583-006D-0003	1,674	B	554	•		
583-007D-0001	2,597	E	406	•		
583-007D-0002	3,814	G	26	•		
583-007D-0003	2,806	E	530	•		
583-007D-0004	2,531	D	61	•		
583-007D-0005	2,336	D	538	•		
583-007D-0006	2,624	E	193	•		
583-007D-0007	2,523	D	84	•		
583-007D-0008	2,452	D	116	•		
583-007D-0009	2,716	E	221	•		
583-007D-0010	1,721	C	273	•		
583-007D-0011	2,182	D	226	•		
583-007D-0013	1,492	A	65	•		
583-007D-0014	1,985	C	543	•		
583-007D-0015	2,828	F	527	•		
583-007D-0016	3,850	F	283	•		
583-007D-0017	1,882	C	229	•		
583-007D-0027	654	AAA	561	•		
583-007D-0028	1,711	B	423	•		
583-007D-0029	576	AAA	108	•		
583-007D-0030	1,140	AA	373	•		
583-007D-0031	1,092	AA	233	•		
583-007D-0032	1,294	A	393	•		
583-007D-0037	1,403	A	268	•		
583-007D-0038	1,524	B	245	•		
583-007D-0039	1,563	B	562	•		
583-007D-0040	632	AAA	564	•		
583-007D-0041	1,700	B	370	•		
583-007D-0042	914	AA	549	•		
583-007D-0043	647	AAA	582	•		
583-007D-0044	1,516	B	263	•		
583-007D-0046	1,712	B	259	•		
583-007D-0047	2,730	E	338	•		

Plan Number	Square Feet	Price Code	Page	Material List	Right Read. Reverse	Can. Shipping
583-007D-0048	2,758	E	131	•		
583-007D-0049	1,791	C	21	•		
583-007D-0050	2,723	E	122	•		
583-007D-0051	2,614	E	577	•		
583-007D-0052	2,521	D	303	•		
583-007D-0053	2,334	D	235	•		
583-007D-0054	1,575	B	63	•		
583-007D-0055	2,029	D	53	•		
583-007D-0056	3,199	E	441	•		
583-007D-0057	2,808	F	603	•		
583-007D-0058	4,826	G	40	•		
583-007D-0059	3,169	F	502	•		
583-007D-0060	1,268	B	16	•		
583-007D-0062	2,483	D	112	•		
583-007D-0063	3,138	E	366	•		
583-007D-0064	2,967	E	161	•		
583-007D-0066	2,408	D	143	•		
583-007D-0067	1,761	B	86	•		
583-007D-0068	1,384	B	4	•		
583-007D-0070	929	AA	322	•		
583-007D-0071	3,657	F	74	•		
583-007D-0072	2,900	E	463	•		
583-007D-0075	1,684	B	365	•		
583-007D-0077	1,977	C	625	•		
583-007D-0079	2,727	E	2	•		
583-007D-0080	2,900	E	163	•		
583-007D-0083	3,510	F	342	•		
583-007D-0084	3,420	F	480	•		
583-007D-0085	1,787	B	88	•		
583-007D-0086	2,231	D	599	•		
583-007D-0088	1,299	A	255	•		
583-007D-0089	2,125	C	80	•		
583-007D-0098	2,397	D	308	•		
583-007D-0101	2,384	D	390	•		
583-007D-0102	1,452	A	586	•		
583-007D-0103	1,231	A	403	•		
583-007D-0105	1,084	AA	383	•		
583-007D-0107	1,161	AA	184	•		
583-007D-0110	1,169	AA	253	•		
583-007D-0113	2,547	D	409	•		
583-007D-0114	1,671	B	389	•		
583-007D-0117	2,695	E	362	•		
583-007D-0118	1,991	C	420	•		
583-007D-0119	1,621	B	544	•		
583-007D-0121	1,559	B	442	•		
583-007D-0123	1,308	A	241	•		
583-007D-0132	4,370	G	416			
583-007D-0137	1,568	B	7			
583-007D-0140	1,591	B	506	•		
583-007D-0150	2,420	D	92			
583-007D-0155	2,636	E	593			
583-007D-0162	1,519	B	28			
583-007D-0164	1,741	B	204			
583-008D-0004	1,643	B	402			
583-008D-0010	1,440	A	81	•		
583-008D-0013	1,345	A	275	•		
583-008D-0045	1,540	B	91	•		
583-008D-0079	2,253	D	66			
583-008D-0098	1,980	C	232			
583-008D-0101	1,820	C	542			
583-008D-0110	1,500	B	531			

Plan Number	Square Feet	Price Code	Page	Material List	Right Read. Reverse	Can. Shipping
583-008D-0134	1,275	A	111	•		
583-008D-0150	1,680	B	419	•		
583-008D-0162	865	AAA	545	•		
583-010D-0006	1,170	AA	237	•		
583-011D-0001	1,275	C	379		•	
583-011D-0002	1,557	C	67		•	
583-011D-0003	1,693	C	548		•	
583-011D-0004	1,997	D	107		•	
583-011D-0008	1,728	C	239		•	
583-011D-0009	2,840	F	428		•	
583-011D-0010	2,197	C	234	•	•	
583-011D-0013	2,001	D	396		•	
583-011D-0014	3,246	G	412		•	
583-011D-0015	1,893	D	578		•	
583-011D-0016	1,902	D	575		•	
583-011D-0017	1,805	D	563		•	
583-011D-0018	1,500	C	405		•	
583-011D-0019	1,978	E	372		•	
583-011D-0021	1,464	C	103		•	
583-011D-0022	1,994	D	125		•	
583-011D-0025	2,287	E	287	•	•	
583-011D-0026	2,320	E	407		•	
583-011D-0028	2,871	E	266		•	
583-011D-0029	2,689	E	425		•	
583-011D-0030	2,476	E	632		•	
583-011D-0031	2,613	E	17		•	
583-011D-0032	3,565	G	587		•	
583-011D-0033	3,398	G	90	•	•	
583-011D-0035	6,088	H	23		•	
583-011D-0036	2,986	F	144		•	
583-011D-0037	2,262	E	305		•	
583-011D-0038	2,797	F	218		•	
583-011D-0039	3,118	G	278		•	
583-011D-0041	3,231	G	445	•	•	
583-011D-0042	2,561	F	605		•	
583-011D-0043	2,196	E	118		•	
583-011D-0044	2,420	E	165		•	
583-011D-0045	2,850	F	327		•	
583-011D-0046	2,277	E	230		•	
583-011D-0047	2,120	E	532		•	
583-011D-0048	2,383	E	391		•	
583-011D-0049	2,079	D	111		•	
583-013D-0001	1,050	AA	533			
583-013D-0003	1,296	B	630			
583-013D-0009	1,598	C	271			
583-013D-0010	1,593	C	32		•	
583-013D-0012	1,647	B	81			
583-013D-0015	1,787	B	429			
583-013D-0019	1,992	C	42		•	
583-013D-0020	1,985	C	591			
583-013D-0021	1,982	C	227			
583-013D-0022	1,992	C	71		•	•
583-013D-0024	2,088	C	549			
583-013D-0025	2,097	C	85			
583-013D-0026	2,187	C	403			
583-013D-0027	2,184	C	89			
583-013D-0030	2,288	D	401			•
583-013D-0031	2,253	D	64			
583-013D-0033	2,340	D	541		•	
583-013D-0035	2,484	D	236			
583-013D-0036	2,546	D	491			

Home Plan Index

Plan Number	Square Feet	Price Code	Page	Material List	Right Read. Reverse	Can. Shipping
583-053D-0029	1,220	A	129	•		
583-053D-0030	1,657	B	438	•		
583-053D-0037	1,388	A	529	•		
583-053D-0057	3,427	F	615	•		
583-055D-0012	1,381	A	555	•	•	
583-055D-0016	2,698	E	73	•	•	
583-055D-0017	1,525	B	12	•	•	
583-055D-0024	1,680	B	537	•	•	
583-055D-0026	1,538	B	247	•	•	
583-055D-0029	2,525	D	195	•	•	
583-055D-0030	2,107	C	95	•	•	
583-055D-0032	2,439	D	251	•	•	
583-055D-0038	2,247	D	359	•	•	
583-055D-0043	1,654	B	571	•	•	
583-055D-0053	1,978	C	492	•	•	
583-055D-0055	1,739	C	377	•	•	
583-055D-0064	1,544	B	399	•	•	
583-055D-0081	1,880	C	619	•	•	
583-055D-0088	2,261	D	173	•	•	
583-055D-0093	1,965	C	59	•	•	
583-055D-0131	1,461	B	198	•	•	
583-055D-0137	2,444	D	369	•	•	
583-055D-0158	1,636	C	250	•	•	
583-055D-0162	1,921	C	497	•	•	
583-055D-0170	2,148	D	596	•	•	
583-055D-0174	2,755	E	240	•	•	
583-055D-0188	1,525	C	274	•	•	
583-055D-0192	2,096	D	499	•	•	
583-055D-0193	2,131	D	598	•	•	
583-055D-0194	1,379	B	206	•	•	
583-055D-0195	1,746	C	385	•	•	
583-055D-0196	2,039	D	29	•	•	
583-055D-0197	2,742	E	203	•	•	
583-055D-0198	2,186	D	276	•	•	
583-055D-0199	2,951	E	501	•	•	
583-055D-0200	2,784	E	602	•	•	
583-055D-0201	1,927	C	47	•	•	
583-055D-0202	3,108	F	208	•	•	
583-055D-0203	2,388	D	282	•	•	
583-055D-0204	2,534	E	504	•	•	
583-055D-0205	1,989	C	524	•	•	
583-055D-0206	2,606	E	568	•	•	
583-055D-0208	2,147	D	145	•	•	
583-055D-0209	2,029	D	210	•	•	
583-055D-0210	2,624	E	323	•	•	
583-055D-0211	2,405	D	511	•	•	
583-055D-0212	2,603	E	360	•	•	
583-055D-0213	1,921	C	521	•	•	
583-055D-0214	2,373	D	169	•	•	
583-056D-0001	1,624	E	156			
583-056D-0002	2,135	H	363			
583-056D-0003	2,272	G	458			
583-056D-0004	2,317	G	249			
583-056D-0005	2,111	H	170			
583-056D-0006	2,136	G	216			
583-056D-0007	1,985	G	263			
583-056D-0008	1,821	E	469			
583-056D-0013	1,404	E	525			
583-056D-0015	2,287	G	182			
583-056D-0018	3,422	F	519			
583-056D-0023	1,277	E	559			
583-056D-0026	1,761	E	214			
583-056D-0027	1,580	E	373			
583-058D-0002	2,059	C	261	•		
583-058D-0010	676	AAA	413	•		
583-058D-0014	416	AAA	381	•		
583-058D-0016	1,558	B	215	•		
583-058D-0020	1,428	A	286	•		
583-062D-0016	4,087	G	626			•
583-062D-0031	1,073	AA	553	•	•	•
583-062D-0033	1,286	A	251	•	•	•
583-062D-0036	1,018	AA	379	•		•
583-062D-0039	2,493	D	512	•		•
583-062D-0041	1,541	B	253	•		•
583-062D-0042	2,582	D	604	•	•	•
583-062D-0043	2,750	E	175	•		•
583-062D-0045	2,516	D	217	•		•
583-062D-0046	2,632	E	485	•		•
583-062D-0047	1,230	A	190	•	•	•
583-062D-0048	1,543	B	385	•		•
583-062D-0049	1,292	A	329	•		•
583-062D-0050	1,408	A	563	•		•
583-062D-0052	1,795	B	517	•		•
583-062D-0053	1,405	A	267	•		•
583-062D-0054	1,375	A	487	•		•
583-062D-0056	1,924	C	194	•		•
583-062D-0058	1,108	AA	537	•		•
583-062D-0059	1,588	B	513	•	•	•
583-062D-0061	1,092	AA	105	•		•
583-062D-0062	1,298	A	393	•		•
583-062D-0063	1,455	A	571	•		•
583-062D-0065	1,601	B	196	•		•
583-065D-0002	2,101	C	318	•		
583-065D-0005	1,782	B	478	•		
583-065D-0006	2,082	C	158	•		
583-065D-0009	2,403	D	290	•		
583-065D-0012	2,738	E	387	•		
583-065D-0013	2,041	C	320	•		
583-065D-0014	2,388	D	585	•		
583-065D-0019	4,562	G	588	•		
583-065D-0024	4,652	G	179			•
583-065D-0026	2,269	D	101	•		•
583-065D-0035	1,798	B	552	•		•
583-065D-0036	2,587	D	197	•		•
583-065D-0037	2,241	D	496	•		•
583-065D-0039	1,794	B	229	•		•
583-065D-0041	3,171	E	455	•		•
583-065D-0042	2,362	D	269	•		•
583-065D-0043	3,816	F	167	•		•
583-065D-0045	2,085	C	199	•		•
583-065D-0048	2,576	D	437			•
583-065D-0058	2,797	E	498			•
583-065D-0059	2,773	E	202			•
583-065D-0063	2,248	D	507			•
583-065D-0068	2,449	D	528			•
583-065D-0069	1,697	B	555			•
583-065D-0072	1,770	B	608			•
583-065D-0074	1,640	B	389			•
583-065D-0077	4,328	G	339	•		•
583-065D-0078	3,421	F	330	•		•
583-065D-0080	2,160	C	500	•		•
583-065D-0083	2,338	D	98	•		•
583-065D-0084	1,896	C	177			•
583-065D-0087	3,688	F	514	•		•
583-065D-0089	3,168	E	343	•		•
583-065D-0092	2,292	D	252	•		•
583-067D-0006	1,840	C	418			•
583-067D-0008	2,327	D	205			•
583-067D-0009	2,198	C	78			•
583-067D-0010	2,431	D	505			•
583-067D-0011	2,433	D	123			•
583-067D-0014	2,599	D	220			•
583-067D-0015	2,571	D	294			•
583-070D-0001	1,300	A	510			•
583-070D-0004	1,791	B	561			•
583-070D-0006	1,841	C	422			•
583-070D-0007	1,974	B	75			•
583-070D-0008	2,083	C	209			•
583-070D-0009	2,153	C	516			•
583-070D-0011	2,198	C	381			•
583-071D-0001	2,920	E	493			•
583-071D-0002	2,770	E	185			•
583-071D-0003	2,890	E	483			•
583-071D-0004	3,085	F	353			•
583-071D-0005	3,688	G	100			•
583-071D-0006	3,746	G	451			•
583-071D-0007	4,220	G	620			•
583-071D-0008	4,100	G	22			•
583-071D-0009	4,650	G	211			•
583-071D-0010	5,250	H	172			•
583-071D-0011	5,800	H	114			•
583-072D-0001	1,724	B	124			
583-072D-0002	1,551	A	594			
583-072D-0003	1,317	A	257			
583-072D-0004	1,926	C	341			
583-072D-0005	2,729	E	466			
583-072D-0007	2,143	C	397			
583-072D-0008	2,272	D	160			
583-072D-0009	2,464	D	556			
583-072D-0010	2,198	C	200			
583-072D-0011	2,445	D	335			
583-077D-0001	1,638	C	257	•		
583-077D-0002	1,855	D	346	•	•	
583-077D-0003	1,896	D	296			
583-077D-0004	2,024	D	567	•		
583-077D-0005	2,207	D	509	•		
583-077D-0006	2,307	D	539	•		
583-077D-0007	2,805	E	565	•		
583-078D-0002	1,925	D	575	•		
583-078D-0004	1,425	D	424	•		
583-078D-0006	4,000	D	624	•		
583-078D-0007	2,600	D	189	•		
583-078D-0011	950	D	391	•		
583-078D-0013	1,175	D	573	•		
583-078D-0014	2,070	D	77	•		
583-078D-0050	2,300	D	355	•		
583-078D-0051	2,000	D	447	•		
583-078D-0058	2,245	D	628	•		

What Kind Of Plan Package Do You Need?

Once you find the home plan you've been looking for, here are some suggestions on how to make your Dream Home a reality. To get started, order the type of plans that fit your particular situation.

Your Choices:

THE 1-SET PACKAGE - We offer a 1-set plan package so you can study your home in detail. This one set is considered a study set and is marked "not for construction." It is a copyright violation to reproduce blueprints.

THE MINIMUM 5-SET PACKAGE - If you're ready to start the construction process, this 5-set package is the minimum number of blueprint sets you will need. It will require keeping close track of each set so they can be used by multiple subcontractors and tradespeople.

THE STANDARD 8-SET PACKAGE - For best results in terms of cost, schedule and quality of construction, we recommend you order eight (or more) sets of blueprints. Besides one set for yourself, additional sets of blueprints will be required by your mortgage lender, local building department, general contractor and all subcontractors working on foundation, electrical, plumbing, heating/air conditioning, carpentry work, etc.

REPRODUCIBLE MASTERS - If you wish to make some minor design changes, you'll want to order reproducible masters. These drawings contain the same information as the blueprints but are printed on erasable and reproducible paper which clearly indicates your right to copy or reproduce. This will allow your builder or a local design professional to make the necessary drawing changes without the major expense of redrawing the plans. This package also allows you to print copies of the modified plans as needed. The right of building only one structure from these plans is licensed exclusively to the buyer. You may not use this design to build a second or multiple dwellings without purchasing another blueprint. Each violation of the Copyright Law is punishable in a fine.

MIRROR REVERSE SETS - Plans can be printed in mirror reverse. These plans are useful when the house would fit your site better if all the rooms were on the opposite side than shown. They are simply a mirror image of the original drawings causing the lettering and dimensions to read backwards. Therefore, when ordering mirror reverse drawings, you must purchase at least one set of right-reading plans. Some of our plans are offered mirror reverse right-reading. This means the plan, lettering and dimensions are flipped but read correctly. See the Home Plans Index on pages 635-638 for availability.

Other Great Products...

The Legal Kit - Avoid many legal pitfalls and build your home with confidence using the forms and contract featured in this kit. Included are request for proposal documents, various fixed price and cost plus contracts, instructions on how and when to use each form, warranty statements and more. Save time and money before you break ground on your new home or start a remodeling project. All forms are reproducible. The kit is ideal for homebuilders and contractors. **Cost: $35.00**

Detail Plan Packages - Framing, Electrical and Plumbing Packages - Three separate packages offer homebuilders details for constructing various foundations; numerous floor, wall and roof framing techniques; simple to complex residential wiring; sump and water softener hookups; plumbing connection methods; installation of septic systems, and more. Each package includes three dimensional illustrations and a glossary of terms. Purchase one or all three. Note: These drawings do not pertain to a specific home plan. **Cost: $20.00 each or all three for $40.00**

More Helpful Building Aids...

Your Blueprint Package contains the necessary construction information to build your home. We also offer the following products and services to save you time and money in the building process.

Express Delivery - Most orders are processed within 24 hours of receipt. Please allow 7-10 business days for delivery. If you need to place a rush order, please call us by 11:00 a.m. Monday-Friday CST and ask for express service (allow 1-2 business days).

Technical Assistance - If you have questions, please call our technical support line at 1-314-770-2228 between 8:00 a.m. and 5:00 p.m. Monday-Friday CST. Whether it involves design modifications or field assistance, our designers are extremely familiar with all of our designs and will be happy to help you. We want your home to be everything you expect it to be.

Material List - Material lists are available for many of the plans in this magazine. Each list gives you the quantity, dimensions and description of the building materials necessary to construct your home. You'll get faster and more accurate bids from your contractor while saving money by paying for only the materials you need. See the Home Plans Index on pages 635-638 for availability. Note: Material lists are not refundable. **Cost: $125.00**

How To Order

For fastest service, Call Toll-Free
1-800-DREAM HOME (1-800-373-2646) day or night

FOUR Easy Ways To Order

1. CALL toll-free 1-800-373-2646 for credit card orders. MasterCard, Visa, Discover and American Express are accepted.

2. FAX your order to 1-314-770-2226.

3. MAIL the Order Form to: HDA, Inc.
   944 Anglum Road
   St. Louis, MO 63042

4. ONLINE visit www.houseplansandmore.com

Please send me -

PLAN NUMBER 583-_____

PRICE CODE _____ (see pages 635-638)

Specify Foundation Type (see plan page for availability) _____

- ☐ Slab ☐ Crawl space ☐ Pier
- ☐ Basement ☐ Walk-out basement
- ☐ Reproducible Masters $_____
- ☐ Eight-Set Plan Package $_____
- ☐ Five-Set Plan Package $_____
- ☐ One-Set Study Package (no mirror reverse) $_____

Additional Plan Sets*
- ☐ _____ (Qty.) at $45.00 each $_____

Mirror Reverse*
- ☐ Right-reading $150 one-time charge
  (see index on pages 635-638 for availability) $_____
- ☐ Print in Mirror Reverse (where right-reading is not available)
  _____ (Qty.) at $15.00 each $_____
- ☐ Material List* $125 (see pages 635-638 for availability) $_____
- ☐ Legal Kit (see page 639) $_____

Detail Plan Packages: (see page 639)
- ☐ Framing ☐ Electrical ☐ Plumbing $_____

SUBTOTAL $_____

Sales Tax (MO residents add 6%) $_____
- ☐ Shipping / Handling (see chart at right) $_____

TOTAL (US funds only - sorry no CODs) $_____

I hereby authorize HDA, Inc. to charge this purchase to my credit card account (check one):

☐   ☐   ☐   ☐

Credit Card number_____

Expiration date_____

Signature _____

Name _____
                    (Please print or type)

Street Address_____
                    (Please **do not** use a PO Box)

City _____

State _____

Zip _____

Daytime phone number (_____) - _____

E-mail address _____

I'm a ☐ Builder/Contractor ☐ Homeowner ☐ Renter
I ☐ have ☐ have not selected my general contractor.

Thank you for your order!

Before You Order

EXCHANGE POLICIES - Since blueprints are printed in response to your order, we cannot honor requests for refunds. However, if for some reason you find that the plan you have purchased does not meet your requirements, you may exchange that plan for another plan in our collection within 90 days of purchase. At the time of the exchange, you will be charged a processing fee of 25% of your original plan package price, plus the difference in price between the plan packages (if applicable) and the cost to ship the new plans to you.

Please note: Reproducible drawings can only be exchanged if the package is unopened.

BUILDING CODES & REQUIREMENTS - At the time the construction drawings were prepared, every effort was made to ensure that these plans and specifications meet nationally recognized codes. Our plans conform to most national building codes. Because building codes vary from area to area, some drawing modifications and/or the assistance of a professional designer or architect may be necessary to comply with your local codes or to accommodate specific building site conditions. We advise you to consult with your local building official for information regarding codes governing your area.

Questions? Call Our Customer Service Number
1-314-770-2228

Blueprint Price Schedule

Price Code	1-Set	SAVE $110 5-Sets	SAVE $200 8 Sets	BEST VALUE Reproducible Masters
AAA	$225	$295	$340	$440
AA	$325	$395	$440	$540
A	$385	$455	$500	$600
B	$445	$515	$560	$660
C	$500	$570	$615	$715
D	$560	$630	$675	$775
E	$620	$690	$735	$835
F	$675	$745	$790	$890
G	$765	$835	$880	$980
H	$890	$960	$1005	$1105

Plan prices are subject to change without notice.
Please note that plans and material lists are not refundable.

ADDITIONAL SETS* - Additional sets of the plan ordered are available for an additional cost of $45.00 each. Five-set, eight-set, and reproducible packages offer considerable savings.

MIRROR REVERSE PLANS* - Available for an additional $15.00 per set, these plans are simply a mirror image of the original drawings causing the dimensions and lettering to read backwards. Therefore, when ordering mirror reverse plans, you must purchase at least one set of right-reading plans. Some of our plans are offered mirror reverse right-reading. This means the plan, lettering and dimensions are flipped but read correctly. To purchase a mirror reverse right-reading set, the cost is an additional $150.00. See the Home Plans Index on pages 635-638 for availability.

ONE-SET STUDY PACKAGE - We offer a one-set plan package so you can study your home in detail. This one set is considered a study set and is marked "not for construction." It is a copyright violation to reproduce blueprints.

*Available only within 90 days after purchase of plan package or reproducible masters of same plan.

Shipping & Handling Charges

	1-4 Sets	5-7 Sets	8 Sets or Reproducibles
U.S. Shipping - (AK and HI express only)			
Regular (allow 7-10 business days)	$15.00	$17.50	$25.00
Priority (allow 3-5 business days)	$25.00	$30.00	$35.00
Express* (allow 1-2 business days)	$35.00	$40.00	$45.00
Canada Shipping (to/from) - Plans with suffix 032D & 062D - see index			
Standard (allow 8-12 business days)	$25.00	$30.00	$35.00
Express* (allow 3-5 business days)	$40.00	$40.00	$45.00

* For express delivery please call us by 11:00 a.m. Monday-Friday CST

Overseas Shipping/International - Call, fax, or e-mail (plans@hdainc.com) for shipping costs.